Design Drawing

2000 Edition

William Kirby Lockard

W. W. Norton & Company

New York • London

Copyright © 2001, 1982, 1974 by William Kirby Lockard

For information about permission to reproduce
selections from this book, write to Permissions,
W. W. Norton & Company, Inc., 500 Fifth Avenue,
New York, NY 10110

The text and display of this book is composed in Sabon.
Composition and production by Ken Gross.
Manufacturing by Quebecor Kingsport.

Library of Congress Cataloging-in-Publication Data

Lockard, William Kirby, 1929–
    Design drawing / William Kirby Lockard. — 2000 ed.
        p.   cm.
    Includes bibliographical references and index.
    ISBN 0-393-73040-9
    1. Architectural drawing—Technique. I. Title

NA2705 .L62 2000
720'.28'4—dc21   00-053389

Please see pp. 7–9 for a list of illustration credits and
copyright acknowledgments.

W.W. Norton & Company, Inc., 500 Fifth Avenue,
New York, NY 10110
www.wwnorton.com

W.W. Norton & Company Ltd., 10 Coptic Street,
London WC1A 1PU

0 9 8 7 6 5 4 3 2

Dedication

For my students, whose eager appearance, year after year, with the enthusiasm to learn how to design/draw a better world has allowed the development of the ideas in this book.

For my fellow teachers, who have tolerated, supported, and encouraged a nontraditional approach to teaching the introductory drawing courses at the University of Arizona.

and most of all

For Peggy, without whose love this book would never have been written, and whose equal and essential contributions to every phase of the writing, production, and publication make it our book in the deepest sense.

Contents

Illustration Credits

The author wishes to thank the following publishers, institutions, and individuals for permission to reproduce the illustrations, tables, and photographs, as listed:

Page 15. Pablo Picasso—Guernica. © 1999 Estate of Pablo Picasso/Artists Rights Society (ARS), New York.

Page 15. Gearbox Control Surface Lock Casting. From *Graphics—Analysis and Conceptual Design* by A. S. Levins. Copyright © 1968 by John Wiley & Sons, Inc., New York.

Page 15. Le Corbusier—La Chapelle de Ronchamp. From *Le Corbusier 1946–52*. © 1999 Artists Rights Society (ARS), New York/ADAGP, Paris/FLC.

Page 17. A Victorian Drawing Class. From *Nelson's New Drawing Course* by J. Vaughan (Edinburgh 1903). By permission of Thomas Nelson and Sons, Ltd., Publishers, London.

Pages 25, 51, 73, 74, 79, 109, 135. Johnny Hart from the cartoon strip, *B. C.* By permission of Johnny Hart and Field Enterprises, Inc.

Pages 34, 35, and 36. Photographs by Peggy Hamilton Lockard.

Page 39. Charles Schultz *Peanuts* cartoon. United Feature Syndicate.

Page 48. Le Corbusier—Le Modulor. From *Le Corbusier 1946–52*. © 1999 Artists Rights Society (ARS), New York/ADAGP, Paris/FLC.

Page 56. Diagram of the Brain. From *The Dragons of Eden* by Carl Sagan. Copyright © 1977 by Carl Sagan. Reprinted by permission of Random House, Inc., and by permission of the author and the author's agents, Scott Meredith Literary Agency, Inc., 845 Third Avenue, New York, New York, 10022.

Page 59. Schematic Representation of the Organismic Hierarchy from *Janus: A Summing Up* by Arthur Koestler. Copyright © 1978 by Arthur Koestler. Reprinted by permission of Random House, Inc., and by permission of Sterling Lord Literistic, Inc.

Page 63. The Two Modes of Consciousness: A Tentative Dichotomy taken from *The Psychology of Consciousness* by Robert E. Ornstein, copyright © 1972 by Harcourt Brace & Company, reprinted by permission of the publisher.

Page 72. Express Text Cycle from *Experiences in Visual Thinking*, Second Edition, by R. H.

McKim. Copyright © 1980 by Wadsworth, Inc. Reprinted by permission of the publisher, Brooks/Cole Publishing Company, Monterey, California.

Page 77. Nancy Strube—Fig. 21–50, Scroll. From *Experiences in Visual Thinking*, Second Edition, by R. H. McKim. Copyright © 1980 by Wadsworth, Inc. Reprinted by permission of the publisher, Brooks/Cole Publishing Company, Monterey, California.

Page 82. Piranesi—Illustration 28, Carceri: Plate 3. From *Giovanni Battista Piranesi. Drawings and Etchings at Columbia University*. Copyright © 1972 by the Trustees of Columbia University of the City of New York. By permission of Columbia University.

Page 82. Canaletto—Piazza San Marco: Looking East from South of the Central Line. From *Canaletto: Giovanni Antonio Canal 1697–1768* by W. G. Constable, Second Edition, edited by J. G. Links. Copyright © Oxford University Press 1976. By permission of the publisher.

Page 82. Leonardo da Vinci—The Costruzione Legittima as it was Drawn by Leonardo from *On The Rationalization of Sight: With an Examination of Three Renaissance Texts on*

Perspective by William J. Ivins, Jr. Copyright © 1973 by Da Capo Press, Inc. By permission of the publisher.

Page 83. Peter Eisenman—Axonometric Drawing. From *Five Architects* by P. Eisenman, M. Graves, C. Gwathmey, J. Hedjuk, R. Meier. Copyright © 1974 by Peter Eisenman, Michael Graves, Charles Gwathmey, John Hedjuk, and Richard Meier. Used by permission of Oxford University Press, Inc.

Page 84. C. Leslie Martin—Multi-view Orthographic Projections. Reprinted with permission of Macmillan Publishing Co., Inc. from *Architectural Graphics*, Second Edition, by C. Leslie Martin. Copyright © 1970 by C. Leslie Martin.

Page 92. Richard Welling—Line Drawing. From *The Technique of Drawing Buildings* by Richard Welling. Watson-Guptill Publications. By Permission of Richard Welling.

Page 92. Paul Stevenson Oles—Tone Drawing. From *Architectural Illustration: The Value Delineation Process* by Paul Stevenson Oles. Copyright © 1979 by Van Nostrand Reinhold Company. Reprinted by permission of the publisher.

Page 93. Mark deNalovy-Rozvadovski—Tone of Lines Drawing. From *Architectural Delineation* by Ernest Burden. Copyright © 1971 by McGraw-Hill Inc. Used with permission of the McGraw-Hill Companies.

Page 93. Helmut Jacoby—Line and Tone Drawing. From *New Architectural Drawings* by Helmut Jacoby. Copyright © 1969 by Verlag Gerd Hatje. Reprinted by permission of the publisher.

Page 111. Projected Perspective Methods. From *Architectural Graphic Standards*, Sixth Edition, by Charles G. Ramsey and Harold R. Sleeper. Copyright © 1970 by John Wiley & Sons, Inc. By permission of the publisher.

Page 115. Leonard da Vinci—Studio del Corpo Umano O "Canone di Proporzioni." By permission of Scala New York/Florence.

Page 135. C. Leslie Martin—Shadows on Plans and Elevations. Reprinted with permission of Macmillan Publishing Co., Inc. from *Design Graphics*, Second Edition, by C. Leslie Martin. Copyright © 1968 by C. Leslie Martin.

Page 155. Ted Kautzky—Pencil Drawings. From *The Ted Kautzky Pencil Book* by Ted Kautzky. Copyright © 1979 by Van Nostrand Reinhold Company. Reprinted by permission of the publisher.

Page 195. Paul Laseau—Problem Solving Diagrams. From *Graphic Problem Solving for Architects and Builders* by Paul Laseau. Copyright © 1975 by CBI Publishing Company. Reprinted by permission of the publisher, CBI Publishing Company, Inc., 51 Sleeper St., Boston, MA 02210.

Pages 202, 207, 212. Paul Laseau—Drawings from *Graphic Thinking for Architects and Designers* by Paul Laseau. Copyright © 1980 by Van Nostrand Reinhold Company. Reprinted by permission of John Wiley & Sons, Inc.

Page 204. Edward de Bono—Illustrations on p. 179 and specified excerpts from *Lateral Thinking: Creativity Step by Step* by Edward de Bono. Copyright © 1970 by Edward de Bono. Reprinted by permission of HarperCollins Publishers, Inc.

Pages 205 and 206. Edward T. White—Programming Diagrams. From *Introduction to Architectural Programming* by Edward T. White. Copyright © 1972 by Edward T. White. By permission of the author.

Page 211. Francis D. K. Ching. Regular and Irregular Forms. From *Architecture: Form, Space and Order* by Francis D. K. Ching. Copyright © 1979 by Van Nostrand Reinhold Company. Reprinted by permission of John Wiley & Sons, Inc.

Page 222. Edward T. White—The Variables of Presentation. From *Presentation Strategies in Architecture* by Edward T. White. Copyright © 1977 by Edward T. White. By permission of the author.

Page 223. Documents de L'Ecole Nationale Supérieure des Beaux-Arts, Paris. From *The Architecture of the Ecole Des Beaux-Arts*, The Museum of Modern Art, New York, edited by Arthur Drexler.

Page 227. Cartoon from *Shaping the City* by Roger K. Lewis.

Pages 253, 254, 255, 258. Photographs and drawings by Les Wallach, Bob Clements, and John Birkinbine of Les Wallach's office, Line and Space.

Page 259. Photographs by Bill Timmerman.

Page 259. Drawings by Rick Joy.

Page 276. Photograph by Douglas Mazonwicz. From *Prehistoric Art* by T. G. E. Powell.

All other drawings in *Design Drawing* are by the author.

Acknowledgments

The author wishes to thank the following publishers and authors for permission to reprint material copyrighted or controlled by them.

Brooks/Cole Publishing Company, Monterey, California, for permission to quote from *Experiences in Visual Thinking,* second edition, by R. H. McKim. Copyright © 1972, 1980 by Wadsworth, Inc.

Jerome S. Bruner for permission to quote from *A Study of Thinking* by Jerome S. Bruner, Jacqueline J. Goodnow, and George A. Austin. Copyright © 1956 by John Wiley & Sons.

Edward de Bono and Harper & Row, Publishers, Inc. for permission to quote specified excerpt on pages 63–64, 197, and 203 abridged from *Lateral Thinking: Creativity Step by Step* by Edward de Bono. Copyright © 1970 by Edward de Bono.

James J. Gibson, *The Ecological Approach to Visual Perception.* Copyright © 1979 by Houghton Mifflin Company. Reprinted with the permission of Dr. Eleanor J. Gibson.

James J. Gibson, *The Perception of the Visual World.* Copyright © 1950 by Houghton Mifflin Company. Used with permission.

James J. Gibson, *The Senses Considered as Perceptual Systems.* Copyright © 1966 by Houghton Mifflin Company. Reprinted with permission.

"Excerpts" from *The Hidden Dimension* by Edward T. Hall. Copyright © 1966, 1982 by Edward T. Hall. Used by permission of Doubleday, a division of Random House, Inc., and Edward T. Hall Associates.

William H. Ittelson and Seminar Press, Inc. for permission to quote from *Environment and Cognition,* edited by William H. Ittelson. Copyright © 1973 by Seminar Press, Inc.

Sterling Lord Literistic, Inc. for permission to quote excerpts from *Karl Popper* by Bryan Magee. Copyright © 1973 by Bryan Magee.

W. W. Norton & Company, Inc. for permission to quote from *Conceptual Blockbusting* by James L. Adams. Copyright © 1974, 1976 by James L. Adams.

Random House, Inc. and Sterling Lord Literistic, Inc. for permission to quote from *Janus: A Summing Up* by Arthur Koestler. Copyright © 1978 by Arthur Koestler.

Edward T. White for permission to quote from *Introduction to Architectural Programming* by Edward T. White. Copyright © 1972 by Edward T. White.

John Wiley & Sons, Inc. for permission to quote from *Graphic Thinking for Architects and Designers* by Paul Laseau. Copyright © 1980 by Van Nostrand Reinhold Company.

I also would like to thank two people for their help in producing the 2000 editions of *Design Drawing* and *Design Drawing Experiences:* Nancy Green, the editor at Norton to whose interest in the books, loyalty to the ideas, and insistence on quality this edition owes its existence; and to Casey Ruble, who not only tightened up the writing and eliminated most of its redundancies, but also challenged me to clarify the ideas and explanations.

Preface

I am grateful for this opportunity, twenty-seven years after *Design Drawing*'s first edition, to revise the book again. The revisions consist of a condensation of the original text; I have left what I think is still valid and important to know for a designer learning to draw and made room for new techniques that were unknown when the book was originally written.

This 2000 edition also offers new chapters on applications and combinations, which spell out how the drawing abilities promoted in the book can best be applied in school and in practice, and which contain two new color sequences illustrating the use of overlays and the combination of hand drawing with computer drawing and coloring. It is a great pleasure to have the sections on combining hand drawing with digital color and on computer-based presentations done by my son, Scott Lockard. The skill you see in that sequence has nothing to do with genetic inheritance. It is the result of Scott's diligence and intelligence, and I am pleased and grateful to have his work in this revised edition.

The revised chapters on perception and conception eliminate some of the speculative writing of the original edition, and the chapters on perspective and shadow-casting are simplified and made more clear. I have also eliminated many of the cartoon drawings with which the original text was illustrated. They were fun to draw for the original book, but I decided it was time to put them in retirement.

Since the first edition of *Design Drawing* twenty-seven years ago, there have been many changes in the way drawing is used in the design professions and taught in professional design schools. The use of the computer has revolutionized drawing in ways that, in the long term, will be clearly beneficial. In the short term, however, the benefits of the computer are not nearly as clear.

Computer-aided drafting has been embraced by students who don't want to take the time to learn to draw and by schools who don't want to take the time to help their students learn to draw. The most radical computer advocates have assumed that the computer will do all our drawing for us and that the ability to draw and the collateral learning that accompanies learning to draw are no longer necessary.

Computer-aided drafting has begun to take over the more boring, repetitive tasks of drawing, beginning with the construction drawings for large, repetitive designs. Computers also can do many things that are impossible or very difficult for human draftspersons. They can, for example, keep track of quantities, verify dimensioning, and confirm that changes on one drawing have been made on all related drawings.

The downside to the use of computers can be seen in computer drawings that employ no difference in line weights or tones and in presentation drawings with awkward computer-generated entourage or none at all.

There is also disagreement as to whether it is desirable or necessary for professional designers to use the computer to make drawings or whether that role is better filled by a technical person trained at a community college or technical school.

The use of computers is beginning to make even more clear what kinds of drawing are still worth learning. It is probably no longer worth learning to make the very accurate and beautifully legible drafted construction drawings of past generations of designers. Experienced CAD operators can make them even more accurately and almost as legibly, and the office standards for drafting can be programmed into the computer.

The value of spending time learning to hand draft with a skill rivaling the computer seems increasingly questionable. But it is highly worthwhile to spend time learning to make quick, freehand, precomputer, conceptual sketches and a freehand layer of drawing that can be combined with computer drawing and coloring in final presentation perspectives. Letting the computer do what it can do best gives us even more time to learn to do what human designers do best.

The two new color sequences in this revised edition are added to show these two uses of freehand drawing. Since we no longer need to learn to draft our orthographic drawings by hand, we should rededicate ourselves to learning the freehand drawing skills that are essential at both ends of the design-drawing spectrum.

We will always need to represent our design concepts in their earliest stages, especially with their three-dimensional, subjective, experiential qualities. And if we care about the quality of the images that represent our final designs, we need to be able to make the layer of freehand drawing that gives them the personal character designers have always aspired to.

For these reasons the kind of drawing advocated in this book will be even more worthwhile in the future than it has been in the past.

Kirby Lockard

Introduction

This book is for students entering the environmental design professions: architecture, landscape architecture, and interior design. Most beginning environmental design students already have some understanding of drawing as art or as drafting. However, compared to their understanding of English, mathematics, or science, beginning design students' attitudes toward drawing could hardly be more disparate, depending on whether they have been introduced to drawing as art or drawing as drafting. Design schools often do no more than polish whatever drawing abilities the student happens to have. They accompany this with either an extravagant and undeserved appreciation of the students' supposed "talent" or an equally undeserved deprecation of their lack of it. For these reasons, learning to draw and to use drawing in design is often unnecessarily difficult, frustrating, and humiliating for students who are well prepared for design education in every other way.

I have written a previous book on drawing called *Drawing As a Means to Architecture* (1968). The success of that book, and a deepening conviction that the confident ability to draw is indispensable and should be taught by designers, led me to undertake *Design Drawing* and the present revised edition. The main claims of this book are:

- Design drawing is clearly different from conventional, formalized art and drafting in its purposes, methods, and values, and to limit environmental design students to the conventional attitudes and methods of art or drafting is to limit their understanding of the most valuable tool in the design process.

- Design drawing most differs from conventional drafting in the way it describes a design. While drafting considers a design an object and uses traditional orthographic plans, sections, and elevations to describe it, design drawing considers a design an environment and uses perspectives to study the subjective experience of it.

The greatest difficulty of which I am aware as an author is the Western intellectual tradition of linear, logical argument—how to categorize and relate what you have to say. Unfortunately, stream-of-consciousness prose is only accepted from authors of fiction. This is particularly difficult when much of what you have to say involves the breaking and remaking of traditional categories. The new category of drawing—design drawing—that this book begins to establish is best understood by first considering its relationship to the two traditional kinds of drawing: art and drafting.

Design Drawing's Relationship to Art and Drafting

TRADITIONAL SPLIT

The differences between art and drafting begin to become evident to students from the time mechanical drawing is introduced in junior high school. This kind of precisely accurate drawing, with its own special orthographic form, comes after a much earlier and quite different introduction in elementary school to drawing as art. The difference is reinforced by a culturally indoctrinated split based on the student's gender. Although society's notion of proper "male" and "female" types of drawing is weakening, you still find few boys in high school art classes and fewer girls in mechanical drawing classes.

VISUAL/GRAPHIC COMPONENT OF REASON AND CREATIVITY

Art and drafting are well-established, useful traditions, and for the draftsperson, the artist, and the illustrator, their approaches, values, and methods are adequate. Unfortunately, however, the two poles represented by drawing as art and drawing as drafting bypass a way of thinking about and using drawing that is potentially more valuable than either of the conventional concepts. This third approach to drawing considers it as the visual or graphic component of reason and creativity. Vision is our best-developed sense, and the unique linkage of remarkable vision with a facile hand is the source of the intelligence that

makes us human. If we develop this visual/graphic potential, we can often "see" the most correct or reasonable choice in representative drawings more directly than if we used our minds alone to sort through the semantics of reason. Our eyes are very wise and we trust them more than our other sense organs. Anyone who has agreed to a verbally described blind date knows what I mean. Our language is filled with trite but true phrases that illustrate this: "I see," "It looks good to me," "Show me," "Let me see," "I can visualize," etc.

Drawing the problem or tentative solutions to it allows the designer and all others involved in the design process to see and evaluate proposals in the most direct way possible. This kind of drawing is used or should be used by all those who design the built environments on which our convenience, safety, delight, and sanity depend. We have known for some time now that we are irrevocably shaped by whatever environment we inhabit, but we have been slow to take seriously the responsibility for the design of that environment. Knowing what it will be like to be surrounded by a proposed environment is absolutely basic to this kind of design responsibility.

I am not prepared to make an argument here for the use of drawing in philosophic or scientific inquiry, although I believe drawing could be very useful in those endeavors. There is, unfortunately, a prejudice against graphics in most of the higher human endeavors. As our children mature, we take away their pictures, deliberately inhibiting the strong evolutionary link between eye and mind. Any illustrated book suffers a cer-

tain stigma. The use of graphics is degraded to selling or persuading some presumably intellectually inferior group whose approval is needed but whose real understanding is presumed to be limited or undesired.

A related attitude holds that drawings or pictures are misleading and strike emotional responses that are not to be trusted in serious matters. My experience is that, on the contrary, drawings are much more dependable and honest than words.

Drawing is also mistrusted as either a mysterious intuitive activity or discounted as automatic and mindless by many design-methods theorists. Most designers who are confident of their drawing ability and use drawing consciously in the design process find such a paranoia of the supposed evils of drawing more irrational than the ritual it seeks to avoid.

DRAWING AS SEEING

An argument can be made that one of the great benefits of language, beyond its communicative use, is that it promotes more precise thought. There is a parallel argument for drawing. Reproducing a spatial environment accurately and making evaluations from such drawn representations promotes a more precise "seeing" and experiencing of the environment. Such a drawing ability allows us to propose precise changes in the environment and "see" them in an evaluative way. The ability to draw complex objects and spaces leads to a deeper understanding and appreciation of the spatial structure of our environment.

THREE KINDS OF DRAWING

The best way I have found of illustrating the differences between design drawing, art, and drafting is to compare their uses, methods, and value systems.

As *art*, drawing values self-expression, choice of subject, virtuoso technique, many levels of communication (often deliberately obscure), and, above all, the drawing itself as a unique, one-of-a-kind original. The drawing itself is the product. Reality, in terms of color, perspective, and subject matter, is often deliberately distorted, and this distortion is a part of the expressionistic value of the work. Creating a drawing as art is also often considered to be a complete, finite act, and any redrawing or change degrades the particular drawing because it indicates indecision or weakness on the part of the artist. Art places no demand for efficiency on drawing. It may, in fact, value the laboriousness of the drawing.

Picasso, Pablo—*Guernica*—1937 (May–early June).

Drawing as art is the product of a single creative act valued according to its juxtaposition to reality and convention.

As *drafting*, drawing values mechanical accuracy and efficiency and relates to reality through a rigidly formal set of orthographic abstractions (plan, elevation, section, and isometric). These are only records of, or patterns for, the making of an existing or already-determined object. Excellence in drafting or mechanical drawing is judged exactly as you would judge the excellence of a copying machine. There is no room for self-expression or creative thinking, except perhaps in lettering style or choice and placement of the north arrow.

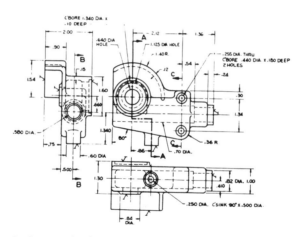

Gearbox control surface lock casting. (Adapted from a drawing by Convair Division of General Dynamics Corp.)

Drawing as drafting is an efficiently made pattern or record that is mechanically accurate and obeys rigid, formal rules.

As *design drawing*, drawing must satisfy several paradoxes. Design drawings should be committed to clear, complete representation of a design and simultaneously tentative and open to improvement. They may be informal but they must be accurate. They should show the design as it will exist in its surrounding context and also show the design itself as an environment surrounding the viewer. Design drawings should represent the design at once objectively and quantitatively as an integrated object and also subjectively and qualitatively as an environment to be experienced. And finally, although they are absolutely essential in generating, evaluating, improving, and recording the design, design drawings are of no value in themselves—their only role is to serve the design process.

Design drawings should be made primarily for the designer and only secondarily for others. They exist as "transparent viewers" through which designers can see what they are designing.

Le Corbusier—*Sketches for the chapel at Ronchamp.*

The most valuable design drawings are those that extend and shape the design process and accurately represent the experiential qualities of the design.

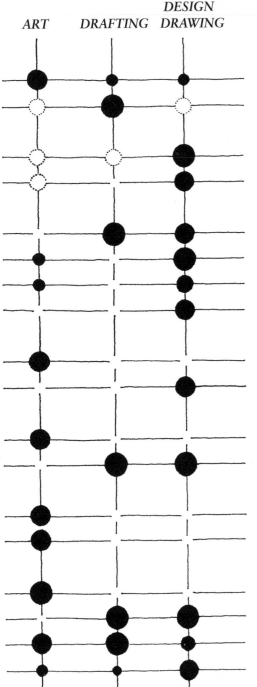

	ART	DRAFTING	DESIGN DRAWING	TECHNIQUE

Choice of media

Conformity to formal rules

Realism

Direct relationship to reality—realism

Inclusion of specific context

Time

Efficiency

Relationship to a decision-making process

Iterative drawing

Choice of when to make a particular drawing

Innovation

Inventing new ways of drawing

Inventing new uses for drawing

Perceiver

Open to various individual interpretations

Universal unambiguous interpretation

Delineator

Intended to demonstrate the skill
of the delineator

Self-expressive choice of subject matter

Purpose

To be admired as an end in itself

A means toward another end

Primarily communicates with others

Primarily for designer's self-communication

Size of circle indicates the relative importance of the characteristics.
Dotted circles indicate when a characteristic may or may not be present.

The table at left clarifies the differences between the three kinds of drawing. Design drawing shares certain characteristics with art and drafting, but it is clearly a different kind of drawing. Perhaps the differences between the three kinds of drawing can be summed up as follows:

ART: RESPONDING AND EXPRESSING

When artists draw they are *responding* to their environment, freely *expressing* their experience. When the drawing is finished they hope it will communicate a personal expression of something about their experience, variously interpreted in turn through each viewer's experience. Artists hang their drawings in galleries.

DRAFTING: DESCRIBING AND INSTRUCTING

When draftspersons draw they are *describing* a predetermined built or to-be-built object. When the drawing is finished they must count on its *instructing* precisely, without any freedom of interpretation, how the described object is or should be built. Draftspersons duplicate their drawings as instructions and then file them as records.

DESIGN DRAWING: GENERATING, EVALUATING, AND IMPROVING

When designers draw they are designing an environment that does not exist and has not yet been determined. They are directly *generating, evaluating,* and *improving* what they see in the crystal ball of the drawing. Their drawings may never be finished, but designers count on them to accurately represent the experience of the proposed environment to themselves and to those for whom they are designing. Designers may throw their drawings away.

The future of the three kinds of drawing will probably exaggerate their present differences. Drafting increasingly will be taken over by computers because of its repetitive mechanical nature. This possibility seriously jeopardizes traditional, noncomputerized "mechanical" drawing courses. The very name implies a machine-made ideal and it seems futile to continue training humans to produce something that has mechanical perfection as its goal.

Drawing as art will certainly continue, but the realism that in the past demanded precise delineation has been largely forsaken, and many artists use drawing as a predictive representation, with the final work being done by a painting process quite different from realistic representation.

Design drawing has perhaps the most potent future of the three. In his book, *Future Shock* (1970), Alvin Toffler suggests:

> Multiplying our images of possible futures is important; but these images need to be organized, crystallized into structured form. In the past, utopian literature did this for us. It played a practical, crucial role in ordering men's dreams about alternative futures. Today we suffer for lack of utopian ideas around which to organize competing images of possible futures.

Architects, landscape architects, and interior designers should take the lead in proposing the physical forum of alternative futures. Wright's Broadacre City, Soleri's Archologies, Archigram's various urban proposals and the recent *New Urbanism* were flawed but influential. Design drawing should be able to show us many better alternatives so that we can imagine what it would be like to inhabit them without having to build them.

Teaching and Learning Drawing

THE COMPUTER CHALLENGE

In the first edition of *Design Drawing* I argued that the conventional ways of teaching drawing, especially perspective drawing and shadow-casting, were so technical and tedious that the techniques were seldom actually used in practice. Today I must also argue against the misuse of drafting and rendering computer programs, which are rapidly growing in number. Instead of being welcomed as helpful supplements to design drawing, they are too often hailed as total replacements that make learning hand drawing unnecessary.

Freehand eyelevel perspectives that show the experience of the environment being designed are still the quickest and best representations on which to base a commitment to a particular design solution. Unfortunately, commitments to particular design solutions are too often made with little or no three-dimensional exploration. The rationalization is that the perspectives can't be drawn until the plans and sections are finalized or until the final design has been completely programmed into the computer.

Instead of improving our ability to study the three-dimensional experiential qualities of our designs, computers have helped us to add to the excuses for limiting the use of perspectives to that of nondesign presentation drawings. But designers still need to learn to draw by hand to make at least three kinds of drawings:

- freehand, precomputer, conceptual plan-and-section diagrams that explore the range of potential solutions to problems

A Victorian drawing class.

- perspectives, overlays, and the hand or digital coloring that helps to develop and win commitment to the best design solution
- layers of freehand drawing that humanize and give character and life to final presentation perspectives

It is unlikely that computers will ever take over these essential kinds of drawing because the well-trained human hand and eye will always be faster, better, and more beautiful.

TEACHING DRAWING

All concepts about teaching and learning drawing are based on assumptions about the nature, origin, and development of drawing ability. One of the few points on which I agree with the behavioral psychologists is that what appears to be drawing talent is actually the unrecognized product of years of reinforced behavior. Students who have not had drawing reinforced as a behavior may be discouraged in their first drawing or design class when they compare their drawings with those of other students who, with little apparent effort, draw much better than they.

TALENT

The conventional cop-out is to assume that such effortless drawing skill is a God-given or "natural" talent. This is a comfortable assumption for students, since it excuses their poor drawings or, worse, their dropping the whole idea of becoming a designer because they apparently don't have a "gift" for drawing. It is also a convenient excuse for teachers, since they can assume that students who draw clumsily are untalented and therefore unteachable. Little teaching or learning is possible where the assumption of innate or natural ability prevails. Talent is a myth, comfortable perhaps, but surely untenable for those who teach and attend drawing courses.

When a student exhibits what commonly passes for talent, his fellow students and teachers do not see the ten or fifteen years of reinforced drawing behavior. In every case I know of, this so-called talent is the product of reinforcement by parents, teachers, and friends and has become very self-rewarding. The talent myth also discredits the hours of concentrated effort it takes to learn to draw, which isn't fair to those who have made that effort. It similarly strips good drawing teachers of any credit they might deserve for the drawing abilities of their students.

MOTIVATION

The development of drawing ability does require a great deal of actual drawing. There are not many shortcuts to learning to draw. One of the paradoxes is that learning to draw quickly and confidently requires drawing slowly and tentatively over a long period of time. Clear, comprehensive explanation, graphic examples, and a patient, supportive attitude are teaching essentials, but perhaps the greatest single influence on a student's learning to draw is the self-rewarding experience of success. The completion of a difficult drawing that the student recognizes as successful and is proud of having drawn will do more to help a student learn to draw than all the books and lectures in the world. It doesn't matter if the student began with a half-finished drawing or received help from a teacher or fellow student. What is important is that the student understands how to produce a similar drawing—the help he or she received will be forgotten in the glow of realizing that such a self-rewarding experience can be repeated and improved. If a teacher can simply turn a student on to drawing as an enjoyable activity, that teacher has done the most important thing any teacher can do.

The companion book of drawing exercises, *Design Drawing Experiences*, is intended to provide the kind of successful drawing experiences that support the success of students' efforts to learn to draw. Reasonable diligence and applied intelligence should always be rewarded by success in drawing courses.

COGNITIVE DRAWING

While learning to draw may begin with making drawing rewarding, as much of the learning as possible should be raised to the cognitive, verbal level. The ability to draw must be more than a mere physical routine that a well-coordinated animal or robot could be programmed to do.

Too many books and courses rush into drawing as if it were a physical education class, with little recognition that drawing ability somehow extends above the shoulder and that there is a growing body of knowledge about drawing and its relationship to reality and to the design process. Most drawing mistakes are head mistakes, not hand mistakes.

Because I am interested in the intellectual side of drawing, I have included more arguments and rationale than are normally found in a book on drawing. The arguments are intended to expose you to—and perhaps persuade you to accept—certain ideas concerning design drawing's uses, methods, and values. But more than this, the arguments are intended to encourage you to think about the way you draw and make it conscious and communicable. The myth of talent or innate ability is of no service to the design disciplines, design schools, or individual designers. It is much more valuable to know as much as possible about the alternative uses, methods, and values of drawing, and to consciously choose and develop them for yourself as a designer.

TEACHING DESIGN DRAWING

The establishment of design drawing as a distinct practice has several implications for teaching design students to draw:

- Design drawing tasks should always include design decisions, even if it's only where to place the furniture or figures, choose the materials, or make minor changes in the design. There should always be some room for the student's creativity. The design opportunities may be quite limited, but there must be some responsibility for the delineator beyond just acting as a copying machine. Otherwise the drawing becomes an end in itself and ceases to be a design drawing.

- Design drawing courses should be taught by practicing designers who use drawing in the design process.

- Drawing landscapes and still lifes has only limited potential for teaching design students how to draw, for what is needed in design drawing is the ability to draw what doesn't exist, or exists only in the designer's mind. Drawing examples and details of well-designed environments, however, is extremely valuable in building a design vocabulary as well as drawing skills.

- Design drawing should be accurate but not mechanical.

- Design drawing should focus on environmental design choices, using entourage and drawing technique to make the drawing more real, but never letting them become the focus.

- Design drawings should always include the surrounding context, considering how the design will appear in its place.

- Design drawing tasks should teach speed and efficiency so the drawing can keep pace with the mind.

- Design drawings should be vehicles through which designers directly, clearly, and honestly communicate with themselves.

- Design drawing students should be encouraged to learn to make both personal and broadly shared kinds of design drawings, and to make intelligent, free use of whatever graphic representations might be helpful in a particular design process.

- Design drawing students should be aware of and practice making choices about what and how to draw in various situations.

The understanding and skills involved in design drawing could be learned at the junior high school level. I believe that the ability to represent the built environment, either as it exists or as it might exist, and the ability to diagram various concepts graphically is at least as useful as learning to make orthographic patterns of predetermined objects.

If we use writing as an analogy for drawing, *drawing as art* might be poetry and *drawing as drafting* might be a set of specifications, a scientific description, or a completed questionnaire. *Design drawing*, however, would be more basic, for it is no more than a vocabulary and syntax.

Design drawing has little to do with what is said, or even how it is said; it is simply the vocabulary, the grammar, or the voice. In this analogy, design drawing could even be thought of as preverbal, for whatever the designer wishes to say will be said and read in concrete and wood and steel and glass—not in drawings.

FREEDOM AND DISCIPLINE IN DRAWING

When students are given freedom in design or drawing classes they often ask, "You mean we can draw it any way we want?" The question poses a logical or semantic paradox, for the answer is, "No, for a long time you will be unable to draw it any way you want, unless you are prepared to have an experienced observer assume you intended to draw it inaccurately, ineptly, naively, or crudely. You can only draw it the ways you *can* draw it." Freedom in drawing begins with the disciplined ability to make more than one kind of drawing in more than one technique. It is only then that a designer can be said to have any freedom at all. Freedom and discipline in drawing are two sides of the same coin, they cannot occur alone.

STRUCTURED FREEHAND DRAWING

The kind of drawing advocated throughout this book can be called structured freehand drawing. It is structured in four ways:

- by an understanding of the purpose and potential of any particular drawing in the design process and an awareness of the varied choices of what and how to draw

- by a mastery of the spatial structure underlying perspectives and shadow-casting, drafted in critical cases as a basic framework

- by a mastery of a perceptual and procedural structure in drawing certain graphic indications so that they can be dependably replicated

- by the building up of an underlying structure of progressively refined studies so that the final drawing is always supported by previous drawings

This way of drawing is influenced by years of trying to teach young people who have little drawing experience to use drawing as a design tool. I believe it is the best way to teach the majority of students to understand the underlying structure and rationale of the various drawing techniques and their relationship to reality and to the design process. Teaching this way of drawing does not raise the drawings of the best students to their highest peaks, but it supports and raises the average and weak students' drawings to a point where they are no longer a handicap in communicating the proposed environment. I also believe the approach promotes the continued open-ended learning *of* drawing and *about* drawing because it is knowledge-based—based broadly on what is known about perception, conception, and the design process. It is not limited to art's *on-the-paper* technique or media application or by drafting's equipment and compulsion toward mechanical accuracy. It is in many ways a combination of art and drafting, but I believe the combination is synergetic—unexpectedly different and in many ways more

valuable for designers than either art or drafting.

Another characteristic of design drawing is its irreverence for drawing tools. One of the mistaken ideas that students carry over from drafting is that discipline and accuracy somehow reside in the T square and triangle or, more recently, the computer. This is not true of design drawing. There is an essential accuracy to be mastered, but it has nothing to do with tools. You can construct a perspective and cast the shadows on it freehand in the sand with your finger and make an essentially accurate, disciplined design drawing.

For those who have been indoctrinated into the disciplines of art or drafting, this book may seem at first to offer a diluted or permissive approach to drawing. This is not my intention. I do not believe today's environmental design students need less drawing skill or discipline—they need more—and you will find the skills presented here at least as demanding as those of traditional art or drafting courses. What I hope to add to the discipline of drawing is more *understanding* of how the drawing skills they are learning can be used in the design process.

THE FREE HAND

The free hand is the only fit companion to the free mind. The term has special significance: it is precisely because we walk upright, freeing our hands for more important tasks, that we have developed the intelligence called human. In the design process, we need to generate tentative design proposals that can be continually compared to the restated design problem. These graphic representations should suggest restatements of the problem, and those restatements should in turn suggest more drawings. Design is essentially a stream-of-consciousness process, and the reliance on tools, even a sophisticated tool like a computer, is inhibiting. It is possible to sketch the diagrams and the graphic representations of tentative design proposals with a free mind, free hand, and any simple drawing tool.

THE FREE MIND

The goal in design drawing is the freedom that comes from being able to draw the environment as variously as possible, so that all drawing decisions are free. To make decisions out of a fearful, defensive incompetence is surely a miserable way to draw, design, or live. To make a particular drawing in a particular way because you are afraid of perspectives, ink, or color is the most regrettable of limitations in the design process.

The glory of design education is that it asks students to visualize an environment better than the one surrounding them, and for which there are no answers at the back of the book. Environmental design students enjoy a unique form of education for life, which probably should be the general form of all education: to visualize, propose, advocate, and practice making the choices about their future, always with the possibility that they might be wrong. Drawing ability, like our environment and ourselves, is not received as a gift, or discovered, or found, but must be consciously, deliberately, freely, joyously *made*. The purpose of this book is to help in that making.

The Value of Learning to Draw

After centuries of being considered an essential skill for environmental designers, drawing has been challenged in several very different ways in the past fifty years. These challenges have resulted in a diminishing and weakening of drawing courses in the curriculum. However, it recently has become apparent that, in spite of the illusions of some design educators and their graduates, practicing designers still draw and want the graduates they hire to be able to draw by hand. Most of them consider CAD skills essential, but only in addition to basic traditional drawing ability, not as its replacement. Despite the devaluation of drawing by many design educators, most environmental designers continued using drawing as the best representational tool available to designers. Even in the professional schools some teachers continued to teach students how, and even why, to draw. We can come out in the open now and speculate as to why the teaching of drawing was mistakenly abandoned.

All these attacks on the learning and teaching of drawing ability began with the misconception I discussed earlier—that drawing ability is a God-given or hereditary talent and therefore very difficult or impossible to learn or teach. My experience, in almost forty years of teaching, is that drawing is one of the most learnable skills any designer needs, and if it is in any sense a gift, it is the gift of parents, siblings, friends, and teachers.

I am also convinced that it is much easier to learn to draw today than when I began my design education because there are so many excellent teachers and books available to today's design students. In spite of the procession of great designer/delineators, from Michaelangelo to Louis Sullivan, few have ever bothered to document how they learned to draw or how they thought a design student should learn to draw.

When I started my design education at the University of Illinois in 1948, the only books on drawing were by the artists Kautzky and Guptill, neither of whom was a designer. Their beautiful books were written entirely for artists whose final products were to be the drawings, not the designs represented by the drawings. I had a role in beginning to change that with *Drawing As a Means To Architecture* in 1968. Since then, the books of Edward T. White III, Paul Laseau, Paul Stevenson Oles, Michael Doyle, Kevin Forseth, and Frank Ching, all practicing designers, are infinitely better than Kautzky and Guptill. They cover all the kinds of drawings made during the design process, from the programming and precept diagrams of Tim White and the conceptual and development sketches of Paul Laseau, through the comprehensive collections and explanations of Frank Ching and the basic graphic geometries and beautiful analytical renderings of Kevin Forseth, to the gorgeous color drawings and clear instructions for their making by Mike Doyle and the masterpiece tone renderings of Steve Oles. These brief descriptions of their works don't begin to do them justice. You should spend a weekend with these books and then buy the ones that interest you most—it will be the start of your personal professional library. They amount to as substantial a literature as you are likely to find on any category of design education. It is much easier to learn to draw today because of the contribution of these teachers, and more of a shame when design students come to believe that drawing isn't important or isn't worth their while to learn.

Historically, elementary and secondary education valued handskills as an integral part of education and spent time teaching penmanship, drawing, woodworking, and sewing. This attitude in the schools was solidly reinforced in the home, where skills like quilting and carpentry were valued for their necessity and their pleasure. This meant that design education could get away with merely selecting and encouraging students who could already draw, because such a society produced plenty of people with a "talent" for drawing. Professional design schools often delegated drawing instruction to the engineering or art faculties, or, when this support wasn't available, assigned it to the most junior faculty, who abandoned the courses the moment a newer faculty member appeared.

Both home life and education have changed profoundly in the last fifty years. The handskills that once were a distinguishing characteristic are today simply curious or perhaps even embarrassing. Time-consuming handwork has been in a steady decline, along with the value and dignity of all physical labor. To spend long periods of time alone making anything by hand, particularly if the skill itself takes a long time to master, is generally considered to be eccentric and certainly is not associated with satisfaction and pleasure as it once was.

Our schools also seem to have lost the will or the patience to teach abilities like handwriting—or even grammar or spelling for that matter—that require repetitive correction on an individual basis. It is much easier to show films or discuss ideas verbally than to take great stacks of papers home for correction. With all these changes, it is hardly surprising that so few students nowadays seem to have the "gift" of drawing.

Concurrently, the last thirty years have seen a steady devaluation of drawing in the professional design schools. There are a number of reasons for this, all of them understandable and some justifiable. First there was the realization that the traditional emphasis on drawing ability was unfair to students who happened to have little previous drawing experience. Instead of trying to equalize these individual differences by taking on the responsibility for teaching everyone to draw, the equalization was attempted through the promotion of other forms of communication: verbal descriptions, analytical diagrams, and models. These changes were rationalized by claims that drawings are misleading and generally less dependable than models or even analytical diagrams.

Drawing was also denigrated because it was associated with the academic formalism of the École des Beaux-Arts, and the overemphasis on elaborate presentation drawings was taken to be symptomatic of an overemphasis on formal visual qualities, which were seen as cosmetic and superficial. In its most extreme form this new view of architecture held that beautiful drawings were the first clue to design decadence, and the ability to make beautiful drawings and especially to enjoy their making was to be avoided and denied.

The design methodologists found it easy to build on this devaluation of drawing and the misunderstanding of drawing's relationship to the design process. Most methodologists assume that drawing is or should be simply the neutral printing out of decisions already made in the clear light of logical "problem solving." They generally mistrust drawing as some sort of irrational ritual, preferring various quantitative analytical models, and their influence has contributed to the general devaluation of design drawing.

Underlying all these reasons for drawing's de-emphasis is the persistent attempt to turn environmental design into a science. Scientism would replace the cultural certainty of tradition or the academic certainty of a particular style with the scientific certainty of method—what Colin Rowe has called "physics envy." And this latest search for certainty is just as futile as the others. It has affected drawing by assuming that, like science, we need a series of metalanguages representing certain unseen but ever-present and all-important environmental qualities. Just like the neutrinos of subatomic physicists and the black holes of astronomers, scientism insists that there are unseen environmental problems that we must identify, analyze, represent, and solve. We thus get matrices, graphs, decision trees, interaction nets, endless box-and-arrow diagrams, and other pseudoscientific notations that supposedly represent critical, but invisible, characteristics of an environment or the design process. The analysis these various graphic tools allow is certainly beneficial, but it cannot replace the synthesis represented in traditional design drawings. What the proponents of the various problem-solving languages seem to forget is that, unlike the explorations of science beyond the macro- and micro-scales of human vision, environmental design manifests at human scale. Environmental qualities must be directly perceivable by human beings, and we have had the graphic means to represent such environmental qualities for a long time.

A more recent challenge to the value of learning to draw is the computer. In spite of the persistent claims of computer advocates and the obvious benefits of computer graphics, however, it is increasingly clear that computers are only another tool, albeit a very sophisticated one, for helping us make uncreative, automatic, and repetitive graphic images for communicating and constructing a design once it has been determined. Computers show little or no signs of being much help in making the personal conceptual drawings that explore, synthesize, and lead a designer to commit to a particular design.

The speed with which all these changes in the teaching of drawing occurred is perhaps unique to American academia. Bright young students who never learned to draw could, within a year or two, have earned a master's degree and be telling a whole classroom full of slightly younger students that they really didn't need to learn to draw because drawings are essentially misleading and, when absolutely necessary, can be produced by underlings or machines. These young teachers never needed to actually say anything about the value of learning to draw because their lack of respect for the ability was very apparent in their design teaching and, as far as they knew, was correct, since they usually hadn't experienced the absolute necessity of drawing in practice. Meanwhile, back at the office, the typical architect, landscape architect, or interior designer kept wondering why recent graduates couldn't draw and weren't even convinced they needed to learn.

From time to time we see the publication of the design drawings of prominent designers like Helmut Jahn or Frank Gehry in our professional periodicals. Such publications make it clear that famous designers still draw, but the editors' interest in their drawings seldom extends to how the drawings were used in the design process. The drawings are simply viewed as interesting artifacts to illustrate the articles.

If this recurring interest in design graphics is to be more than merely part of the ebb and flow of fashion or the editorial recycling of interest, we must use it as an occasion to reconsider some of our attitudes toward drawing. We need to begin by dropping the talent myth. By bringing the ability to draw out of the realm of giftedness and personal idiosyncrasy and acknowledging that it has a fundamental relationship to designers' thinking processes, we can initiate a serious dialogue. I believe such a dialogue will make clear the differences between design drawing and the traditions of art and drafting. It also will soon replace the hybrid collection of myths and inappropriate notions we have mindlessly accepted from artists and draftspersons. If we raise drawing to this level of serious discussion, we might remember that the ability to draw is absolutely basic for environmental designers.

Anticipation being one of the mixed blessings we gained from the evolution of our big forebrains, humans worry a lot about the consequences of their future actions. You probably remember your first date and how you tried to visualize what it would be like—what you or your date would say or do in the various situations that might occur.

Like any other human anticipation, environmental designers worry about the effects of their professional actions in designing environments because they know that whatever they design will affect the lives of its occupants for many years. Being able to draw the environment you are designing so that it is believable and so that you can imagine it built and being used by people is fundamental in visualizing its success. Until we can accept and believe our own representations of the environment, we can never be sure about the success of our proposed designs.

Just as the ability to correctly anticipate and visualize critical human situations is a source of great personal confidence, the ability to make drawings that you can accept as reliable predictors of the qualities of any environment you are designing is one of the surest foundations of conceptual confidence for a designer. Accurately anticipating a future for which you are professionally responsible is the primary purpose of design drawing.

We must rededicate ourselves to the serious teaching of drawing in the early years of design education for three reasons: First, because drawing remains the best way to visualize what you are designing. Second, because drawing is even more learnable today thanks to the many excellent books on the subject. And third, because drawing can be the source of creative confidence for any designer. Drawing courses should be taught by experienced designers, perhaps aided by student assistants, and must have student/teacher ratios that allow the kind of personal attention real learning requires.

On a more basic level I believe, as parents of today's schoolchildren, environmental designers must take the lead in insisting that writing and drawing skills be restored as integral parts of elementary and secondary education and that the skilled hand and eye be recognized as indispensable partners of the skilled mind.

1 Perception

The transactional process by which we experience the world is called perception. An understanding of perception is particularly important for environmental designers because the environments we design and the design drawings we make will be experienced by ourselves and by others through this process. We may make the best analysis and conceive the best solution, but unless the qualities we see in the design can also be perceived by others, especially the clients or users, the design will be a failure. Environmental designers' entire enterprise hinges on perception, and we should develop a deep and deserved confidence in our own perception as well as a sensitive anticipation of the perceptions of others, which will always be different from our own.

Psychology's concept of perception has changed over the years from a simplistic and passive stimulus/response model to a recognition that (1) all perception occurs in concrete situations loaded with interdependent relationships; (2) that we actively, even compulsively, seek perceptions; and (3) the perception of the environment is fundamentally different from the perception of an object. There is not space in this book, nor do I have the credentials, to consider perception comprehensively, but environmental designers should read the available literature on perception in order to understand themselves, and the people for whom they will be designing, as perceivers.

Although perception includes the input from all our senses, I will concentrate on visual perception, not just because it is the most critical sense involved in drawing, but also because our sense of vision is dominant in our perception of and interaction with the environment.

The Dominance of Vision

EVOLUTION'S LEGACY

A human being may be thought of as part genetic inheritance, part cultural indoctrination, and part conscious, self-directed experience. Of these three, genetic inheritance, or the legacy we are left by evolution, is the most pervasive, and we can do little to change it in a lifetime; but by increasing our understanding of this ancient inheritance we may learn to respect its useful characteristics and somewhat mitigate its prejudices.

All our senses have served in our survival, but our sense of sight has made the biggest contribution. Visual perception dominates the perceptions of our other senses for several reasons:

• Vision operates at a greater distance than the other senses, and thus is our early warning system. Our evolutionary ancestors, once mauled by saber-toothed tigers, undoubtedly found it valuable to recognize the species at a distance—without having to get close enough to smell, hear, feel, or taste it. In *The Intelligent Eye* (1970), R. L. Gregory proposes:

> Eyes give warning of the future, by signaling distant objects. It seems very likely that brains as we know them could not have developed without senses—particularly eyes —capable of providing advance information, by signaling the presence of distant objects. . . .

• Vision is our best-developed sense. The visual world is incomparably richer in information than the worlds available to our other senses. This is because the eye, unlike some of our other senses (which have actually deteriorated over the years), has continued to evolve with the brain. To quote Gregory again:

> As we shall see, eyes require intelligence to identify and locate objects in space, but intelligent brains could hardly have developed without eyes. It is not too much to say that eyes freed the nervous system from the tyranny of reflexes, leading to strategic planned behavior and ultimately to abstract thinking. We are still dominated by visual concepts. . . .

In *Experiences in Visual Thinking* (1972), Robert H. McKim explains the pervasiveness of visual thinking:

> Visual thinking pervades all human activity, from the abstract and theoretical to the down-to-earth and everyday. An astronomer ponders a mysterious cosmic event; a football coach considers a new strategy; a motorist maneuvers his car along an unfamiliar freeway: all are thinking visually. You are in the midst of a dream; you are planning what to wear today; you are making order out of the disarray on your desk; *you* are thinking visually.

Donald D. Hoffman in *Visual Intelligence*: *How We Create What We See* (1998) supports the dominance of visual intelligence:

Vision is normally so swift and sure, so dependable and informative, and apparently so effortless that we naturally assume that it is, indeed, effortless. But the swift ease of vision, like the graceful ease of an Olympic ice skater, is deceptive. Behind the graceful ease of the skater are years of rigorous training, and behind the swift ease of vision is an intelligence so great that it occupies nearly half of the brain's cortex. Our visual intelligence richly interacts with, and in many cases precedes and drives, our rational and emotional intelligence. To understand visual intelligence is to understand, in large part, who we are.

• Our minds have been built on an evolutionary linkage of vision and touch so strong as to make our other three senses secondary. Our world looks like it feels and feels like it looks and this correspondence is the foundation of our successful interaction with the environment. In his book *Man's Emerging Mind* (1965), N. J. Berrill explains:

> Sight for us is vision in action, and memory of things seen is memory of visual images and of our own optic muscle movements. Close your eyes for a moment and picture a triangle: you can sense your eyes moving from point to point. And to all of this we add all the sensory impressions gathered from the skin and muscles of fingers and palms. The brain is enlarged between the regions set apart for vision and touch so that records of their past associations can be neatly stored. We have in fact a type of brain as highly distinctive as it can be, in which seeing and doing are in some ways indissoluble. . . .

• Vision is the feedback loop by which we manipulate our bodies, particularly our hands. All mental activity is visual/actual in the sense that we actually seek perceptions that promise some beneficial potential for action. Bronowski, in *The Ascent of Man* (1973), proposes:

> We are active; and indeed we know, as something more than a symbolic accident in the evolution of man, that it is the hand that drives the subsequent evolution of the brain. . . . we can oppose the thumb precisely to the forefinger, and that is a special human gesture. And it can be done because there is an area in the brain so large that I can best describe its size to you in the following way; we spend more gray matter in the brain manipulating the thumb than in the total control of the chest and the abdomen.

For the preceding reasons vision has become our most trusted sense and our basic arbiter of value. What we call *mind* would better be called *eyemind*, or, more correctly, *eyemindhand* because of the eye/hand linkage on which our brains are built.

Although vision is the last sense to be developed in our evolution, its leading role in the development of the mind makes it the source of most of our information about the world. As Gibson has pointed out, psychologists have seemed obsessed with optical illusions, forgetting that the main reason our vision can be tricked is because it is so dependable. Abstractly perverting the visual cues that serve us so well in the real world easily misleads us, not because our perception is faulty, but precisely because our vision is so trustworthy it seems beyond suspicion.

PERCEPTION'S PREJUDICES

Visual perception is never neutral and its prejudices are linked to the evolution of the eyemindhand system.

• *Perception is selfish,* selectively perceiving information that promises survival, pleasure, personal gain, or adulation.

• *Perception focuses,* using foveal vision to sharpen the center portion of our visual field at the expense of the peripheral context, making it difficult for us to comprehend complexity.

• *Perception separates,* seeing a world of objects separate from one another in time and space, making it difficult for us to see relationships.

• *Perception forms wholes,* or gestalts, jumping to conclusions from partial evidence.

• *Perception discriminates,* seeking subtle differences in form and pattern.

• *Perception judges instantly,* in the first impression, and verbal explanation merely serves as a "rational" justification, making it difficult to withhold judgment.

• *Perception chooses dominance over equivalence,* seeing the figure before the field rather than seeing an object and background as equivalent, making it difficult to consider the context or maintain balanced interest.

• *Perception demands new input,* becoming saturated as in the color after-images resulting from over-stimulation or starved resulting from sensory deprivation, making it difficult to stay with a design long enough to complete it.

While all these prejudices have served in our evolutionary survival, they form our most persistent perceptual/conceptual blocks. Our compulsions to stereotype, discriminate, make premature decisions, and endlessly sort and classify the world can be traced to the way we see.

Perception of the Environment

SPATIAL PERCEPTION

The visual cues by which we perceive space are particularly important for environmental designers, in relation to both the environments they design and the drawings they make to represent those environments. Spatial perception depends on surfaces, edges, and various perspective cues. This is demonstrated in the perspectives at right, in which the four geometric shapes, which are the same size in each drawing, appear to vary in size and distance depending on the background surfaces that form their context.

SURFACES

From its crude beginnings our perceptual system has always seen a visual field divided at the horizon. The upper half of this field has always been a bright sky, and the lower half, the earth's surface, with a textural gradient going from coarse to fine as it recedes into the distance. The perception of this textured horizontal surface and continuous background surfaces is essential to our understanding of space. In *The Perception of the Visual World* (1950), Gibson argues:

there is literally no such thing as a perception of space without the perception of a continuous background surface. . . .

The 'basic' idea is that visual space should be conceived not as an object or an array of objects in air but as a continuous surface or an array of adjoining surfaces. The spatial character of the visual world is given not by the objects in it but by the background of objects. . . .

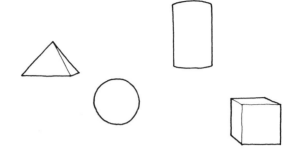

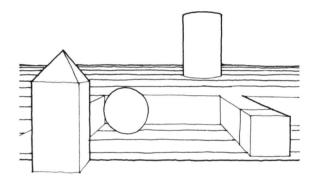

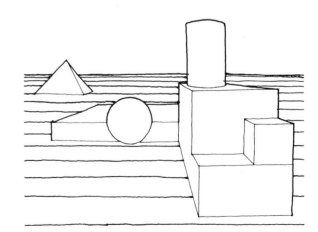

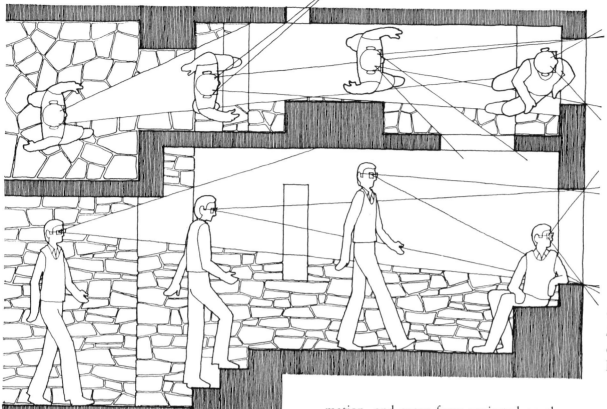

EDGES

The shape or conformation of the space and especially the kinesthetic experience of moving through the environment is conveyed by the perception of edges. In *The Senses Considered as Perceptual Systems* (1966), Gibson explains what happens in our kinesthetic experience of the world:

> whenever an observer moves, the array changes. Every solid angle of ambient light—each one of the adjacent pyramids in the diagram—is altered. Every form that would be projected on a sphere centered at the eye is altered by a perspective transfor-

mation, and every form projected on the retina, of course, undergoes a corresponding transformation. . . .

> . . . Introspectively, the field is everywhere alive with motion when the observer moves.

In addition to being sensitive to the apparently changing sizes and inclinations of surfaces, the kinesthetic experience of space depends on the movement of spatial edges against their backgrounds—the striptease of space, or what Gibson calls "kinetic optical occlusion and edge information." To quote Gibson further:

> The edge of a surface in the room is specified by a discontinuity in the flow of optical texture, as at the table top. The corner of a surface in the room, the angle of two planes, is

specified by another kind of discontinuity in the flow. . . . As I will phrase it, texture can undergo "wiping" or "shearing" at a margin. That is, one texture can be "wiped out" by another or "cut across" by another. This kind of optical discontinuity corresponds to a separation of surfaces in the world. . . . The motion perspective for an environment is theoretically loaded with information about its layout, and the experimental tests that have been made so far agree in showing that this information is effective for human perception.

One last series of quotations from Gibson's *The Senses Considered as Perceptual Systems* describes the extension of what we learn from the kinesthetic experience of space:

> When the individual goes from one place to another, . . . he has a different *vista*. What is the connection between one vista and another? The answer is interesting; the transition is another edge phenomenon, an "emergence-from-behind."

> When the man in the room walks up to and through the door, the edge of the door frame expands to uncover the new array of the next room. The same unwiping of the new array (or wiping out of the old one) occurs in reaching the corner of a street or the brow of a hill. If the man had panoramic vision, he could see the old array gradually being wiped out behind his back. The specification for a hole in the world, an aperture, window, or space between obstacles, is that it "opens up" on an optically denser array. . . .

. . . One vista leads to another in a set of continuous connected sequences. Over time, as the individual moves about the house, the street, the town, and the country, the sequences come to be perceived as a scene, and the fact that the transformations all make a group becomes evident to him. The individual is then able to find his way from place to place, but more than that, he is able to see one place behind another on a larger and larger scale. He is then geographically oriented. Even when he is shut into the room he is able to apprehend the house, the street, the town, and the countryside in relation to the room. . . .

The information provided by kinetic occlusion and its variants is extremely rich. It specifies the existence of an edge in the world, and the depth at the edge, but it does even more. It also specifies the existence of one surface behind another, that is, the continued existence of a hidden surface. . . .

PERSPECTIVE

For too long philosophers and psychologists thought that the perception of space or depth was entirely the result of binocular vision. There are at least twelve other visual clues that help us to perceive space. In the appendix to his book *The Hidden Dimension* (1969), Edward T. Hall abstracted the list that follows from James J. Gibson's *The Perception of the Visual World*.

A. Perspectives of Position

1. *Texture perspective.* This is the gradual increase in the density of the texture of a surface as it recedes in the distance.

2. *Size perspective.* As the objects get farther away they decrease in size. (Apparently not fully recognized by the Italian painters in the twelfth century as applying to humans.)

3. *Linear perspective.* Possibly the most commonly known form of perspective in the Western world. Renaissance art is the best known for its incorporation of the so-called laws of perspective. Parallel lines like railroad tracks or highways that join at a single vanishing point at the horizon illustrate this form of perspective.

B. Perspectives of Parallax

4. *Binocular perspective.* Binocular perspective operates very much out of awareness. It is sensed because, owing to the separation of the eyes, each projects a different image. The difference is much more apparent at close distances than at great distances. Closing and opening one eye and then the other makes the differences in the images apparent.

5. *Motion perspective.* As one moves forward in space, the closer one approaches a stationary object, the faster it appears to move. Likewise, objects moving at uniform speeds appear to be moving more slowly as distance increases.

C. Perspectives Independent of the Position or Motion of the Observer

6. *Aerial perspective.* Western ranchers used to have fun at the expense of dudes unfamiliar with regional differences in "aerial perspective." Untold numbers of these innocents would awaken refreshed and stimulated, look out the window and, seeing what looked like a nearby hill, announce that it was such a nice, clear morning they were going to walk to the hill and back before breakfast. Some were dissuaded. Others took off only to discover that the hill was little closer at the end of half an hour's walk than when they started. The "hill" proved to be a mountain anywhere from three to seven miles away and was seen in reduced scale because of an unfamiliar form of aerial perspective. The extreme clarity of the dry, high-altitude air altered the aerial perspective, giving the impression that everything was miles closer than it really was. From this we gather that aerial perspective is derived from the increased haziness and *changes in color* due to the intervening atmosphere. It is an indicator of distance but not as stable and reliable as some of the other forms of perspective.

7. *The perspective of blur.* Photographers and painters are more likely than laymen to be aware of perspective of blur. This form of visual space perception is evident when focusing on an object held out in front of the face, so that the background is blurred. Objects in a visual plane other than the one on which the eyes are focused will be seen less distinctly.

8. *Relative upward location in the visual field.* On the deck of a ship or on the plains of Kansas and eastern Colorado, the horizon is seen as a line at about eye level. The surface of the globe climbs, as it were, from one's feet to eye level. The

further from the ground one is, the more pronounced this effect. In the context of everyday experience, one looks *down* at objects that are close and up to objects that are far away.

9. *Shift of texture or linear spacing.* A valley seen over the edge of a cliff is perceived as more distant because of the break or rapid increase in texture density. Although several years have passed since I first saw a certain Swiss valley, I can recall clearly the bizarre sensations it produced. Standing on a grassy ledge, I looked down 1,500 feet at the streets and houses of a village. Blades of grass were sharply etched in the visual field, while each blade was the width of one of the small houses.

10. *Shift in the amount of double imagery.* If one looks at a distant point, everything between the viewer and the point will be seen as double. The closer to the viewer, the greater the doubling; the more distant the point, the less doubling. The gradient in the shift is a cue to distance; a steep gradient is read as close, a gradual gradient as far.

11. *Shift in the rate of motion.* One of the most dependable and consistent ways of sensing depth is the differential movement of objects in the visual field. Those objects which are close move much more than distant objects. They also move more quickly, as noted in Point 5. If two objects are seen as overlapping and they do not shift positions relative to each other when the viewer changes positions, they are either on the same plane or so far away

that the shift is not perceived. Television audiences have become accustomed to perspective of this type because it is so pronounced whenever the camera moves through space in a manner similar to the moving viewer.

12. *Completeness or continuity of outline.* One feature of depth perception that has been exploited during wartime is *continuity of outline*. Camouflage is deceptive because it breaks the continuity. Even if there is no texture difference, no shift in double imagery, and no shift in the rate of motion, the manner in which one object obscures (eclipses) another determines whether the one is seen as behind the other or not. If, for example, the *outline* of the nearest object is unbroken and that of the obscured objects is broken in the process of being eclipsed, this fact will cause one object to appear behind the other.

13. *Transitions between light and shade.* Just as an abrupt shift or change in the texture of an object in the visual field will signal a cliff or an edge, so will an abrupt shift in *brightness* be interpreted as an edge. Gradual transitions in brightness are the principal means of perceiving molding or roundness.

Since surfaces, edges, and perspective form the basis of our perception of space, they are especially important for design drawings, which represent kinesthetic space. This will be discussed in depth in chapter 3.

PERCEPTION AS TRANSACTION

The scientific study of perception is the province of psychology, and while I believe that designers should never uncritically accept what others, even scientists, tell them about human behavior when it conflicts with the designer's own experience, psychologists have established a body of theory and research that has direct implications for anyone wanting to design or draw the environment.

The psychologists whose work has the most direct bearing on environmental design are the transactional psychologists (not to be confused with transactional analysis, a psychotherapy technique). Transactional psychologists trace their name to John Dewey and A. F. Bentley's 1949 book *Knowing and the Known*, from which William H. Ittelson has abstracted the following quotations in his 1973 book *Environment and Cognition*.

"Observation of this general [transactional] type sees man-in-action, not as something radically set over against an environing world nor yet as something merely acting 'in' a world, but as action *of* and *in* the world in which man belongs as an integral constituent [p. 52]." Under this procedure we treat "all of [man's] behavings, including his most advanced knowings, as activities not of himself alone, nor even as primarily his, but as processes of the full situation of organism-environment [p. 104]." "From birth to death every human being is a *Party*, so that neither he nor anything done or suffered can possibly be understood when it is separated from the fact of participation in an extensive body of transactions—to which a given human being may contribute and which he modifies, but only in virtue of being a partaker in them [p. 271]."

The transactionalists have made us aware that what appears to our prejudiced perception as a simplistic world of separate pieces is actually something much more complex. I will refer to the distinctions they make between object perception and environment perception in chapter 3, but here I want to touch on the richness and complexity they have identified in our perception of the environment. The best I can do is quote directly from *Environment and Cognition*.

The distinction between object and environment is crucial. . . .

Environments surround . . .

The quality of surrounding—the first, most obvious, and defining property—forces the observer to become a participant. One does not, indeed cannot, observe the environment: one explores it. If the observation is the object then the exploration is the environment. The problem of exploratory behavior, its nature, function, and its relation to the individual's larger purposes, becomes central to the study of environment perception. The limits of the exploration, moreover, are not determined; the environment has no fixed boundaries in space or time, and one must study how the explorer himself goes about setting boundaries to the various environments he encounters. The exploratory aspects of environment perception can thus extend over large spaces and long time spans, and require some process of spatial and temporal summation; both long- and short-term memory are essential.

Environments, in addition, are always multi-modal. It may be possible to conceive of an environment which offers information through only one sense modality, but it probably would be impossible to build. In any event, it would be a curiosity. Perceptual experiments have been notably deficient in their study of multi-modal processes, and yet these are essential for understanding environment perception. We need to know the relative importance of the various modalities, the kinds of environmental concepts, and sets of environmental predictabilities associated with each modality. But more important, we need to know how they function in concert: what processes are involved when supplementing, conflicting, and distracting information is presented through several modalities at once.

A third necessary characteristic of environments is that peripheral, as well as central, information is always present, peripheral in the mechanical sense—the area behind one is no less a part of the environment than that in front—and peripheral in the sense of being outside the focus of attention. Both meanings are important and raise questions concerning the process underlying the direction of attention.

Fourth, environments always provide more information than can possibly be processed. Questions of channel capacity and overload are inherent in environmental studies. However, the mere quantity of information does not tell the whole story.

Environments always represent simultaneously, instances of redundant information, of inadequate and ambiguous information, and of conflicting and contradictory information. The entire mechanism of information processing in the nervous system, about which psychologists are only beginning to learn, is brought into play.

The four characteristics of environments which objects either cannot or usually do not possess (their surrounding quality; their multi-modal property; the presence of peripheral stimulation; and the presence of too much information which is simultaneously redundant, inadequate, and contradictory) already suggests that findings in object perception can be applied only with great caution to environment perception. But these characteristics are nevertheless rather traditional in perceptual studies in that they refer to what can very broadly be called stimulus properties. Beyond these properties, however, there is another group of properties of the environment which must be taken into account in any study of environmental perception, and which are almost completely foreign to the field of object perception.

The first of these, or a fifth characteristic of the environment, is that environment perception always involves action. Environments, as we have seen, are not and cannot be passively observed; they provide the arena for action. They define the probabilities of occurrence of potential actions, they demand qualities which call forth certain kinds of actions, and they offer differing opportunities for the control and manipulation of the environment itself.

Environments call forth actions, but not blind, purposeless actions. Of course, what an individual does can be expected to be largely influenced by the particular purposes which he brings to the situation; at the same time, however, the environment possesses the property, a sixth characteristic, of providing symbolic meanings and motivational messages which themselves may effect the directions which action takes. Meanings and motivational messages are a necessary part of the content of environment perception.

Finally, and perhaps most important of all, environments always have an ambiance, an atmosphere, difficult to define, but overriding in importance. One can at this point only speculate on some of the features of the environment which contribute to this ambiance and which thereby become of central significance for the study of environment perception. First of all, environments are almost without exception encountered as part of a social activity; other people are always a part of the situation and environment perception is largely a social phenomenon. Second, environments always have a definite esthetic quality. Esthetically neutral objects can be designed; esthetically neutral environments are unthinkable. Last, environments always have a systemic quality. The various components and events relate to each other in particular ways which, perhaps more than anything else, serve to characterize and define the particular envi-

ronment. The identification of these systemic relationships is one of the major features of the process of environment perception.

Thus, to the first four characteristics dealing roughly with stimulus properties, three others must be added: the role of action and purpose as defined, delimited, and called forth by the environment; the presence of meanings and motivational messages carried by the environment; and the concept of ambiance, related to the esthetic, social, and systemic qualities of the environment. . . .

Ittelson makes clear that environments and the perception of environments are much more complex than we might assume. His thoughtful analysis of any environment's characteristics and their interrelationships makes it clear that environmental perception is both more common to our experience and more promising to research than object perception.

Environmental Interest

The brains of human babies require a certain amount of visual stimulation from the environment for adequate development and, if deprived of any sensory stimulation, the brain will actually manufacture visual patterns. There is a threshold to visual environmental interest; we judge content below that threshold as not worthy of our attention.

Beyond this minimum threshold extends a wide variation of visual environmental interest that will hold a perceiver's attention. The clue to holding a perceiver's attention is to promise and deliver successive levels of visual interest or information.

I will now categorize the information available in the visual environment, beginning with basic sense data and progressing through innocent and informed perception of natural and built environments.

INNOCENT INTERACTION with the environment depends on the interactive potential of the environment that demonstrates Ittelson's statement that one does not, indeed cannot, observe the environment: one explores it. Children at play perhaps provide the best example of this uninhibited interaction with the environment.

I had the good fortune of growing up in a very small midwestern town and our house was perhaps half a mile from the grade school. Over the years, the boys from my side of town made the most interesting route to and from school. This route changed as our bodies and our sense of adventure strengthened; it also depended on the

Photograph by Peggy Hamilton Lockard.

Photograph by Peggy Hamilton Lockard.

time available, the season, and the mood and makeup of the group. We didn't passively find the path, we deliberately created it, putting the experience together from what was available each day.

The choices we made were based almost entirely on participatory interactions with our environment and had nothing to do with cleanliness, efficiency, or safety, which society lays on us as we grow up. Rather, we valued getting dirty, spending great amounts of time, and taking physical risks as valid ways of interacting with the environment.

If I went home with a playmate from the other side of town, we took his way home, which he was very proud to show me. Turn an active, uninhibited group of children loose in any environment and they will find the special interactive opportunities it offers in a few minutes.

SPATIAL INTEREST is the most dynamic interest category and the richest source of interest for most environmental designers. The spatial interest of any environment is potential kinesthetic interest—that is, the variety of exploratory experiences that can be anticipated.

Specifically, the sources of spatial interest are the aforementioned edges that hide various volumes of space. Interesting spatial environments abound in partially hidden spatial volumes and extend space ahead, to the sides, and up and down. The simplest test of good spatial interest is whether the environment is likely to be chosen by a group of children as a place to play hide and seek.

TEXTURAL INTEREST is primarily tactile, a matter of touch or potential touching. Evolution has given us a particularly close coupling of our eye and hand. We can sense how things will feel by looking at them and recalling what similar textures felt like. We can almost "touch" or "feel" a surface with our eyes. By looking at an environment and the textures of its surfaces, we can sense what it will feel like to stand barefoot on a sheepskin rug, lean against a stone wall, or grasp an oak handrail. Textures promise perhaps the most intimacy in experiencing an environment.

Photograph by Peggy Hamilton Lockard.

TONAL INTEREST is perceived at the greatest distance and under the poorest illumination; tonal information is the last to disappear when we lose our sight, making it the most basic category of environmental/visual interest. Tonal interest derives from the relative darkness or lightness of the various surfaces of a space or object. This variety may be caused by the play of sunlight, shade, and shadow or the result of color or material selections. Tonal interest can be judged simply by squinting your eyes when viewing a space or object. If, when you squint, all the interest or definition is squinted out, you are probably looking at a space or object that has little or no tonal interest.

The tonal interest that comes from sunlight is the most dynamic because it changes as the sun moves, making the morning experience of a space quite different from the late-afternoon experience. A strong example of this is the casting of shadows by the grandstands on a baseball diamond as the afternoon lengthens. Another example of tonal interest is the difference between a brightly lit exterior space and dim interior space. Sunlight provides not only tonal interest but also kinesthetic interest because the viewer can anticipate the sensual experience of moving out of shade into sunlight or from sunlight into the coolness of shade.

Material and color afford a secondary opportunity for tonal interest. They can be used to exaggerate or correct the proportions of spaces, as light surfaces tend to recede while dark surfaces advance. Another approach is to tone-code the space or object in such a way that all surfaces oriented similarly have the same relative tone—all ceilings light, all floors dark, and all walls somewhere in between.

COLOR INTEREST is perhaps the most arbitrary, personal, and emotional of the interest categories. This is apparent in the way we are manipulated by clothing and decorating fashion—our ideas often change according to which colors are "in" or "out" this spring or fall. Color is also arbitrary in that a painted surface can be any color; paint as a material has no intrinsic color, unlike other materials such as stone or wood. We also have come to look down on institutional color schemes, which are both ubiquitous and unimaginative. "Eyestrain green" and "hospital beige" are examples of innocuous color schemes. By contrast, the powerful impact of entire walls of strong color in modern Mexican architecture is impossible to ignore.

Color varies in importance with the designer, from the entirely white buildings of Richard Meier to Luis Barragan's color-saturated surfaces. Color schemes may also vary from the integral colors of natural materials like stone, brick, or wood to the applied surface treatments and paints that today can be almost any color.

Color helps to suggest reality in quick sketches, as illustrated in the overlays in the chapter on applications. A few strokes of blue become a sky; a trunk and a few branches with a green smudge make a tree; a brick red indicates a floor or roof; and a quick brown tint will communicate wood. This kind of coloring makes no design statement and takes advantage of natural or traditional colors to communicate reality.

In a similar way color can also substitute for distant sidewalk-level details, figures, cars, signs, or window displays, which take so long to draw. A few well-drawn figures, cars, and signs in the foreground can be suggested as extending into the distance by combining color with very sketchy drawing. This is demonstrated in the digital coloring of the perspectives in chapter 7.

What I can say or show about the use of color in design drawing is severely limited in what is basically a book in black and white. For further information on color, I recommend Michael Doyle's *Color Drawing*.

These four interest categories—spatial, tonal, textural, and color—are integral to any designed environment and should be included in the design drawings we make to study the environments we are designing. While most designs will emphasize some interest categories over others, you should be sure that any imbalance among the four categories is the result of deliberate design decisions and not a weakness in your design concepts or in your design drawing ability.

Photograph by Peggy Hamilton Lockard.

ADDITIONAL INTEREST, unlike the four previous interest categories, is not integral to the designed environment. It refers to that collection of stuff with which we furnish any space: furniture, trees and landscaping, cars, and human figures. In modern buildings this category helped replace the integral ornament that was stripped away because it was considered superficial and cosmetic. But in design drawings additional interest adds much more than just ornamentation. Well-drawn, carefully integrated entourage can specify the scale, indicate the use, and demonstrate the space of any drawing, especially perspectives. These humanizing elements make the drawing come alive as a believable representation of a designed environment. Additional interest is one of the last categories the computer will do for you, and mastery of it is sure to improve your drawings and make drawing more enjoyable.

Intention and Meaning

One side of our humanness, we are told, is our compulsive search for intention and meaning in the world. This is true on several levels when we perceive the built environment and also helps to explain why we become designers. We believe that the environments we design will be appreciated by those who inhabit them—that our intentions for the environments we design will be perceived.

Although certain environmental qualities are rather obvious, the deeper levels of meaning and intention in the built environment and natural world are only available to those who have learned to see them. We can easily recognize that a rosewood table with a marble top is an elegant piece of furniture, but we may not appreciate the elegance, simplicity, and economy of a Hardoy canvas butterfly chair.

NATURE

When we perceive nature we may find it interesting or dull, beautiful or ugly. But whether we believe in a creator God or the natural selection of evolution, we inevitably accept what we see as beyond or above the assignment of design responsibility. We may perceive a tree of a certain species as being a misshapen specimen, but it would seldom occur to us to seriously criticize the entire species as being a bad design. And even if we did decide that hyenas or camels are unfortunate evolutionary results, it would remain a passive perception; we would hardly recommend their extinction based on that perception.

THE BUILT ENVIRONMENT

When we perceive the built environment, we assign design responsibility. One of the main reasons our cities often become ugly and unworkable is that the design responsibility is fragmented—traceable only to unquestioned and inflexible regulations. Because the design responsibility is obscured, we tend to accept the entire built environment as "natural" and inevitable—just as we accept nature. We forget that people deliberately wrote the regulations, set the utility poles, and erected the billboards.

We should be very careful in deciding what to call natural, for the word tends to provide a protective mantle that allows us to circumvent criticism and assignment of design responsibility. If we view the natural or built environments as irrevocable and inevitable, we will never perceive them critically or consider the possibility of correcting them.

THE FIRST IMPRESSION

The first and perhaps most important level on which the manmade environment communicates is that of the instantly pervasive first impression. At one point in our evolutionary history this immediate reflex may have helped us to instantly judge the danger or safety of a situation, but I'm not sure it serves us well in situations that require in-depth study and evaluation, for the first-impression prejudice dies hard. Nevertheless, the almost-instant formation of an evaluative perception is part of our perceptual legacy.

Exactly what is perceived in that first impression is difficult to define, but perhaps the immediate and dominant impression of any built environment is of the designer's skill—the record not just of brute effort, but also of ability, care, and intelligent intention.

The reason this first impression of human skill or intelligence is so important is that it determines, more than anything else, our interest in spending more time discovering the various levels of design intention communicated.

DESIGN INTENTION

The discovery of design intention is the key to all further perception of the environment and is one of the most exciting realizations a person can have while perceiving a human product. Furthermore, man-made products can communicate their makers' intentions long after he or she is gone: an archeologist can read the design intentions of an ancient people; musicians can appreciate Bach or Beethoven by playing their music and understanding the composers' intentions. The following list, while not complete, demonstrates the variety of factors that have impact on design intention.

1. *Craftsmanship* communicates the skill of the maker, but the appreciation of craftsmanship demands that you be familiar with the particular skill, by having done it yourself, by having watched it being done, or by having seen other examples of similar work. The appreciation of design intention in craftsmanship depends on how well the design extends or demonstrates the craft. Does the aria extend and demonstrate a coloratura soprano voice? Does the brick wall extend and demonstrate a mason's skill? Does the design of the wall reveal what can be done with brick at openings, corners, and cap or does it simply use masonry as a type of wallpaper?

2. *Construction process* can be communicated by leaving a record of the process in the finished work. Exceptions to this, such as the pyramids, may also be interesting and lead to endless speculation as to how they were made. Deliberately designed curiosities, however, like concealed bookshelf doors or panels that open to the touch, must be considered a luxury. The motion of the potter's wheel recorded in a pot, the imprint of form work or tie holes for concrete, and the exposed trusses of a roof all add to the understanding of the construction process and tell us more about the intention and skill of the designers and builders.

3. *Function* can also be read in a well-designed place or object. How something is to be held, opened, or moved through can be communicated by its form, material, and particularly by the design of its parts. For example, most objects that are intended to sit or stand are impossible to place upside down or on their sides. Similarly, a good design articulates the handle of an object meant to be held. Design quality can be assessed by determining whether the object's use is visually predictable.

4. *Budget* refers to the information about the economy or richness of the design of any human product. This information is communicated not only by the materials and ornamentation, but also by the permanence or lasting quality of the design. Remembering that the budget is normally beyond the control of the designer, however, sophisticated perceivers never equate a fat budget with good design. Shaker furniture and farm implements are examples of excellent design, perhaps *because* of a severe budget limitation.

5. *Structural order* (internal relationships) is communicated by the relationship or lack of relationship of a design's constituent parts. Relationships can be made by geometry, proportion, material similarity or contrast, and joint articulation and arrangement, to name a few. The skeleton and circulatory system of the human body and the table of contents of a book are good examples of structural order. This internal ordering always occurs in relationship to the entire design—the parts relate to one another and to the whole.

6. *Contextual order* (exterior relationships) communicates how well designs relate to their context. The context includes the designed object or environment's immediate physical surroundings and climate, the cultural or regional tradition, the prevailing technology, and the contemporary esthetic. Designers may choose to follow or adapt to some of these and disregard or challenge others, but their designs will always communicate the combination of those relationships.

7. *Unity* is another way of thinking about structural and contextual order and can be achieved in at least two ways. Traditionally, unity is thought of as being closed or exclusive. The internal parts of a composition are designed to relate so strongly that they form a closure that excludes contextual relationships and especially additions or mutations. A sym-

phony, a Greek temple, and a limerick all defy addition. The other form of unity is open or inclusive. It relies on an internal structure that has little to do with spatial or temporal boundaries and can easily be extended and added to. Either of these ways of obtaining unity may be valid for a particular design. The designer's decision regarding unity will be communicated in the design.

8. *Reaction* may be thought of as a factor in communication and is closely related to contextual order. By reaction, I mean the appeal of novelty for novelty's sake, or, similarly, the appropriation of a historic style for whatever that identification may add to the design. The perception of this type of communication depends completely on the perceiver's prejudices, just as its inclusion in any design depends on the designer's prejudices.

9. *Classic patina* is something for which most designers strive, but it is only achieved by years of human use. It is the quality that some designers try to acquire cheaply by recalling historic design styles, but it can only truly evolve in designs that function for a long time as they were intended.

All these factors in design communication contribute to the richness of information inherent in everything made by human beings. If we learned to look for them, we could undoubtedly find other types of communication to add to this list.

Perceptual Experience

CULTURE'S INDOCTRINATION

Cultural indoctrination gives its members a set of operating instructions for the eyemindhand system inherited from evolution. The instructions include an interpretation and categorical naming of the environment and experience, and a set of inhibitions and guilt structures designed to enforce a culturally correct way of using the eyemindhand system.

All perception—even that of a newborn—is informed by past perceptions and by purposes and intentions. The perceptual prejudices we inherit from evolution, the culture we are born into, and our individual experience quickly add to the selectivity of the experience network through which we perceive the world. Our developing attitudes influence all our perceptions. It is in what we expect to perceive that perception and conception become indistinguishable. Our cultural indoctrination can lead us to preconceive our perceptions. This correspondence of perception and conception will be discussed further in the next chapter, but is demonstrated by the fact that we refer to any conceptual framework in which we think or act as our *worldview*.

Anthropologists have clearly established that different cultures inhabit different perceptual worlds. In his book *The Hidden Dimension* (1969), Edward T. Hall says:

Space itself is perceived entirely differently. In the West, man perceives the objects but not the spaces between. In Japan, the spaces are perceived, named, and revered as the ma, or intervening interval.

Cultures with different worldviews explain the visual world differently, and languages further reinforce these cultural differences. In *A Study of Thinking* (1956), Bruner, Goodnow, and Austin write:

The categories in terms of which man sorts out and responds to the world around him reflect deeply the culture into which he is born. The language, the way of life, the religion and science of a people: all of these mold the way in which a man experiences the events out of which his own history is fashioned. . . .

Because of its dominance and accuracy, visual perception might seem to be beyond any kind of cultural censorship. Precisely because of its dominance, however, vision is our most carefully censored sense and carries most of our cultural prejudices.

Our visual indoctrination is doubled in that we are not only taught how to see the world but also what to show the world. Our manners are very much matters of appearance. We are taught to respond to certain visual cues and ignore others. Fortunately, by adolescence, we often strongly counter cultural standards in matters of personal appearance—vision's dominance as a tool of cultural indoctrination is nowhere more clear than in the threat this rebellion always poses to the older generation.

Perception reinforces, or perhaps is the source of, all these mechanisms of cultural indoctrination. We *see* a world that is differentiated, but culture's indoctrination assures that we *perceive* a world of categories structured in the hierarchies and polarized in the dualities that the culture has found useful.

In *The Crack in the Cosmic Egg* (1971), Joseph Chilton Pearce sums up our cultural indoctrination:

> Our world view is a cultural pattern that shapes our mind from birth. It happens to us as fate. We speak of a child becoming "reality-adjusted" as he responds and becomes a cooperating strand in the social web. We are shaped by this web; it determines the way we think, the way we see what we see. . . .

PLURAL PREJUDICES

Cultures pluralize the prejudices built into the visual perceptual system we inherit from evolution.

- Perception's selfish tendency is extended into a group selfishness that serves the culture's long-term survival.
- Perception's focusing tendency is extended into a preference for simplistic causes and effects and a compulsive search for scapegoats and enemies.
- Perception's separating tendency helps us accept the endless inclusive/exclusive boundaries of the categories and hierarchies in which cultures direct us to see the world.
- Perception's tendency to form wholes or gestalts gives us perhaps our most powerful cultural esthetic and ethic: unity. This begins with the family and ends with the nationalism celebrated in the phrase "united we stand, divided we fall."

- Perception's tendency to discriminate is extended into all the abuses of discrimination and privilege within a culture.
- Perception's instant judgment is extended into the demand for partisan loyalty on which cultures have thrived: "You are either with us or against us."
- Perception's choice of dominance is extended into all the forms of competition within and between cultures.
- Perception's need for new input becomes a culture's need for change, expressed superficially in fashion or entertainment and most deeply in conversion or revolution.

Opportunity Seeking

EXPERIENCE'S OPPORTUNITIES

Because perceivers' cultural indoctrinations, past experiences, and the contexts in which perceptions take place are never identical, perceptions will always be different; identical perceptions are impossible. Even a second glance at the same object is different from the first because the perceiver has been changed by the first perception. This explains why repeated experiences are never quite the same as the originals and why eye-witness accounts inevitably vary. Perception, knowledge, and truth are transitory and different for each of us.

Perhaps the most basic distinction in perceptual attitude is whether our experience leads us to anticipate success or failure in our interactions with the environment. A history of success will lead perceivers to see the world as a field of opportunities for further success, while a history of failures can cause them to spend most of their energy avoiding responsibility or identifying potential excuses for their anticipated failures.

Anticipated success and opportunity-seeking are the keys to education. When either education or society fails to offer perceived opportunities, they fail together. The heightening of perception based on perceived opportunity accelerates learning. If an opportunity is perceived, it sharpens perception, and the sharpened perception itself promotes perception of further opportunities.

On the other hand, children who fail to perceive any opportunity for pursuing their self-interests, in school or in society, will experience a dulled perception, and this will foreclose perception of other opportunities. The presence of perceived opportunity is exhilarating and the absence of perceived opportunity is debilitating, in education and in life. The basic goal of education and of society should be to make perceived opportunity abundant and equal for everyone.

Most designers are optimists and their optimism is usually sufficient to withstand several years of intensely critical design education. The traditional optimism in the design professions makes me wonder at the increasing use of the phrase "problem solving" to describe what a designer does. "Problem solving" sounds more like the motto for an exterminating company than for any creative activity.

Unlike mathematical problems, so-called design problems are never fixed or absolute. Experienced designers' solutions to design opportunities are more sophisticated and creative because their experience has given them the ability to perceive both their responsibilities and their freedom more comprehensively and flexibly. They simultaneously see a much more complex "problem" and have much greater flexibility in restating that "problem" to match a broader range of "solutions."

It is important for designers to self-educate themselves perceptually. In designing for others, designers must learn as much as possible about how perception works and develop a sensitivity to the perceptions of others. The main thing to remember about other perceivers is that while they share a similar evolutionary heritage and may share a similar cultural indoctrination, their perceptions are prejudiced by their experiences and self-interests, and their prejudices will never be the same as yours.

The legacy from our evolutionary eyemind-hand system and our cultural worldview is not ours to choose, but we *are* free to choose many of our perceptual experiences. If there is one thing I have learned as a teacher trying to hold the attention of a group of students, it is that human beings exercise perceptual freedom. Our responsible use of this freedom, however, is never quite as apparent.

John Locke proposed that the mind is a blank slate, a *tabula rasa,* on which our senses write the experiences of our lifetime. It seems clear now that the slate can only accept certain messages because of the evolutionary eyemindhand system and the cultural worldview we inherit; it is equally clear that we actively hold the chalk as it writes by choosing our perceptual experiences. Our grip on the chalk is much stronger today than in the past, when perceptions were forced on us by the responses necessary for survival, but our grip on the chalk is also uncomfortable because we are responsible for the perceptions we choose and learn from in our lifetime.

The effect of the positive perceptual attitude involved in opportunity seeking is clearly demonstrated in most designers. While negative perceivers collect "problems," positive perceivers compulsively collect "solutions," confident that they will have the opportunities to use them. Creative people, including successful designers, tend to choose their perceptions carefully. They are often more selective in what they show themselves, where they travel, what they read, and whom they listen to. They also find ways to relate more of what they perceive to their work.

A lifetime may be thought of as the sum of a person's consciousness, and today we are remarkably free in choosing how to fill our consciousness. Just as dietitians or nutritionists claim "you are what you eat," most designers know that "you are what you have seen."

RELATIVITY OF PERCEPTUAL EXPERIENCE

All perception is relative, to what is perhaps an infinite range of variables. Only three of the more obvious variables will be considered here.

1. *Past experience* affects subsequent perceptions. Our past visual experience and our cultural indoctrination make us believe that things have inherent qualities. However, our perception of both quality and quantity are entirely relative to our past experience.

   It is pointless then to consider either quality or quantity as inherent characteristics of what we are perceiving. We can, however, examine some of the variables that affect our perception of what is presented.

   The perception of the quality of a specific environment is entirely dependent on the quality of the environments you have experienced in the past and also perhaps on your sophistication at the time. Thanks to color photography and reproduction technology we can know many environments, at least superficially, without experiencing them directly. But to fully experience a building or garden you must visit the site in person. Most great designers visit and study the creations of those they admire.

2. *The role of the perceiver* is another potent variable in the relativity of perception. A bull is quite differently perceived by a bullfighter, a butcher, and a tanner. The perception of a building is quite different for a contractor, a realtor, an owner, or an architect. Our perceptual attitudes also change in response to whether we are actively associated with the thing perceived or just a passive observer. A contractor's perception of a building is certainly heightened by his direct association with it—he expects to act on what he perceives, not just ponder it at his leisure.

   Our attitude toward perception may also be affected by our confidence in our own perception. This is one reason why many people commission designers—they lack a confidence in their own evaluative visual perception or "taste." Other people who are unsure of their own perception may rely on the opinions of friends and be very afraid of wearing, driving, or occupying anything of which their friends might disapprove. This is also sometimes seen in design education, when beginning students frequently ask for their teacher's opinion or approval. Later, if they work at sophisticating their perception, they won't need to ask for approval as often, and much later, as they develop confidence in their own perception, they will find the teacher's approval completely unnecessary.

3. *Context.* All perception occurs in a specific psychological context and the context may strongly influence that perception. Because perceptual contexts vary widely, it seems worthwhile to consider these variations.

- *Preparation* for perception is one of the contextual variables. By preparation, I mean the immediate circumstances that may have prepared you or left you unprepared for a particular perception. Preparation depends primarily on how you come to a particular perception. Whether you perceive voluntarily or involuntarily can make quite a difference. (Chance perception allows no preparation and so can carry no preparatory prejudice.)

  Voluntary perception, like the decision to see an exhibition of paintings, involves a certain preparation or expectation. The experience may have been recommended by a friend or by a favorable review, or you may have seen other paintings by the same artist. In most cases of voluntary perception, the decision to perceive carries with it a prejudice that favors the perception. On the other hand, involuntary perception, like being coerced into seeing a movie in which you have no interest, is something to be endured and the perceiver is not likely to be sharpened by the same anticipation.

  Preparation further prejudices perception by the anticipation of certain qualities and exclusion of others. Reading a critical review before you see a movie may focus your perception on the movie's faults or strong points, and focused perception always excludes other information. Professional athletes and coaches well know that when they tell a football official to "Watch their tackle, he's holding our guard," he can hardly keep from doing it—which means he may miss other infractions.

At first, such prejudicing of perception may seem negative, but all knowledge is prejudicial and the very aim of education is to change your perception. There is no such thing as informed innocence. What is important is to be careful of whom and what you allow to influence you and to become as aware as you can of all your perceptual prejudices.

- *Pressures* vary dramatically and also strongly influence perception. One kind of pressure is what we feel when we are perceiving for others. This varies from the perception involved in selecting a gift for someone to the pressure a sentry might feel in wartime, when the security of an army depends on his perception. In all cases, perception is affected by the perceiver's relationship and sense of responsibility to those for whom he is perceiving.

This second-hand perception wastes immense amounts of time in bureaucracies and other management hierarchies where underlings neglect their own perceptions in favor of trying to second-guess what their superiors' perception will be. Perceiving for others also allows a kind of dishonest appraisal. For instance, the perceiver may blame his rejection on his superior by saying, "Well, it looks good to me, but J.C. will never approve it because. . . ." The kind of second-hand perception that occurs when a designer is kept from dealing directly with the user or decision-maker is often very frustrating.

Another kind of pressure is that of convention or manners. This pressure doesn't influence perception so much as it inhibits what we say about our perception. The opinions of designers are often sought as expert in matters of visual "taste."

Persuasion is another pressure that may influence perception. Saturated as we are today with advertising, persuasion may as easily turn our perception off as on.

The author or presenter of what we perceive will also influence our perception. "Look at the picture I drew, Daddy," is a sure setup for favorable perception. The reputation or associations of the presenter may also affect perception. Bosses, for instance, usually benefit from this. Good teachers also enjoy a similarly heightened perception from their students.

Time and age also exert pressure on perception. The leisurely, dawdling perception of childhood is too soon replaced with the hurried perceptions that must be made in order to cope with the adult world. Although we perceive visual information almost instantaneously, in-depth seeing requires time. One of the ways psychologists exaggerate optical illusions and perceptual errors is by decreasing the time allowed for visual perception.

Other peoples' opinions can also influence your perception. Strong, confident perceivers may be influenced little by what others think. Many people, however, are counter-punch perceivers; they need to know what someone else has perceived before they feel their perception is complete.

- *Consequences* that may follow from perception (or misperception) are perhaps the most important contextual influences. Tightrope walkers, mountain climbers, and gunfighters all know that the consequences of perception may be extreme. Designers are introduced to this kind of heightened perception when they are commissioned to design a very prominent public environment.

The relativity of perceptual experience is what gives "experience" its meaning. Knowing that a brick wall is laid correctly depends on having seen or laid other brick walls. Knowing that a particular exterior space you are designing will have an intimate human scale depends on having experienced or designed similar spaces. Being confident that a drawing you are making will have an acceptable or exceptional professional quality depends on your having seen and made similar drawings.

Perception of Design Drawings

In addition to a general grasp of visual perception, designers need a specific understanding of the perception of design drawings—both the perception of the designer who is making them and that of colleagues, clients, and others to whom they must communicate—and not only the perception of a designer's own drawings, but those of other designers.

THE DESIGNER'S PERCEPTIONS

Perception, not hand skill, is the key to drawing ability, and designers' practiced perception of their own drawings is crucial in developing design ability.

Design students should learn to look critically at all design drawings—especially their own. You should respect a peer's or teacher's opinion and learn to perceive what they perceive in a drawing, but you should never passively accept any evaluation of your design drawings.

The development of this critical attitude toward your own work should be tempered with patience and understanding. Because your perceptual ability has been operating much longer than your drawing ability, you will always see more flaws in your drawings than you can ever correct, but don't be too hard on yourself. Be especially careful not to think of your drawing ability as inferior to that of another student until you understand that student's drawing background. You will usually find that a fellow student who, with little apparent effort, draws much better than you has been drawing a lot longer and/or a lot more intelligently than you

have. Differences in drawing ability can almost always be explained by variations in experience and motivation.

TRANSPARENCY

Design drawings represent successive attempts at drawing a congruence between the design problem and its solution. The drawings themselves are not the congruence, but are simply representative "transparencies" through which the real congruence can be judged. The importance of the transparency of design drawings cannot be overemphasized and perhaps is best understood in comparison to a drawing intended as a work of art.

When we look at anything, the completion or meaning of the perception requires a synthesis of whatever we are looking at with our expectations and our past experience in our eyemind. When we view a painting, this perceptual synthesis is initiated at the plane of the canvas. There is nothing beyond the canvas.

In contrast, design drawings must be neutrally transparent representations of an attempted congruence between the problem and its solution. Unlike a painting, a design drawing forms a window through which the real environment it represents can be perceived. A design drawing must be honest, direct, and undistorted, and the perceptual synthesis must be consummated beyond the drawing—in the reality of the environment the drawing represents.

OPACITY

A major problem for designers can be the opacity of their drawings. When a design drawing becomes opaque the designer is unable to see *through* the drawing to the reality of the environment being designed. Drawings can become opaque in two quite different ways.

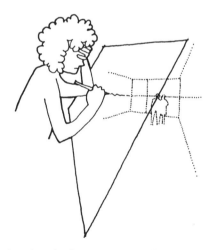

The first kind of opacity, usually encountered by beginning designers, occurs when designers loathe their own drawings. By the time most students enter professional design education, they are rather sophisticated judges of "beauty" or "good drawing" and their own first attempts at making design drawings are often so repulsive to them or so poor in relation to some of their fellow students' drawings that they are unable to look through them to the reality of what they are designing. You should be patient, though never satisfied, with your drawing ability. As your perception improves, so will your drawing, and you will be able to look through even the crudest sketches and see the design content they represent.

The opposite kind of opacity, while less painful, can be even more damaging to a designer. This kind of opacity comes not from a loathing, but from a love of the drawing *as a drawing*—at the level of drawing technique and cliché graphic cosmetics. Students who draw very well are most subject to this perceptual error. These students often become more interested in a virtuoso drawing technique and its superficialities then in communicating the real environment the drawing represents and for which they are responsible.

Both kinds of opacity are often encouraged in drawing courses by assignments that have no design content and therefore have no reality *beyond the drawing* for which the student is responsible. Both kinds of opacity stop designers' perceptions at the level of the drawing and keep them from perceiving the reality of what they are representing with the drawing. As long as designers see and think of their design drawings as only relatively clumsy or elegant compositions of lines on pieces of paper, they will misunderstand and misuse drawing.

TWO-CIRCUIT CYBERNETICS

Another way of looking at the problem of privileging the drawing over the reality is to remember that the eyemindhand system has two feedback loops. One feedback loop allows your eyemind to monitor and continually control your hand as you draw. This circuit, which helps us draw and could be called the drawing loop, stops at the surface of the drawing. The second feedback loop goes beyond the drawing and keeps it transparent. This circuit allows your eyemind to monitor and continually evaluate the design as your hand draws it. While it may operate more slowly, it is your main means of evaluating and improving the design. To make design drawings, both circuits must be turned on.

OPPORTUNITIES

The perception of design opportunities in design drawings is one of the central ideas of this book. The perception of such opportunities depends on:

- the assumption of a participatory role for drawing in the design process
- the anticipation of the appearance of design opportunities in the drawings

- the perceptual experience to recognize them when they appear
- willingness and confidence to keep drawing until they appear

If you believe that drawing is nothing more than the direct printout of a full-blown conception, you won't expect to gain much from the perception of your design drawings. If, on the other hand, you have learned from experience that drawings are much more than just a conceptual print-out—that they are an integral part of conception—then you will perceive design opportunities as you draw. You will seldom finish a drawing without changing it or starting a new one based on opportunities you see in the drawing.

Design opportunities appear only to those who are prepared to recognize them. You must have saturated your perceptual experience with design solutions, with ways of making environments, by reading about and visiting as many well-designed environments as you can, if you hope to recognize similar potentials in your drawings. The opportunities aren't announced with fanfares and blinking neon signs. You must recognize them as potential patterns, or relationships, or forms, and the recognition only comes from study and experience.

If design opportunities are to "appear" in your drawings, you must also learn to enjoy drawing. This means that the activity of making the drawings and the drawings themselves must be a source of pleasure. Designers who use drawing confidently in the design process surround themselves with their drawings and spend hours looking for opportunities in the drawings. The drawings themselves, although they may be rather mysterious multicolored patterns on buff tracing paper, inevitably develop a certain vitality and are also displayed with a certain pride *as drawings*. Although I have warned against overly self-conscious drawings in which graphic cosmetics obscure the design content, rough design study drawings are a different matter. The haste and intensity with which such design drawings are made will almost always make them immune to the evils of narcissism.

Design drawings are special examples of what Newell and Simon (*Human Problem Solving,* 1972) have called EMs, or external memories (as opposed to STM—short-term memory—and LTM—long-term memory). Like any other drawn or written matter that serves a creative process, these external memories are drawn simultaneously in our consciousness and in the world. Once externalized, they become part of what Karl Popper has called World 3—the product of minds (as distinguished from World 1—material things—and World 2—subjective minds). Design drawings have a life of their own and may contain more than we ever intended in making them. Brian Magee explains in his book *Karl Popper* (1973):

> In man, some of the biological characteristics which developed to cope with the environment changed that environment in the most spectacular ways: the human hand is only one example. And man's abstract structures have at all times equaled in scale and degree of elaboration his transformation of the physical environment: language, ethics, law, religion, philosophy, the sciences, the arts, institutions. Like those of animals, only more so, his creations acquired a central

importance in the environment to which he had then to adapt himself, and which therefore shaped him. Their objective existence in relation to him meant that he could examine them, evaluate and criticize them, explore, extend, revise, or revolutionize them, and indeed make wholly unexpected discoveries within them. . . .

Through our hand's drawing them, and our eye's seeing them, drawings also allow the participation of all the elements of human intelligence and include the unconscious layers of our experience network. We may draw and recognize potentials in the drawing for patterns and relationships that we "know"—preverbally, intuitively, illogically. We may realize that a collection of small spaces that need to be near one another functionally don't need to be physically separated from one another as we have been drawing them, but can instead be spatially connected in one continuous space, like the living spaces of Frank Lloyd Wright houses.

Exploratory design drawings also legitimately offer the kind of random stimulation recommended for creativity by Edward de Bono (*Lateral Thinking,* 1970).

DECISIONS

The choice of which drawings will best represent designers' ideas to themselves should be made consciously and carefully. Mindless habit or convention in the choice of drawings dulls our eye-minds and can critically inhibit the design process.

The order in which we perceive design drawings is critical because subsequent perceptions are limited by the information gained in initial

perceptions. The habit of always beginning with a plan drawing should be questioned in relation to the particular design problem.

Another mistake is to underestimate the information processing potential of our eye-minds. Design drawings should be loaded with as much graphically encoded meaning as possible. Color, line weight, and texture can be interrelated and used to represent various functions or design qualities. We waste our time when we don't draw and perceive to our potential.

ENVIRONMENTAL DESIGN DRAWINGS

The drawings through which we perceive the reality of our designs should represent the designs as environments, not objects. Just as psychologists have spent too much time studying object perception instead of environmental perception, designers, especially architects, have spent too much time drawing and perceiving their designs as objects, separated from their context and never to be entered or occupied.

Ittelson and the environmental psychologists have pointed out that the more basic mode of perceptual experience is that of environmental perception and that, unlike object perception, the perception of environments is more complex, interactive, and full of meaning.

DESIGN EDUCATION'S INDOCTRINATION

Design students can experience serious frustration in adapting to the indoctrination of the design discipline or to the particular school they have chosen. Most schools try to avoid narrow approaches but even the most liberal design or drawing education is essentially an indoctrination. Students may discover that both the design discipline (architecture, landscape architecture, or interior design) and the particular school or university they have chosen contradict their parents', friends', former teachers', and their own ideas of what constitutes good design or good drawing.

If students can weather the frustration, they will learn a great deal from this doctrinal shift. They will learn a new design and drawing discipline and, more importantly, they will learn that there are many possible approaches to design and drawing and that they must make their own. Perceptually, such a shift in indoctrination can be shattering because the student must master a whole new set of visual cues. An example of this in architectural design education is the difficulty of getting students to look at the *space*—and its shape, structure, surfaces, openings, and relationship to other spaces—rather than at the *things* in the space or on its surfaces.

Although few design schools today indoctrinate their students in any single style, the teachers and advanced students usually favor a general esthetic, which may be foreign to the student's previous experiences. Unfortunately, such a style is the first thing students master because it is easy to identify; the deeper levels of design may take much longer to understand and some students never move beyond the superficial "school" method of drawing trees or figures.

WHAT YOU SEE IS WHAT YOU GET

The validity of the design professions turns on the assumption that anything that is designed will be better, in some sense, for having been designed. This designed value relies on the communication of designed qualities to the viewer and user. When we look at a chair we may find it beautiful in its structure, workmanship or materials, or in relationship to its context. Then we sit in the chair and it communicates its physical comfort, which then colors our future visual appraisal of it and other chairs.

This communication takes place on several levels but remains narrowly, though not exclusively, focused in the viewer's or user's visual sense. The direct experience of an object or place by the other senses tends to verify or modify our visual evaluations, but the visual sense remains dominant in succeeding evaluations of similar objects or places.

The fact that our evaluation of environments predominantly hinges on the visual sense is why drawing should be used in designing an environment.

The value in learning and using drawing in the design professions does not lie in the usefulness of drawings as patterns for construction or quantity surveys. The production of construction documents has been largely taken over by computers. Nor should a designer learn drawing primarily to sell the design for an environment. This function may almost as happily be turned over to professional delineators. Rather, drawing should be used by a designer to predict, evaluate, and improve the visual communication of design qualities. If these qualities aren't communicated by the drawings, they probably won't be communicated by the environment.

I have heard arguments that put down drawings or three-dimensional models as misleading and deceptive. Such arguments undoubtedly have some validity. Drawings and models are misleading, but they are the best we have. Words, I think, are much more misleading. Our language is highly value-colored and I have found the eye to be much more trustworthy than either the ear or mouth.

James L. Adams argues for drawings over words in *Conceptual Blockbusting* (1974):

> Visualization, as expressed through the use of drawings, is almost essential in designing physical things well. One reason for this is that verbal thinking, when applied to the design of physical things, has the strange attribute of allowing one to think that he has an answer when, in fact, he does not. Verbal thinking among articulate persons is fraught with glib generalities. And in design it is not until one backs it up with the visual mode that he can see whether he is fooling himself or not.

Language is more broadly understood and accepted as the almost exclusive media of intelligence and reason. Drawing and other nonverbal forms of expression, like music, have been denigrated as unreliable and warped by fashion, emotions, and personal expression. However, designed environments are experienced directly and pervasively by our most accurate sense—sight .

We cannot read a building, a garden, or an interior. The designer does not have the opportunity to give every user or viewer a guided tour or hand out a descriptive brochure in persuasive prose. The users of an environment experience it directly, without benefit of language, so designers must communicate their intentions directly and primarily visually.

The validity of using drawing in the design process, then, seems undeniable. Designers must be masters of visual/spatial communication, both as delineators and perceivers, for the visual qualities of their designs must speak for them. The best way to predict the experience of a designed environment is to draw accurately and perceive carefully what appears in design drawings.

DRAWINGS BY OTHER DESIGNERS

Drawings by other designers can be a great source of frustration when you are learning to draw, but if you can get over seeing them as threatening, they will greatly help you to improve your drawing ability.

Many design students are discouraged early in their education by experiencing something like this: You arrive at the design studio on time, well prepared, and with the proper equipment. You have read the assigned material and begin to work with great diligence and seriousness on the assigned design or drawing project. The person at the next desk arrives late, asks what the assignment is, borrows equipment from neighbors, sings or whistles, and spends very little time actually drawing but a great deal of time apparently admiring the drawing. After some time you cast a curious glance at the next desk to see what could possibly result from this less serious neighbor's behavior. What you see is shattering: the drawing emerging on that student's drawing board is nothing short of miraculous. Much better than anything ever made at Diligence High School or Sincerity Summer Studio. In that instant the unfairness of the world seems crushing.

This end of innocence about drawing is crucial. You may invoke the talent myth and tell yourself that you were somehow excluded when drawing ability was distributed, or you may begin to build another myth as to why drawings are misleading or unimportant and have little to do with design. What you should try to understand, however, is that what you saw was a performance. Your neighbor was performing—just as anyone practiced in dancing, tennis, or telling stories enjoys doing it and having others watch. What you didn't see, and what is visible only in the miraculous drawing, is perhaps fifteen years of drawing, drawing, drawing, with steady encouragement from parents, teachers, and friends; the drawing performance you saw became a self-rewarding activity for your classmate long ago.

There is an opposite but equally shattering experience for the diligent but naive design student. This usually happens when the first big design or drawing assignment is due. About a week before the due date the student on the other side of you disappears, only to reappear a half hour before the project is due with twice the number of required boards, all rendered in the most breathtakingly meticulous technique. The student is well-groomed, bright eyed, and rested. Meanwhile, you have been working at school with the other students, stayed up all last night, haven't washed or eaten, and still haven't finished the required drawings.

Your prolific neighbor mentions that "I was going to do one other board, but I knocked off last night and caught a movie." As in the first example, you're not seeing the whole story. Your second neighbor has been working steadily at home in every spare moment for the last three weeks and those drawings that look like they took hours and hours *did* take hours and hours. She cut all her classes the last week and worked at home because she needed more room and more quiet than was available at school. As in the first case, there is no magic involved, and the talent myth is only a comfortable cop-out. If you want to make beautiful drawings you must have the motivation to spend the time drawing—over many years or in intensely concentrated efforts, or both.

If you can survive such experiences with other designers' drawings and understand that drawing ability is learnable and worth learning, you will find the drawings of others to be your best teachers. You should look at all drawing as the record of an activity over time and try to discover what was done first, second, and third and what the controlling rules were. As you become a practiced perceiver of other designers' drawings, apply what you have seen to your own drawings. This actual application of what you have learned to see is crucial. No amount of casual admiring will help. Your scrutiny must have the intensity of an undercover agent's. You must look for ways of drawing that you can copy and begin to use immediately. We learn from one another. Accounts of the Renaissance, when painting, sculpture, and architecture made great advances, abound in stories of how artists overtly or covertly studied one another's work. If you doubt this, check the sign-out slips for your school's library books on drawing or rendering. You will probably find that they have been checked out by your fellow students who already draw very well.

OTHERS' PERCEPTIONS

Communicative responsibility belongs to the designer. Failure to communicate is a failure of the designer's perception, not the perception of those with whom we must communicate. The design-proposal drawings designers show to their teachers, bosses, and clients are an integral part of design responsibility. To blame the perceiver for not seeing the qualities in a design is to duck your design responsibility.

This is one of the most difficult responsibilities a designer has to accept. The responsibility for communicating your designs to others begins, however, in the development of your own perception. Designers must learn to perceive how their designs, and the drawings that represent those designs, will be seen by others.

This communicative responsibility means that designers' drawing abilities may either promote or inhibit their ability to get their designs built. Someday you may be able to afford to have someone else make the drawings you present to a client, but junior designers are seldom assigned a delineator as their personal slave. This means that whatever *you* design *you* are going to have to draw, and draw in such a way that someone will want to build it.

Le Corbusier developed a system of proportions based on the dimensions of the human figure and his drawings of the system illustrate the point I am trying to make. If we take the vertical axis as ability, the designer's hand should be as good, or as high, as his or her head, for it is the hand that will have to communicate the head's creativity. Actually, they are integrally connected and I believe that for the designer, the head must help the hand draw and the hand must help the head design.

The two possible imbalances of head and hand are equally frustrating. A facile hand that makes beautiful empty-headed drawings is comparable to a brilliantly creative mind that must communicate with a clumsy hand.

FIRST IMPRESSION

When any human product, like a drawing, is presented to our perception, the first impression is crucial. In the first few seconds of perception, we absorb a rush of information that is difficult and sometimes impossible to correct in subsequent perception.

Whatever is presented will instantaneously communicate the amount of human effort and skill that went into its creation. If the perceiver judges it as adequate or more than adequate (based on past experience and on the context in which it is presented), she or he will eagerly look further for design intention. If, on the other hand, the perceiver is put off by any inadequacy seen during the first instants of perception, subsequent perception will already be negatively prejudiced.

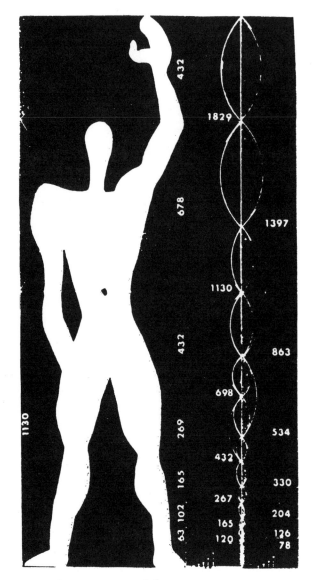

Le Corbusier—*Le modulor.*

TRANSPARENCY

In the first impression of design drawings, the actual drawing should have the same kind of transparency for the "other" perceiver that it has for the designer. The perceiver should immediately accept the drawing as realistic and competently drawn and look through it to the design content. It is difficult to overemphasize this point and it deserves careful explanation.

If the drawing technique is clumsy and distorted or inaccurate, the perceiver is put off by the ineptitude of the delineator and will be hesitant in accepting the drawing as a true representation of the design.

Most drawings that a designer uses to communicate to others, especially clients, need to be drawn rather explicitly in order for the client to see the design. Design drawings can easily be overdrawn, however; an overworked or virtuoso technique, or a technique that is loaded with drawing clichés, actually inhibits the communication of the design. If you make design drawings to demonstrate how well you can draw, you may obscure the transparency of the drawing in such a way that the design content is pushed into the background.

THE FORM OF DRAWINGS

The title of Marshall McLuhans' book, *The Medium is the Message* (1967), sums up my point. Just as the form of books, radio, or TV communicates as much as their content, so too does the form of drawing—conceptual diagram, rough sketch, working drawing, or slick rendering—communicate as much as what is drawn.

The choice of drawing form can invite or discourage participation during the stages of the

design process when the participation of teacher, consultant, boss, or client is necessary. If the drawing is diagrammatic or tentative, and particularly if alternative designs are shown, the design process will appear open and participation will be invited. If the drawing is a working drawing or a slick "final" presentation, the design process will appear closed, prompting only approval or rejection, not participation.

This impression is communicated entirely by the form of drawing used. It is also related to the adequacy of effort mentioned earlier, but rough sketches can invite perception and participation if they are well done. I have had the most success when I've shown clients the first conceptual diagrams and invited them to participate in the design process from its earliest conceptual stages.

This early involvement of the client and the opportunity it affords a designer to understand the client's perceptions proves invaluable to the success of later communications.

PROFESSIONAL PERCEIVERS

Designers must be professional perceivers. They must learn to perceive their environment comprehensively and predict other's perception of the environments they design. Drawing is a primary means of developing this needed perceptual ability.

In architectural education, this function was traditionally served by the field sketch. Students and architects carried sketchbooks and recorded their experience of buildings and urban spaces. After years of such training, students and architects can recall these buildings and spaces and draw them months later and miles away with remarkable accuracy.

Photographers, painters, archaeologists, and animal trackers also have trained perception. This gives them a special kind of access to the visual world. The ability to draw similarly gives perceivers a special, structured way of looking at the world. They look at the world as a potential drawing and see themselves as the delineators.

By permission of Johnny Hart and Field Enterprises, Inc.

2 Conception

The synthesis by which we relate and apply what we know is given various names: cognition, thinking, problem solving, etc. I will call it conception because that name reinforces its relationship to perception.

Design drawing is, potentially, one of conception's most valuable tools. While the ability to draw helps perception indirectly, drawing directly promotes conception by externalizing concepts in graphic form, which can then be evaluated and manipulated with all the human tools of intelligence: eye, mind, and hand.

Our conceptual ability has gradually moved from serving our immediate survival to planning our futures to the comparative luxury of thinking about our thinking. This development of our conceptual ability has not been achieved without a cost. The abilities and patterns that have allowed us to survive and on which our minds are built also form our deepest conceptual blocks.

We inherit the experience of the entire human race throughout its evolutionary history. Very early in life we are also subjected to a lengthy indoctrination by a prejudiced language into the collective experience of whatever culture happens to have produced us. To this massive legacy we add the experience of our lifetime, much of which is unconscious. The conscious experience that we add to this mostly inherited framework might seem of little value, but it is preeminently worth understanding and managing, for it is, after all, all we can call our own.

Self-Conception

In the range, direction, and depth of our thought, perhaps the most important of all the variables involved in the conscious experience of a lifetime is self-conception. Whether thought through and held consciously or adopted at an unconscious level, a self model can do more to influence the way we think about our lives or the way we design an environment than any other factor. Self models are either inhibiting or liberating depending on what they assume is a possible and proper use of the conceptual abilities we inherit from evolution.

The most crucial difference in the various mindmodels is to what extent human conceptual functioning is free or determined—whether the mind works in certain predetermined, inevitable ways or is free and largely under the control of the individual to whom it belongs. Most people acknowledge our evolutionary inheritance and cultural indoctrination and believe that we can never have complete conceptual freedom, but the argument over the extent to which our thoughts are determined remains very much alive.

Determinism has many forms and much of the argument over the various mindmodels is actually over these conflicting forms of determinism. Future-based determinism suggests that future events will unfold according to a plan or script that we call fate, destiny, divine will, or secular historicism. Proponents of past based determinism believe that events are controlled by the unfolding of various natural laws set in motion by science's "big bang." The nature-versus-nurture debate is also actually over alternative forms of determinism. The various deterministic models of the mind are based on either the historical conditioning of past experiences, proposed by Freud and Skinner, or on the deity-determined fate or predestination favored by religion. Both these models support the status quo by suggesting that the free, creative use of the mind is either an impossibility or a heresy. Technology has given us the perfect analogy for the deterministic models—the robot.

THE CULTURALLY PROGRAMMED ROBOT, the oldest of the deterministic models, serves the survival of most members of the animal world and many nominally human cultures. There are cultural and political systems in which the individual members are expected simply to memorize a set of rules and doctrines, live their lives by them, and pass them on to their children—unquestioned, unchanged, and unbroken. In animals and insects much of the programming is carried by heredity as instinct, which is nature's most perfect form of preprogramming. Humans may have escaped this hard-wiring only because of their relatively premature birth and their necessarily long period of acculturation. Ants, bees, lemmings, and some of the oldest and newest of human societies depend on this strict control of their members.

Today we have infinitely more flexibility and capacity in our programmable memory than our ancestors or animals. It is not a question of *whether* to program the human child or not, for extensive programming is obviously necessary for survival. The question is *how* the programming should be done, and all cultures approach this responsibility with great care. There is little disagreement as to the awesome responsibility involved, because the culture's future clearly depends on how well each new robot is programmed. What is arguable is the kind and extent of the programming needed to prepare the individual for life in a changing world. Some cultures' programs consist of detailed specifications that attempt to cover every situation, while others rely on relative principles that the individual is expected to apply to varying situations.

THE STIMULUS-RESPONSE ROBOT is an alternative automaton proposed by the school of psychology known as behaviorism. This set of notions was initiated early in this century by John B. Watson and his better-known follower, B. F. Skinner. Behaviorists deny or ignore such concepts as *mind* or *consciousness* and insist that the only basis for psychology is observable human behavior. Strangely, however, most of their theories are based on observations of rats' or pigeons' behavior. They assume that the complex functioning of humans is nothing more than an additive collection of the simple stimulus/response/reinforcement patterns observable in much simpler animals.

This deterministic model restricts even the cultural programming discussed in the previous model to the kind of behavior modification demonstrated in various laboratory animals subjected to reinforcing punishments and rewards. It also completely rules out any self-modification or self-determined behavior. The stimulus-response robot's hard-wiring exists inside a closed console—this robot can only be "trained."

Howard Gruber (*Darwin On Man—A Psychological Study of Scientific Creativity,* 1974) describes and names this kind of determinism:

> A view of human life has arisen in which the individual is subject both to deterministic and probabilistic laws in such a way as to make the idea of free and purposeful creativity meaningless. To the extent that life is governed by deterministic laws, the argument runs, there is no way of affecting the future because it has all been determined by circumstances beyond personal control. Meanwhile, wherever probabilistic laws prevail, there is no way of intelligently influencing the future because things are chancy and unpredictable.
>
> It may help to give this view a name. Because it combines determinism and chance in a thoroughly materialistic way, and proceeds on this basis to deny any significance or reality to mental processes, we may label it *hyper materialism.* . . .

THE HISTORICALLY PROGRAMMED ROBOT

is perhaps a very old deterministic model but has rather recently been given a very convincing form by Sigmund Freud. This robot is assumed to have been largely programmed by its earlier experiences, which it can do little about, especially since much of this programming occurred below the level of consciousness. The robot's past experiences have programmed its future in a subtly different way than in the cultural robot, since this robot's history was not the deliberate work of cultural indoctrination but primarily the random experiences suffered in the relationships of the immediate family.

THE HEREDITY VS. ENVIRONMENT CONTROVERSY

over whether our minds are predetermined by heredity or conditioned by environment obscures the underlying determinism of both these notions. Neither heredity nor environment, nor their compromised combinations can account for some of the human race's most creative individuals. Hereditary determinism and environmental determinism are simply alternative forms of a claim culture seems to need to make about the creativity of its individuals.

GIFTEDNESS

is is an even more remote deterministic explanation. It cannot be proven and is not even a useful idea, especially in education, since it becomes a cop-out for student and teacher alike. The idea that our minds are largely predetermined at birth even seems to deny the usefulness of the cultural indoctrination of which it is a part.

Elsewhere in this book I have argued against the notion of giftedness and have taken the side of the environment, or, more specifically, experience, in explaining the "talent" or ability to draw. My quarrel with environmental explanations of abilities, including drawing ability, is that they often treat the environment as something that inevitably *happens* to individuals, leaving no room for their free choice of experiences and thus no responsibility for their own abilities.

SCIENCE

promises the last and perhaps most threatening deterministic model of the mind. While some scientists have contributed to the arguments supporting various deterministic models of the mind, the scientific community has not agreed on any single paradigm for the mind and its functioning. Several branches of science have been busily collecting data for decades or centuries but their data and their discoveries are equally impressive in their diffuse detail and their lack of any comprehensive explanation of the mind.

Most scientists are quite candid about their distance from any comprehensive mindmodel and some talk like they believe or hope that there may indeed be a "ghost in the machine" that defies scientific explanation. But the popular understanding or misunderstanding of science and the faith we, as a culture, have bestowed on it makes many of us believe that science will one day inexorably discover *exactly* how the mind works. This attitude holds that, like with the cure for cancer, we must just wait a little longer for the eventual triumph of this difficult but inevitable deterministic explanation—perhaps we won't live to see it, but some more fortunate future generation might! Meanwhile, we can only greet science's successive revelations with wonder and compliance.

Science's deterministic self-model is of course the general model we have been using—the robot. And the mindmodel of the robot is the triumph of modern technology, the computer. The computer is the perfect analogy, programmable to be indefatigably loyal, accurate, and unforgetful . . . but not creative.

The general adoption of the notion that the computer is analogous to the mind and information processing is analogous to mental function makes it clear, however, that many of our traditional mindmodels have outlived their usefulness, especially as examples of what the human mind should be. The filing cabinet, the unquestioning believer, the infallible calculator, the obedient servant, the fanatic patriot, and the objective analyst have all reached their ideal manifestation in the computer, leaving human minds to find other, better things to do.

All deterministic models have some usefulness. They are not entirely wrong, but they leave little room for the concepts of freedom, responsibility, or creativity, which are the hallmarks of designers.

FREE MODELS of the mind are not entirely correct either, but, conversely, they seem to be much more useful for the future of our species than deterministic models. If we believe the mind is entirely predetermined by fate or external influences over which we have no control, we are indeed doomed to be automatons. Choosing to conceive of at least the conscious part of the mind as free and capable of synthesizing its own values and answers (and accepting the responsibility commensurate with such a conception) seems to be proof of a free mind and the only hope for the future of human intelligence.

Human intelligence and free will turn on an insistence that while there may be some generalized patterns that are our legacy from evolutionary and cultural responses to the environment, we are always in the process of changing these patterns—in our individual lifetimes and over the long-term evolution of our species. While most of our history has been directed by our environment or the outside, we do have the opportunity to self-direct an increasing part of our future.

THE CHOICE OF MINDMODEL to believe in probably has more potential for influencing the way we use our minds than any other factor. Models are very powerful in their paradoxical potential for both extending and limiting our thinking about what they are modeling. We will be best served by a model that proposes a mind very carefully and individually made and remade: free, open, responsible, and mature enough to be self-motivating and self-rewarding.

The archenemy of the free mind is determinism in all its forms. The determinism that was once advocated by religions now largely has been inherited by science. Science has also documented, however, that our inherited mental equipment is extremely flexible. The range and variety of conceptual worlds that have developed in diverse cultures suggests that the mind may be a do-it-yourself kit of near-infinite flexibility and undreamed-of potential. If this is true, or even partly true, the mindmodel we adopt does more to promote or inhibit the use of our minds than anything else.

We continue to look longingly over our shoulders for approval or at the back of some book for the answers. We are slow to understand that both the answers and the approval must be *made* and continually remade synthetically in our own consciousness. They are ours *only* for the making.

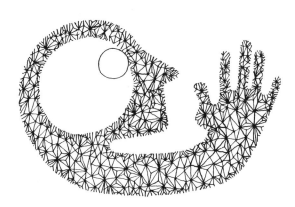

A Modest Mindmodel Proposal

In the absence of any definitive scientific description of the workings of what we have come to call our "minds," I offer the following model to understand and begin to increase conscious control of the mind. I will call the total system *eyemindhand* as a reminder that it includes the body, is dominated by vision, and functions best as a whole.

My model for the human eyemindhand system is free rather than deterministic. The system's basic structure is the inherited evolutionary result of our species' interaction with the environment, and our use of the system is both promoted and inhibited by our cultural indoctrination. Neither heredity nor environment, however, can completely determine or excuse our minds because our consciousness is free.

The proposed mindmodel consists of three parts:

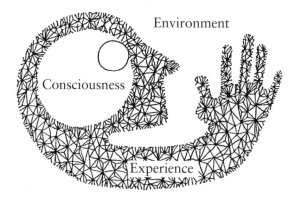

ENVIRONMENT—THE CONTEXT

This element in the model represents everything that is outside us. This includes the natural and built environments, other people, and all forms of communication—books, conversation, and drawings among them.

EXPERIENCE—A NETWORK

This element is the interrelated network of all our accumulated knowledge and experience. In the model, this experience network surrounds and forms the third part of the model, consciousness. The experience network is represented as a system that integrates our evolutionary heritage, our cultural indoctrination, the conscious and unconscious experience of our lifetimes, and such phenomena as emotion and will. The experience network is everything we are *except* consciousness.

The hand is used in the mindmodel to represent the experience network of the whole body, and justly so because the hand is so much a part of our intelligence. Frank R. Wilson suggests in *The Hand* (1998):

The more one looks, the more it appears that the revolutionary hand-brain marriage qualifies as one of *the* defining and unifying themes of human paleoanthropology, of developmental and cognitive psychology, and of behavioral neuroscience.

. . . I would argue that any theory of human intelligence which ignores the interdependence of hand and brain function, the historic origins of that relationship, or the impact of that history on developmental dynamics in modern humans, is grossly misleading and sterile.

CONSCIOUSNESS—A SPACE

In contrast to all nature's other forms of life, the hallmark of human intelligence and freedom is the development and free individual use of consciousness, even though we seem to be a long way from understanding how best to use it. C. G. Jung explained, "Consciousness is a very recent acquisition of nature and is still in an experimental state."

This element of the mind is represented as the space of our attention. Consciousness is the most uniquely human part of the mind and is limited in three ways: in the quantity of information it can hold at any particular time, the extent to which it can be opened up or closed off to sensory input from the environment, and the length of time it can be held either fully open or fully closed.

The most characteristic use of human intelligence is the making of synthetic congruences between problem/solution, past/future, real/ideal, etc. Our sense of reality, our identity, and all our day-to-day conscious thoughts are the products of such syntheses. According to the mindmodel proposal, design drawings are the manifestations

of these synthetic congruences that exist along the interface of consciousness and experience; we draw them simultaneously in our consciousness, on the surface of our experience network, and on the paper in the environment. The forming of such synthetic congruences is both the highest and most common use of human intelligence, and the hand's drawing of them includes and legitimizes the unconscious layers of our experience network. The model now represents and integrates the whole human being, and one of the central ideas of this book is that we function better whole—using all the tools of human intelligence. Drawing is an example and a symbol of that holistic functioning.

THE MODEL'S FORM

The model's form, in addition to separating and naming the three constituents of environment, experience, and consciousness, establishes two interfaces: environment/experience and experience/consciousness.

The spatial arrangement of the three elements and their two interfaces rules out any interface between consciousness and the environment, except by a transition through our experience. This means that our perception of the environment is only possible through the mediation of our experience. It also means that any perceptions or conceptions that develop in our consciousness can only be communicated or acted out in the environment through the same experience network. The network of our experience thus translates or mediates both the input and output of the system.

The model thus correctly represents the difficulty we encounter in understanding ideas that are beyond our experience, or in saying what we think, or in doing what we intend.

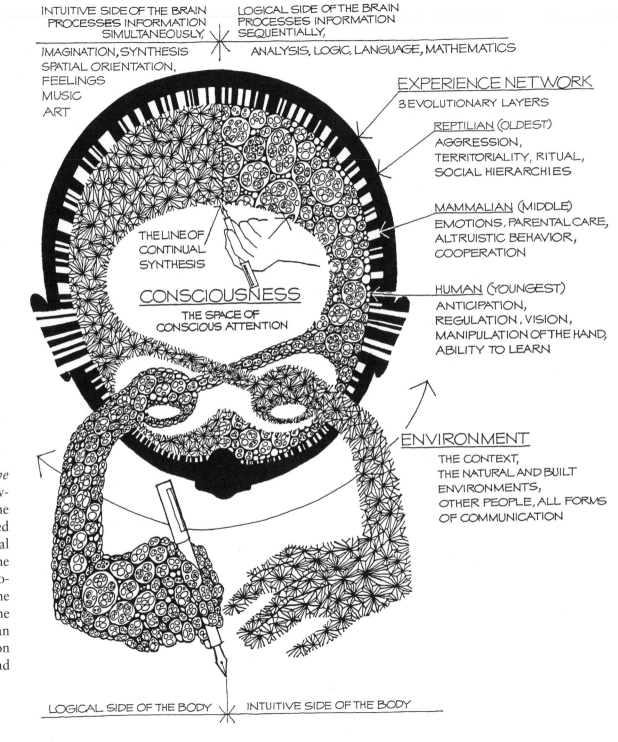

NEOCORTEX

LIMBIC SYSTEM

REPTILIAN COMPLEX

From *The Dragons of Eden* by Carl Sagan.

INTUITIVE SIDE OF THE BRAIN PROCESSES INFORMATION SIMULTANEOUSLY,

LOGICAL SIDE OF THE BRAIN PROCESSES INFORMATION SEQUENTIALLY,

IMAGINATION, SYNTHESIS SPATIAL ORIENTATION, FEELINGS MUSIC ART

ANALYSIS, LOGIC, LANGUAGE, MATHEMATICS

EXPERIENCE NETWORK
3 EVOLUTIONARY LAYERS

REPTILIAN (OLDEST)
AGGRESSION, TERRITORIALITY, RITUAL, SOCIAL HIERARCHIES

MAMMALIAN (MIDDLE)
EMOTIONS, PARENTAL CARE, ALTRUISTIC BEHAVIOR, COOPERATION

THE LINE OF CONTINUAL SYNTHESIS

CONSCIOUSNESS
THE SPACE OF CONSCIOUS ATTENTION

HUMAN (YOUNGEST)
ANTICIPATION, REGULATION, VISION, MANIPULATION OF THE HAND, ABILITY TO LEARN

ENVIRONMENT
THE CONTEXT, THE NATURAL AND BUILT ENVIRONMENTS, OTHER PEOPLE, ALL FORMS OF COMMUNICATION

LOGICAL SIDE OF THE BODY

INTUITIVE SIDE OF THE BODY

Evolution's Layered Legacy

Paul MacLean, quoted in Carl Sagan's *The Dragons of Eden*, has described the brain as having successive layers laid down by evolution. The oldest and innermost layer is reptilian, concerned with aggression, territoriality, ritual, and social hierarchies. Next is what can be thought of as the mammalian layer, which introduces the emotions, altruistic behavior, and parental care. The last and by far the largest layer of the brain is the neocortex, which can be thought of as the human layer. This layer is concerned with anticipation and regulation, vision, bipedal posture, and manipulation of the hand.

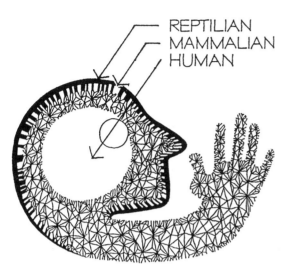

REPTILIAN
MAMMALIAN
HUMAN

On the proposed mindmodel, the evolutionary layers are reversed. The reptilian brain is the outermost layer in direct contact with the environment and least subject to conscious control. Next is the mammalian layer, and last of all, surrounding consciousness and most controlled by it, is the neocortex or "human" layer of the brain. This reversal of the layering is a result of the model's giving consciousness a central position.

Another factor that the proposed mindmodel attempts to indicate is that the left and right cerebral hemispheres of the neocortex are specialized in their functioning. The right hemisphere processes information instantaneously and is generally described as the intuitive or creative half of the brain, concerned with pattern recognition, spatial orientation, and instant holistic judgments—synthesis. The left hemisphere processes information linearly or sequentially and is generally described as the rational or logical half of the brain, having the abilities of reason, language, and mathematics—analysis. Interestingly, the right half of the brain is connected to the left side of the body, including the left eye, while the left half of the brain is connected to the right side of the body and the right eye.

The drawing at left represents the right hemisphere as an open and complexly interconnected network—a unified relational pattern. The left brain, on the other hand, is represented as being organized in exclusive categories and hierarchies—a classified diversity.

The proposed model indicates some of the real limitations of our minds, like the impossibility of anything (including environmental design) coming out of our minds unless it was previously taken in; or the impossibility of anything entering or exiting our consciousness without passing through the three evolutionary layers of our experience network. These real limitations are not nearly as inhibiting as those of deterministic models, which tell us what we should or must think.

The model is not intended to be physiologically correct or scientifically verifiable. Its value lies in its usefulness as an analogy for the brain's functioning and its ability to help us conceive of the mind in richer, clearer ways.

Categories and Hierarchies

In *A Study of Thinking* (1956), Bruner, Goodnow, and Austin propose that "virtually all cognitive activity involves and is dependent on the process of categorizing." The world we perceive seems differentiated, or made up of different kinds of things. Seeing differences in the world is perhaps part of perception's prejudice. The focus of our vision, our tendency to form gestalts or wholes, the eyehand correspondence that sees and feels separate objects, and our ability to discriminate between subtly different patterns all promote seeing a differentiated environment.

In *An Ecological Approach to Perception* (1979), Gibson points out that this differentiated world seems to be organized into parts and wholes by the nesting of some patterns or elements within others:

Now with respect to these units, an essential point of theory must be emphasized. The smaller units are embedded in the larger units by what I will call *nesting*. For example, canyons are nested within mountains; trees are nested within canyons; leaves are nested within trees; and cells are nested within leaves. There are forms within forms both up and down the scale of size. Units are nested within larger units. Things are components of other things. They would constitute a hierarchy except that this hierarchy is not categorical but full of transitions and overlaps. Hence, for the terrestrial environment, there is no special proper unit in terms of which it can be analyzed once and for all. There are no atomic units of the world considered as an environment. Instead, there are subordinate and superordinate units. The unit you choose for describing the environment depends on the level of the environment you choose to describe.

Our vision not only separates the world into potential categories, but also begins to break them down into constituent parts.

The collection of the differentiated elements into conceptual categories and the arrangement of these categories into hierarchies, however, is a task assumed by culture and is largely carried out by the culture's language. Our language names the separate elements we perceive, tells their qualities and characteristics, and describes their actions and their relationships to one another. The culture into which we are born literally tells us what we are perceiving, and this indoctrination is so pervasive in structuring the way we see and the way we think that we can never be free of it.

Bruner, Goodnow, and Austin (*A Study of Thinking*, 1956) explain that categorizing "reduces the complexity of [the] environment, . . . is the means by which objects of the world about us are identified, . . . reduces the necessity of constant learning, . . . provides [the direction] for instrumental activity, . . . [and] permits [the] ordering and relating [of] classes of events. . . ."

Before considering cultures' uses of categories and the influence of language, let us look at the patterns involved in categorization.

PATTERNS

All categorization is accomplished by drawing inclusive/exclusive boundaries through the world, including some things in certain categories and excluding others. This seems simple enough until we consider how these boundaries are drawn and understand that the drawing of a single categorical boundary usually infers three relationships to other categories.

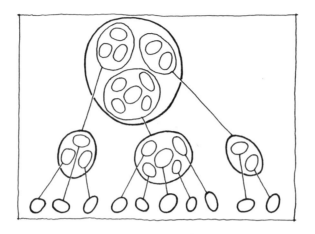

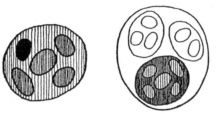

1. As a *part*—most categories are parts of some larger category.

2. As a *whole*—most categories are collections of parts, which themselves may be categorized.

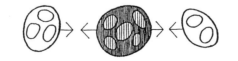

3. As a *sibling*—most categories have equal rank with potentially competitive brother or sister categories.

Any category has these relationships, not as a *consequence* of its being a category, but as *criteria* for its becoming a category in the first place.

We are born into this categorical patterning and grow accustomed to the successive boundaries that seem to surround us. As we look out at them these categorical boundaries extend the concentric layers of the mindmodel suggested earlier. They protectively articulate our environment into a succession of friendly circles within which we can be assured of the company of others who share our interests and values and, above all, have a similar way of categorizing the world. Family, gender, age group, occupation, religion, political preference, nationality, and race are all protective concentric categorical rings we may draw around ourselves, and many have outlived their usefulness.

All categorizing can be thought of as occurring within one grand pattern, although there are several ways of diagramming that pattern. I have been diagramming it in a way that emphasizes our experience of the categorical boundaries and only implies the hierarchical relationships. The more conventional diagram for this same pattern is the branching "tree" pattern, which, taken in one direction, looks like binuclear cell division, and in the other like a family tree. It is interesting that this single conceptual pattern is as ancient a part of our evolutionary heritage as the subdivision of cells and the coupling reproduction of higher organisms. This pattern is also the one recurring diagram in Darwin's notebooks.

Perhaps the most active spokesman for the pervasiveness and conceptual value of hierarchical organization is Arthur Koestler (*Janus: A Summing Up*, 1978):

All complex structures and processes of a relatively stable character display hierarchic organization, regardless of whether we consider galactic systems, living organisms and their activities, or social organizations. The tree diagram with its series of levels can be used to represent the evolutionary branching of species into the "tree of life"; or the stepwise differentiation of tissues and integration of functions in the development of the embryo . . . .

. . . the branching tree illustrates the hierarchic ordering of knowledge in the subject-index of library catalogues—and the personal memory stores inside our skulls.

While Koestler's diagram does not model the experience of living within the set of concentric hierarchical boundaries I proposed earlier, it makes clear the linear organizational patterns on which categorizing relies: larger wholes sit above smaller parts and items of equal rank sit side by side. Vertically it diagrams two aesthetic concepts often invoked in design: unity and diversity.

Unity collects diversity, while diversity articulates unity. To move in a unifying direction is to ascend toward some grand collector, be it the cosmos, nature, or God. To move in the direction of diversity is to descend to the bewildering articulations of our environment. Between these poles of ultimate unity and intimate diversity we have stretched a chain of conceptual categories.

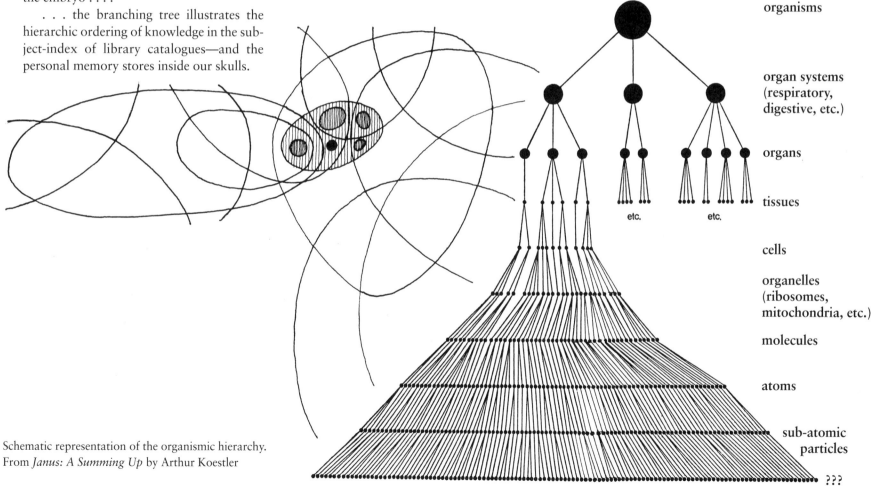

Schematic representation of the organismic hierarchy.
From *Janus: A Summing Up* by Arthur Koestler

organisms

organ systems (respiratory, digestive, etc.)

organs

tissues

etc.   etc.

cells

organelles (ribosomes, mitochondria, etc.)

molecules

atoms

sub-atomic particles

???

It is interesting to speculate that the interdependent relationship between these complementary concepts has inevitably led us to search for either end of the hierarchy. This would explain both our compulsion to investigate and classify diversity and to postulate and deify unity.

Koestler has also written about what the vertical dimension of the social hierarchy means in terms of human behavior (*The Ghost in the Machine,* 1967). He explains that humans exhibit two conflicting tendencies because they are both an individual *whole* and an integral *part* of a biological and social hierarchy. Their "wholeness" as individuals leads them to *self-assertive* behavior, while their "partness" leads them to *integrative* behavior.

It is this integrative tendency (our apparent need to identify with causes and beliefs that transcend us) that leads us to accept cultural indoctrination and abdicate conceptual freedom and responsibility.

The horizontal dimension of the conventional diagram represents the other linear relationship —that between equally ranked, potentially competitive categories.

In its simplest form, the "sibling rivalry" between these brother/sister categories can be seen as a set of mutually exclusive dualities: mind/body, heredity/environment, liberal/conservative. A more balanced view is that this lateral dimension represents a continuum that accommodates polar opposites but also offers a range of positions between those opposite ends.

Interestingly, it seems that this is the only pattern that organizes our conceptual world. It is rather clearly anthropomorphic in its correspondence to the higher/lower, left/right axes of our body and is easily described by our language. The

fact that it is difficult to imagine another pattern for a conceptual framework is testimony to the omnipresence of hierarchical organization. It is also evidence that patterns are more powerful conceptually than the names we write in them.

CULTURE'S CATEGORIES

Cultural indoctrination begins with a categorization of the world. Categorization or separation is never done innocently. When we categorize and separate, we assign meaning and usually a value to the distinction. The differentiated world that we perceive is collected into categories, named and arranged in hierarchies, and valued. Claude Levi-Strauss (*The Savage Mind,* 1962) has made it clear that even the most primitive cultures have systems that name and classify the world, and many of them are more comprehensive than our own. While the variations between these "primitive" categorizations and our own "scientific" ones are staggering, they all follow the same hierarchical patterns discussed previously and depend on similar "axes of reference" and mutually exclusive pairs.

The differences in various worldviews prove that the categories with which we structure the conceptual world are never objectively or necessarily "given" by the environment. To quote Bruner, Goodnow, and Austin (*A Study of Thinking,* 1965) once more:

The categories in terms of which we group the events of the world around us are constructions or inventions. The class of prime numbers, animal species, the huge range of colors dumped into the category "blue," squares and circles—all of these are inven-

tions and not "discoveries." They do not "exist" in the environment. . . .

. . . Science and commonsense inquiry alike do not discover the ways in which events are grouped in the world; they invent ways of grouping. The test of the invention is the predictive benefits that result from the use of the invented categories. . . .

The categories in terms of which man sorts out and responds to the world around him reflect deeply the culture into which he is born. The language, the way of life, the religion and science of a people: all of these mold the way in which a man experiences the events out of which his own history is fashioned. . . .

Most cultural indoctrinations promote one set of fixed, authoritative answers: to challenge the tenets is to commit heresy. These cultural conceptual sets range from the general to the specific and address matters ranging from dress, eating, drinking, and personal and group behavior to notions about the origin of the world and the purpose of life.

The danger of the conceptual categories of any culture is that they inhibit conceptual freedom by implying that there are fixed, correct answers that need only be memorized, and that the answers to all human problems are a matter of "knowing" that correct answer. Today our fixed answers don't seem to be serving us very well. What we need is the ability to make new answers, the flexibility to try them out, and the attitude that this making and testing is the highest use of human intelligence.

The conceptual framework of any culture extends to ethical and esthetic value systems that are established by the culture's institutions and enforced by cultural sanctions. If you are a design student you are currently undergoing an indoctrination into a subculture. You should be aware of the categories into which your curriculum is divided and of their hierarchical arrangement.

LANGUAGE

The medium that carries a culture's indoctrination is its language. The language names the conceptual categories into which the world is sorted. Its syntax limits what can be said and even, as some linguists believe, what can be thought. Language and literacy in any culture are privileged, even today. Those who developed and used language throughout history were undoubtedly at the top of their cultural hierarchy. Language, like categorization, cannot be used innocently. It retains the prejudices of the people who historically used language to carry out their selfish interests.

THE OPEN CATEGORY

A design problem is like an open category. The designed solution will take its place, like any category, in several established hierarchies. It is as if your clients had made an opening in the hierarchy of their lives for the environment you will design for them; or like the hillside had made a place in its hierarchy of sun, wind, and view; or the neighborhood had made a place in the previously built environment; or like your maturation as a designer had prepared a place for this next design in the body of your work. There are several other hierarchies into which any design may be placed by a sensitive designer, and your designs will always be perceived as a part of these hierarchies, never as an isolated act or object.

Just like any conceptual category, every design solution is defined by three relationships:

1. As a *part*—any building, exterior, or interior space belongs to a larger whole, a natural environment, a street, a neighborhood, a city, and a geographical region. Any designed environment also becomes a part of people's lives and you and your profession's work.

2. As a *whole*—any built environment also is a composition of parts. Most environments include a spatial/circulation system, one or several environmental control systems, an illumination system, a materials system, and, if it is a building, a structural system and an enclosure system. The new category must try to integrate all these subcategories into a convincing whole.

3. As a *sibling*—each environmental design takes its place in a lateral rank of environments of similar date, function, budget, site, and technology and also along several shifting, arguable continua: modern/postmodern, natural/high-tech, site-integrated/site-dominant.

Like all categories, the open category presented by a design problem is defined by these three relationships. The designer has the opportunity to establish all these relationships and the choice of whether to make them clear and distinct or leave them interestingly ambiguous.

THE DANGERS OF CATEGORIZATION

We must have categories. Thinking is inconceivable without them, but they should always be questioned and deliberately accepted or broken and reformed. Robert H. McKim (*Experiences in Visual Thinking*, 1980), in an excellent section on the dangers of verbal categories, quotes Schachtel and then offers an example of relabeling:

> Schachtel, however, notes the inherent danger of labels: "The name, in giving us the illusion of knowing the object designated by it, makes us quite inert and unwilling to look anew at the now supposedly familiar object from a different perspective."

> Since perception is object-oriented, one way to recenter perception is to abandon object labels and to relabel the environment according to another method of classification. . . . Instead of labeling your perceptions according to the usual object categories, label them according to qualitative categories such as color. In place of seeing groupings of furniture in a room, for instance, see and group first all things that are red, then all things that are yellow. In other words, look for the "rediture" instead of the "furniture." Recenter again by other relabelings: look only for the "cubiture" (all things cubic), the "rounditure," the "smoothiture," and so on. Notice how a familiar room becomes new again: colors become brighter and richer; patterns, shapes, and textures suddenly emerge from the shadows of familiarity. Realize also how often you have allowed the "veil of words" to obscure and stereotype your vision.

If we adopt the categories of our culture, language, and profession without question, we severely limit our conceptual potential.

LIMITED SYNTHESES

One danger in categorization is the way it limits new syntheses. The way you take something apart determines the forms into which it may be reassembled. Synthesis is always prejudiced by analysis. If, in designing a house, you only conceive of it in the real estate shorthand categories of 3 br, 1-1/2 b, you are already limiting design syntheses. To accept any particular categorization is to surrender part of the structuring of your intelligence to whomever sets those categories. You can't open the same limited cupboard of ingredients every day and prepare an interesting succession of meals, as any dieter knows.

OVERSIMIPLIFICATION AND AUTHORITY

Our cultural categories carry our values and our prejudices, and while their generalizations make it possible for us to deal with the world, they are seldom innocent or fair. The greatest danger of categorization is not its pattern or form, which seems inevitable, or its content, which varies from culture to culture, but the overall authority of its structure. The seamless fabric of a culture's categories is intimidating. To look for and pick or pull vigorously at the loose threads of any hierarchy takes a lot of courage. It is much easier to sink back into the intellectual indolence that just accepts the most conventional categories.

THE OTHER PATTERN

Even though there seems to be only one general hierarchical form that relates all our categories, there are at least two complementary ways of diagramming it. The conventional pattern works to separate the world into closed, exclusive categories by focusing analytically on the categorical boundaries. The other pattern is complementary to the first and strives to comprehend the network that connects, relates, or structures the separate categories of the first pattern. This second pattern is more concerned with similarities than differences.

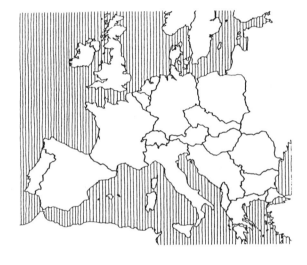

The first pattern is like a political map of the world that delineates national boundaries, while the second pattern is more like an airline's map showing connections between capital cities. The first pattern cuts the world into smaller and smaller pieces, measures them, and names them—this pattern can be called absolute-quantitative.

The second pattern stitches the world back together, thereby producing relations and patterns that can be named and evaluated—this pattern can be called relative-qualitative.

Our conceptual world seems to oscillate between these two interdependent patterns. Like figure/field reversal demonstrations of visual perception reveal, we tend to focus on only one pattern at a time. But a balanced oscillation is both possible and desirable. Western culture and its science-dominated intellectual world have been built on the exclusive, verbal, mathematical,

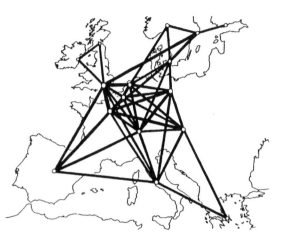

linear, logical, quantifiable, left-brained pattern definitive boundaries. We must learn to look for the other pattern in order to repair the imbalance of our cultural indoctrination. The other pattern is more often identified with Eastern cultures and is more concerned with inclusive, intuitive, qualitative, relative, right-brained unifying connections.

The complementary relationships between the two patterns are apparent in the list shown at right, assembled by Robert Ornstein (*The Psychology of Consciousness*, 1972) to demonstrate the difference in consciousness of the left and right sides of the brain.

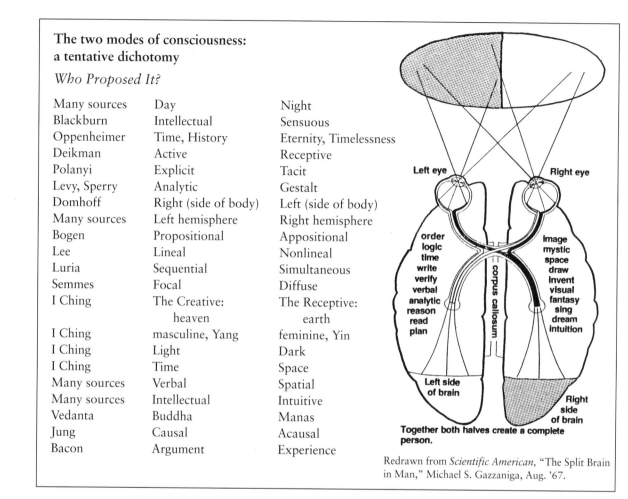

The two modes of consciousness: a tentative dichotomy

Who Proposed It?

Many sources	Day	Night
Blackburn	Intellectual	Sensuous
Oppenheimer	Time, History	Eternity, Timelessness
Deikman	Active	Receptive
Polanyi	Explicit	Tacit
Levy, Sperry	Analytic	Gestalt
Domhoff	Right (side of body)	Left (side of body)
Many sources	Left hemisphere	Right hemisphere
Bogen	Propositional	Appositional
Lee	Lineal	Nonlineal
Luria	Sequential	Simultaneous
Semmes	Focal	Diffuse
I Ching	The Creative: heaven	The Receptive: earth
I Ching	masculine, Yang	feminine, Yin
I Ching	Light	Dark
I Ching	Time	Space
Many sources	Verbal	Spatial
Many sources	Intellectual	Intuitive
Vedanta	Buddha	Manas
Jung	Causal	Acausal
Bacon	Argument	Experience

Left eye   Right eye

order
logic
time
write
verify
verbal
analytic
reason
read
plan

corpus callosum

image
mystic
space
draw
invent
visual
fantasy
sing
dream
intuition

Left side of brain

Right side of brain

Together both halves create a complete person.

Redrawn from *Scientific American*, "The Split Brain in Man," Michael S. Gazzaniga, Aug. '67.

Conceptual Function

It may seem inappropriate to make a verbal argument against verbal conception, and as designers you probably don't need to be convinced that words are not the primary medium of creative thought. However, any book about the relationship between drawing and thinking must make an argument for nonverbal conception. The following excerpts make my case.

In *Visual Thinking* (1969), Rudolf Arnheim argues that:

> The great virtue of vision is that it is not only a highly articulate medium, but that its universe offers inexhaustibly rich information about the objects and events of the outer world. Therefore, vision is the primary medium of thought.

Edward de Bono, in *Lateral Thinking* (1970), argues for the superiority of visual or graphic conception:

> The advantage of a drawing is that there is far more commitment than with a verbal explanation. Words can be very general but a line has to be put in a definite place. . . .
>
> The advantages of a visual format are many.
>
> 1. There has to be a definite commitment to a way of doing something rather than a vague generalized description.
>
> 2. The design is expressed in a manner that is visible to everyone.

QUESTIONING CATEGORIES

We are just beginning to understand the pervasive influence of our categories and to question the usefulness of some of those categories. While such groupings have allowed the development of our minds and our language, they have also left us with our destructive compulsions toward competition, discrimination, and all the abuses of privilege and power. It is clear that many of our traditional categories have outlived their usefulness, if indeed they ever had any. The continual remaking of more useful patterns and conceptual frameworks with which to organize our world is probably the most critical task we face as designers and human beings.

3. Visual expression of a complicated structure is much easier than verbal expression. It would be a pity to limit design by the ability to describe it.

These concepts and this material is from the book *Lateral Thinking* by Edward de Bono who is regarded as a leading authority in the field of creative thinking, and the inventor of "Lateral Thinking." Toronto: (416) 488-0008. Web: www.edwdebono.com.

Michael Polanyi (*The Tacit Dimension*, 1966) argues persuasively for another mode of knowing:

I shall reconsider human knowledge by starting from the fact that *we can know more than we can tell*. This fact seems obvious enough; but, it is not easy to say exactly what it means. Take an example. We know a person's face, and can recognize it among a thousand, indeed among a million. Yet we usually cannot tell how we recognize a face we know. So most of this knowledge cannot be put into words. . . .

. . . The declared aim of modern science is to establish a strictly detached, objective knowledge. Any falling short of this ideal is accepted only as a temporary imperfection, which we must aim at eliminating. But suppose that tacit thought forms an indispensable part of all knowledge, then the ideal of eliminating all personal elements of knowledge would, in effect, aim at the destruction of all knowledge. The ideal of exact science would turn out to be fundamentally misleading and possibly a source of devastating fallacies.

In their beautiful book, *Seeing with the Mind's Eye* (1975), Mike and Nancy Samuels propose:

The human mind is a slide projector with an infinite number of slides stored in its library, an instant retrieval system and an endlessly cross-referenced subject catalog. . . .

In a sense man has long been in conflict between the power his visual images have over him and the control he can exert over his environment through the spoken word. Both of these faculties, the visual and the verbal, are basic mental processes. Man sees; he also talks. When he talks to others, he calls it communicating; when he talks to himself, he calls it thinking. When he sees the world around him, calls it reality; when he sees in his mind's eye, what is it?

It is only recently that this powerful, often fearful, question is beginning to be answered. What is it that goes on when we see in our mind's eye? Are we going crazy? Are demons possessing us? Are repressed terrors from the night, from our past, haunting us? These questions are so anxiety-provoking that the rise of civilization in the last 2000 years reads like a history of the social suppression of visualization and therefore a denial of one of our most basic mental processes. For visualization is the way we think. Before words, images were. Visualization is the heart of the bio-computer. The human brain programs and self-programs through its images. Riding a bicycle, driving a car, learning to read, bake a cake, play golf—all skills are acquired through the image-making process. Visualization is the ultimate consciousness tool.

One final witness for preverbal, intuitive conception may suffice. Arthur Koestler (*The Act of Creation*, 1964) documents Albert Einstein's description of the way his own mind worked:

In 1945 an inquiry was organized among eminent mathematicians in America to find out their working methods. In reply to the questionnaire which was sent to him, Einstein wrote:

"The words or the language, as they are written or spoken, do not seem to play any role in my mechanism of thought. The physical entities which seem to serve as elements in thought are certain signs and more or less clear images which can be 'voluntarily' reproduced and combined. . . .

". . . Taken from a psychological viewpoint, this combinatory play seems to be the essential feature in productive thought—before there is any connection with logical construction in words or other kinds of signs which can be communicated to others.

"The above-mentioned elements are, in any case, of visual and some of muscular type. Conventional words or other signs have to be sought for laboriously only in a secondary stage, when the mentioned associative play is sufficiently established and can be reproduced at will.

"According to what has been said, the play with the mentioned elements is aimed to be analogous to certain logical connections one is searching for.

"In a stage when words intervene at all, they are, in my case, purely auditive, but they interfere only in a secondary stage as already mentioned."

MODELS OF CONCEPTION

Cultural indoctrination tends to explain concept formation in two ways: (1) that creative ideas are revealed to gifted individuals by divine providence or that they are the genetic result of having gifted parents, or (2) that concepts are discovered by a diligent search using the latest methods of science. Unfortunately the apparent choice between these two alternatives masks the fact that they both assume concepts already exist, preformed, waiting to be either revealed or discovered.

REVEALED CONCEPTS

This explanation is an extension of the doctrine of giftedness. The donors of conceptual "gifts" are various: gods, ancestors, the subconscious, or the environment. In all cases the conceiver is simply the passive recipient of conceptual favors. The recipient may ingratiate the various donors by certain actions and rituals, but these are often indirect in that they require an intermediary "revealer"—a priest, a psychologist, etc. The assumption is that new, preformed concepts exist in some realm remote from the average human mind and that they are revealed to certain individuals in some random or predetermined (but unknowable) way. The idea of revealed concepts does not threaten the cultural status quo because by its definition creativity cannot be taught or sought directly by questioning traditional concepts.

DISCOVERED CONCEPTS

This explanation also assumes the existence of preformed concepts—or ultimate truths—but suggests instead that they can be discovered through the use of scientific, analytical methods. Unlike revealed concepts, discovered concepts can be sought directly, but many of the assumptions we have made about that search are questionable: that there are preexisting, correct concepts waiting to be discovered, that we are progressing in our search for scientific certainty toward some goal (such as truth), and that the correct kind of searching method will ensure our success.

Thomas S. Kuhn (*The Structure of Scientific Revolutions*, 1962) proposes:

> We may . . . have to relinquish the notion, explicit or implicit, that changes of paradigm carry scientists and those who learn from them closer and closer to the truth.
>
> . . . The developmental process described in this essay has been a process of evolution *from* primitive beginnings—a process whose successive stages are characterized by an increasingly detailed and refined understanding of nature. But nothing that has been or will be said makes it a process of evolution *toward* anything. Inevitably that lacuna will have disturbed many readers. We are all deeply accustomed to seeing science as the one enterprise that draws constantly nearer to some goal set by nature in advance.
>
> But need there be any such goal? Can we not account for both science's existence and its success in terms of evolution from the community's state of knowledge at any given time? Does it really help to imagine that there is some one full, objective, true account of nature and that the proper measure of scientific achievement is the extent to which it brings us closer to that ultimate goal? If we can learn to substitute evolution-from-what-we-do-know for evolution-toward-what-we-wish-to-know, a number of vexing problems may vanish in the process. . . .

The *Origin of Species* recognized no goal set either by God or nature. Instead, natural selection, operating in the given environment and with the actual organisms presently at hand, was responsible for the gradual but steady emergence of more elaborate, further articulated, and vastly more specialized organisms. Even such marvelously adapted organs as the eye and hand of man—organs whose design had previously provided powerful arguments for the existence of a supreme artificer and an advance plan—were products of a process that moved steadily *from* primitive beginnings but *toward* no goal. . . .

Discovered concepts likewise pose no severe threat to the cultural status quo except during periods of conceptual revolution. In the relatively much longer periods of normality between revolutions, the method, direction, and object of the search are all rather narrowly prescribed.

MADE CONCEPTS

A more useful model assumes a free mind and suggests that humans are personally responsible for the concepts they create. This explanation of creativity or concept formation denies that there are any preformed or preexisting concepts that may either be bestowed upon certain deserving recipients or discovered by diligent searchers. It also denies that there is any particular recipe or procedure by which concepts should be made.

This notion that concepts can be, should be, and must be created rather than bestowed or found recognizes that most creativity makes use of existing ideas by generating new ways of perceiving, relating, or combining those ideas. The human potential for making new, creative syntheses from old, familiar ideas is infinite.

This model of conception also recognizes that there are many techniques that encourage creativity and that they, like the conceptual realm itself, must remain infinitely open-ended.

Karl Popper's thoughts on the origin of scientific concepts are explained in Bryan Magee's *Karl Popper* (1973):

> If Newton's theory is not a body of truth inherent in the world, and derived by man from the observation of reality, where did it come from? The answer is it came from Newton. . . .
>
> The fact that such theories are not bodies of impersonal facts about the world but are products of the human mind makes them personal achievements of an astonishing order. . . .

CONCEPTUAL MODES

We have at least three distinctly different uses of our minds: *recall, concept attainment*, and *concept formation*.

The first two uses are focused upon in our educational systems, our intelligence testing, and our research into cognition. Only the third mode of mental functioning can be considered free or creative and one of the unique characteristics of design education is that it asks students to function freely and creatively in this third mode. For some students this is a very confusing transition from their customary role in education, but for others it is a welcome opportunity, an isolated example of what education should be.

RECALL

Recall is simple rote memory and its criterion is the ability to retain and repeat information verbatim. There is no denying the continuing need for this ability and scientists tell us that the storage space it takes in our long-term memory is insignificant. In our age of tape recorders and instant copiers it is difficult to persuade students that learning to spell and multiply or to develop the concentration required to retain verbal or visual information is still very important.

CONCEPT ATTAINMENT

Concept attainment is beyond the ability of most of our machines and therefore may be more worthy of our mental effort than memory recall is. The attainment of a concept requires an understanding of a set of principles or criteria that can be expressed "in your own words" and applied to varying or novel situations. The identification of new examples of animal life as mammals, for instance, or of a building as Gothic or Romanesque, requires the much deeper, yet more flexible, level of intelligence we call understanding.

While concept attainment is much more sophisticated than recall, it is still based on a given set of "correct" answers. This "correct" categorization of ideas, actions, and people is a device of indoctrination used to insure that the members of a group will be able to tell the good guys from the bad guys and know how to react correctly in all situations.

Concept attainment, acceptance of a paradigm, is what Thomas S. Kuhn (*The Structure of Scientific Revolutions*, 1962) has called the necessary climate for normal science.

> Transformations . . . though usually more gradual and almost always irreversible, are common concomitants of scientific training. Looking at a contour map, the student sees lines on paper, the cartographer a picture of a terrain. Looking at a bubble-chamber photograph, the student sees confused and broken lines, the physicist a record of familiar subnuclear events. Only after a number of such transformations of vision does the student become an inhabitant of the scientist's world, seeing what the scientist sees and responding as the scientist does. The world that the student then enters is not, however, fixed once and for all by the nature of the environment, on the one hand, and of science, on the other. Rather, it is determined jointly by the environment and the particular normal-scientific tradition the student has been trained to pursue. . . .

Both recall and concept attainment are ideally suited for conventional education because they allow for testing and because they help to "program" the youth according to a body of information and a standard set of behaviors. The fledgling robots can be easily tested for compliance and then sorted on the basis of the testing. The comfortable measurability or quantification that concept attainment makes possible explains why most education, intelligence testing, and psychological research stays within the limits of concept attainment.

CONCEPT FORMATION

Concept formation is unlike recall and concept attainment in that there are no fixed answers that can be learned or discovered. This conceptual mode correlates with the made-concept model; concepts must be synthetically formed and evaluated by a free mind. Such concepts may provoke lively discussion or criticism, as there are many different points of view and no absolute authorities. This is the highest function of the human mind, but it is bound to threaten the status quo and the conventional wisdom that cultural indoctrination preserves.

Unless we assume that humans are completely passive beings to whom life "happens" or preprogrammed robots capable only of knee-jerk responses to life's stimuli, then we must assume that we are to some extent in control of and responsible for our actions. And since life is too complex to be covered by the recall and concept attainment of cultural indoctrination, our dominant mental mode in day-to-day experience is concept formation. We conceive and act out a day's work, a night on the town, or a two-week vacation in relative freedom and in the absence of many fixed answers. Such a view of experience makes no distinction between planning a weekend or designing a building. They both involve concept formation and are potentially creative.

The three kinds of conceptual functioning correspond roughly to a story my dad tells: A sportswriter was interviewing three major league umpires and asked how they called balls and strikes. The first umpire replied, "I call them like they are" (recall). The second answered, "I call them like I see them" (concept attainment). Then Bill Clem, the dean of umpires at the time, allowed that "They ain't nothin' 'till I call 'em" (concept formation).

EXPERIENCE'S OPPORTUNITIES

The opportunities of experience offer our only chance of claiming conceptual freedom or responsibility. While evolution seems to favor freedom, cultures are generally uncomfortable with conceptual freedom and believe that one's responsibility is limited to learning, maintaining, and transmitting the culture's particular conception of the world.

In *The Ghost in the Machine* (1967), Arthur Koestler explains:

> Coghill has demonstrated that in the embryo the motor-nerve tracts become active, and movements make their appearance, before the sensory nerves become functional. And the moment it is hatched or born the creature lashes out at the environment, be it liquid or solid, with cilia, flagellae, or contractile muscle fibre; it crawls, swims, glides, pulsates; it kicks, yells, breathes, feeds on its surroundings for all it is worth. It does not merely adapt to the environment, but constantly adapts the environment to itself—it eats and drinks its environment, fights and mates with it, burrows and builds in it; it does not merely respond to the environment, but asks questions by exploring it. The "exploratory drive" is now recognized by the younger generation of animal psychologists to be a primary biological instinct, as basic as the instincts of hunger and sex; it can on occasion be even more powerful than these. . . .

This exploratory drive, which is apparently part of our evolutionary heritage, serves us well in opening cracks in our cultural indoctrination. The restlessness of youth helps us to discover that many experiences prohibited by culture are harmless or even pleasant.

Confident conceivers have experienced the rewards successful conception can bring. If their parents, teachers, or friends valued their first efforts at "original" conceptions, by the time they reached a professional design school "conception" had become fun because they knew that they were good at it.

The first attempts at this kind of conception may be making jokes or wisecracks, providing nicknames for buddies, or suggesting how to make a Saturday afternoon interesting to a gang of friends. Children's first attempts at humor, first drawings, or first ideas about anything are usually offered very tentatively. The reception of these first conceptual offerings is more critical to their confidence in their conceptual ability, and therefore their *actual* conceptual ability, than perhaps anything else. The reception can of course be overdone, as it is when parents insist on endlessly retelling or displaying a child's creative efforts to the point of embarrassment. The trick is to accept children's first creative efforts, teach them to build on those efforts, and, most of all, to let them know that you think this kind of behavior is worthwhile by participating with them in joking, storytelling, drawing, or just plain thinking, without enforcing any doctrine that puts down their ideas.

Ideas with which conceivers have been indoctrinated, or that they have accepted from any other source, regardless how sophisticated they might be, contribute little to experience in concept formation. Individuals may exhibit high conventional intelligence, but have little more of the conceptual ability needed in design than a filing cabinet or an encyclopedia.

This is one of the reasons that some of the best designers in professional design schools have undistinguished academic records in high school. They may have judged, correctly, that it was much more challenging and creative to figure out how to date the prettiest girl or the best-looking boy, or to become the class clown, or to succeed at any number of other activities, than to become a human photocopy machine or tape recorder, which is often required to get good grades.

Experience offers few conceptual opportunities without an initial assumption that the mind is potentially free and that concepts are made rather than given or discovered. Just as perception influences conception, so, too, a free mind able to make concepts influences perception, as it leads us to perceive the world and the traditional concepts of the world critically and as capable of improvement. Conversely, if we expect experience to be nothing more than a lifelong verification of our traditional cultural indoctrination, we will probably not be disappointed.

Gibson furthered perceptual studies by criticizing the assumption that a fixed lens on a tripod can represent our vision. Ittleson has similarly criticized experiments involving the perception of artificially isolated objects rather than environments. Both theorists point out that in reducing the complexity of perception for the purposes of scientific measurement, the experimental conditions lose their similarity to conditions of actual perception.

Most of the psychologists who have studied conception have done little better. They have qualified for Abraham Maslow's (*The Psychology of Science, A Reconnaissance*, 1969) comment about the behaviorists: "If the only tool you have is a hammer, you tend to treat everything as if it were a nail." Most studies of intelligence or conception are limited to tests of memory (recall) or the kind of problem solving that applies known categories and concepts (concept attainment).

The reason for avoiding the mind's most common functional mode is that the absence of fixed verifiable answers means there are no standards for the quantitative measurement on which "scientific" inquiry relies. This leaves concept formation awash in the sea of relative value while respectable academic or scientific research prefers the solid ground of measurable certainty.

Bruner, Goodnow, and Austin (*A Study of Thinking*, 1956) admit, "There is, first of all, the act of concept or category formation—the inventive act by which classes are constructed. Of this process, we have had relatively little to say here. . . ."

Measuring human intelligence by testing a person's recall and concept attainment is as misleading as the conventional experiments in perception. In the stream of consciousness of day-to-day experience we do not normally use our minds to solve problems that have fixed answers, and we spend very little time recalling verbatim information. Our minds were developed to prepare for the future, and while that preparation certainly includes the remembrance and application of lessons from the past, the relationship is a link, not a chain.

Unless my consciousness is incredibly unique, the normal conceptual mode is concept formation, a continual synthesis of or congruence between what I want to do and what I should or can do. Unlike with recall or concept attainment, it is not a *compliance* with some fixed standard set by science or society. I must make and take responsibility for both sides of this congruence—the side that represents what I should do and/or can do and the side that represents what I want to do.

One of the great benefits of design education, and the catalyst for a painful transition for many design students, is the challenge of creatively analyzing a problem *and* creatively solving it. They are suddenly criticized for *both sides* of the congruence—not just how they solved the design problem, but also their perception/conception of the problem to be solved.

Many of the great conceptual advances in human knowledge have come about because the thinkers redefined the problem side of the congruence, or, in other words, saw a different problem to solve.

Another inhibiting habit that we carry over into free conception is the idea that the "problem" side of the congruence is antecedent to the "solution" side and that once established, it should remain fixed. In normal, everyday concept formation it doesn't work that way. Early success on the solution side of the congruence will raise my goals or aspirations on the problem side. I may begin willfully with what I want to do and change my definition of what I should do to fit it. It is only with reverse order congruences like this that I will ever raise or redefine my idea of what I can do.

The congruences involved in the normal concept formation mode can best be understood by considering an average day in our lives.

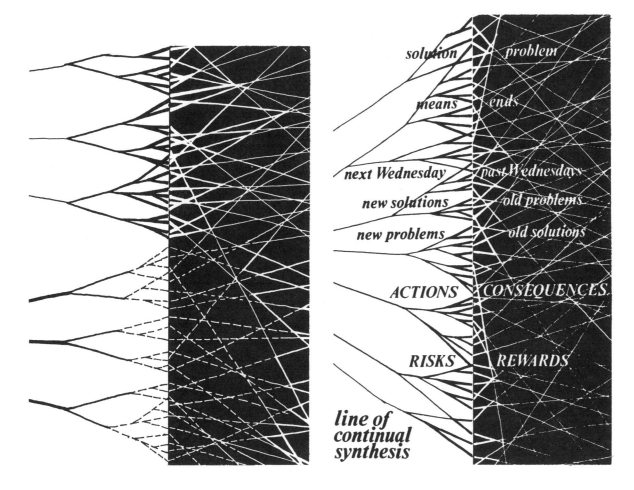

solution   problem

means   ends

next Wednesday   past Wednesday

new solutions   old problems

new problems   old solutions

ACTIONS   CONSEQUENCES

RISKS   REWARDS

*line of
continual
synthesis*

WEDNESDAY

Each of us in each week of our lives has a category called "Wednesday" and, unless we are content to rise every Wednesday morning like a new goose and let Wednesday happen to us, we actively *perceive/conceive/achieve* our Wednesdays. On Thursday morning when we awake we can never say that we "correctly" did Wednesday. We can count our money, note how well we slept, and check our bodily functions, but our Wednesday is not capable of any kind of objective measurement.

Wednesday can only be measured against what we, individually, set out to accomplish on that day. No one else can ever tell us whether we successfully perceived/conceived/achieved Wednesday or not, except within very narrow categories, like "legally," "financially," "physically," or "morally," and there is an obvious argument against letting others decide most of these. The fact that we can never measure Wednesday does not excuse our ignorance of the kind of conception involved in perceiving/conceiving/achieving a great Wednesday.

Wednesday, any Wednesday, is like the open category of any design problem. It will be established by its relationship to the larger whole of the week, year, or lifetime, to the smaller moments that make up its twenty-four-hour duration, and to its lateral relationship to Tuesday and Thursday or to other Wednesdays.

Wednesdays will have certain invariables (rise, bathe, breakfast), some periodic variables (design committee luncheon meeting), and some specific variables (client meeting at 4:00 P.M.); but except in the most extremely regimented environments, Wednesday will be mostly ours to conceive and, even within our regular or specific tasks, will include all sorts of opportunities for conceptual freedom (what to have for breakfast, what to discuss at the luncheon meeting, and what to think about when only our physical presence is required).

What we expect to accomplish or experience on a given Wednesday will vary according to what we can conceive based on our resources, our abilities, our experience, and our environment.

I know from experience that it is difficult for a country boy to conceive of the set of experiences that can be strung together on a Wednesday in New York, London, or Paris if you do not have the resources, the energy, and some knowledge of what is available. These simple, everyday, commonsense variables still make more difference in conception than do the labyrinth of methods, strategies, and tactics into which some psychologists and design methodologists have led us.

Conception is only one function of the eyemindhand triad of human intelligence and thus is interdependently related to perception and action. Experienced conceivers who are confident of their resources, their abilities, and their environment perceive a much richer potential for any Wednesday; if they are accustomed to success in matching what they want to do with what they should or can do, they anticipate Wednesdays as an opportunity for satisfying achievement. The concept of Wednesday, which they form, is fundamentally different from those for whom Wednesday is only another boring or threatening period of time.

Most design "problems" are as open as most Wednesdays and they are subject to the same kind of concept formation, varying wildly with the experience, resources, and abilities of the conceiver or designer and the context of the so-called problem. To call such design opportunities "problems" and to call the activity that responds to them "problem solving" is to make the same error that psychologists do when they oversimplify mental functioning by removing all the complex variables in which any real-world conceptual task is wrapped.

Conceptual Drawing

The succeeding chapter on representation contains a detailed discussion of drawing's relationship to the design process, including the conceptual phase. Here I would like to discuss the role of drawing in conception in a more general way by looking at the complementary kinds of synthesis it promotes and by considering the external sequence it catalyzes.

THE ROLE OF DRAWING in conception varies widely among designers, depending on their confidence and experience with drawing. There seem to be at least six different roles that drawing can play in the design process:

- to sell the product
- to neutrally record the results of a mental process that occurs separately, privately, and previously
- to communicate the process
- to participate in the process
- to lead the process
- to be the process

Even prescriptions for the design process that mistrust drawing do concede its usefulness in graphically presenting certain analytical relationships through graphs and matrices. Later in the process, the similarly neutral recording of ultimate design decisions in plans, sections, and elevations can serve as patterns from which to estimate costs and construct the design.

These views of drawing are essentially the same as those an executive would hold of the activity of typing or key-punching—that it is some sort of automatic activity that demands accuracy and competence but is best delegated to some underling and is not really an opportunity for creativity.

Another view of drawing's relationship to the design process is that its most useful role is to sell the products of the process. In this view, drawing is similarly separated from the decision-making process and may easily be farmed out to another kind of underling, a professional renderer, just as the responsibility for a firm's public relations may be given to an advertising agency.

If drawing is relegated either to the role of a neutral recording mechanism or of selling the designed product, it is essentially excluded from any significant role in the design process. If, on the other hand, we assume that the activity of drawing is an inseparable part of designing anything that will be experienced and evaluated visually—that drawing at least *participates in the process*—then a whole range of much more useful roles for drawing emerges.

Such an expanded role for drawing in the design process raises our expectations for what may happen *while we are drawing*, and this anticipation allows us to see conceptual opportunities that might otherwise be overlooked.

THE DOUBLE SYNTHESIS

When we begin to draw whatever we are designing a very unique phenomenon occurs. It is as if the drawing were made with a pantograph (a device that, when one of its two heads is used to draw or write, produces, by a connecting armature, a remote image of variable size that is an exact copy of the original drawing or writing). The original drawing is an overt image, in the world, on the paper for all to see; but there is a simultaneous second drawing—the covert image drawn on our consciousness, on the surface of our experience network or memory.

Two kinds of syntheses occur in this double drawing. Each is seeking a kind of congruence, and this double synthesis and the congruences it seeks deserve careful consideration.

THE OVERT SYNTHESIS occurs in the world, on the paper, and is open to everyone. When we begin to make representative drawings of our designs, we must collect all the separate precepts, concepts, notions, and hunches we have about a design problem into a committed whole. Without drawing we could endlessly speculate verbally about what the design should be, but the moment of truth represented by those first drawings cuts through all the verbiage. For the first time the design solution must undergo a physical synthesis. For the first time it can be seen and evaluated by the designer and by others.

This synthesis in itself is very beneficial because of the holistic commitment it requires. The synthesis also makes possible the evaluation by the other participants in the design process— the client, the consultants, the other members of the design team—and begins to test the congruence between the physical solution proposed and its supporting rationale.

Once the design is represented by drawings it becomes a member of Karl Popper's World 3, the product of minds, and can be evaluated and tested logically. Popper makes clear the importance of objectifying ideas so that they can be openly criticized. His thoughts on the matter are summarized by Brian Magee (*Karl Popper*, 1973):

Throughout his account of the evolution of life and the emergence of man and the development of civilization, Popper makes use of the notion not only of an objective world of material things (which he calls World 1) and a subjective world of minds (World 2) but of a third world, a world of objective structures which are the products, not necessarily intentional, of minds or living creatures; but which, once produced, exist independently of them. . . .

World 3, then, is the world of ideas, art, science, language, ethics, institutions—the whole cultural heritage, in short—insofar as this is encoded and preserved in such World 1 objects as brains, books, machines, films, computers, pictures, and records of every kind. . . .

. . . This underlines the enormous importance of objectifying our ideas in language or behavior or works of art. While they are only in our heads they are barely criticizable. Their public formulation itself usually leads to progress. And the validity of any argument about them is again an objective matter: it is not determined by how many individuals are prepared to accept it. . . .

THE COVERT SYNTHESIS occurs in the designer's consciousness, imprinted on the experience network, and is a very separate and private matter. When we begin to draw our ideas we integrate the third component of human intelligence, the hand (as representative of the body), with the eye and the mind. Drawing completes the eyemindhand triad so that we become a perceptual/conceptual/ actual whole. We no longer have the artificial detachment of the observer or the critic who just talk about a design. We have now represented our ideas by making drawings of them *with our hands* and that simple action commits our whole selves to an identity with the proposed solution in a way that just describing the design verbally never could.

This second synthesis also seeks a congruence, but not with a logical, communicable rationale like the overt synthesis. The private congruence sought by the covert synthesis in our consciousness is immediately felt, not reasoned. But it is this private inner synthesis and its congruence with our hopes, wishes, and feelings for the solution that is more important. The overt synthesis of our design can be a disaster in terms of matching the verbal or mathematical criteria of a problem's program, or in terms of being able to support it with any even remotely reasonable rationale. Yet, in our gut, or in our heart, or in whatever body part you want to represent that inner synthesis that includes *all* of whatever we are, we may feel or *know* we have the best solution. The reverse may also be the case and this is perhaps even more painful. Our solution may match the words and numbers of the problem's program flawlessly, and the rationale that supports the design may be so obvious and logical that the client grasps it immediately, but somewhere deep inside us the inner congruence is awry and we know the design stinks.

The separateness of the double synthesis is critical. A designer must cultivate the difference between the two because the dimension that separates what satisfies clients or the general public and what satisfies the designer is in many ways the measure of the designer's ability and integrity.

When we surrender the separate opinion of that inner synthesis and are content whenever others are content, we will have lost much of the value we have as designers.

THE SIMULTANEITY of the two drawings is demonstrated by the process of conceptual drawing. In many cases we know *as we draw* whether the line we are drawing is congruent or incongruent with our intentions for the design. This is because our intentions for the design are represented somehow in our experience network (from the mindmodel offered earlier). When we attempt to draw the design, we are drawing *on* the surface of the experience network, which holds the vague intentions, wishes, and hunches we have for the solution.

Robert H. McKim explains this simultaneity and the feedback loop (*Experiences in Visual Thinking*, 1972):

> drawing and thinking are frequently so simultaneous that the graphic image appears almost an organic extension of mental processes. . . .

Graphic ideation utilizes seeing, imagining, and drawing in a cyclic feedback process that is fundamentally iterative. I have given this "feedback loop" the acronym ETC (etcetera) to dramatize the importance of repetitive cycling to the graphic development of visual ideas.

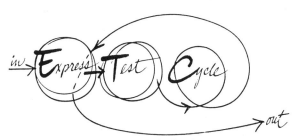

From *Experiences in Visual Thinking* by R. H. McKim

Fluent and flexible ideation, deferred judgment, and unhesitating translation of idea into sketch are important ways to open the gates that hold back ideas. However, the importance of *drawing skill* to the full expression of visual ideas must not be overlooked. Inadequate drawing ability has three negative effects on the Express phase of ETC: (1) a clumsy sketch usually evokes judgmental processes that restrict or stop idea-flow, (2) ideas that cannot be adequately recorded in sketch form are often lost, and (3) attention devoted to problems of drawing is attention diverted from idea-generation.

The effort at congruence also works in the opposite direction. The drawing often causes us to change the pattern of our intentions in order *to fit the drawing*. We may see opportunities for improving or extending our understanding of the design task as we draw tentative solutions. The act of drawing shows us relationships and opportunities that we would have never discovered verbally. This simultaneous synthesis and search for congruence also explains the spontaneous momentum we feel when drawing *becomes* design.

This is described by William D. Martin, an M.I.T. graduate, in his unpublished master's thesis called "The Architect's Role in Participatory Planning Processes: Case Study—Boston Transportation Planning Review":

> Sketch design manipulation of pattern relationships provides the architect with insights and information which may stimulate the recall of other patterns or may be used to modify the content of patterns currently in use. Such information may also change the architect's perception of the problem itself resulting in shifts in objective, appropriate methods and form requirements, and thereby suggesting new, more appropriate patterns and programs.

Congruences that occur from a changing perception of the design task may also be delayed. In looking over week-old or month-old drawings we may suddenly recognize a congruence or potential congruence that wasn't there before, because our perception/ conception of the problem to be solved has changed in the week or month since we made that drawing—perhaps *because* we made the drawing.

EXTERNALIZATION

Instead of representing a distinct division between the internal and external phases of conception, externalization is better conceived as a transition. Design drawing begins to participate directly in the design process at this point and is, in fact, one of the criteria of externalization. When a design can be represented by a drawn form, pattern, or diagram, we say it has been externalized.

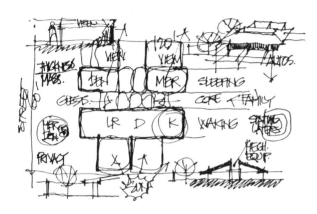

Strictly speaking externalization begins during the *internal* phase in the form of the graphic note-taking illustrated in Edward T. White's books. This is a very natural way to break the blockage of giving your ideas physical form in drawing. This ability may be developed by trying to make as many of your notations to yourself as graphic as possible.

ANALOGICAL DRAWING is another way of beginning to externalize conception so that it involves the hand. It also can be a rich source of conceptual relationships. Analogical drawing entails a search for relationships between the "problem" or its parts and similar (or even dissimilar) problems that already have been solved. W. J. J. Gordon (*Synectics*, 1968) has identified specific analogical categories (direct, personal, fantastic, and symbolic), which will be discussed in chapter 6.

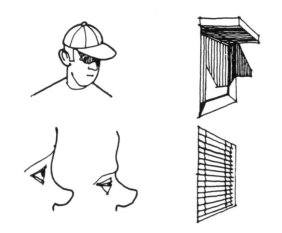

The act of drawing an analogy usually deepens our understanding of how much it is like what we are working on. If the analogy is a good one its correspondence to the problem at hand may have an unexpected richness, which is extended by drawing it. It is also surprising how many facets of any design problem may be drawn analogically. The site, the function, the climatic context, the construction process, even the overall problem (not just its solution) offer analogical opportunities that will deepen a designer's understanding and provide unsuspected conceptual opportunities.

One final reason for drawing analogies is that they are so beautifully efficient in communicating design ideas to clients and consultants. Creative analogies synthesize the essential qualities of the design concept and make them much more accessible to anyone whose understanding and approval you need.

Externalization is, to use an analogy of my own, like a computer "printout." This externalized printout may be graphic or verbal. I am convinced that its purest, truest form is graphic and that verbal printouts are only distorted translations in a prejudiced, if remarkable, secondary symbol system.

Robert H. McKim (*Experiences in Visual Thinking*, 1972) argues,

The dichotomy that mistakenly links verbal thinking with abstraction and visual thinking with concretization was undoubtedly conceived by individuals who identified visual imagery with postcard realism and failed to observe visual abstraction as expressed in contemporary art and abstract graphic-language forms. Abstract graphic languages encode abstract ideas, not concrete things. . . .

THE EYEMINDHAND WHEEL

The externalization of a design concept can be thought of as a rolling eyemindhand wheel. Strong concepts roll into reality out of the externalization starting gate in an upright position,

By permission of Johnny Hart and Field Enterprises, Inc.

By permission of Johnny Hart and Field Enterprises, Inc.

while weak concepts may be pushed out on one flat side. The rolling of the wheel represents a chain reaction where the eyemindhand conceives, presents, perceives, evaluates, reconceives, represents, reperceives, and reevaluates, like in McKim's *ETC*. During this chain reaction a designer is using the three evolutionary tools that make us human—if our eyes, minds, and hands have been carefully sharpened and we know how to use them as one confident intelligence, a real pleasure accompanies the process.

William D. Martin ("The Architect's Role in Participatory Planning Processes: Case Study—Boston Transportation Planning Review") witnesses:

Sketch design in this manner might continue for only a few moments or perhaps some several hours with perceptions of form relationships between current patterns providing continuous feedback and stimulating the recall of additional patterns and pattern linking programs from LTM [long-term

memory]. The process stops when the architect reaches a desired point of design development or when he has posed questions which require informational inputs from outside his current problem space, or perhaps when he finds he has no appropriate patterns in LTM for the form relationships suggested by current problem requirements.

Adel Foz, another M.I.T. graduate, noted in his master's thesis "Some Observations on Designer Behavior in the Parti" (1972):

he continually strives to externalize his ideas and form proposals into external memory devices thereby keeping STM [short-term memory] clear. By not requiring STM to hold both an object and tests of its significance simultaneously, its capacity is freed for invention and testing activities.

. . . he uses EM [external memory] devices [design drawings] to display and correlate information automatically, again freeing STM from having to perform a task and retain its results. He uses representational media as analogous as possible to the final physical product, i.e. perspective drawings and models.

The design process can be triggered by any of the three components of the eyemindhand wheel or by indistinguishable combinations of the three components. Teachers encourage all three components, but they most enjoy working with students who can really roll the wheel so that they can spend most of their time talking about the direction of the wheel's movement rather than whether it is even upright.

Students respond to this pushing of their conceptual wheel in various ways, depending mostly

on the experience and confidence they have in using the three components of the wheel. Some students begin to draw right away, but have difficulty explaining or justifying what they are drawing. Other students begin to make verbal notes or outlines or talk about their ideas. Others begin looking in libraries and at real situations.

Most of what is written about the design process or design methodology assumes that drawing is or should be delayed until there is "something to draw" in the form of an internal verbal or visual image. This view assumes that the hand can never initiate the rotation of the eyemindhand wheel. There are also writers, deBono for instance, who advocate random verbal stimulation as a creativity technique—opening a dictionary and choosing a word at random and then generating conceptual connections between the word and the problem you are trying to solve. Random graphic stimulation is even more valuable and needn't undergo any artificial translation from words.

Drawing allows the participation of our subconscious or preconscious in ways that are not fully understood. If we look at our design drawings carefully and expectantly, in anticipation of recognizing unintended patterns and relationships, we can learn to find them. Whether that illogical, preverbal recognition is the participation of our subconscious or is only the recognition of our subconscious participation in making the drawings is not clear. But there is no reason why such pattern recognition cannot be stimulated initially and directly by random drawing.

Difficulty in overcoming the inertia of the conceptual wheel may indicate a flat side that represents the student's area of least confidence. Teachers' responsibility is to help the design student build up the flat parts of the wheel so the student can roll it confidently and smoothly. They may then spend most of their time deciding what is the most promising direction in which to roll it.

Design teaching depends on the externalized printout of the conceptual process in the form of external memories or design drawings. Little communication is possible during the internal phase of conception—it is only after the drawings are made that teaching can begin, because until then there is no common referent for discussion. There are two main blockages to externalization that cause drawings to be withheld.

The search for a perfect, full-blown concept is perhaps the most prevalent blockage to externalization. The mythology that surrounds creativity promotes this extension of the internal phase and inhibits the open, communicable process that is necessary for the clients' participation and students' learning from discussion with peers or teachers. In my experience, it is also a sign of weakness, since the confident designers externalize a concept quickly and manipulate it vigorously through an extended external conceptual phase. They draw or talk about the concept throughout this external phase and they are in confident control of the changes and refinements that take place.

A second blockage to externalization is the inability, or lack of confidence in the ability, to printout the concept in an acceptable verbal or graphic form. Design students may feel that their first attempts at verbal or graphic communication are unworthy of representing the qualities they see in their eyemind. Even though they feel their concept is as good as those of their fellow students, they may be intimidated by the verbal or graphic eloquence they see in their peers' externalization of their concepts.

James L. Adams (*Conceptual Blockbusting*, 1974) describes the difficulties he has experienced in getting his students to use drawing as a conceptual tool:

> As I have previously mentioned, we work with an extremely verbal group of students at Stanford. A great deal of effort has been put into their verbal (and mathematical) abilities during their formal education, but little into their visual ability. When they come to Stanford many are, in Bob McKim's frustrated terminology, "visual illiterates." They often are not used to drawing, or to

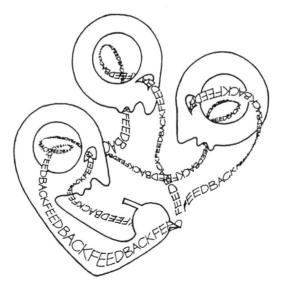

using visual imagery as a thinking mode. Although their drawing is generally not good, it is usually good enough (especially with a few helpful hints) to use as a thinking aid. Nonetheless, they are usually extremely reluctant to draw because their drawings compare so badly with drawings made by professionals (intended for communication with others). We try to encourage crude but informative drawings for the student's own purposes. We also try to encourage improving one's drawing skills, since we find that good drawing skill is a powerful conceptual aid. . . .

Both the blockages are expressions of a more basic fear of failure or ridicule, which is one of the first obstacles encountered in design education. Unfortunately, the obstacle is increased by the pressure of deadlines and the compulsive grading and sorting of students that accompanies most design education. Students must somehow cope with externalization, however, or they will miss a great deal of the teaching and learning they need. The early externalizers automatically get more teacher and peer attention because they have something to see and talk about.

Design drawing is the most helpful catalyst of externalization. The internal searching of the perceptual/conceptual network is a search for images and patterns, but if we are unaided by external graphics, only a limited number of these patterns can be found, held, and compared in our eyeminds. During this internal searching, it is natural and normal that the images and patterns with which a designer is working begin to be externalized piecemeal in the form of conceptual doodles and diagrams. The advantage of beginning externalization at this very early stage is that externalized doodles and diagrams can be evaluated for design playback, displayed and compared with alternative diagrams, and manipulated, revised, and kept as a record of the conceptual process.

Experienced designers, who habitually and confidently use conceptual diagrams early in the process, learn to represent and see a great deal from these simple graphic images. With intelligent use, they can become a shorthand that is superior to verbal language.

The basis of the superiority of diagrams is that they involve the eyemindhand—all the evolutionary tools of intelligence. The eyemind can perceive and evaluate more than the mind alone and when the hand has made the visual images, the eyemindhand is imprinted with the conceptual patterns. The drawing of the conceptual diagrams also allows a better understanding of the concept because our eyemindhand interactively works with it.

The conceptual process is led by, and literally runs on, design drawings. The eyemindhand wheel turns, and each rotation brings a deeper understanding of the concept's relationships and a refinement of its form. This process strips the concept of extraneous details and distills it into its most meaningful and efficient form. For the confident designer, the conceptual diagram becomes the concept, and the designer's eyemind learns to see in the externalized diagrams qualities and relational possibilities that were impossible to discover in the concept's internal form.

The external phase has been reached when designers experience what is called "analogue takeover." When asked about the design, they let

their drawings speak for them; instead of thinking about the design without any graphic referents, they actively draw the design and spend considerable time scrutinizing those drawings. Regardless of the means we used to trigger externalization, the externalized conceptual image can be manipulated, evaluated, and communicated to others. The drawings have become an analog for the design solution.

Robert H. McKim (*Experiences in Visual Thinking*, 1972) explains the advantages of ideas that have been externalized as drawings:

> Drawing not only helps to bring vague inner images into focus, it also provides a record of the advancing thought stream. Further, drawing provides a function that memory cannot: the most brilliant imager cannot compare a number of images, side by side in memory, as one can compare a wall of tacked-up idea-sketches.

Adams (*Conceptual Blockbusting*, 1974) argues for the necessity of graphic externalization:

In order to take full advantage of visual thinking ability, *drawing* is necessary. Drawing allows the recording, storage, manipulation, and communication of images to augment the pictures one can generate in his imagination. In the Design Division, we find it useful to divide drawing into two categories: that which is done to communicate with others, and that which is done to communicate with oneself. . . .

These drawings should include a variety of graphic languages as they progress from conceptual diagrams to realistic perspective representations. One of the most handsome demonstrations, ranging over several design disciplines, is collected in Robert H. McKim's *Experiences in Visual Thinking* (1972) in which he proposes:

> indeed, ability to move from one graphic language to another, along the dimension of abstract-to-concrete, is probably the most useful kind of graphic-language flexibility. . . .

In his chapter "Out of the Language Rut," McKim demonstrates the fantastic range of conceptual graphic languages by giving beautiful examples from a great variety of designers.

The rolling of the eyemindhand wheel through these design-drawing manipulations will eventually begin to leave a track of words with which the design can be explained verbally. Teachers, bosses, and clients will inevitably ask questions that your personal conceptual process hasn't covered, and these questions will need to be answered.

From *Experiences in Visual Thinking* by R. H. McKim.

As the designers roll the wheel toward more realistic, representational design drawings, they look back over the ground they have covered for a supporting rationale. If they perceive a track of verbal rationale, the wheel settles into and deepens that track. If no track of rationale is perceived, the designer must change the direction of the rolling wheel in search of more impressive ground. Some design methods imply that the design process proceeds on the basis of verbal or mathematical logic, although none can explain the "magic leap" from words to three-dimensional form. I believe it is much more honest to admit that the words are literally an afterthought. Words can describe a conceptual design task and, after the conceptual design solution is established, they can frame its rationale, but in the white heat at the core of the conceptual synthesis words are only in the way and are replaced entirely by groans, whistles, sighs, expletives, and the scratch of pen or pencil. Words may also mislead by the many glowing, honorific adjectives that carry our hopes for the design solution. The eye is little persuaded by verbal eloquence,

however, and may not see these qualities in the drawings. Verbal descriptions may also be spatially impossible—you may say you are going to organize the house around an atrium, but until you draw it you won't know if you have enough rooms or budget to go around. As long as design concepts remain in designers' minds or words they may be impossible or irrational. It is only when they are synthesized in drawings that they become subject to open, objective, rational argument.

Drawing can make at least six contributions to the conceptual sequence of externalization.

- It can make graphic notes that efficiently record spatial or temporal relationships and clear our short-term memory for more important tasks.

- It can record and extend the analogies for various aspects of the design task; the analogies deepen understanding and are the source of unexpected creative relationships.

- It can trigger, provoke, symbolize, and record formative images, some of which may change the designer's perception of the conceptual task.

- It completes the integration of the eyemind-hand triad of human intelligence.

- It allows the participation of the subconscious in the forms and patterns it offers for recognition and inclusion in the design synthesis.

- It synthesizes the various precepts, concepts, wishes, and hunches about the design task in concrete physical forms that can then be openly evaluated and manipulated by the designer and others during the external phase of the design process.

By permission of Johnny Hart and Field Enterprises, Inc.

3 Representation

This section of the book is concerned with the various drawings we make as representations of whatever we are designing, from concept to finished product. These drawings are important because they represent the design to our eye-minds, and we must be very careful to understand their limitations and the prejudices they carry. Of all the strongholds of dogma in design education, the conventional drawings and the order in which they are undertaken are the most strongly defended, if indeed they are ever questioned at all. It is time we critically evaluate traditional representational drawings and their relationship to experience and to the design process, as well as alternative techniques for making them. The ways of thinking about and making the drawings advocated here are not proposed as the most technically accurate or artistically admired. I use them, however, because I have found they can be understood and applied by design students with little previous background in drawing—they work. My aim is to help students of design learn to use drawing as a design tool, not to teach students who already know how to draw to make masterpiece renderings, nor to demonstrate how well I can draw.

In order to see drawings in a more useful way it is necessary to rethink the conventional categories we normally use to describe and think about drawings. Traditionally we categorize drawings by their media and form, and we believe when we have described a drawing as a pen-and-ink plan or a pencil perspective we have said something very significant about the drawing. These two traditional categories, media and form, are a hybrid inheritance from art and drafting. From art we have adopted the notion that the chemical composition of the drawing (ink, graphite, charcoal, etc.) is of great importance. In art schools the curriculum is normally categorized, at least in part, in terms of the media used, with courses called "beginning watercolor" or "advanced oil painting." From drafting we have accepted the idea that the formal naming of a drawing (plan, section, elevation, etc.) is as significant as the medium. This traditional categorization is almost useless for design drawings. The *medium* in which a design drawing is made is of no significance whatsoever, even secondarily, and unless the designer is aware of and deliberately chooses a particular drawing for its relationship to experience or to the problem or solution, the *form* of the drawing may also be meaningless. I believe it is more appropriate to categorize design drawings according to:

- the drawing's relationship to experience; and
- the drawing's relationship to the design process.

In light of these two relationships (the first I will cover in this chapter, the second in chapter 6), the conventional ways of thinking about design drawings in the categories of form and media seem trivial.

These relationships are the best way I have found for designers to think about representational drawings, but it is much more important that you, as a designer, create and continually recreate your own best way of thinking about them, so that you can make intelligent choices. Never mindlessly accept and use any kind of drawing without questioning its value, and never assume that the drawings you are making have any particular or necessary relationship to experience or to the design process. The choices you make about how those drawings are made and used are your responsibility as a designer. To always make the same drawings in the same way and in the same order is to continue unquestioningly to use the same method, when choice of method may be our greatest freedom and most useful tool.

Drawing's Relationship to Experience

The word "design" or "designing" implies an activity that is separate from "making." Sculptors, painters, or poets enjoy a direct interaction with their creations through the clay, paint, or language that forms their means of expression. They do not *design* their sculptures, paintings, or poems so much as they *make* them. In contrast to this immediate experience of making, we environmental designers are always separated from the reality of what we are designing. Separated from our design process by time and space, the making of our designs is normally carried out by other people and, increasingly, by machines.

This separation requires us to use representations of reality to propose, see, evaluate, change, and communicate our designs. We must clearly understand the relationships these graphic representations have to the experience of the built environment. It is important to remember that design drawing is *always* representational. A design drawing represents a thought or a synthesis of several thoughts, which is one of many possible alternatives to be evaluated in the design process. Design drawings must communicate honestly, openly, and with extreme accuracy. This also means that design drawing should be as quick and free as your thought process. Like the verbalization of an idea, a design drawing is a statement, more or less congruent to a thought, whose truth and eloquence can only be evaluated visually.

TRANSCENDENCE

The goal of all representational drawing should be to make the environment being designed real to the designer's eyemind. Representational drawings must be more than just an assemblage of lines and tones on paper. They must take on a separate reality of their own in space or as space, and in relationship to their context and their users. They must transcend all the trivia of technique and their physical form and become a believable presence in the consciousness of the designer.

TRANSPARENCY

The best way of achieving the desired transcendence is to learn to accept your drawing ability, wherever it is at the moment, and look *through* your drawings to the potential reality of whatever you are designing. This transparency is promoted by drawing very credibly, so that the accuracy of the representation is unquestioned, and by drawing very simply, in a way that calls little or no attention to the drawing *as a drawing*.

This neutral transparency can be illustrated by an analogy using our written language. In reading these words you are probably unaware of the form or style of the typeface. The letters are *transparent* as letters, and you look right through them to the meaning of the words they form. It is possible, however, to begin a series of *CHANGES* that will make the LETTERING PROGRESSIVELY CALL MORE & MORE ATTENTION TO ITSELF,

lose its transparency and become almost opaque TO ANY MEANING BEYOND the style of the lettering.

Design drawings must retain their transparency so that the attention of the designer is always focused *beyond* the drawing, on the reality of what is being designed, not at the level of the drawing itself. To be separated from what we are designing by time and space is difficult enough; we mustn't allow the form or technique of our representative drawings to separate us even further from reality.

RELATIVE REALISM

In the design professions, the sequence of the orthographic drawings is always "plan, section, and elevation," enjoying the same dogmatic invocation as "Father, Son, and Holy Ghost" in the Christian religions. This sequence is so firmly entrenched that finding the three words written in any other order—in our literature, in our schools, or anywhere—is nearly impossible. This conventional order is determined by how a design will be constructed, and the sequence in which the set of construction drawings will be arranged. We have mindlessly adopted it as the best or only way of thinking about the drawings. Perspective's place is always last, added almost as an afterthought: plan, section, elevation, and perspective.

When drawings are arranged in a descending hierarchy based on their relationship to experience, however, the traditional order in which they are discussed, taught, or even named is reversed.

Our experience of reality is intimately tied to our perception of our surroundings as an environment, but architects, and perhaps other designers, have for too long conceived of and represented their buildings as objects, viewed from outside, and concentrated their efforts on the perception of their designs as built objects. This has always seemed to me (*Drawing As a Means to Architecture*, 1968) a strange way to design and evaluate buildings, since the entire reason for creating the building is to enclose space. The quality of the enclosed space would seem to be much more important than the exterior of the enclosure.

While viewing what we are designing as an object is an indispensable part of the design process, what I am concerned with here is the perception and representation of the building's interior or exterior space as an *environment*. Environment perception is fundamentally different from object perception. The reality we experience every day is perceived as an environment that surrounds us, and in which we actively participate. Any representation of the built environment that artificially separates the experiencers from the building and makes them merely observers of a separate object denies reality.

PERSPECTIVES

When we consider drawing's relationship to experience, perspectives immediately surface as the most realistic drawings. Their closeness to experience depends on the skill with which they are drawn, but even the crudest perspectives show more of the experiential qualities of an environment than do elaborate plans, sections, or elevations. In the representational phase of any design process, perspectives most accurately predict what the environment will be for several reasons.

1. Perspectives are more qualitative than quantitative. The experiential qualities of an environment can be perceived directly from a perspective. Light and texture, which are the main qualities of surfaces, are much better depicted in perspective. The qualities of the space/time/light continuum are also better represented and understood in perspective.

2. Perspectives represent the third dimension realistically. The depth or thickness of objects or spaces contributes more than anything else to their achieving a real presence in the designer's eyemind. This three-dimensional quality helps the drawn environment to transcend the flatland of lines on paper and become a believable reality.

   The third dimension allows the perception and study of inside and outside corners both vertically (wall-wall corner), and horizontally (wall-floor corner or wall-ceiling corner). These three-dimensional corners are key to the making of environments and they can only be seen and studied in perspective.

3. Perspectives represent, more than any other drawing, the human, kinesthetic experience of an environment. Correctly drawn perspectives can predict much of the interest that will be available in moving through a space or around an object.

From Giovanni Piranesi. Drawings and etchings at Columbia University.

From *Canaletto: Giovanni Antonio Canal, 1697–1768* by G. W. Constable.

The Construzione Legittima as it was drawn by Leonardo da Vinci.

While multiple perspectives are needed to show extended spatial sequences, a clear sense of the experience of moving through an environment can be shown in a single perspective. This anticipated kinesthetic experience is what gives environments much of their experiential interest, and it can be sensed from the single viewpoint a perspective provides.

4. Perspectives include the viewer by presenting the environment from a particular viewpoint. The perspective's viewpoint is a place made especially for the viewer by the drawing, into which he or she steps in a way not possible in any other drawing. This inclusion of the viewer is uniquely like actual experience. Unlike other drawings, in which reality is a separate object at which we look, perspectives always include us in the experience.

5. Perspectives need no artificial supporting propaganda about their relationship to experience. The qualities of the environments they represent can be judged in an instant. They are subject to less misinterpretation because the qualities are either there or not, and their presence or absence is sensed directly in almost exactly the same way we perceive environments in reality. This direct communication allows us to use our highly evolved senses, not the conjuring developed to overcome the obscure communication of orthographic abstractions.

The drawing of perspectives was first mastered during the Renaissance and developed, according to Bronowski, from the insights of the Moorish mathematician Alhazen. Brunelleschi, Alberti, Ghiberti, da Vinci and Michelangelo all knew and eagerly used perspective in representing their designs. Albrecht Durer traveled to Italy to learn the method and wrote a treatise on it upon his return to Germany. Bronowski states that the development of the rules of perspective was one of the significant discoveries of the underlying structure of reality. In *On the Rationalization of Sight* (1938), William M. Ivins, Jr. proposes that perspective construction allowed all the successive discoveries of science by accounting for the changes in the external appearances of the world, so that objects might retain the internal integrity that science assumes.

The remarkable ability of perspectives to represent the experience of existing environments has been largely forgotten with the subsequent invention and development of photography. There is no longer any reason to draw an existing environment, and the ease with which any environment may be photographed makes us forget the relatively brief period during which the cityscapes of Canaletto or the vast interiors of Piranesi demonstrated the excitement of being able to reproduce the visual experience of an environment with perspective drawing.

Although we no longer need to draw the existing world, the *only* way to propose environments for the future (other than making large, meticulous models) is to draw perspectives.

AXONOMETRIC OR PARALINE DRAWINGS

Next in the hierarchy of realism come the other three-dimensional drawings: the axonometric or paraline drawings. They are much easier to draw than perspectives because the parallel lines of the building remain parallel in the drawing, and all the orthogonal lines are directly measurable. These advantages, however, eliminate the convergence and foreshortening we perceive in reality.

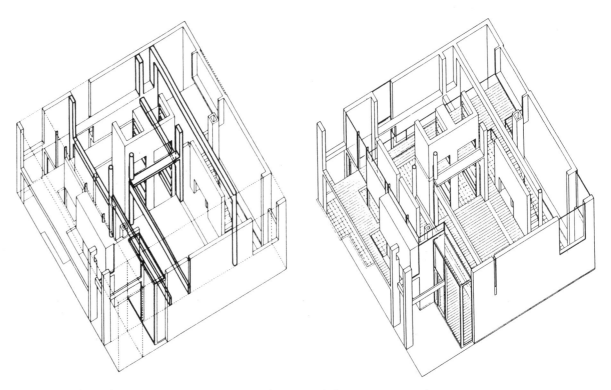

From *Five Architects* by P. Eisenman, M. Graves, C. Gwathmey, J. Hedjuk, R. Meier. Copyright © 1974 by Peter Eisenman, Michael Graves, Charles Gwathmey, John Hedjuk, and Richard Meier. Used by permission of Oxford University Press, Inc.

When considered in the hierarchy of realistic drawings, axonometric drawings are clearly a regression from experience toward quantification; their lack of convergence and foreshortening distorts reality, and their mandatory aerial viewpoint and exclusion of viewer position further sacrifice the experiential quality that perspectives offer. Axonometric drawings are currently enjoying a renewed popularity because, in addition to requiring less drawing skill, they make a very nice *set* of drawings when formally published with orthographic plans and sections. They are visually consistent with orthographic projections precisely because they have retreated a similar distance from experience. They, like plans, sections, and elevations, are drawings of objects, not environments.

PLAN, SECTION, AND ELEVATION

The drawings we conventionally use in the design process are the traditional orthographic abstractions. In the hierarchy of drawing's relationship to experience, however, they run dead last. These drawings are valuable for surveying quantities of materials, for ordering certain structural and mechanical systems, and for studying certain functional relationships. They were developed as patterns from which to build a space or object and have a very distant relationship to experience. They are inadequate and misleading as representative design drawings for several reasons:

1. Plans, sections, and elevations are entirely quantitative, not qualitative. The qualities of a designed environment cannot be read directly from the conventional drawings. We talk endlessly about these qualities and supposedly value them above anything else, but in the drawings we conventionally use to represent our designs, they are completely invisible. The orthographic abstractions do not directly indicate functional pattern or anything about the qualities of privacy, light, sound, or tactility. The plan shows an object or space that is this shape—this orientation—this wide—this long—with these openings—in this location. The section shows, in addition, that this volume has these thicknesses, is this high, and has this relationship to the ground. The elevation shows an object or space this long—this high—with these openings. These are very clear instructions for building something and that's about all they are.

   The ability to deduce qualities from a quantitative drawing can supposedly be acquired, but I seriously question the extent to which they can ever be seen. Similarly the idea of deliberately using an obscure form of communication seems perverse to me.

2. Plans, sections, and elevations give no indication of the third dimension. Plan, section, and elevation can be compared to a fold-out box. This is an excellent way to explain the drawings and their limitations as design drawings.

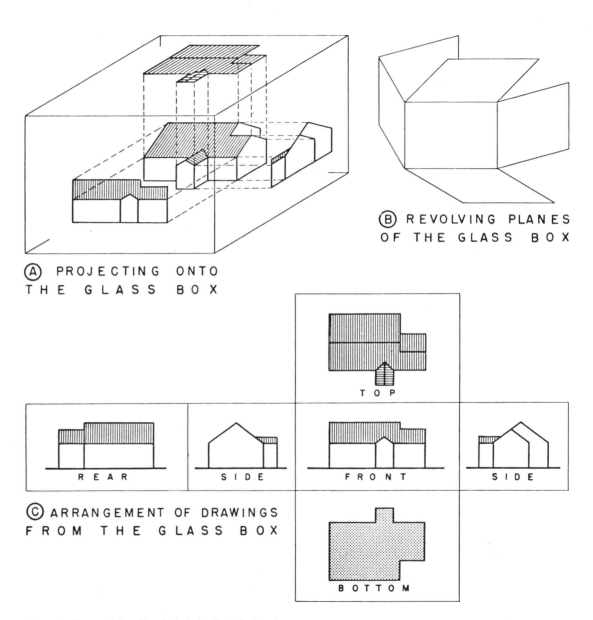

Ⓐ PROJECTING ONTO THE GLASS BOX

Ⓑ REVOLVING PLANES OF THE GLASS BOX

Ⓒ ARRANGEMENT OF DRAWINGS FROM THE GLASS BOX

REAR SIDE FRONT SIDE TOP BOTTOM

From *Architectural Graphics*, 2nd ed., by C. Leslie Martin.

They present a flat face that is an abstraction, since the actual space or object can never be viewed in a similar way. Because of this two-dimensional flatness, they tend to just lie there on the paper, incapable of becoming a real three-dimensional presence in the designer's eyemind. Further, the evaluation of these two-dimensional drawings tends to degenerate into sheet borders, line weight, north arrows, and the many trivia connected with the abstract formality of such drawings—trivia related to the paper, the graphite or ink, and the formal rules for making the drawing.

3. Plans, sections, and elevations offer fragmented views of what would in reality be experienced as a three-dimensional whole. The obscurity of such fragmentation is made clear by the common drafting assignment "puzzle" in which students are given two of the three orthographic views of an object and asked to "discover" the correct form of the object and draft the missing view. Such exercises seem to me more appropriate for cryptographers than for environmental designers.

4. Unlike perspectives, where space *envelops* and *includes* the viewer, plans, sections, and elevations *exclude* the viewer and are perceived as separate objects in space. Our perceptual prejudice for seeing wholes and for perceiving a dominant figure on a recessive field results in our manipulating such drawings as separate, formal, visual images. This perception of the conventional drawings results in configurations that are *of the drawing* and that make little sense in reality. T-, H-, and I-shaped buildings and all symmetrically

designed arrangements probably result from this preoccupation with overall form as seen in the plan abstraction.

5. Plans, sections, and elevations have little to do with human experience. Perhaps the most damning of all their inadequacies is that they are almost impossible to evaluate experientially, especially by the layman. Yet we say that we are designing environments primarily for our fellow human beings. We hope they will participate in the design process and we wonder why they have difficulty relating to the environments we design.

By drawing human figures in elevation, you can tell the viewer how high a window sill is, but there is no way to tell him if it is deep enough to sit in. A light line in plan might indicate a floor-material change, a step, or a 36"-high counter. There is no indication of whether a human will trip over it or lean against it. The entire future experience of the environment must be imagined with very little qualitative help from the drawings.

6. Plans, sections, and elevations are particularly weak in conveying any sense of time or movement—the kinesthetic experience of space or objects. Some vague notion of the experience of movement can be perceived in looking at the plan, but a section or elevation tells us absolutely nothing about the experience of moving toward, through, or around the spaces they represent.

If the ultimate evaluation of designed spaces and objects is to be the experience of the human senses, then it is perverse to limit the predictive representative drawings to orthographic drawings.

7. Plans, sections, and elevations are supported by centuries of unquestioned dogma that often misleads us. This dogma implies that orthographic drawings are the best, most proper, easiest, and often *only* representative drawings for the design of an environment. I will concede that they are the easiest, but the unquestioned propriety of tradition and convention does not persuade me that they are the best.

WHY WE DON'T DRAW PERSPECTIVES

There are three reasons why we cling to plans, sections, and elevations as the primary or only design drawings and all of them are invalid excuses. The first grows out of historic tradition, the second is the result of mistaken teaching, and the third asks the orthographic drawings to do more than they can.

1. Construction drawings were historically used as design drawings. Initially, the design professions were not separated from the construction or craft professions. The functions for which spaces or products were designed were uncomplicated, the forms and ways of making environments were traditional, and the range of innovation was very limited. In addition, the people involved in any decision-making process were fewer—they included the owner or patron and his chosen builder or craftsman. In such a context there was perhaps no need for an extensive investigation of alternatives, and the conventional drawings used to make the space or object

could adequately predict and communicate whatever slight modifications were proposed.

Most important of all, the practice of using the orthographic construction drawings to represent designed spaces or objects was firmly established centuries before the drawing of perspectives was developed during the Renaissance.

2. We are incompetent in drawing perspectives, which is understandable, if inexcusable. Perspective drawing has been taught as a complicated procedure that can only be initiated after the design's structure has already been determined in plan, section, and elevation. It has generally been badly taught in drawing courses that are usually too large to give individual attention to perspective drawing. Subsequently, design teachers often allow the skill to atrophy by never assigning more than one perspective—if they assign any at all. All this amounts to a tacit agreement that perspective drawing is too difficult and time-consuming to teach and is beyond the ability of most students anyway. This attitude leads to the mistaken notion that requiring students to present their work in perspectives is discriminatory because it gives those who already happen to be able to draw perspectives an unfair advantage. We have now completed one of those elaborate excuse systems we use to convince ourselves that incompetent teaching is morally mandatory.

The ambivalence of our attitude toward perspectives often shows up in exhibitions of students' design projects. The projects selected

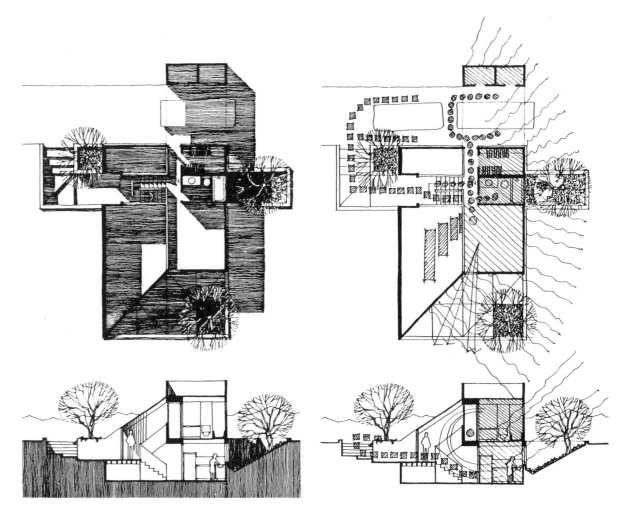

for exhibition usually display a balanced set of presentation drawings. Even in the best projects, however, the lonely perspective is often the weakest drawing, has had the least design and drawing attention, and was obviously drawn last.

In the projects that receive mediocre or low grades and are never displayed, this weakness in perspective is even more exaggerated and very clearly shows an inept design. I think this says several things about design teachers and students. It indicates that the students who produce the best designs are those who understand perspectives well enough to use them in the design process. It also indicates that design teachers appreciate perspectives as much as other drawings, even though they spend little time teaching the skill and require only one or two to communicate each design.

3. We mistakenly embellish orthographic drawings. The over-rendering of plans, sections, and elevations is often promoted to extend or improve their lack of experiential quality. This embellishment takes two forms: an elaborate, tedious rendering of materials and shadows or an applied, supposedly qualitative, notation system.

This tedious, pseudo-realistic rendering of plan, section, or elevation is a waste of time. These drawings are basically abstractions and valuable as such, but trying to make them into drawings that represent reality is nonsense when you can draw perspectives.

Notation systems applied to plan, section, and elevation are also valuable at the conceptual level to symbolize the designer's intentions. But during the representation phase on the orthographic abstractions they signify nothing about whether the design intentions they symbolize could actually be experienced in the built space or product. I have wasted hours in architectural design reviews listening to students' glowing descriptions of the experiential qualities that supposedly exist in their floor plans, and neither they nor I will ever know whether they were there or not.

Drawing Techniques

Having explored the relationships of various drawing forms (plan, section, elevation, axonometric, perspective) to experience, we can now consider technique: the variety of different techniques, their relationship to experience, and how to choose one technique over another.

Because we gain most of the information about our environment through visual perception, it seems most appropriate to classify drawing techniques according to how they correspond to the way we perceive space. As Gibson points out, our perception of space relies upon perceiving continuous surfaces and the discontinuities between surfaces at their edges. Thus, the most basic division in drawing techniques is into two complementary categories:

1. Edge drawings, which draw a line along the edge of every surface. This is the simplest and most efficient way to represent the environment.

2. Surface drawings, which render every surface with a continuous tone, relatively dark or light depending on the surface's relationship to the sun or light source. This is the most realistic way to represent the environment.

The combination of these technique results in a third way of drawing the environment:

3. Edge-and-surface drawings, which delineate both surfaces and edges, combining the perceptual cues by which we perceive space rather than choosing between them. This is the most manageable method of representing the environment because of the way it allows the drawing to be developed in layers.

Although the various techniques can be made with a wide variety of media, I have drawn them in what I believe is their purest and simplest form. All the lines were drawn with technical pens using two or three different line weights, with each line being of a constant width from point to point. All the tones were applied with black Prismacolor™ pencils.

SPATIAL PROFILING

The use of heavier lines to indicate spatial edges serves two purposes. First, it helps the viewer understand the space of the drawing by emphasizing the moving edges that carry our kinesthetic experience of space. The second reason may be much more important, especially for beginning students. Spatially profiling a drawing insures that the delineator perceives the drawing as a spatial representation. Completing graduated spatial profiling requires seeing and thinking about the drawing as a real environment. The drawing can never again be a flat collection of lines on a two-dimensional surface, and this establishment of the drawing as a transparent, transcendent means of seeing a real environment is the primary purpose of design drawing.

TONAL APPLICATION

The discipline of stroking surfaces in the direction of their orientation has several purposes beyond lending consistency to the drawing. Stroking horizontal surfaces to the far vanishing point (VP) avoids two pitfalls—one perceptual, the other technical. If horizontal surfaces are stroked toward the near VP, there will be too much attention focused toward that point and, technically, too much graphite or ink will be accumulated in the convergence. The stroking discipline also has a much more important purpose for beginning drawing students. Like spatial profiling, disciplined tonal application forces delineators to get spatially involved with the drawing, because in order to understand the orientations of the various surfaces, they *must* perceive the drawing as a real environment.

An alternative to stroking the pencil tones in a direction that matches their orientation is to stroke them all, whether they are vertical or horizontal, in a 45-degree direction, from upper right to lower left (for right-handers). This alternative will add a great consistency to the overall drawing, but it is *of the drawing* and has nothing to do with the environment being depicted.

TIME AND SKILL

One of the most dramatic differences between various drawing techniques is the time and skill they require. This may already seem obvious but it is only by actually drawing in each of the techniques that you can really experience these differences. Since drawing is such an integral part of design and facilitates or inhibits design in so many ways, designers should try all the techniques. Only then will they be able to make intelligent choices about which techniques correspond to the time available, the subject matter, and their drawing ability.

DRAWING FOR REPRODUCTION

One last variable in understanding drawing techniques is the relative ease or difficulty involved in their reproduction. In general, line drawings, including tone-of-line drawings, will be easier and less expensive to reproduce. Ink line drawings will endure several steps of enlargement or reduction on any decent photocopier and retain their quality. The reproduction of tone drawings continues to improve, with the latest being color copies (even for black-and-white drawings) but it is still generally more risky and more expensive to reproduce tone drawings.

EXAMPLES

The following six examples illustrate the most basic techniques in their purest forms, give the rules for each technique, and rate them according to relative time and skill, based on a scale of 1 to 10, with the lower numbers indicating the quickest and easiest techniques and the higher numbers indicating the most time-consuming and difficult.

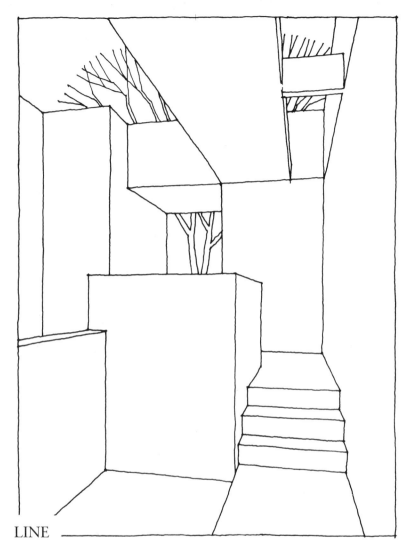

LINE

- spatial edges and planar corners defined with lines
- surfaces unrendered

time factor: 1
skill factor: 1

LINE—SPATIALLY PROFILED

- spatial edges and planar corners defined with lines
- spatial edges profiled—the farther an edge lies in front of its background the heavier the line should be, but its heaviness should be lightened in proportion to its distance from the viewer
- surfaces unrendered

time factor: 1½
skill factor: 1

TONE

- surfaces toned evenly in relation to their differential reflectance of light
- spatial edges and planar corners defined by a change in tone—no lines
- stroking direction should respond to vertical or horizontal orientation of the surfaces, with the horizontal stroking always toward the farthest vanishing point
- surface tones may be graduated within the surface to heighten contrasts with other tones at the surface's edges

time factor: 9
skill factor: 9

TONE-OF-LINES

- surfaces toned in relation to their differential reflectance of light
- tones made up of evenly spaced lines
- spatial edges and planar corners defined by a change in line spacing—no spatial edge lines
- direction of lines should respond to vertical or horizontal orientation of the surfaces, with horizontal lines always going toward the farthest vanishing point

time factor: 10
skill factor: 7

LINE-AND-TONE

- spatial edges and planar corners defined with lines
- spatial edges profiled—the farther an edge lies in front of its background the heavier the line should be, but its heaviness should be lightened in proportion to its distance from the viewer
- surfaces toned evenly in relation to their differential reflectance of light
- stroking direction should respond to vertical or horizontal orientation of the surfaces, with the horizontal stroking always going toward the farthest vanishing point

time factor: 7
skill factor: 4

LINE-AND-TONE
ON MIDDLETONE

- spatial edges and planar corners defined with lines
- spatial edges profiled—the farther an edge lies in front of its background the heavier the line should be, but its heaviness should be lightened in proportion to its distance from the viewer
- surfaces toned evenly in relation to their differential reflectance of light—black for shadow, white for sunlight, unrendered middletone paper for shade
- stroking direction should respond to vertical or horizontal orientation of the surfaces, with the horizontal stroking always going toward the farthest vanishing point

time factor: 7
skill factor: 4

COMPARATIVE EXAMPLES

Renderings of similar building types in the various techniques may help demonstrate how these techniques are used as well as the variations often introduced by individual architectural delineators.

The examples also make clear how the choice of technique is related to the characteristics of the building or environment being represented. Richard Welling's line drawing of the Flatiron building is uniquely able to represent the articulation of the masonry coursing of the building and how it progresses up the building in changing horizontal bands. The indication of shade and shadows and the reflections in the windows are given up in favor of the meticulous delineation of the masonry.

The Welling line drawing couldn't differ more from Steve Oles's beautiful tone drawing of the modern, flush-detailed, reflective/transparent monolith. The powerful gradations of the building and the sky dramatize what the tone technique can do to depict a building whose emphasis is the slick surface of an overall form rather than the articulation of individual pieces.

The following pages indicate the three remaining techniques, and while they don't offer the dramatic contrasts of the first two, it is clear that each technique contributes a great deal to the perceived character of the building.

Drawing by Richard Welling from *The Technique of Drawing Buildings*.

Drawing by Paul Stevenson Oles from *Architectural Illustration: The Value Delineation Process*.

LINE DRAWING delineates *edges* and not *surfaces*. All the edges in the environment are represented directly with line; the relative depth of edges is indicated by variations in line weight. Surfaces are not directly rendered, although their overall shape is indicated by their edge lines.

TONE DRAWING delineates *surfaces* and not *edges*. The texture and relative illumination of the various surfaces is rendered. Edges are not directly delineated with an edge line, but rather remain simply a discontinuity between two surfaces.

Drawing by Mark deNalovy-Rozvadovski from *Architectural Delineation* by Ernest Burden. © 1971 by McGraw Hill Inc. Used with permission of The McGraw-Hill Companies.

TONE-OF-LINES DRAWING is an alternative way of making a tone drawing. The smooth, flat tones are replaced by tones built up of individual lines. The line weight is constant, with the relative lightness or darkness of the tone depending on the spaces between the lines.

Drawing by Helmut Jacoby from *New Architectural Drawings*.

LINE-AND-TONE DRAWING is a combination of the two basic techniques. It exploits the strengths of each and offers more flexibility and manageability than any other drawing technique. This technique is discussed at length on pages 96–104.

Drawing by William Kirby Lockard.

TONE-OF-LINES-ON-MIDDLETONE is a variation that can be applied to all three tone techniques: tone, tone-of-lines, and line-and-tone. It begins with a middletone paper and goes both toward white and toward black. It always appears impressively efficient and the middletone adds a finished look even to drawings that are incomplete. For that reason it is a great technique to use when you are short on time.

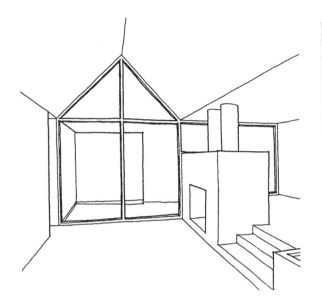

Interest Categories

The various qualities that make a drawing interesting correspond directly to the visual interest categories proposed in chapter 1. If you conceive of drawing interest as consisting of these separate categories it gives you a way of breaking down the overall graphic interest of any drawing into separate, manageable categories. This will help you:

- balance the interest in any drawing;
- evaluate and improve your drawing skills; and
- manage any drawing task better by applying the interest categories in layers.

SPATIAL INTEREST is the most basic of all the categories because it structures or forms the framework for all the other interest groups. The three categories that follow occur on or within a spatial framework, and they can be greatly limited or enhanced by this initial interest category.

Spatial interest is promised kinesthetic interest—the anticipated experience of objects, spaces, and vistas that are only partly seen but will be revealed as we move through the environment. Spatial interest sources are the hidden spaces created when an object sits in front of another object or surface. The sum of these partially revealed spaces indicates the degree of spatial interest.

TONAL INTEREST is the result of light reflecting differently off the various surfaces that make up the environment. Visually, tonal interest is the most powerful of the interest categories—the last to be squinted out, diluted by distance, or lost as we cross the threshold into blindness. In the environment, tonal interest depends primarily on a rich collection of surfaces that have various orientations to light, and secondarily on material selections and color schemes. The composition of variously oriented surfaces that provide strong tonal interest is directly dependent on the previous category of spatial interest.

TEXTURAL INTEREST is tactile interest—our enjoyment in touching various materials and surfaces. While we often directly experience this type of interest by contacting the surfaces on which we are standing or sitting, most textural interest is the promised or potential interest of the distant surfaces we perceive *visually*.

ADDITIONAL INTEREST is the interest we find in all the additions we, and nature, make to any built environment. In contrast to spatial, tonal, and textural interest, which are all integral parts of any environment, additional interest is a separate "additional" category made up of those things we add to an environment. These additions may include trees, plants, furniture, automobiles, or human figures.

The line-and-tone drawing technique is unique in that it allows the four interest categories to be applied in a series of discrete layers, which the other techniques do not. The following section demonstrates how line-and-tone can be used to make the most of the time you have available to make a drawing.

DRAWING AS AN INVESTMENT HIERARCHY

Earlier I suggested that designers should visualize a drawing task not as a single drawing, but as a stack of potential drawings progressing from a quick sketch at the bottom to a slick, detailed rendering at the top. This is one way of thinking of drawing as an investment hierarchy.

Another way of thinking of drawing as an investment hierarchy is based on the procedure for making any individual drawing. The idea here is to invest your effort in the more important aspects of the drawing first. This is similar to the up-front way journalists are trained to write newspaper stories. Journalists can never be sure how many column inches their stories will be given, so they cover everything of importance in the lead paragraph, with successive paragraphs filling in details in a hierarchy of importance. If you can learn to draw in this way your effort will always be a solid investment even when you don't finish. As we learned earlier, the line-and-tone technique's flexibility makes it ideally suited for such phased management.

This investment hierarchy is best understood in terms of the drawing interest categories: spatial, tonal, textural, and additional. When a rough design sketch is selected to be made into a more finished drawing, it may need to be given an accurate drafted framework, like the drawing to the right. This accurate underlying spatial structure is the first investment on which everything else will stand and should include possible shadow patterns and the placement of figures, furniture, and trees, so that they will have the benefit of refinement along with everything else.

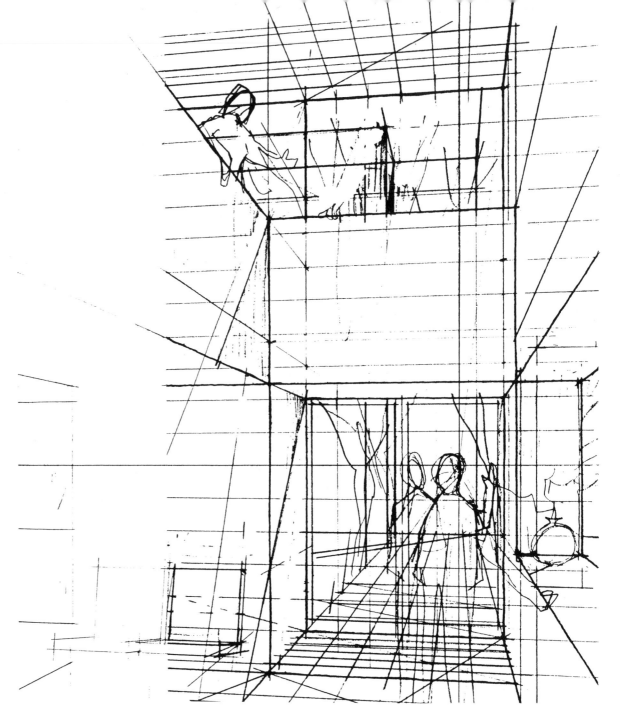

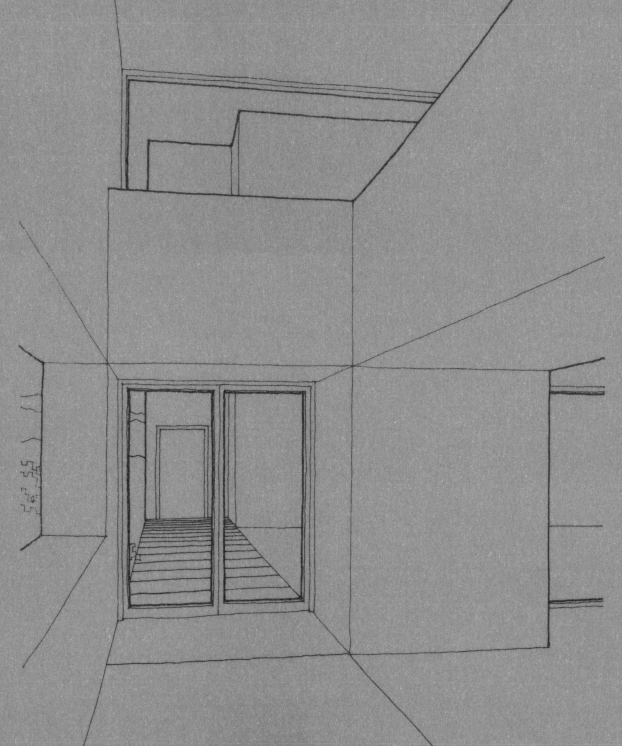

SPATIAL INTEREST

The most basic category of environmental interest for designers is the interest offered by the spatial configuration of any environment. In a drawing, the hidden spaces that constitute spatial interest are all partially hidden/revealed by a profiled spatial edge, and the total spatial interest will be the sum of these edges. Spatially interesting drawings may have stacks of these spatial overlaps that are ten or twelve deep.

While it is valuable to be able to select the perspective view that will have the most interest in its prepared spatial layering, it is even more important to improve the spatial interest of a design based on what any perspective of that design shows you. Spatial interest can never be reduced to a problem of clever selection of views, nor can its lack ever be adequately compensated for by overemphasizing the other interest categories. If the space looks dull in the drawing, it probably is dull.

The spatial interest of a perspective will be enhanced by adjusting the view so that it shows a maximum number of spatial overlaps and planar intersections. The representation of the environment should promise the revelations that movement through it would bring, but the view chosen should never be deliberately mysterious or confusing. Corners, intersections, edges, stairs, and floor-level and ceiling-level changes should always be visible.

SPATIAL INTEREST

The most basic category of environmental interest for designers is the interest offered by the spatial configuration of any environment. In a drawing, the hidden spaces that constitute spatial interest are all partially hidden/revealed by a profiled spatial edge, and the total spatial interest will be the sum of these edges. Spatially interesting drawings may have stacks of these spatial overlaps that are ten or twelve deep.

While it is valuable to be able to select the perspective view that will have the most interest in its prepared spatial layering, it is even more important to improve the spatial interest of a design based on what any perspective of that design shows you. Spatial interest can never be reduced to a problem of clever selection of views, nor can its lack ever be adequately compensated for by overemphasizing the other interest categories. If the space looks dull in the drawing, it probably *is* dull.

The spatial interest of a perspective will be enhanced by adjusting the view so that it shows a maximum number of spatial overlaps and planar intersections. The representation of the environment should promise the revelations that movement through it would bring, but the view chosen should never be deliberately mysterious or confusing. Corners, intersections, edges, stairs, and floor-level and ceiling-level changes should always be visible.

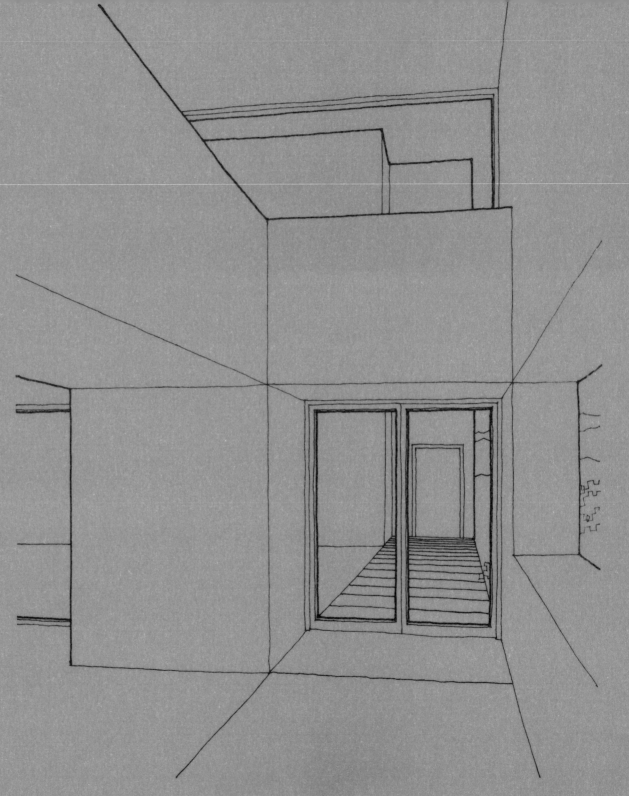

SPATIAL AND ADDITIONAL INTEREST

Additional interest is not an integral part of environmental design, but in the sequential adding of
layers of interest it comes second, because trees,
plants, and furniture are needed to make the
design come alive and seem real. Intelligently integrated into the drawing, elements of additional
interest specify the scale, indicate the use, and
demonstrate the space of the design. The placement of this "entourage", as it is traditionally
known, can also increase the spatial interest of the
drawing by adding additional spatial layers.

There are two practical reasons for making
additional interest the second stage. First, it
allows the tones and textures that come later to
be added around the items of additional interest,
avoiding the erasing that would be necessary if it
came after the tones and textures. The second
and more important reason is that the two
remaining interest categories, tonal and textural,
take much more time.

Although many of our additions to the environment are frankly ornamental, we must be
careful not to reduce them to mere decorations in
our drawings. Objects that provide additional
interest must be carefully placed so that they do
not cover the planar intersections that help us to
perceive spatial volumes; generally, they also
should be textureless so they contrast with the
background surfaces.

This spatially profiled open-line drawing is
the first mandatory "plateau" of any line-and-
tone drawing—the first complete overlay over
the previous perspective framework, which combines spatial and additional interest. It is very
much like the simple line drawings in a child's
coloring book, but everything is spatially defined
and it is a very committed, unequivocal drawing
that will communicate clearly to a client as it is.
It is a solid investment of your time and effort,
and it won't tell on you if you had intended to
add the tones and textures but ran out of time.

SPATIAL AND ADDITIONAL INTEREST

Additional interest is not an integral part of environmental design, but in the sequential adding of layers of interest it comes second, because trees, plants, and furniture are needed to make the design come alive and seem real. Intelligently integrated into the drawing, elements of additional interest specify the scale, indicate the use, and demonstrate the space of the design. The placement of this "entourage," as it is traditionally known, can also increase the spatial interest of the drawing by adding additional spatial layers.

There are two practical reasons for making additional interest the second stage. First, it allows the tones and textures that come later to be added *around* the items of additional interest, avoiding the erasing that would be necessary if it came after the tones and textures. The second and more important reason is that the two remaining interest categories, tonal and textural, take much more time.

Although many of our additions to the environment are frankly ornamental, we must be careful not to reduce them to mere decorations in our drawings. Objects that provide additional interest must be carefully placed so that they do not cover the planar intersections that help us to perceive spatial volumes; generally, they also should be textureless so they contrast with the background surfaces.

This spatially profiled open-line drawing is the first mandatory "plateau" of any line-and-tone drawing—the first complete overlay over the previous perspective framework, which combines spatial and additional interest. It is very much like the simple line drawings in a child's coloring book, but everything is spatially defined and it is a very committed, unequivocal drawing that will communicate clearly to a client as it is. It is a solid investment of your time and effort, and it won't tell on you if you had intended to add the tones and textures but ran out of time.

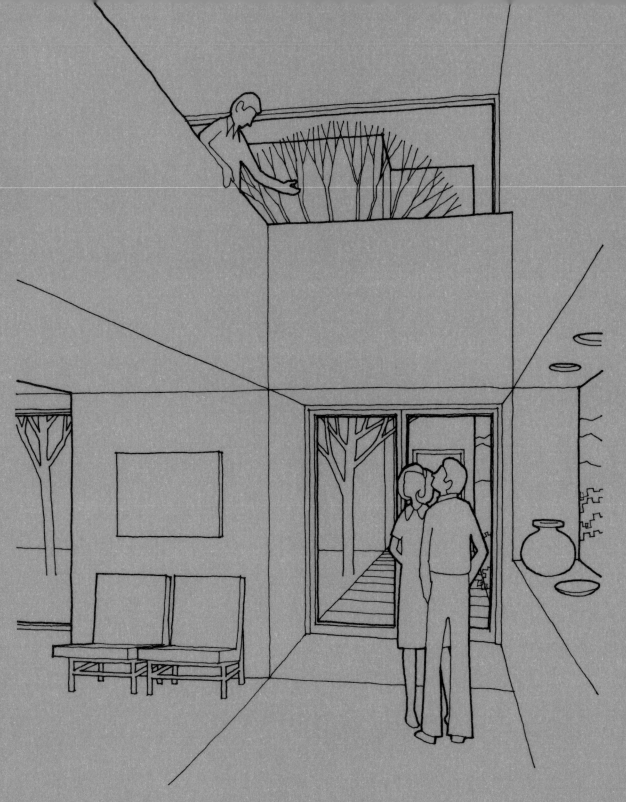

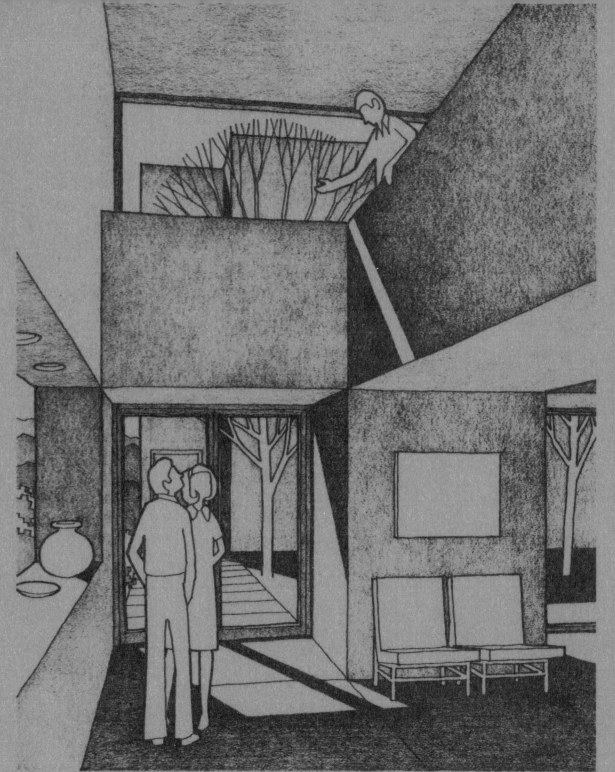

TONAL INTEREST

In drawings, tonal interest depends on using the full range of grays—from pure white to solid black—over broad areas of the drawing. The main sources for this tonal range are the light conditions on the various surfaces: sun, shade, and shadow. Color and material variations are much less important, since many drawings must remain black and white and the textural interest of materials is generally more important than their lightness or darkness.

Both tonal and textural interest are very time-consuming, but tonal interest should be applied next because its main source—light—is not as arbitrary as the main source of textural interest—materials—and because tonal interest lends itself to various technological shortcuts, including Ozalid prints, middletone drawings, and mounted tracing-paper drawings on a black background that are then colored on the back with white pencil or with white-paper cutouts.

In this technique, the tones, including color, should be smooth, flat, and characterless. Don't draw or render with the tone-making tools; all rendering should be done with a pen. This will preserve the distinction between edge-indicating lines drawn with a pen and surface-indicating tones drawn with a pencil or marker.

The pattern of the tonal interest—the shade and shadows—is a matter of choice and deserves careful study. It greatly affects the way a space is read and it should be carefully integrated with figures and other elements of additional interest.

TONAL INTEREST

In drawings, tonal interest depends on using the full range of grays—from pure white to solid black—over broad areas of the drawing. The main sources for this tonal range are the light conditions on the various surfaces: sun, shade, and shadow. Color and material variations are much less important, since many drawings must remain black and white and the textural interest of materials is generally more important than their lightness or darkness.

Both tonal and textural interest are very time-consuming, but tonal interest should be applied next because its main source—light—is not as arbitrary as the main source of textural interest—materials—and because tonal interest lends itself to various technological shortcuts, including Ozalid prints, middletone drawings, and mounted tracing-paper drawings on a black background that are then colored on the back with white pencil or with white-paper cutouts.

In this technique, the tones, including color, should be smooth, flat, and characterless. Don't draw or render with the tone-making tools; all rendering should be done with a pen. This will preserve the distinction between edge-indicating lines drawn with a pen and surface-indicating tones drawn with a pencil or marker.

The pattern of the tonal interest—the shade and shadows—is a matter of choice and deserves careful study. It greatly affects the way a space is read and it should be carefully integrated with figures and other elements of additional interest.

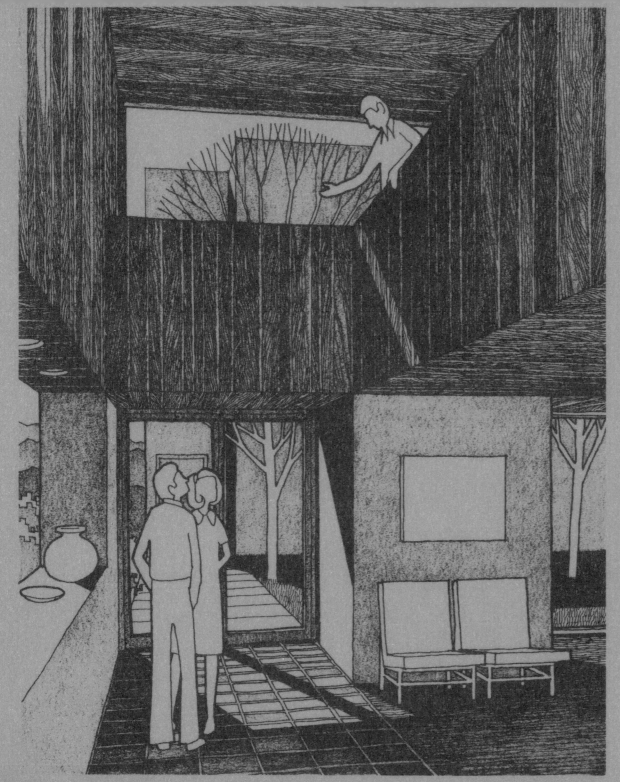

While the touching associated with textural interest makes it the most intimate of the interest categories, the memory of what something feels like can be triggered visually at a distance and represented in drawings. The main source (and virtually the only source) of textural interest in design drawings, as in environments, is the collection of materials of which they are made. Textural interest should always begin with the space-bounding surfaces, most importantly the floor. These surfaces establish our perception of space and are also the critical and permanent material choices in any environment.

In the hierarchy suggested here, textural interest is the last category to be added. This is because the addition of textural interest is very time-consuming and, unlike tonal interest, it must be applied by hand with no technological shortcuts. It also tends to be the interest category most subject to change, since materials are often considered late in the design decision-making process and frequently are adjusted to meet the construction budget.

In line-and-tone drawings, textural interest should be applied only with a pen, and applied first to the space-defining surfaces. These surfaces should always be rendered continuously because intermittent texturing destroys the perception of the surface as a continuous background. Objects standing in front of these textured surfaces should never be textured; rather, they should remain open silhouettes, so the viewer's perception always continues past them to the textured surface beyond.

TEXTURAL INTEREST

While the touching associated with textural interest makes it the most intimate of the interest categories, the memory of what something feels like can be triggered visually at a distance and represented in drawings. The main source (and virtually the only source) of textural interest in design drawings, as in environments, is the collection of materials of which they are made. Textural interest should always begin with the space-bounding surfaces, most importantly the floor. These surfaces establish our perception of space and are also the critical and permanent material choices in any environment.

In the hierarchy suggested here, textural interest is the last category to be added. This is because the addition of textural interest is very time-consuming and, unlike tonal interest, it must be applied by hand with no technological shortcuts. It also tends to be the interest category most subject to change, since materials are often considered late in the design decision-making process and frequently are adjusted to meet the construction budget.

In line-and-tone drawings, textural interest should be applied only with a pen, and applied first to the space-defining surfaces. These surfaces should always be rendered continuously because intermittent texturing destroys the perception of the surface as a continuous background. Objects standing in front of these textured surfaces should never be textured; rather, they should remain open silhouettes, so the viewer's perception always continues past them to the textured surface beyond.

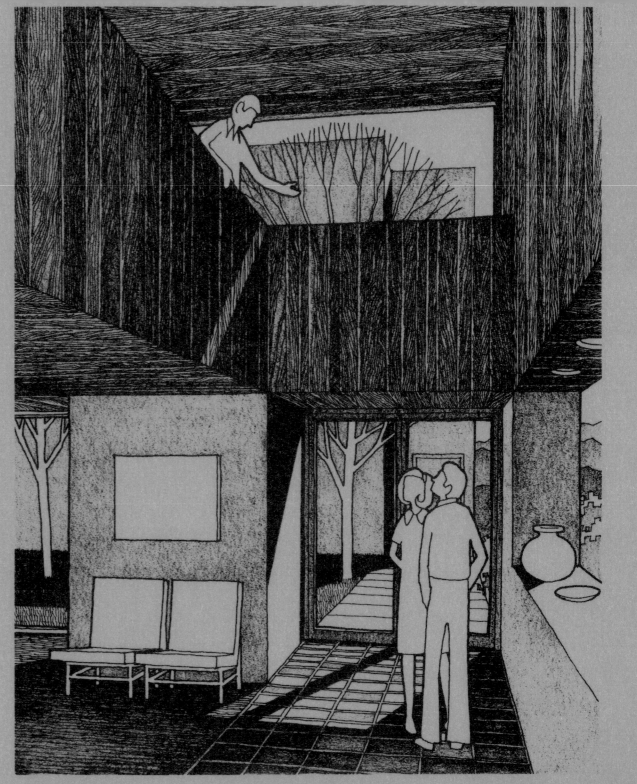

CHOOSING
THE RIGHT TECHNIQUE

While the categorization of drawing techniques may be interesting intellectually and necessary in order to consistently represents the environment, the main reason to master several different ways of drawing is so that you have alternatives from which to choose when you are making a particular drawing. There are at least five variables that might affect the choice of technique: the problem, its solution, the time available, the skill required, and presentation and reproduction alternatives.

The type of problem or solution may indicate the appropriate drawing technique for a particular drawing. If light is an important criterion for the design, as in a museum or gallery, you must draw in a tone technique that represents light. A line drawing wouldn't respect the problem or solution.

However, if you are designing a street or an airport, which incorporate continuing sequences of different views, you might choose to make a series of line drawings to quickly show the visual variety and vitality you are proposing.

Available time is often the most inflexible criteria. Deadlines or limited fees often demand the quickest techniques. In these situations it is important to conceive any drawing task as flexibly as possible, so that you may expand or contract the number or detail of the drawings depending on how the drawing process unfolds.

Always have a plan B and, ideally, plans C and D. This means planning a hierarchy of drawings or drawing tasks, so that you get the most important drawings or aspects completed first, and then can reconsider each successive phase in

respect to the remaining time. If you have extra time, you can then extend the drawings, or do more of them, but it is crucial to build in as much flexibility as possible.

The skill required is also somewhat inflexible. In rare cases you may be able to test a new technique for a drawing or set of drawings, but more often you should stick with what you know. Even then things can go wrong if you don't know and manage your skills very well.

It is wise to have a forgiving attitude toward your drawing ability, but when you have to meet a tight deadline, you must be realistic about your drawing abilities and never try to do more than you know you can. Your ability and confidence will thrive on successful drawings, but neither your ability nor your confidence will benefit from failures caused by overly optimistic decisions about which technique to use.

You may decide that a certain design rich in material textures would be most dramatically rendered in a tone-of-lines drawing, with the stone, wood, and fabrics drawn very explicitly, but forget that it will take hours to make the drawing and, more importantly, that you have never tried drawing a couple of those materials in tone-of-lines. Unfortunately, failing for the best of reasons is still failing.

The ways in which the drawing is liable to be presented or reproduced should affect the choice of technique. Whether the drawing will be seen only in the original, be a part of a multimedia presentation, or be reproduced as an illustration for a black-and-white brochure will certainly affect the choice of technique. If the drawings are to illustrate a black-and-white folder, for instance, it would be pointless to make them in color or, perhaps, even in tone. A line or a tone-

of-lines drawing might be best, because tone drawings are generally more difficult and expensive to reproduce.

Making a decision about drawing technique based on reproduction requires your being as familiar with reproductive processes as you are with the drawing techniques. The most flexible presentation techniques today are offered by the computer. Once digitally captured, the drawing may be "outputted" in various ways, from prints to slides to videotape.

Actually drawing in each technique is the only way to really experience the time and skill they require. As drawing is such an integral part of design, designers should experience all the techniques. Only from such experience can you make intelligent choices about which techniques will correspond to your time, subject matter, and drawing ability.

IN PRAISE OF LINE-AND-TONE DRAWINGS

I strongly advocate line-and-tone as the most useful drawing technique for designers, especially for beginners. There are several reasons for this advocacy of the line-and-tone technique.

The potential for separating the entire drawing task into layers that can be added sequentially (as in the investment hierarchy proposed earlier), is the greatest difference between line-and-tone and the other tone techniques and makes possible the four advantages that follow.

FLEXIBILITY. Line-and-tone drawings are the most flexible of the tone techniques, since their basic line framework represents space very well by itself, making added tones bonuses. A line-

and-tone drawing never looks incomplete once it has become a line drawing because the completion of the tones has no particular optimum and is therefore very flexible. An unfinished drawing in the tone or tone-of-lines techniques, on the other hand, always looks conspicuously incomplete.

The unique layering allowed by the line-and-tone technique offers the flexibility of interrupting the drawing process at various points and shifting to other media, which saves time and enhances the drawing. For instance, you can photocopy an open line drawing onto middle-tone paper and color the sunlit surfaces white.

MANAGEABILITY. Being able to break down the drawing task into discreet phases also allows much tighter management of the drawing process. Decisions to add shade and shadows, textures, or colors can be made during the process as the amount of time available becomes more apparent. This is extremely important because even experienced delineators can underestimate the time a drawing will take, and it is comforting to be able to manage the process by adjusting the degree of detail during the process.

LEARNABILITY. In learning to draw and to use drawing in the design process the most useful technique will require as little skill as possible. This is because the first hurdle is getting beginning designers to accept their own drawings and see through them to whatever they are designing.

The separation of the drawing task into at least four layers allows the student to see more clearly the strengths and weaknesses of his drawing ability. The drawing may look fine, for instance, until the trees, shadows, or figures are added, making it clear which points in the student's skills need improvement. Like practicing the hands separately in beginning piano lessons, this suboptimization allows students to master the subroutines independently as well as promoting a structured perception of the drawing so that the constituent parts of the technique can be balanced.

In the other, more monolithic tone techniques a drawing's weaknesses may never be clear, prompting the student to be generally dissatisfied with the drawing without ever understanding that it is weak in spatial, tonal, textural, or additional interest.

COMBINABILITY. The flexibility described above is even more dramatic when line-and-tone drawings are combined with the graphic abilities of computer software. The open line drawing, which is a combination of spatial and additional interest, can be scanned into a computer (see chapter 7). Tones, colors, and textures can then be added digitally and worked with as separate layers. In this way the separation of simple line-and-tone drawings anticipates the layering that is so effective in managing the most complex computer-aided drawings.

HUMILITY. The humility of line-and-tone drawing may be the most important advantage of all, and the goal of all design drawings. They should strive to be the honest brokers of design communication—accurate, believable, and trustworthy, but always deferring to the design they represent.

Because it is a mixed-media technique with the lines ideally drawn with a pen and the tones applied with a pencil, it has largely been ignored by artists who tend to draw in the more demanding pure-media techniques: pencil or charcoal tone, or pen-and-ink tone-of-lines. These techniques tend to be vehicles for virtuoso drawing.

If your client raves about the quality of the drawing, you know your drawing technique is getting in the way of the design communication. The client should look right through the drawing to the reality of the design and become excited about the design. When asked about the quality of the drawing she might allow that it is a good drawing but return to questions about the design. This means the client has accepted the drawing as an accurate representation of a designed environment, not considered it as a masterpiece rendering suitable for framing.

Of all the techniques in the previous categorization, line-and-tone uniquely meets the criteria for the most useful drawing technique.

4 Perspective

3 MUTUALLY PERPENDICULAR LINES

3 MUTUALLY PERPENDICULAR PLANES

You might expect that perspectives would be the most frequently used drawings in the design process and in design education for two reasons:

because the built environment is designed primarily for human experience and perspectives best represent experience, and because we have understood how to draw perspectives since the Renaissance. However, this is not the case. There are many reasons for this failure, but they boil down to the fact that perspective has been taught in a way that dooms perspective drawings to being tertiary, postdesign drawings. But to relegate perspectives to this subordinate position is to overlook one of the most valuable design tools at your disposal.

This chapter presents an analysis of the principles, methods, and frameworks of drawing perspectives. I then introduce a better method and framework for drawing perspectives quickly and at any time in the design process. I believe this will help perspectives to become what they should be—the dominant design drawing.

STRUCTURING AND LIGHTING EXPERIENTIAL SPACE

The goal of all perspective drawing is to make a flat, two-dimensional drawing appear to have a third-dimension depth, and whether we like it or not, western civilization inhabits a rectangular world. The fact that we speak of an object or space as having width, height, and depth reveals that we conceive of space as being orthogonal. Our language (top, bottom, front, back, right, left), our bodies (head, foot, front, back, right side, left side), our orientation (up, down, north, south, east, west), the Cartesian coordinates (X, Y, Z), the measurement and subdivision of land reflected in our street grids, and the rectilinearity of our spaces and objects all reinforce our understanding of the environment, and perspective, on the three axes of rectangular space.

All the relationships of rectangular space can be represented in an open cube consisting of three contiguous, mutually perpendicular planes and three contiguous, mutually perpendicular lines. The three lines represent the three axes of any rectangular environment. In beginning to understand perspective, you should build such an open cube and draft a grid of constituent lines on each of the three planes. I will use the same cube to analyze and explain shadow-casting in the next chapter.

Tonal interest's relationship to perspective is not as obvious as that of spatial interest. Tonal interest is normally taught as "shade and shadow" or "shadow-casting" and is traditionally introduced in a fragmentary way on plans and elevations. I believe, however, that the lighting of the environment is a natural extension of perspective and is much better understood in three dimensions. After this more holistic understanding is achieved, shadows on plans and elevations can be easily deduced.

Principles, Methods, and Frameworks

Three often-confused categories should be understood in learning to draw perspectives: the principles of perspective, the methods of drawing perspectives, and the frameworks on which perspectives are drawn.

Principles of perspective apply to all the methods of drawing perspectives and all the frameworks on which they are drawn. Both the methods and frameworks offer fundamental choices about how the perspective is to be used in the design process, and for design drawing I advocate a better method and a better framework than those that have been traditionally taught.

Methods of drawing perspectives, as traditionally taught, use drafting procedures based on fixing the exact position, or "station point," of the viewer, projecting lines of sight from that point, and establishing a "picture plane," a "true line of heights," and other complexities (shown on page 111) for an absolutely accurate perspective drawing. The complexity of these traditional perspective methods and their prerequisite of a completed plan and elevation have inhibited the use of perspectives as design drawings. It has never been worth going through all that hocus-pocus more than once, after all the design decisions have been made.

Frameworks (arrangements of vanishing points and vanishing lines) on which perspectives are traditionally drawn are also questionable for design drawings, since they cannot give us the most dramatic and characteristic views of an object or space. The differences in perspective frameworks come from their assumptions about the viewer's relationship to the space, and traditional frameworks in which vanishing points are always located on the drawing board are limited because they cannot offer views that depend on unreachable vanishing points.

I will return to methods and frameworks, but it is most important to first understand the principles of perspective that apply to all methods and all frameworks.

THE PRINCIPLES OF PERSPECTIVE

The first, most basic, and most ignored principle of perspective is:

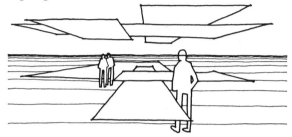

1. SETS OF PARALLEL PLANES CONVERGE INTO A COMMON LINE—which we call a *vanishing line* or VL.

The most familiar example of this principle is the way the surface of the ocean converges toward the horizon, which is animated beautifully by the prologue of the first *Star Wars* movie, which scrolls off, in perspective, toward the distant horizon, a horizontal VL, which we call the *eye-level line.*

Another analogy for the way parallel planes converge toward and vanish into the eyelevel line is the way we slip letters into a mail slot.

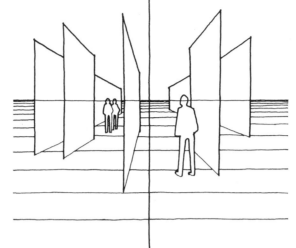

Sets of parallel vertical planes also converge into a common vertical line, which we call a *vertical vanishing line* or VVL.

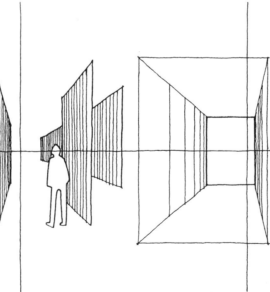

Examples of vertical planes converging into a vertical line are more rare. It may help to imagine very long board fences or the side walls of an underground tunnel.

The second, and more familiar, principle of perspective is:

2. SETS OF PARALLEL LINES CONVERGE TO A COMMON POINT *ON THE VANISHING LINE FOR THE PLANE IN WHICH THEY LIE*—which we call a vanishing point or VP.

This principle seldom includes the last phrase, "on the vanishing line for the plane in which they lie."

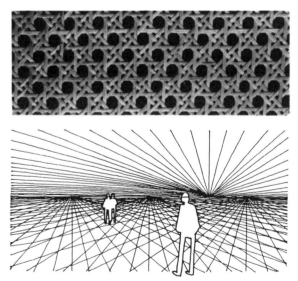

This understanding is crucial, however, because each plane should be conceived as containing an infinite number of sets of parallel lines—suggested by the cane chair bottom above—and each set converges to its own VP on the VL for the plane in which it lies.

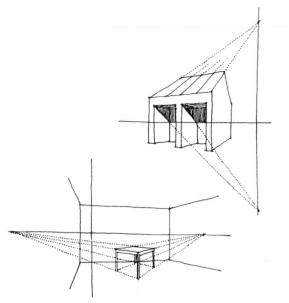

This understanding is necessary in locating the VP for angular shadows (in the next chapter), or the angular placement of furniture, or the seams of a sloping standing-seam roof.

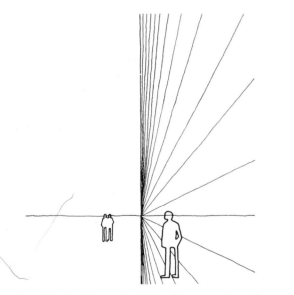

As with the first principle of perspective, the second principle also applies to parallel lines in vertical planes, like the horizontal joints in a masonry wall.

PERSPECTIVE METHODS

A common misunderstanding of traditional perspective drawing is to confuse methods and frameworks.

Unfortunately, perspective methods are usually identified by the frameworks on which they are drawn (one point, two point, or three point). But the framework of a perspective, which will be discussed on pages 117–120, is simply the arrangement of VLs and VPs on which the drawing is made.

Frameworks have little to do with method, which normally means a procedure, process, or technique for accomplishing some goal. This misunderstanding obscures the most basic methodological choice in perspective drawing, which is between traditional plan-projected methods and the direct method I advocate. The dimensional measurability demanded by traditional methods makes perspectives dependent on other drawings and keeps designers from drawing perspectives directly and independently, based on relative, proportional measurability.

Limiting discussions of perspective methods to the frameworks on which they are drawn encourages the misperception that plan-projected methods are superior—indeed, the *only* way to draw perspectives. This continued misunderstanding and prejudice greatly damages the teaching of perspective to environmental designers.

The supposed superiority of projected perspective methods is based on their claim to optical and dimensional accuracy, and their privileged status is largely the result of the attitudes of many drawing teachers. Perspective is usually introduced in "technical" drawing courses in the first year of professional design education or in similar community-college or high-school courses. These courses are usually taught by "technical" drawing teachers and concentrate mostly on traditional drafting procedures. Such courses produce competent technical draftspersons who can accurately *draft* a built or predetermined environment, but the perspective methods taught in such courses are inadequate and inappropriate for the *design* of the environment.

The concern for optical and dimensional accuracy and the way we have allowed it to prejudice the teaching of perspective has greatly inhibited the use of perspectives in the design process. Environmental design students who are introduced to the conventional projected procedures come to associate perspective with drafted projection and technical accuracy. Because students are seldom taught the basic principles and structure of perspective frameworks, or any direct way of drawing accurate perspectives, they have only two choices: they can "eyeball" or "fake" perspectives (which usually results in inaccurate, distorted drawings), or they can wait until they have completed plans and sections and then project perspectives (as after-the-fact presentation drawings) by the traditional methods. Environmental design students (or graduates) often have no choices between these two extremes because of the way perspective is taught. But this doesn't have to be the case—there is a way to create freehand perspectives that are directly drawn, correctly structured, and made relatively measurable and usable as design drawings.

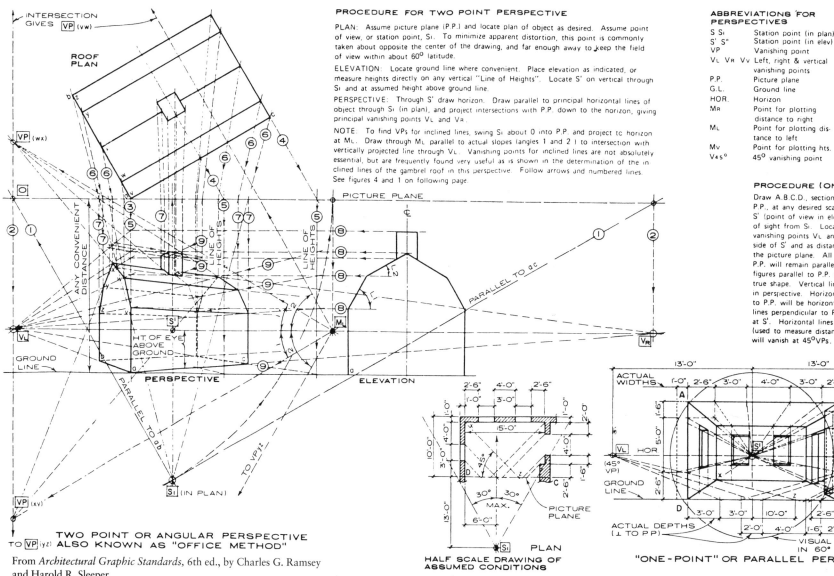

PROCEDURE FOR TWO POINT PERSPECTIVE

PLAN: Assume picture plane (P.P.) and locate plan of object as desired. Assume point of view, or station point, S₁. To minimize apparent distortion, this point is commonly taken about opposite the center of the drawing, and far enough away to keep the field of view within about 60° latitude.

ELEVATION: Locate ground line where convenient. Place elevation as indicated, or measure heights directly on any vertical "Line of Heights". Locate S' on vertical through S₁ and at assumed height above ground line.

PERSPECTIVE: Through S' draw horizon. Draw parallel to principal horizontal lines of object through S₁ (in plan), and project intersections with P.P. down to the horizon, giving principal vanishing points Vʟ and Vʀ.

NOTE: To find VPs for inclined lines, swing S₁ about 0 into P.P. and project to horizon at Mʟ. Draw through Mʟ parallel to actual slopes (angles 1 and 2) to intersection with vertically projected line through Vʟ. Vanishing points for inclined lines are not absolutely essential, but are frequently found very useful as is shown in the determination of the inclined lines of the gambrel roof in this perspective. Follow arrows and numbered lines. See figures 4 and 1 on following page.

TWO POINT OR ANGULAR PERSPECTIVE
ALSO KNOWN AS "OFFICE METHOD"

From *Architectural Graphic Standards*, 6th ed., by Charles G. Ramsey and Harold R. Sleeper.

ABBREVIATIONS FOR PERSPECTIVES

S S₁	Station point (in plan)
S' S"	Station point (in elev)
VP	Vanishing point
Vʟ Vʀ Vᵥ	Left, right & vertical vanishing points
P.P.	Picture plane
G.L.	Ground line
HOR.	Horizon
Mʀ	Point for plotting distance to right
Mʟ	Point for plotting distance to left
Mᵥ	Point for plotting hts.
V₄₅°	45° vanishing point

PROCEDURE (ONE POINT)

Draw A.B.C.D., section which is cut by P.P., at any desired scale, and locate S' (point of view in elevation) on line of sight from S₁. Locate the 45° vanishing points Vʟ and Vʀ on either side of S' and as distant as S₁ is from the picture plane. All lines parallel to P.P. will remain parallel and all plane figures parallel to P.P. will show their true shape. Vertical lines will be vertical in perspective. Horizontal lines parallel to P.P. will be horizontal. Horizontal lines perpendicular to P.P. will vanish at S'. Horizontal lines at 45° to F.P. (used to measure distances ⊥ to P.P.) will vanish at 45°VPs.

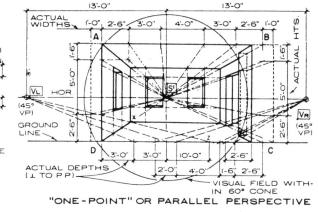

HALF SCALE DRAWING OF ASSUMED CONDITIONS

"ONE-POINT" OR PARALLEL PERSPECTIVE

PROJECTED PERSPECTIVE METHOD
based on projected, dimensional measurability

The most common "one-point" and "two-point" perspective methods are reproduced here as examples of the projected methods. I will not explain the methods as they are well known, appear with only slight variations in many books on drawing, and actually have the procedures drawn or described in the reproductions above.

While these projected perspective methods have been very valuable for drawing highly accurate perspectives, there are now computer programs based on the same kind of orthographic projection that will draw perspectives for us.

After the dimensional data has been entered, the computer "builds" a model of the environment. (This data entry requires a substantial investment of time, but it often is time well spent, as the data may need to be entered anyway for the production of construction documents.) The computer will draw an unlimited number of perspectives from any point you choose. There are even pro-

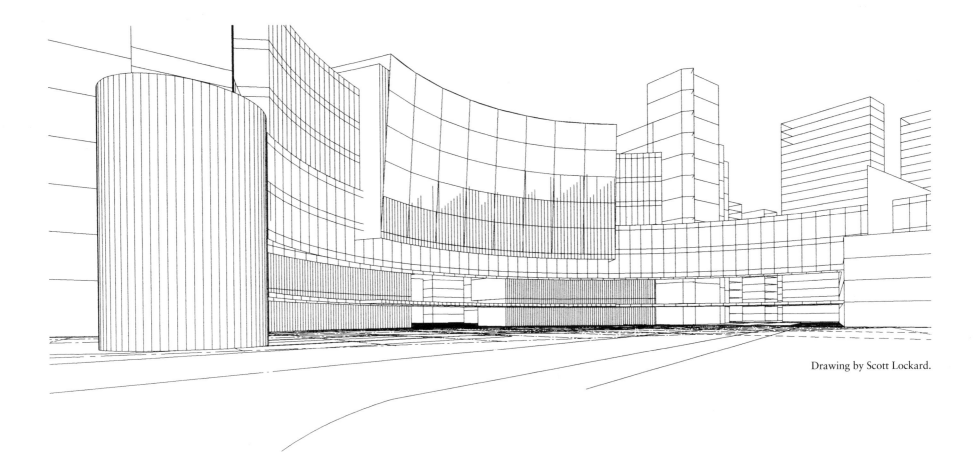

Drawing by Scott Lockard.

grams that will fly you through the environment and a few that will let you walk through the designed environment interactively, choosing your own path or direction.

My objection to the traditional projected methods and the newer computer methods is the same: they are too complex and take too long to be used as conceptual design drawings, which are used to conceive and manipulate early design concepts. The time and effort they take is such that they are seldom undertaken until all the major design decisions are made. This dooms them to a quite different role. Instead of being design drawings, which are still alive with the possibility of beneficial change, they are the dead drawings of persuasion, created after all the important design decisions have long been made.

If perspective drawing is to be of any use in the actual design of the environment, then perspectives must be free of the dependent position of being the third or fourth drawings made because they have waited for plans, sections, elevations, or computer models to be completed first.

A BETTER METHOD:
DIRECT PERSPECTIVE

based on relative, proportional measurability

The direct method of drawing perspectives that follows is based on the use of the diagonal to proportionally subdivide and extend rectangular space. The principles involved are best understood in two-dimensional geometry.

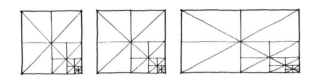

PROPORTIONAL SUBDIVISION

The diagonals of any rectangle subdivide it into quarters, and quarters again, and quarters again, infinitely—limited only by the sharpness of your drawing instrument and your eyesight.

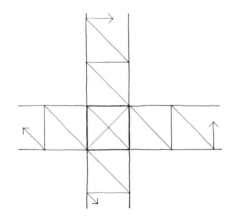

PROPORTIONAL EXTENSION

Successive diagonals will mark off successive identical rectangles along the extensions of either pair of the original rectangle's boundary lines.

THE INITIAL SPATIAL UNIT

This subdivision and extension of rectangular space by diagonals can be applied directly to any perspective framework. Spatial extension is shown on the three conventional frameworks at right, and I will demonstrate it on the recommended two-line/two-point framework in the colored pages that follow.

First, however, we must learn to draw an initial spatial unit, which takes a little practice. A cube is the easiest spatial unit to create and extend, but even such a simple spatial unit is not that easy to draw in perspective.

Jay Doblin (*Perspective: A New System for Designers*, 1956) first proposed that drawing an acceptable cube in various perspective views is a basic part of drawing perspectives. Drawing an accurate cube depends on the ability to draw acceptable squares in all three mutually perpendicular planes, and to understand to which VLs the squares recede and how to establish the VPs for the squares' diagonals.

The ability to draw such squares, identify the VLs to which they recede, and locate the VPs for their diagonals allows us to extend three-dimensional space with a structured accuracy.

Notice that, as with the two-dimensional examples at left, any square in perspective can be extended in the square's two axial directions by using either diagonal. The VP for successive parallel diagonals in any plane is located by extending either diagonal until it intersects the VL for the plane in which it lies (see drawing at top right). This procedure is an application of the second general principle of perspective: *all sets of parallel lines converge to VPs on the VL for the plane in which they lie.*

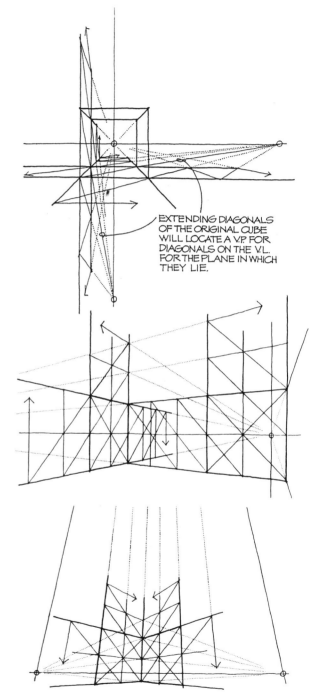

EXTENDING DIAGONALS OF THE ORIGINAL CUBE WILL LOCATE A V.P. FOR DIAGONALS ON THE V.L. FOR THE PLANE IN WHICH THEY LIE.

Either pair of boundary lines of any square in perspective can be extended toward or away from its appropriate VP, and successive duplications of the initial square can be marked off in either direction by extending successive diagonals from the VP for diagonals. This principle of extension by diagonal works for any square, in any of the three mutually perpendicular planes, in any of the perspective frameworks (*except* in the transverse vertical planes of two-line/one-point perspectives, which are so flatly two-dimensional that the diagonals can be drafted with a 45° triangle). The one limitation of such extension is that extending the space more than one or two squares into the foreground usually results in unacceptable distortion.

SHORTCUT

It is necessary to understand the principle behind locating the VP for diagonals on the VL for the plane in which they lie, because when you begin shadow-casting you will need to bring shadows from a similar VP. There is, however, a way to shortcut the diagonal extension procedure when diagonal VPs are distant and difficult to reach.

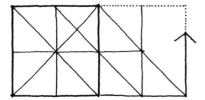

The principle is best illustrated in two-dimensional geometry and is called the *diagonal through the bisector*. The drawing above shows how an initial spatial unit can be extended using the shortcut. If the drawing is accurate, the results will be identical to projections from a VP for diagonals.

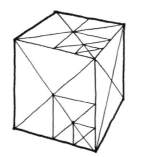

The subdivision of squares into quarters and quarters again by using diagonals is much simpler than extension, since no VP need be found. Drawing the diagonals is a simple matter of connecting the diagonal corners of any square in perspective.

Once the ability to dependably draw acceptable squares in perspective has been mastered, drawing cubes becomes merely a matter of assembling the squares.

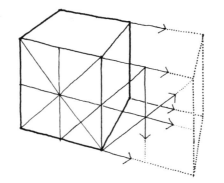

It is easy to see how the extension of any face of an initial cube can be extended to become an identical cube.

We now have all the procedures to draw, extend, and subdivide rectangular space in *direct* perspective, without being dependent on plans or sections. We no longer need to stoop to plan projection but can draw three-dimensional space straight up, erect, in the perceptual posture that is uniquely human.

The only arbitrary step in the direct perspective method is the estimation of the depth of the initial squares and the 90° plan angles involved in locating multiple VPs and assembling the squares into cubes. But these judgments need no defense or apology; rather, they are one of the most valuable steps in the direct perspective method. These judgments insure that the delineator's perception (rather than rules or procedures) is responsible for the accuracy of the perspective, and the delineator's perceptual ability will actually improve with the drawing of each perspective.

Some students, especially those who have already been introduced to the dimensional certainty of plan-projected perspective methods, find the need to guess, estimate, or judge the initial unit of depth in direct perspective uncomfortable or unacceptable. I try to persuade these students that they should develop a little more confidence in their own perception—that in the construction-supervision phase of architectural practice, they can't walk through the job with a level and a plumb-bob; instead, they will have to learn to trust their eye to tell them what is straight and level and plumb. Also, if they are going to expect clients to trust their judgment in spending millions of dollars constructing additions to the environment, they should learn to trust their own perception in judging what a square would look like in perspective.

RELATIVE MEASURABILITY

Notice that the subdivision and extension of space just explained is dimensionless and still only proportional to the initial spatial unit. Making direct perspectives measurable is usually one of the first steps in the procedure, but I have deliberately separated it here so that the constituent parts of the method can be seen independently.

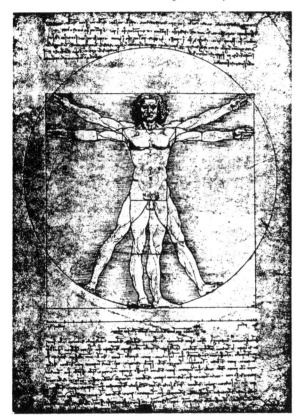

All meaningful measurement is anthropometric. Leonardo's "Man is the measure," though sexist in expression, is still true. The critical scale involved in environmental design is human scale, not metric scale, English scale, or any other *dimensional* scale.

One of the interesting observations you may make in surveying the books on projected perspective methods is that they seldom include the human figure in their perspective examples. This is perhaps because their emphasis is on *dimensional* precision, not *human* scale.

Just as we understand our orientation in space and give directions in terms of our own bodies, our bodies are the most natural, *direct* way of measuring space. The best way to make perspectives measurable is to draw them at the level of the human eye. Direct vertical measurability is possible anywhere in the space of an eyelevel perspective by placing a figure wherever you need a measurement. You may assume human eyelevel to be 5'6", 1.5m, 5', or (seated) about 4'. I use 5', even though it is lower than my own eyelevel, because of the convenience of the 5' module.

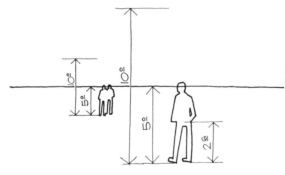

Twice 5' is 10', which comfortably conforms to our base-10 mathematics. Half of 5' is 2'6", or 30", which is an excellent module for furniture: 30" is the height of desks and dining tables; a 30" cube contains a club chair or card table; two 30" cubes make a standard desk or love seat; and half the 30" height is lounge-chair or coffee-table height.

Using the 5' assumed height from the eyelevel to the feet of the figure, you can directly duplicate or subdivide that distance to reach any needed dimension.

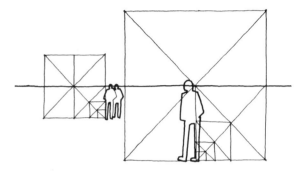

Direct horizontal measurability in the transverse direction is similarly possible anywhere in the perspective by using a 45° triangle (in two-line/one-point perspectives) or by establishing a 5' square receding toward the far VL (in three-line/two-point perspectives) and using its diagonals to extend or subdivide 5' squares.

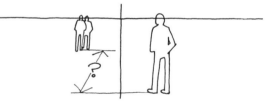

Horizontal measurements in the converging direction (toward the only or near VP) are more difficult and most of the complexities of the various projected perspective methods are caused by the attempt to gain some kind of certainty in these depth measurements.

The direct perspective method advocated here is based on your willingness to estimate—to guess—to *judge*—an initial unit of depth. Like all skills worth learning, this requires practice and self-confidence but once mastered allows perspectives to be drawn freely and directly.

The initial depth judgment is more apt to be accurate if it is made on a vertical plane as far as possible from the near VL. You simply estimate what a 5' square would look like standing in such a converging plane.

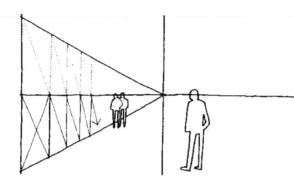

We may also use the shortcut of a diagonal through the bisector explained earlier, if the VP for vertical diagonals is distant or difficult to reach.

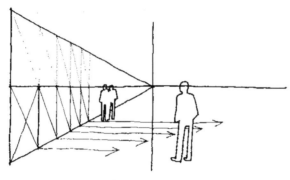

The depth measurements thus determined may then be projected across the floor to wherever they are needed. This horizontal projection is dead horizontal in two-line/one-point perspectives, or from the far VP in two-line/two-point perspectives.

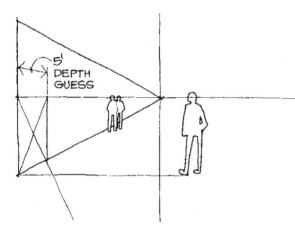

Either diagonal of the initial square can then be extended to find the VP for the parallel set of diagonals on the vertical VL. This is simply following the procedure for spatial extension by diagonals explained earlier. The only difference is that now we have assumed the relative size of the initial unit and its extensions.

In very small perspective sketches the depth judgment can be made on a vertical plane quite near the near VL and without danger of too much distortion.

Or it can be made on the horizontal ground plane, in which case the VP for the set of diagonals will be on the eyelevel VL.

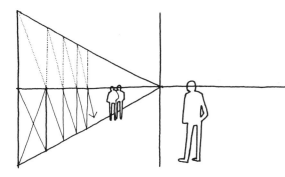

But for deeper, more extensive perspectives, the initial depth judgment and extension should be made on a plane as far from the near VL as possible.

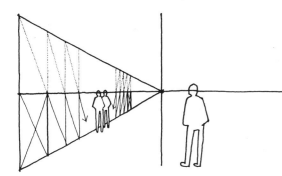

The initial depth judgment should also be made as far forward as possible and the diagonals extended toward the near VL, rather than making the initial depth judgment deep in the space and extending the diagonals forward. Extension of the diagonals more than 10 or 15 feet in front of the initial depth judgment usually results in distortion.

PERSPECTIVE FRAMEWORKS

All perspective frameworks are made up of arrangements of VLs and VPs. Each of the three mutually perpendicular planes of a rectangular environment has a corresponding VL.

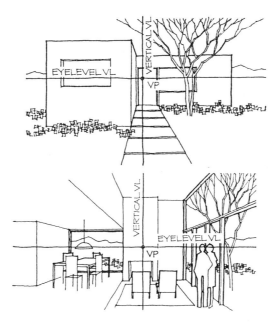

TWO-LINE/ONE-POINT PERSPECTIVES

View is perpendicular to back wall.
Viewer's head held erect.
Transverse planes do not converge.

Advantages:
Easier to draw.
Acceptable for interiors.

Disadvantages:
Static, coincidental view of space.
Dull for exteriors.

The variations of the different perspective frameworks are based on differing relationships between the viewer and the environment. As representations of the experience of the environment, these variations have advantages and disadvantages.

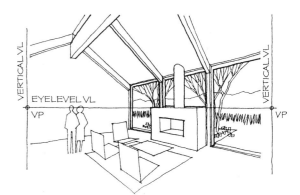

THREE-LINE/TWO-POINT PERSPECTIVES

Viewer free to turn at any angle.
Viewer's head held erect.

Advantages:
Can view the space at various angles.
Consistent with human physiology.
Excellent for exteriors.

Disadvantages:
More difficult to draw.
Conventional interiors set up to reach both VPs don't show the full horizontal extent of the space.

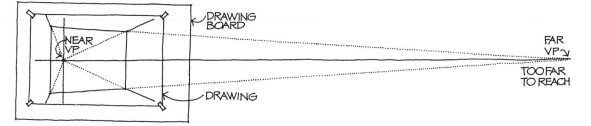

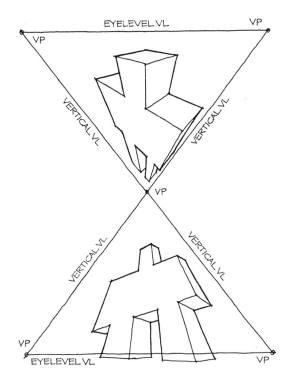

THREE-LINE/THREE-POINT PERSPECTIVES

Viewer free to turn at any angle.
Viewer's head tipped up or down.

Advantages:
Can correctly show dramatic effects of tipping viewer's head.

Disadvantages:
Most difficult to draw.
Misleading as representation of human
    experience.
Relatively useless for interiors.

A BETTER FRAMEWORK: TWO-LINE/TWO-POINT PERSPECTIVES
based on the more dramatic and typical views of space

The perspective framework I strongly advocate for design drawing depicts space in a way that is at once more typical and more dramatic than conventional perspectives. This framework fills the gap between the conventional one-point and two-point plan-projected methods, which only allow views of space that have VPs located on your drawing board.

The framework is called two-line/two-point because transverse horizontal lines converge to a second, "far" VP, even though it can't be physically reached, but the framework does not recognize the far VL as the location for VPs for sets of parallel lines lying in transverse vertical planes because those VPs would be impossible to locate or reach.

Direct perspectives are intended to promote and make the most of confident freehand drawing, but they can be drafted. The tapered width plane can be established by placing a vertical line of ticks at one scale, say 1/4", at the wide end and a slightly smaller line of ticks, say 3/16" at the narrow end. You can even draft a vertical grid of

horizontal lines through those tick marks and then cut across it with diagonals to transfer vertical measurements to transverse horizontal measurements.

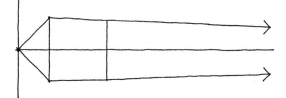

The initial two-line/two-point framework for exterior perspectives consists of an eyelevel line, a 10'-high transverse vertical plane that converges very slightly to an unreachable far VP, a near VP and VL just beyond the wide side end of the building, and an estimated 10' square at the wide end of the transverse plane.

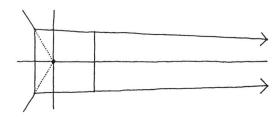

For interior perspectives the framework is equally simple: an eyelevel line, a 10'-high transverse vertical plane converging slightly to an unreachable far VP and VL just inside the wide end of the transverse plane, an estimated 10' square at the wide end of the transverse plane, a near VP and, extending from it, lines representing the intersection of the floor and ceiling, and the side wall of the space being drawn.

These frameworks can be drawn in about ten seconds—less time than it would take you to tape down a plan for projection or boot up your computer. The building can then be sketched on this framework in an additional few seconds and you are now working directly with the reality of what you are designing, in three dimensions. These simple freehand frameworks, combined with the direct method of using diagonals to subdivide and extend the space, let you draw any spatial concept you may have within seconds of thinking of it.

APPLYING THE DIRECT-PERSPECTIVE METHOD TO TWO-LINE/TWO-POINT PERSPECTIVE FRAMEWORKS

The ability to extend space by diagonals lets you make two very useful measuring devices—like the folding gates that confine pets in certain rooms or keep toddlers from falling down stairs—and you can place them in any perspective as a means of measuring the space.

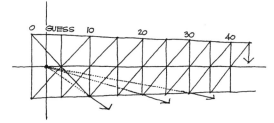

You should set one of the "measuring gates" across your perspective transversely—from side to side—as the major transverse vertical plane of the perspective framework, like the back wall of an interior space you are drawing. This plane is

called the *width* plane. You can measure off 5' increments on this plane and pull the measurements out from the near VP to wherever you need them in the space.

The direct method of using diagonals through the bisector has already subdivided the 10' squares in the width plane and depth plane. By continuing to subdivide using diagonals, we can reach 30", 15", and even 7½" and 3¾" with considerable accuracy—certainly enough for rough conceptual sketches.

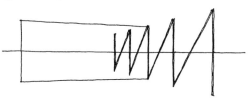

Set the other fold-up measuring gate at right angles to the first one so that it converges toward the near VP and as far away as possible from it, at some convenient place, such as along the far side wall of room or at the end of the building being drawn. This second fold-up measuring gate is called the *depth* plane.

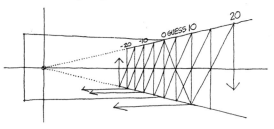

After guessing an initial 10' square standing in the depth plane, you can use diagonals to meas-

ure off 5' depth increments either going back or coming forward on the depth plane and then pull them across the space to wherever you need them.

THE DOWNSIDE OF THE CONVENTIONAL ONE-POINT PERSPECTIVE FRAMEWORK

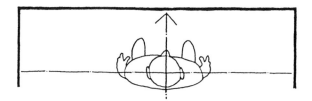

Conventional one-point perspectives are coincidental views of space. By "coincidental" I mean that of all the angles at which an observer might view an object or space, it would be a very unique coincidence to be standing exactly in the center of the space and with your view exactly perpendicular to the end wall, which is what the traditional one-point perspective framework assumes.

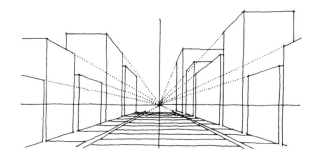

While one-point perspectives do show the extent of one horizontal dimension of the space, they result in dull, static, symmetrical views of even the most dynamic spaces.

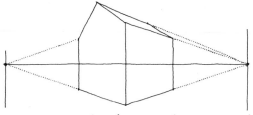

One of the views offered by the two-line/two-point perspective framework is the typical view from an urban sidewalk, which is impossible to draw on either of the traditional frameworks. The view looks sharply down the facades of the buildings along the sidewalk and across the street at the buildings on the other side. It is at once a dramatic perspective angle and the most typical view of our experience of the urban environment.

To draw a conventional one-point perspective of such a street scene would require standing smack in the middle of the street. Besides being a view we seldom have, it is deadly in its static symmetry (see page 119).

The conventional two-point perspective framework is even worse because it is impossible to see both sides of the street and have any sense of the width of the street or square in which we are standing.

This interior perspective is meant to show how dramatic an interior perspective can be on the two-line/two-point framework. It shows the full width of the space and can very quickly convey the qualities of such a space without a finished plan or section or any kind of projection.

THE DOWNSIDE OF THE CONVENTIONAL TWO-POINT PERSPECTIVE FRAMEWORK

Conventional two-point interior perspectives or perspectives of urban streets or spaces are similarly dull because they can't show the extent of either horizontal dimension of the space and often look as if the viewer is being disciplined by having to stand in the corner.

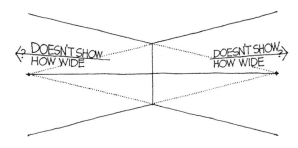

Because conventional two-point perspectives require both VPs to be on the drawing board, exterior perspectives tend to result in dull, equivocal views of buildings, in which the viewing angle stays too close to 45 degrees and results in the two faces of the building being seen at too similar an angle.

The two-line/two-point perspective framework combined with the *direct-perspective* method for extending and subdividing space with diagonals offers a much more useful approach than the traditional methods because it allows us to draw three-dimensional space directly, viewed from the uniquely human erect stance without bowing our heads to the tedium of plan-projection.

The real advantage of direct perspectives, however, is that they can be drawn very quickly, freehand, to study initial ideas in three dimensions. With more careful overlays these freehand perspectives are also perfectly acceptable except for the most formal presentations, as I hope the drawings on these pages demonstrate.

Please remember that these extremely quick, rough, perspectives were drawn without a straight edge or even any kind of scale. I hope you will agree that they can communicate the essential configuration and scale of the space without either the traditional plan-projected methods or the traditional, limited frameworks.

The color coding in this section is a reminder of the first principle of perspective: that the three sets of parallel planes that make up any perspective converge to three separate VLs.

- Horizontal planes and the horizontal eyelevel VL into which they vanish are colored red.

- Near-vanishing vertical planes and the near-vertical VL into which they vanish are colored green.

- Far-vanishing vertical planes and the far-vertical VL into which they vanish are colored blue.

This understanding is necessary in finding VPs for sets of diagonal lines.

Direct Perspective Layout

Deliberate repetition is still a valid teaching technique, especially in learning a skill like drawing. It is also worthwhile to explain procedures or techniques in different ways, with different words and different pictures with the hope that one of those explanations will help the student better understand the concepts. So this section is a somewhat repetitious summary of the principles, frameworks, and methods of perspective drawing, as well as what I hope is a clarifying use of color and a step-by-step procedure for laying out exterior and interior perspectives on the two-line/two-point framework using the direct perspective method. The color is used to clarify the relationships between the three sets of parallel, mutually perpendicular planes and lines that make up rectangular space. It is absolutely mandatory to understand the relationships between these parallel sets of planes and lines and the vanishing lines and vanishing points to which they converge. You need to gain a confident understanding of which lines converge to which vanishing points and, even more importantly, which planes converge into which vanishing lines. I hope the color coding helps.

If environmental designers are to know what the experience of the environments they are designing will be, they must master the drawing of the integrated spatial structure that allows them to represent three-dimensional space in light.

PRINCIPLES

There are only three principles of perspective and they apply to all perspective frameworks and methods.

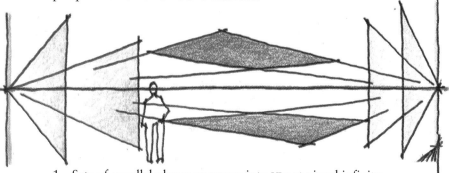

1. Sets of parallel planes converge into VLs at visual infinity.

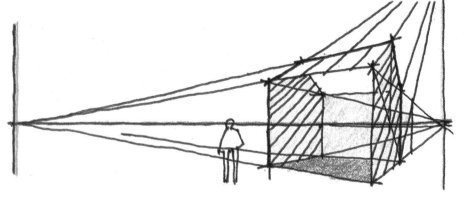

2. Sets of parallel lines converge into VPs on the VL for the plane in which they lie.

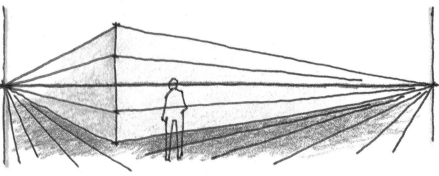

3. VPs for the perspectives of a rectangular object or space are the intersections of the VL for the horizontal planes and the VLs for the vertical planes.

FRAMEWORKS

Perspective frameworks are arrangements of VLs and VPs based on different assumptions about the viewer's relationship to the object or space being drawn.

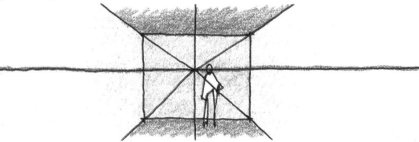

The two-line one-point perspective framework assumes the viewer's line of sight is level and axially aligned with the space or object being drawn.

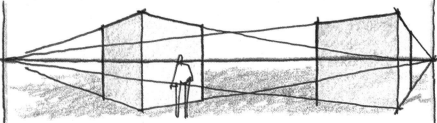

The three-line two-point perspective framework assumes the viewer's line of sight is level but free to turn at any angular relationship to the space or object being drawn.

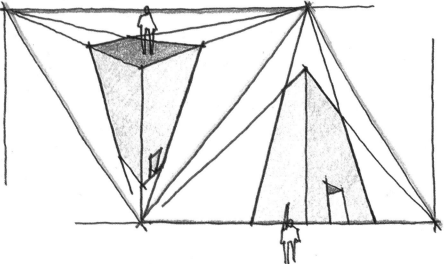

The three-line three-point perspective framework assumes the viewer's line of sight is tipped upward or downward, resulting in a third VP above or below eyelevel.

METHODS

The various perspective methods are all based on the different ways they make the three-dimensional space of the perspective measurable, primarily in the depth dimension.

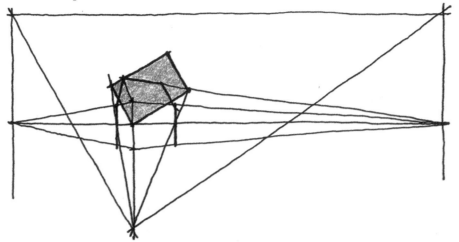

PLAN-PROJECTED METHODS

Conventional perspective methods aspire to an absolute measurability based on laborious drafted projection from a floor plan and section. Projected methods are time-consuming and unpredictable, but their most serious drawback is that they cannot be drawn without a finished plan and section, which dooms them to being tertiary drawings usually completed, if at all, after all design decisions have been made.

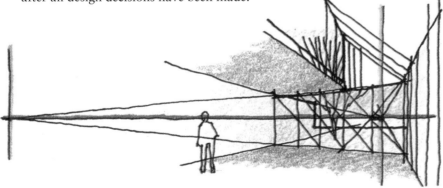

DIRECT-PERSPECTIVE METHOD

The direct-perspective method allows perspectives to be drawn directly, using two vertical planes to measure the width and depth of the space or object to be drawn and requiring only the approximate dimensions and the self-confidence to guess an initial 10' square. Absolute measurability is given up in favor of a relative measurability based on the scale and dimensions of the human figure. This method makes the perspective an equal participant in the design process and allows for study of the experiential quality of the design.

DIAGONALS

Diagonals can be used geometrically to extend or subdivide a rectangular unit. This is best understood on a flat two-dimensional surface.

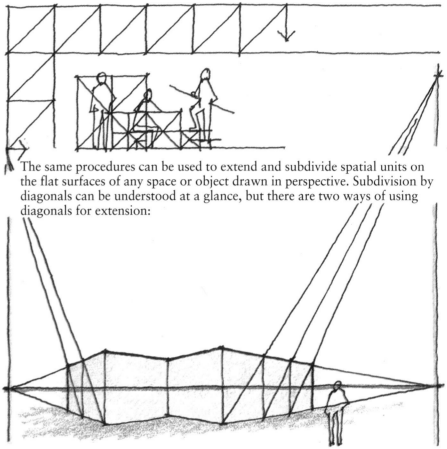

The same procedures can be used to extend and subdivide spatial units on the flat surfaces of any space or object drawn in perspective. Subdivision by diagonals can be understood at a glance, but there are two ways of using diagonals for extension:

1. By finding a VP for diagonals. Use the second principle of perspective to establish a VP for each parallel set of diagonals on the VL for the plane in which they lie.

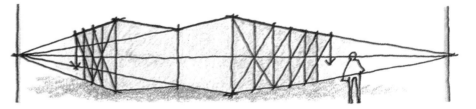

2. By using diagonals through the bisectors of successive 10' spatial units. Use 5' increments so that all spatial units remain square and all diagonals are 45 degrees.

WIDTH PLANE

The width plane is a vertical plane placed across the object or space to be drawn. It is a convenient way of measuring the widths and heights needed to draw a perspective. The plane should be placed at the most convenient measuring position—usually across the most interesting wall of an interior space or the most interesting facade of a building or object.

DEPTH PLANE

The depth plane is a vertical plane placed along the side of the building or space to be drawn. It is a convenient way of measuring the depths and heights needed to draw a perspective. The plane should be placed along the most distant side wall, because the initial depth estimation, on which all successive spatial extensions will be based, is much more accurate if the most distant side wall is used.

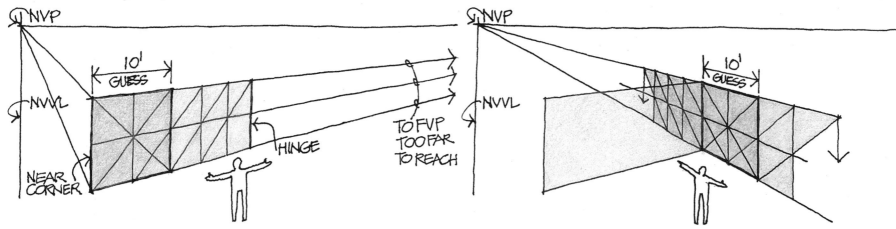

The measuring is done by first guessing a 10' square in the plane and then extending and subdividing the space along the width plane using diagonals, either extended from a VP for diagonals on the far vertical (blue) VL or by using successive diagonals through the squares' bisectors.

The measuring is done by first guessing a 10' square standing in the plane and then extending and subdividing the space along the depth plane using diagonals, either extended from a VP for diagonals on the near vertical (green) VL or by using successive diagonals through the squares' bisectors.

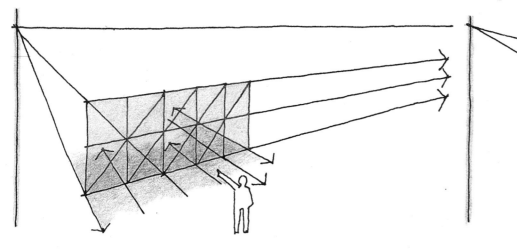

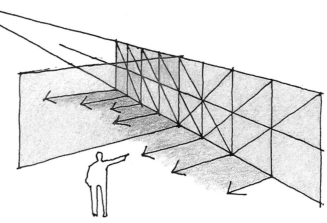

Widths needed in front of or behind the width plane must also be measured off on the width plane and then pulled forward from, or pushed backward toward, the near VP (arrows).

Depths needed at other places in the perspective must all be measured off along the depth plane and then pulled out into the space or object from the far VP (arrows).

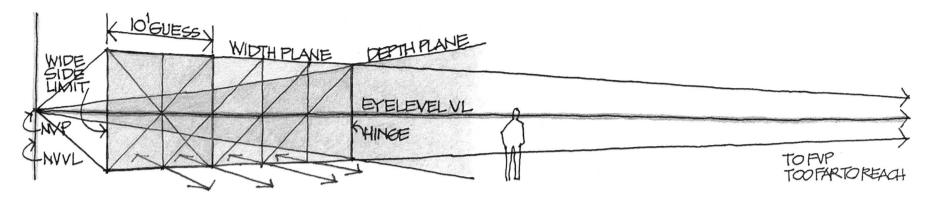

LAYING OUT AN EXTERIOR PERSPECTIVE

1. Draw a horizontal eyelevel line. **2.** Place a VP at each end of the eyelevel line as far apart as possible. **3.** Choose the building's most interesting face and side, placing the corner that is their intersection (the near corner) so the face extends transversely across the drawing toward the far VP. **4.** Extend the near corner an equal distance above and below the eyelevel line. (If we assume that the eyelevel line is at about 5', then the near corner we have just drawn is about 10' tall.) **5.** Draw lines from the top and bottom of the near corner to the two VPs, forming two intersecting vertical planes 10' tall. (The longer of these two planes, extending transversely across the drawing from the near corner toward the far VP, is called the width plane and is colored blue because it converges into the blue far VVL.) **6.** Guess a 10' square standing in the width plane beginning at the near corner and extending toward the far VP.

7. The width of the building's face and all the necessary points within it (windows and doors) can now be measured off by using diagonals. Other width dimensions needed elsewhere in the perspective also have to be measured here and then pulled toward or away from the near VP to wherever they are needed in the perspective (arrows). **8.** Continue measuring along the width plane to the distant corner of the face of the building. This vertical line is called the hinge because this is where the green depth plane (green because it vanishes into the green near VVL) is hinged at 90 degrees to the blue width plane by drawing lines from the top and bottom of the hinge to the near VP (continued on p. 126).

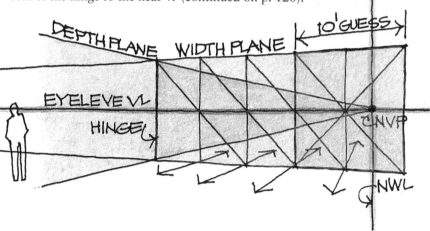

LAYING OUT AN INTERIOR PERSPECTIVE

1. Draw a horizontal eyelevel line. **2.** Choose the space's most interesting end wall and side wall and place the corner that is their intersection (the near corner) so the end walls extend transversely across the drawing toward the far VP. **3.** Having placed the near corner strongly on one side of the drawing, extend it an equal distance above and below the eyelevel line. (If we assume that the eyelevel line is at about 5', then the near corner we have just drawn is about 10' tall.) **4.** Draw lines from the top and bottom of the near corner across the drawing, converging slightly and equally to a far VP (perhaps too distant to reach) and forming two intersecting vertical planes 10' tall. (The longer of these two planes, extending transversely across the drawing from the near corner toward the far VP, is called the width plane and is colored blue because it converges into the blue far VVL.) **5.** Guess a 10' square standing in the width plane beginning at the near corner and extending toward the far VP. **6.** Choose a near VP within the first 10' square, no more than 5' from the near corner.

7. The width of the end wall and all the necessary points within it (windows and doors) can now be measured off by using diagonals. Other width dimensions needed elsewhere in the perspective also have to be measured here and then pulled toward or away from the near VP to wherever they are needed in the perspective (arrows). **8.** Continue measuring along the width plane to the distant narrow end of the end wall of the space. This vertical corner is called the hinge because this is where the green depth plane (green because it vanishes into the green near VVL) is hinged at 90 degrees to the blue width plane by drawing lines from the top and bottom of the hinge to the near VP (continued on p. 126).

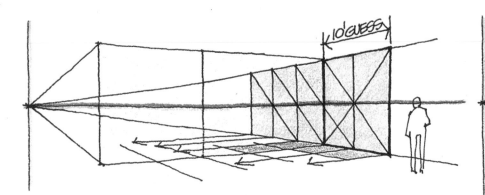

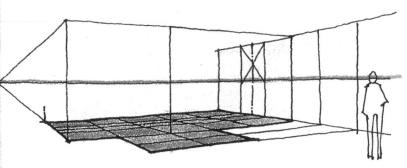

9. Next, guess a 10' square standing in the green depth plane and extending in front of the hinge. 10. Once this square is guessed, all the depths necessary to draw the perspective are measured off along the depth plane by extending one of the diagonals of the 10' square to intersect the near VVL, establishing a VP for diagonals. Successive spatial units can now be marked off by diagonals from this VP. If such a VP for diagonals is inconvenient to reach, the same measuring is accomplished by using diagonals through the bisectors of successive squares. 11. The depths thus measured will have to be pulled across the perspective from the far VP to wherever they are needed (arrows).

12. When the far back corner of the object is reached, the object's depth can be pulled across the floor of the perspective, closing the footprint of the object. 13. The next step is to accomplish this kind of intersecting closure on the red ground plane of the perspective (red because it vanishes into the red horizontal eyelevel VL) wherever it is necessary to establish the footprints of partitions, furniture, or any other elements or convolutions within the space of the perspective (continued on p. 127).

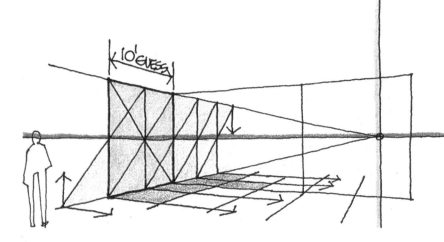

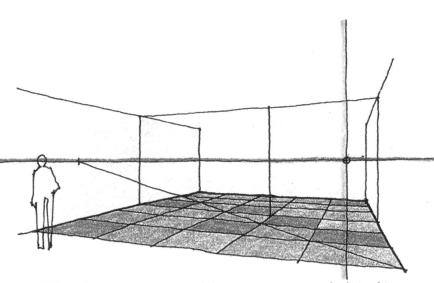

9. Next, guess a 10' square standing in the green depth plane and extending in front of the hinge. 10. Once this square is guessed, all the depths necessary to draw the perspective are measured off along the depth plane by extending one of the diagonals of the 10' square to intersect the near VVL, establishing a VP for diagonals. Successive spatial units can now be marked off by diagonals from this VP. If such a VP for diagonals is inconvenient to reach, the same measuring is accomplished by using diagonals through the bisectors of successive squares. 11. The depths thus measured will have to be pulled across the perspective from the far VP to wherever they are needed (arrows).

12. When the far back corner of the perspective is reached (in this case a patio extending beyond the glass back wall), the space's depth can be pulled across the floor of the perspective, closing the footprint of the space. 13. The next step is to accomplish this kind of intersecting closure on the red floor plane of the perspective (red because it vanishes into the red horizontal eyelevel VL) wherever it is necessary to establish the footprints of the partitions, furniture, or any other elements or convolutions within the space of the perspective (continued on p. 127).

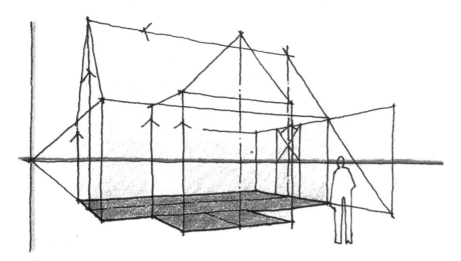

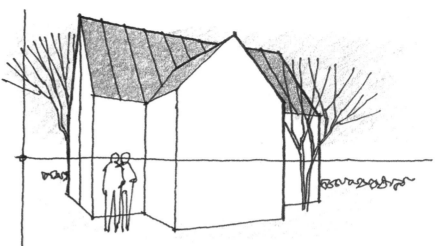

14. Next, the corners of the various footprints are pulled up vertically to their full heights. A vertical dimension is easily determined anywhere in the perspective because the measurement from any point on the floor to the eyelevel VL is always 5'. That distance is easily subdivided or extended to the height needed.

It is important to realize that these perspectives are drawn directly without a drafted plan, elevation, or section, and without an architectural scale. Rather, we relied completely on the 5' height of the human eye level as the basis for all our measurements.

If the resulting perspective is not the view anticipated, we can just as quickly draw another view or change the viewer's eye level or the size of the drawing, as shown on the next page. Most importantly, we have seen the space in three dimensions, as it will actually be experienced, and it is most likely that this visualization will provoke improvements in the design. Drawing perspectives directly and early in the design process can help you discover a need for improvement and provide you with the opportunity to accomplish it.

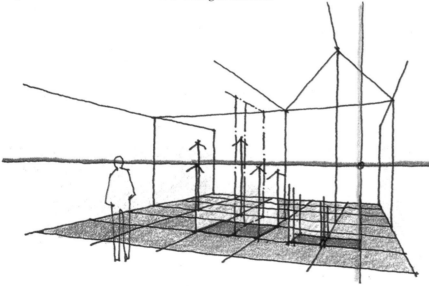

14. Next, the corners of the various footprints are pulled up vertically to their full heights. A vertical dimension is easily determined anywhere in the perspective because the measurement from any point on the floor to the eyelevel VL is always 5'. That distance is easily subdivided or extended to the height needed.

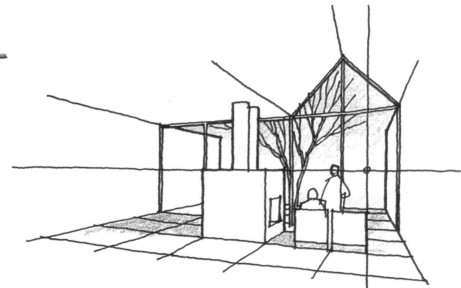

CHANGING EYELEVEL AND SIZE

One of the advantages of the direct perspective method is that vertical and horizontal relationships to the viewer are directly adjustable as the drawing develops, without the repositioning and reprojection necessary with plan-projected methods. This flexibility allows both the vertical position and the size of the drawing to be easily adjusted.

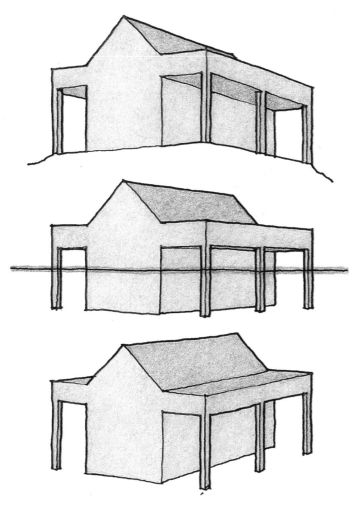

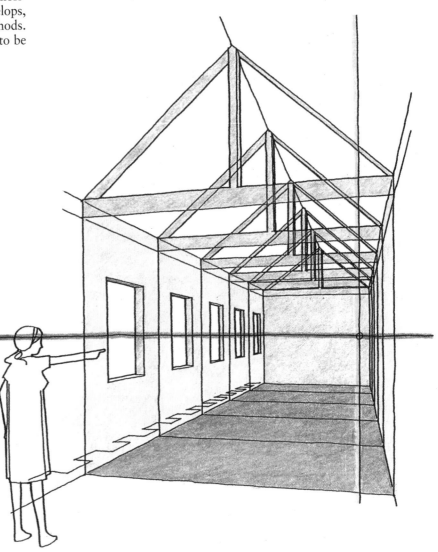

THE ELEVATOR SHAFT: VERTICAL ADJUSTMENT OF DIRECT PERSPECTIVES

The object or environment can be raised or lowered in relation to the viewer and the viewer's eyelevel as if it were an elevator cab moving up or down a vertical shaft. You can select the level you wish by deciding that the floor level be a specific dimension above or below your eyelevel. Remember that the eyelevel remains a horizontal plane through the viewer's eyes.

THE TUNNEL: SIZE OR DEPTH ADJUSTMENT OF DIRECT PERSPECTIVES

The size of a direct perspective is adjusted by moving the width plane or the primary face of an object or space backward or forward, toward or from the near VP, along the tunnel of the perspective framework.

VARIATIONS

There are several variations in the procedure for drawing direct perspectives and the choice of which variation to use should be based on the size or extent of the perspective you wish to draw.

For exterior perspectives or objects it is usually best to use a three-dimensional cube as the initial spatial unit.

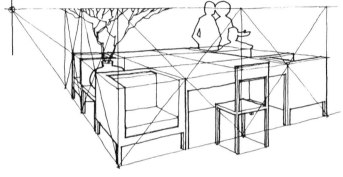

For a single piece of furniture or a furniture arrangement, the initial spatial unit can be a 30" cube. Such a cube may then be extended or subdivided by diagonals as necessary.

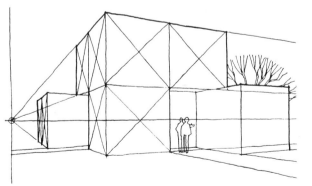

For the exterior of a building, a 10' cube may be the best initial spatial unit, if the building is relatively small and only one story.

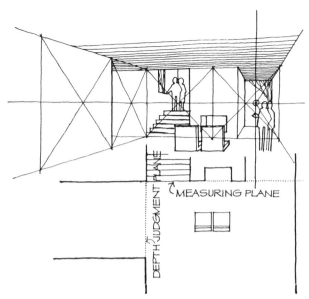

If the building is large and has multiple stories it may be best to begin with a 20', 30', 50', or even a 100' cube.

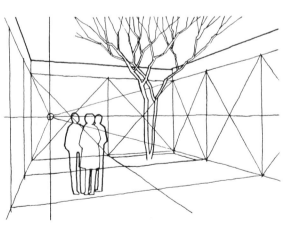

For interior perspectives or exterior spaces that have architectural boundaries, it is probably better to use only two perpendicular vertical planes, one transverse or receding toward the far VL and one converging or receding toward the near VL.

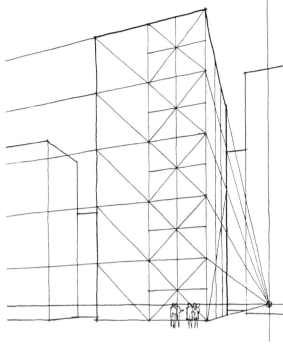

DEPTH JUDGMENT PLANE

↑MEASURING PLANE

These two planes should be placed where they most conveniently measure the space to be drawn. The planes can be any convenient height.

For small or moderate-sized spaces, 5'- or 10'-high planes using 5' or 10' squares as measuring units work well.

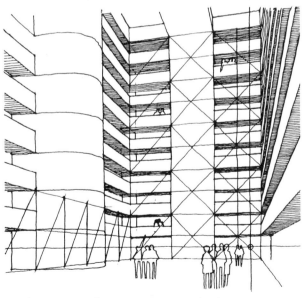

In larger or taller spaces it may be better to use 20'-, 30'-, or 50'-high planes and squares.

CHOICES AND OPPORTUNITIES

CHOOSING THE VIEW

While the wisdom required to choose the best perspective view is largely the product of experience, there is some initial advice that may be worthwhile. First of all, the idea that you are only *allowed* a single perspective view of a space or object is questionable. To try to show all the aspects and qualities of a designed environment in any single view is obviously futile. At least two perspectives are needed to show any rectangular space or object, and complex environments require many more.

THE DIRECTION OF THE VIEW

Choosing the direction of the perspective view is much like choosing the best section; it should always be taken toward the most interesting or characteristic profile of the space.

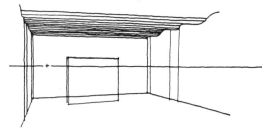

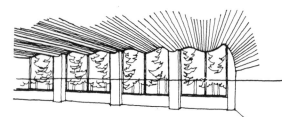

A space with an undulating ceiling, like Alvar Aalto's Viipuri Library, for example, should not be shown head on. A straight-ahead view will obscure half of the undulating profile and not show the real shape of the space.

THE LEVEL OF THE VIEW

Choice of view level offers other opportunities or pitfalls in multilevel space. Generally it is wise to take all perspectives of multilevel environments from the lowest level. This is because stairs and level changes are much easier to draw from the lowest position since the faces of the stair risers or level changes will appear directly. On the other hand, it is almost impossible to show any part of a descending stair in an eyelevel perspective.

For those times when it is necessary to show a multilevel environment from the top or from a midlevel balcony, I offer the following advice. The temptation is to try to draw balcony views head-on, looking over the railing. It requires only a few frustrating attempts to reveal that if the view is taken standing at the railing, the railing will not show in the drawing and there will be no sense of where the viewer is standing. And if you move the head-on balcony view back so the balcony railing shows, it will obscure the view down into the space below. The better alternative is to take the view sideways along the balcony so that both the viewer's position on the balcony and the view into the space below are revealed.

SPATIAL EXTENSIONS

One last piece of advice is to always choose the perspective view that reveals the most interesting spatial extensions. This may seem rather obvious, but we often forget that the most powerful interest in a perspective is spatial interest and that spatial interest is potential kinesthetic interest. This means that perspectives must never be considered as flat, two-dimensional wall decorations that you stand and look *at*. You should rather look/walk into them with your eyemindbody. Never miss the opportunity to show successive layers of space in a perspective, and remember that a poor choice of view can severely limit the promise of the kinesthetic experience of even the most careful rendering.

KINESTHETIC SPACE

Perspectives represent the promise of the potential kinesthetic experience because we normally use vision to predict an experience of a space. Upon entering a room, we can sense, from the doorway, whether further exploration will be rewarding or dull. When drawing perspectives, there are several details to which we must attend if our perspectives are to reach their full potential as representations of kinesthetic space.

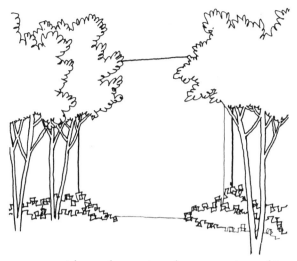

SURFACES

As Gibson has pointed out, the evolution of our visual perceptual system has always included the perception of the earth's surface and its textural gradient from coarse to fine as it recedes into the distance. The perception of this surface and all similar continuous surfaces is essential to our perception of three-dimensional space. For design drawing this means that the bounding surfaces of spaces should be indicated with a graduated texture, in response to their distance from us. Spotty rendering of continuous surfaces can destroy the spatial reality of a drawing. This also means that you should always place textures on continuous *surfaces* (paving, carpet, masonry, paneling, grass, or gravel) rather than on *objects,* which may be on or in front of the surfaces (furniture, people, etc.). At the spatial edges where a surface texture disappears, make sure the texture actually touches the edge. Beginning students often stop textures short and create a "halo effect" around objects that sit on or in front of textured surfaces. Such halo effects completely destroy the spatial quality of the drawing and reduce the drawing to a collection of lines on paper.

VOLUMES

The perception of spatial volumes is dependent on the perception of the intersections of their bounding surface—their *corners*. When placing objects (people, furniture, or plants) in a perspective, especially on or in front of a textured, space-defining surface, be careful not to obscure the edges or corners that define the space. Hiding the resolution of a corner, or the end of a carpet and the beginning of floor tile, for instance, destroys the definitions on which the perception of spatial volumes depend.

This can be illustrated by demonstrating how much of a cube can be removed between the

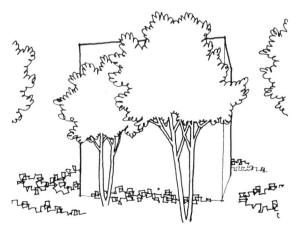

corners without destroying the perception of it, and how quickly the same cube is destroyed when the corners are hidden.

EDGES

When we represent space with a line drawing, the lines we draw represent two quite different constituents of the environment: *planar corners* and *spatial edges*. Planar corners are the intersections of planes where two or three intersecting planes are seen. These corners define spatial volumes and are essential to the perception of space in a drawing. The careful rendering of both surfaces and volumes is essential to the representation of kinesthetic space because they form the backgrounds against which the action of kinesthetic perception occurs. That action is always concentrated at the spatial edges of the environment. Spatial edges are a perceptual phenomena, dependent on where the perceiver is positioned, while planar corners are only a physical fact. An outside physical planar corner also may be a perceptual spatial edge, but only if one of the planes that form it is hidden from the perceiver.

This distinction is critical because a line drawing's only means of expression is line weight; if we draw all the lines the same weight we forfeit

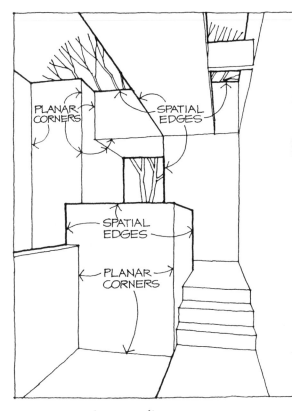

PLANAR CORNERS

SPATIAL EDGES

SPATIAL EDGES

PLANAR CORNERS

ON IRREGULAR FORMS SPATIAL EDGES MOVE GRADUALLY AS THE OBSERVER MOVES

ON GEOMETRIC FORMS SPATIAL EDGES JUMP FROM CORNER TO CORNER

our opportunity to use lines to represent two categorically different things. This is important because the two kinds of edges are in no way the same: as we move through the environment planar corners just lie there passively while spatial edges slide dynamically against their backgrounds, progressively revealing or hiding the surfaces behind them.

So there is no misunderstanding about what constitutes a spatial edge, let me detail the definition. By edge I mean the outline of any form or surface that is separated from its background. In geometric forms this edge will always be one of the form's planar corners, but in curved or irregular forms, like a human figure or a tree, this outline of the form's silhouette shifts freely over the form in relationship to the perceiver's position.

Since we are constantly moving perceptual systems, the edges that carry the most informa-

tion about the environment are the spatial edges. They are the hem lines of kinesthetic perception. The movement of spatial edges against their backgrounds varies in three ways that carry or confirm three kinds of spatial information:

- the edge's relationship to our line of movement,
- the edge's distance in front of the surfaces it partially hides, and
- the edge's distance from us.

Since we swivel our heads and our eyes, there is no predictable relationship between our view of a space and our potential direction of movement into it, but I have found that a hierarchy of line weights based on a combination of the last two variables seems to be very effective in representing the kinesthetic experience of an environment and in assuring that students do perceive their perspective drawings as space.

To represent the kinesthetic experience of an environment, I recommend that planar corners be drawn with the lightest line weight and that all spatial edges be profiled with a darker line. This is the most basic way to indicate these two different kinds of spatial information. To represent kinesthetic space in a more sophisticated way, establish a hierarchy of line weights in which the

heaviness of the line indicates the relative depth of the spatial separation or the distance between the edge and its background. This hierarchy is, however, complicated by another hierarchy in which line weight is used to indicate the edge's distance from us. Edges that are very far away from us should be rendered with a light line weight, while close edges should have a heavier line. At times these two hierarchies will be incompatible. For instance, the edge of a distant mountain range should be of a dark line weight according to the depth-based hierarchy because the spatial separation between it and its background is infinite. According to the distance-based hierarchy, however, the edge should be drawn with a light line because it is far away from us. Experience, and the available time, will govern when the point of diminishing returns is reached in applying such a hierarchy of line weights to a drawing. Even a crude hierarchy, however, will begin to represent the kinesthetic experience of space.

CONTEXT

The peripheral space surrounding a designed environment offers opportunities for design and drawing that should never be ignored. The responses that a designed space or object can make to its context constitute perhaps the richest collection of determinants with which a designer can work. The quality of our collective environment depends on sensitive contextual responses.

The context is what makes a drawing believable as three-dimensional space. We can use the context to make a drawing realistic by:

- establishing the ground plane,
- layering the background, and
- articulating the foreground space.

ESTABLISHING THE GROUND PLANE

As Gibson points out, our perception of space depends on a continuous "ground" that begins at our feet and recedes to the horizon. In *The Perception of the Visual World* (1950), he explains:

> The world with a ground under it—the visual world of surfaces and edges—is . . . the prototype of the world in which we all live. . . .
>
> An out-of-doors world is one in which the lower portion of the visual field (corresponding to the upper portion of each retinal image) is invariably filled by a projection of the terrain. The upper portion of the visual field is usually filled with a projection of the sky. Between the upper and lower portions is the skyline, high or low as the observer looks down or up, but always cutting the normal visual field in a horizontal section. This is the kind of world in which our primitive ancestors lived. It was also the environment in which took place the evolution of visual perception in *their* ancestors. During the millions of years in which some unknown animal species evolved into our human species, land and sky were the constant visual stimuli to which the eyes and brain responded. . . .

We perceive this surface on which we have evolved as a series of horizontal, receding spatial contours, each of which occludes some space behind it. The nearer horizontal contour lines are simply minor ripples in the earth's surface, such as curbs, steps, and walkways in an urban environment. Depending on the terrain, these ripples will generally appear closer together as they recede in the distance. Any simple stack of horizontal lines that progressively get closer together at the top will be perceived as a horizontal plane,

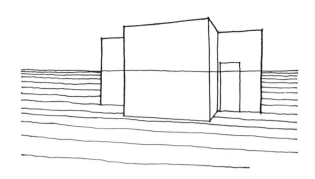

because it abstractly represents the context in which our vision evolved.

This means that the representation of three-dimensional space begins with establishing the ground plane. This can be done by drawing a receding texture that emphasizes, or consists solely of, horizontal lines that cross our visual field. These horizontal lines can be paving textures, joints in a sidewalk, low hedges, or lines of grass blades, and they can be molded to describe slopes or deformations of the ground plane.

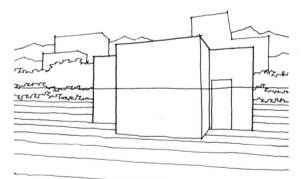

LAYERING THE BACKGROUND

In traditional pictorial composition the contextual space is conceived as containing a foreground and background that provide a setting for the dominant middle-ground. Placing an object such as a building on the ground plane immediately divides the remaining space into a foreground and background. Notice how the horizontal contours with which we established the ground plane disappear behind the building.

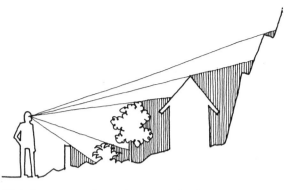

This interrupted continuity is the key to layering the background of any perspective.

Unless the building is sited in the Australian outback or on one of our endless Midwestern planes, there will be something behind the building. In an urban context this background would consist of layers of other buildings. In other contexts the background might be layers of hedgerows, trees, or mountains. Whatever the background, it is best rendered as receding layers of space by simple overlapping outlines. Be sure, however, that the background is consistent on both sides of the building—it is very disconcerting to see a row of trees disappear behind one side of a building and, say, a freight train emerge from behind the other.

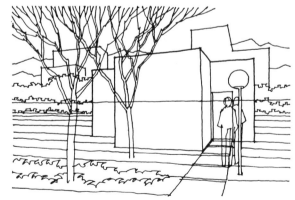

ARTICULATING THE FOREGROUND SPACE

The last way to make a drawing look like three-dimensional space is to place other objects on the ground plane, especially in the foreground, to articulate the distance into various spatial units. Just as the initial placement of the building on the ground plane divides the continuous space into a foreground and background, so too the placement of additional vertical objects subdivides the space further and makes the drawing appear three-dimensional.

Trees, figures, tall shrubs, light standards, and various structures are all potential spatial articulators. Although placing them to the side helps to frame the building, the most dramatic position in which to place these objects is directly in front of the building. Such placements must not, however, obscure the building, especially its volume-defining corners. The effect can be further enhanced by extending horizontal bands (hedges, contours, low walls, etc.) between the vertical objects and the building.

INTERIOR PERSPECTIVES

An indication of the context of interior perspectives is also necessary in order for them to be accurate representations of designed environments. As in exterior perspectives, the enclosed space is the middle ground, the distant outdoor space seen through the doors and windows is the background, and the figures and furnishings articulate the foreground.

It is important that the background's bands of trees, mountains, or buildings disappear and reappear through the various doors and windows, because it will allow the exterior space to be perceived as continuous and surrounding. The figures and furnishings that make up the additional interest of the interior space should be very carefully placed so as few of the corners and space-defining planar intersections are obscured

as possible. Vertical elements like lamps, columns, figures, and plants can help articulate the space by intermittently breaking the horizontal intersections of wall/floor and wall/ceiling. The figures and furnishings should be collected into groups or layers so that their individuality is not emphasized.

Both the continuous layers of exterior space and interior groups of figures and furnishings should be drawn very simply so that the emphasis of the drawing remains on the interior walls of the enclosure.

Use contextual indications reduced to simple but carefully descriptive outlines, because:

- they keep the emphasis on the middle ground,
- they correspond to our focal vision, and
- they take less time to draw.

They also contribute to the believability of the environment's three-dimensional setting.

SLIDE-PROJECTED CONTEXTS

Photographic slides can be used to quickly and accurately draw a context. The back-projected mirror box shown below allows you to project the slide onto a sheet of tracing paper and trace the image. I made such a box years ago and it has become one of the most useful pieces of equipment I own.

It consists of an open plywood box with a mirror mounted at a 45° angle. The mirror reflects the projected image upward onto a piece of tracing paper laid on the clear glass top. A zoom lens on the projector lets you reduce and enlarge the image and the back projection keeps your body or hand from casting a shadow on the projected image. It is handy to make the glass top 11" x 17", which is a little different from the proportions of a slide but the largest dimension that ordinary photocopiers will accept.

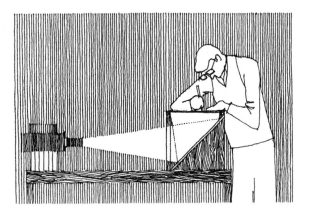

By permission of Johnny Hart and Field Enterprises, Inc.

Tonal Interest and Light

Tonal interest in the environment—the visual array ranging from white through all the shades of gray to black—is the result of light reflecting off the environment's various surfaces. Tonal interest is the most powerful interest category in the environment and the last category to be lost as we cross the threshold into blindness.

The articulation of reflected light into patterns of dark and light has two causes:

- the relative whiteness of the reflecting surface;
- the relative orientation of the reflecting surface to the source of light, and whether or not the light is blocked by some intervening mass.

We will be concerned exclusively with the second kind of reflected light, since relative surface whiteness is a matter of the surface's physical properties—its inherent color and texture—and, as such, only an inevitable additive to the surface's relationship to light.

Light may also be either *direct* sunlight which casts shadows, or the *indirect* light of a cloudy day, a north-facing room, or deep inside a building's interior.

Understanding complex three-dimensional environments from their shadow patterns is an ability we developed long ago and below the level of consciousness. If we are to learn to draw light in the environments we design, however, we must learn the ability consciously, with considerable effort. We must belatedly learn to write or *draw* a language that we read effortlessly.

Books on drawing traditionally call the sections devoted to light "Shades and Shadows" or "Shadow-Casting." This has always seemed backward to me, since it is the light that is the actor, the positive force, while shade and shadow are simply special conditions of the absence of light. To help you see light more correctly, this chapter is printed on a gray background so that the light is emphasized.

Tradition also normally assumes a sun angle of 45° over the viewer's left shoulder, arbitrarily freezing the movement of the sun and reducing shadow-casting to another graphic convention like the north arrow. This rigid convention inhibits any understanding of the freedom necessary for intelligent sun placement.

Shadow-casting is also taught almost exclusively on objects, seldom within spaces, leaving most interior perspectives with no indication of how they would be lit.

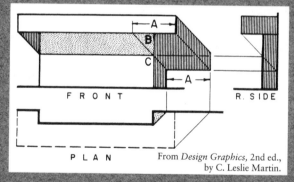

From *Design Graphics,* 2nd ed., by C. Leslie Martin.

It is much more useful to learn shadow-casting three-dimensionally, in perspective, so that the whole shade/shadow system is seen at once, and further, to practice moving the sun and drawing several optional shadow patterns based on alternative sun angles. It is also mandatory to learn shadow-casting for *interiors* instead of exclusively for the *exteriors* of objects.

SUN AND SHADE

The most dramatic and descriptive lighting of the environment is by the direct light of the sun.

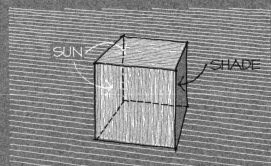

EXTERIOR PERSPECTIVES

The six surfaces of a cube represent the surfaces of any rectangular environment (top, bottom, front, back, left side, right side). When illuminated by direct sunlight, three contiguous surfaces will be lit—in the case above, the top, front, and left side. The remaining three surfaces (bottom, back, and right side) cannot be lit because of their orientation. They are turned away from the sun, and we call the light condition on such surfaces "shade."

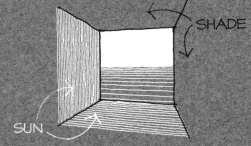

INTERIOR PERSPECTIVES

If we remove the end wall of a cube to let the sun in, it will light the floor and one of the side walls, while the ceiling and the other side wall will be turned away from the sun, in shade.

SHADOWS AND THE CASTING EDGE

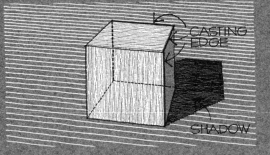

EXTERIOR PERSPECTIVES

The mass of a cube will block the sun and cast a shadow on the ground. The boundary of the shadow will be cast by what is called the "casting edge" on the cube. The casting edge is always the line that separates sunlit surfaces from surfaces in shade.

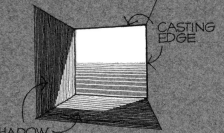

INTERIOR PERSPECTIVES

From the interior, the casting edge will be the edge of the ceiling and the right side wall, even though the sunlit exterior surfaces that meet the interior shade surfaces to form the corner of the casting edge cannot be seen in this view.

In rectangular environments the casting edges are straight lines and any understanding of shadow-casting begins with the shadows of lines on planes. There are only two possible relationships between a line and the plane on which its shadow falls. The line is either perpendicular or parallel to the plane on which its shadow falls, and we will call the shadows cast by those two relationships perpendicular (⊥) shadows or parallel (‖) shadows.

SHADOWS OF LINES ON PLANES

The characteristics of ⊥ and ‖ shadows can be understood using the shadows of an old-time football goal, with the two vertical posts perpendicular to the playing field and a horizontal crossbar that is parallel to the field.

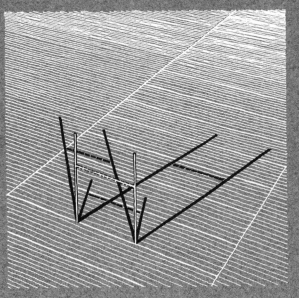

PERPENDICULAR SHADOWS

Perpendicular shadows, while anchored to the bottom of each upright, swing over a great arc as the earth rotates, so that they:

- change dramatically in both their horizontal and vertical angle and their length;
- cut across any rectangular environment at an angle;
- are parallel to one another and converge to their own special VP on the VL for the plane in which they lie;
- are always the ones that begin and end shade/shadow systems.

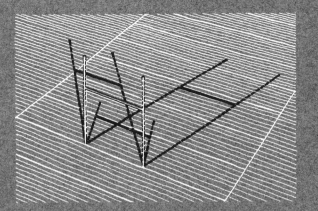

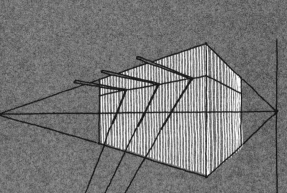

To find the VP for sun's rays requires an understanding of the sun's ray triangle formed by any vertical casting line (flagpole), its shadow on the ground, and the sun's ray that connects the top of the flagpole and the end of the shadow (the triangle's hypotenuse). The VP for sun's rays will always be on the vertical vanishing line for the planes of the sun's rays—a vertical line through the "flagpole" VP.

PARALLEL SHADOWS

Parallel shadows are much more passive. ‖ shadows:

- are always parallel to and the same length as the line that casts them;
- are content to stay parallel to the edges, corners, and joints of the rectangular environment;
- don't need their own VP and are content to converge to one of the VPs of the perspective.

In order to find the VPs for the three ⊥ shadows we need to use two principles of perspective we learned earlier:

Sets of ⊥ shadows cast by near-vanishing horizontal lines on a far-vanishing vertical plane will converge to a VP on the far vertical VL.

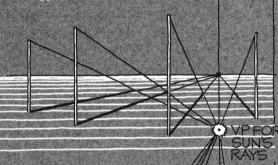

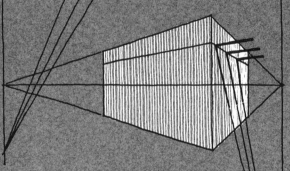

With the sun behind us, the position of the VP for sun's rays is always below the eyelevel VL.

With the sun in front of us, the sun's rays' VP is always above the eyelevel VL.

Sets of ⊥ shadows cast by far-vanishing horizontal lines on a near-vanishing vertical plane will converge to a VP on the near vertical VL.

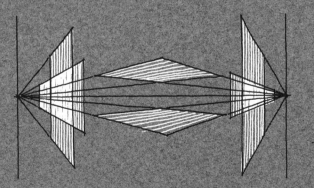

- All sets of parallel planes converge and vanish into VLs at visual infinity.
- Sets of parallel lines converge to single VPs on the VL for the planes in which they lie.

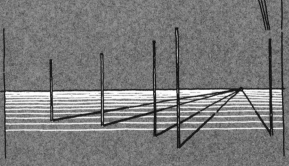

⊥ or "flagpole" shadows of vertical lines falling on a horizontal plane will converge to their own special VP on the eyelevel VL.

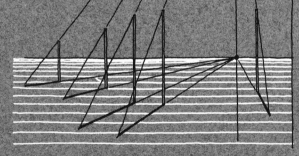

You are free to choose the sun's angle and the sun's rays' VP directly, but it makes more sense to choose them indirectly by choosing the two most critical (of the three) ⊥ shadow angles.

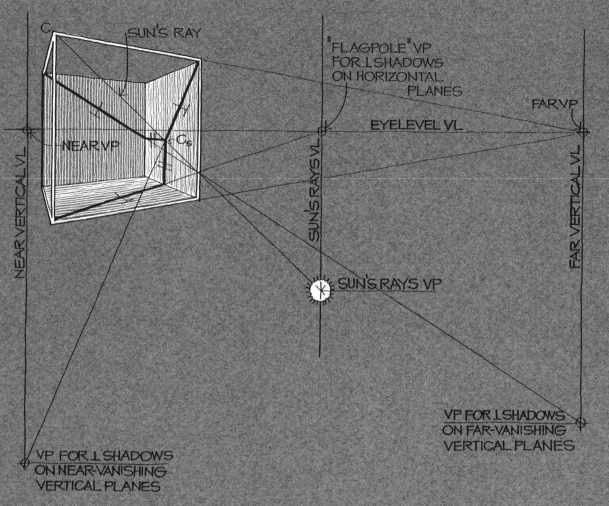

C
SUN'S RAY
"FLAGPOLE" VP
FOR ⊥ SHADOWS
ON HORIZONTAL
PLANES
FAR VP
EYELEVEL VL
NEAR VP
C$_S$
NEAR VERTICAL VL
SUN'S RAYS VL
FAR VERTICAL VL
SUN'S RAYS VP
VP FOR ⊥ SHADOWS
ON FAR-VANISHING
VERTICAL PLANES
VP FOR ⊥ SHADOWS
ON NEAR-VANISHING
VERTICAL PLANES

FREEDOM IN SHADOW-CASTING

When learning the complete framework for casting shadows in perspective, it is important to understand how such shadow-casting ability may be used deductively or inductively.

Shadow-casting in perspective is traditionally taught by specifying the sun angle and then asking students to cast the shadows based on this predetermined sun angle. This makes the student's work easier to grade because there is one single answer against which each shadow pattern may be compared. While this may be understandably expedient for grading stacks of student drawings, it is very misleading because sun angles are never given in reality. Designers are always able to choose the best sun angle, and they may choose it in a variety of ways.

DEDUCTIVE SHADOW-CASTING

The traditional deductive shadow-casting method, in which the sun's angle is determined by establishing the shadow of a particular point in space, has the disadvantage of determining the most critical shadows —the ⊥ shadow angles—as secondary outcomes of the initial choice of sun angle. This may result in weak or awkward shadow patterns and in unreachable VPs.

SHADOW-CASTING IN THREE-LINE/TWO-POINT PERSPECTIVE

We can now assemble the entire framework for shadow-casting in perspective. This consists of establishing the VPs for the three ⊥ shadows and the sun's rays.

You must understand the principles behind the framework, not just the specific geometry of the single case shown here. Test your understanding of the framework by overlaying this framework and changing the angle of one of the ⊥ shadow angles. See how that one change will

change everything: the VP for the changed ⊥ shadow, the angles of the other two ⊥ shadows and their VPs, as well as the sun's ray triangle, the "flagpole" VP and the sun's rays' VP.

Understanding this framework for casting shadows in perspective is worth the effort it takes to master it. Once you understand it you will own that understanding—no one can take it away from you. It will allow you, in moments, to cast the shadows on your perspective sketches, and those shadows will do more to strengthen your sketches than anything else you can learn.

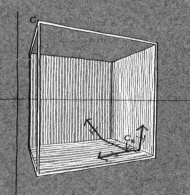

C
C$_s$

INDUCTIVE SHADOW-CASTING

In contrast, the inductive method of shadow-casting allows you the freedom to choose any two of the three ⊥ shadow angles *directly*. This means that those two choices will initiate the strongest and most dynamic shadow pattern possible, because the ⊥ shadows are always the most dynamic members of any shade/shadow system and offer the greatest opportunities in the choice of their length and angle.

The ⊥ shadows are infinitely flexible in angle and length and always cut diagonally across all the other lines and edges of rectangular compositions. The two shadows may be chosen independently of one another to produce two particularly desirable ⊥ shadow angles. The only relationship between the two angles you choose is that those two choices will fix the sun's angle and together determine the third ⊥ shadow angle.

Using the ⊥ shadow-casting relationships to initiate a shadow pattern is more useful because designers often want the shadows to fall at one or two particular angles. You may not care what the precise location of the sun is, instead being content to let it simply be the resultant of the two angle choices.

Taking this method of initiating a shadow pattern step by step, choose any angle you want for two of the ⊥ shadows (in this case the shadows of lines CN and CV). Simply make two choices and then extend them, following the rules for the two shadow-casting relationships

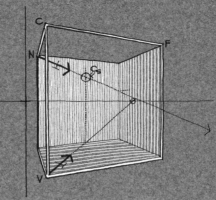

until the two shadows intersect. Their intersection will be the shadow of point C (Cs), because that is the point of intersection of the two lines casting the shadows.

Extend the shadow of each line until it changes planes (and the shadow-casting relationship changes to parallel). You will see that the two shadow routes intersect high on the back, far-vanishing wall.

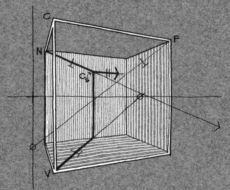

Having found point CS by first determining two of the three ⊥ shadow angles, we can complete the pattern by extending the shadow of line CF from point Cs.

You could just as easily have chosen either of the other two possible combinations of ⊥ shadow angles to determine the sun's position.

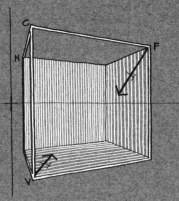

You could have first chosen the ⊥ shadow angles of the far-vanishing line CF on the near-vanishing vertical plane and of the nonvanishing vertical line CF on the eyelevel-vanishing horizontal plane;

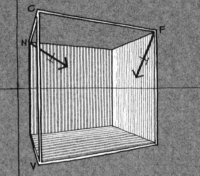

or you could have first chosen the ⊥ shadow angles of the far-vanishing line CF on the near-vanishing vertical plane and of the near-vanishing horizontal line CN on the far-vanishing vertical plane.

Complete these last two shadow patterns to test your understanding of completing shadow patterns initiated by choosing two ⊥ shadow angles.

Introducing students to shadow-casting as a free and flexible way of lighting the environments they design is in every way more useful than introducing shadow-casting as another inevitable convention, leaving students with a rigid set of procedures rather than with the freedom that comes from a deeper understanding.

ANALYZING THE RELATIVE LIGHTNESS AND DARKNESS OF SURFACES IN SUN, SHADE, AND SHADOW

Since each of the three light conditions (sun, shade, and shadow) occurs on three different surface orientations (sun and shadow occur on the same three), and because each surface's relative lightness or darkness varies according to the sun's angular relationship to the surface, you need a way of analyzing the relative lightness and darkness of each surface. This analysis can also be done on the shadow-analysis cube.

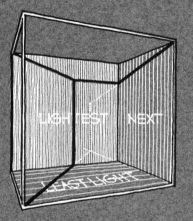

The plane on which the shadow of the corner (Cs) falls is the lightest of the sunlit planes because it is struck most perpendicularly by the sun's rays. This is true because the corner is equidistant from the three planes and its shadow being on a particular plane indicates that the sun's rays travel the least distance to cast that shadow, and the sun's rays are therefore more perpendicular to the surface on which the corner's shadow falls than to the other two. The second-lightest sunlit surface is the one that the sun's rays would strike next if the sun's ray and the plane were extended until they intersected. The third-lightest, or darkest, sunlit surface is the remaining surface, which is reached last by the sun's rays because of their acute angle to the surface.

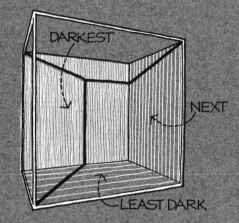

The order of the relative darkness or lightness of the three surfaces in shade is the exact reverse of the sunlit surfaces. The back of the lightest sunlit surface is the darkest shade surface because it is most difficult for reflected light to reach that surface. The darkest of the three sunlit surfaces has the lightest shade surface as its back, and the medium sunlit surface is backed by the medium shade surface.

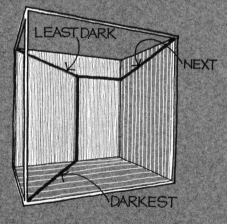

The relative darkness or lightness of shadows is influenced by the relative lightness of the sunlit surfaces on which they occur. The lightest shadows occur on the lightest sunlit surface, the darkest shadows on the darkest sunlit surface, and the medium shadows on the medium sunlit surface.

The shadow-analysis cube below explains the relationships between the nine light conditions on the six surfaces. If we take 1 as the lightest sunlit surface, and 9 as the darkest shadow, the relative order of the nine light conditions from light to dark is as follows:

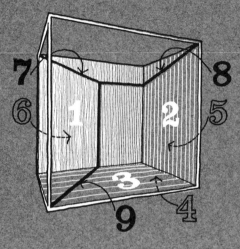

1. lightest sunlit surface
2. medium sunlit surface
3. darkest sunlit surface

4. lightest shade surface
5. medium shade surface
6. darkest shade surface

7. lightest shadow
8. medium shadow
9. darkest shadow

Notice that the sums of the sunlit number and the shade number total 7 on each surface, and the difference between the sunlit number and the shadow number is always 6 on any surface. This kind of detailed analysis is necessary in tone drawings, where the distinction between planes of various orientations to light must be made by a difference in tone alone, without the benefit of a separating line.

SHADE/SHADOW SYSTEMS

Complex shadow patterns may be thought of as assemblages of the simplest kinds of shade/shadow systems, and one of the most useful abilities is to be able to simplify the shadow-casting situation by breaking down complex compositions into their constituent parts.

It is critical to understand that (1) all shadow-casting relationships in a rectangular environment are represented in the shadow analysis cube, (2) every casting edge in the environment is oriented exactly like one of the struts of the cube, and (3) every shadow-catching plane is oriented exactly like one of the shadow-catching planes of the cube.

PROJECTED SYSTEMS

The first system to be understood is a projected system, as if a rectangular object had been pushed up through a plane. Notice that the system is initiated the instant the rectangular solid breaks through the base plane; it immediately has the same characteristics as the taller blocks. The casting edge in a projected system is made up of two lines parallel to the base plane and two lines perpendicular to it, casting two ∥ and two ⊥ shadows. The two ∥ shadows are parallel to and the same length as the lines that cast them. The two ⊥ shadows that initiate the system may vary wildly in angle and length, but they are always the same length and parallel to one another.

INDENTED SYSTEMS

The opposite kind of shade/shadow system involves a rectangular void pushed into a plane. Such a system has the same number of sun and shade surfaces as the previous projected system, but here they occur in a reversed configuration.

Notice that indented systems only have two casting edges (both parallel) because the other edges that separate the sunlit vertical sides from the shaded vertical sides are *inside* corners and cannot cast shadows. And while there are only two casting edges, the shadow pattern again has two ⊥ and two ∥ shadows because the casting relationship of each ⊥ shadow changes to a ∥ shadow on the bottom of the indentation. In indented systems the ∥ shadows are always parallel to the lines that cast them.

STEP SYSTEMS

The third kind of shade/shadow system is different from either the projected or indented systems in that the shadows fall across a series of alternating planes. This causes the shadow-casting relationships to alternate from perpendicular to parallel. This alternation occurs because the planes on which the shadows are falling are perpendicular to one another, so that the relationship of the casting edge to the planes alternates.

In all shade/shadow systems it is important to see clearly the shadows of corners. Always lengthen shadows if you can reveal the shadow of another corner, and never draw the coincidence where the shadow of a corner falls in a corner or on an edge.

Shade/shadow systems are not something *over there* that we look *at*. We rather *occupy* shade/shadow systems, like we inhabit any other part of the environment surrounding us. The interiors of buildings, in their simplest form, are indented shade/shadow systems, and when we are inside the building we are inside the shade/shadow systems as well.

INDIRECT LIGHT

A cloudy day or the interiors of north-facing rooms completely exclude direct sunlight. Without shadows, the representation of the spaces depends entirely on the consistent rendering of the various differently lighted surfaces of the environment. This rendering is based on an analysis or set of assumptions about the sources of light.

Taking a suspended cube as a referent, there are six possible variations in the intensity of indirect light. The first, or brightest, intensity occurs on the side of the cube facing the main source of indirect light, usually a window. The sixth, or darkest, condition occurs on the surface turned 180° away from the main source of indirect light.

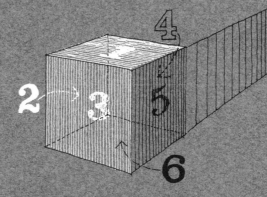

The other four surfaces of the cube (top, bottom, and sides) are lateral to the main source of indirect light and are the middle tones. Of these lateral surfaces the top is generally lighter because sunlight is diffused by the earth's atmosphere and may be thought of as "falling" in such a way that it lights the tops of objects much more brightly than their bottoms. The two remaining sides are illuminated third and fourth brightest depending on the plan angle of the entering light.

If the principle source of light is an overhead skylight, the top surfaces will be brightest and the bottom surfaces (ceilings) darkest, with the sides being the laterally lighted middle tones. A similar analysis of indirect light must be made in rendering the shade/shadow realm beyond the reaches of incoming sunlight or on the various surfaces of a ceiling.

When differentiating between surfaces in indirect light, it is important to make the preceding assumptions and then stick with them consistently for all surfaces. By consistent, I mean that all similarly oriented should have the same relative lightness or darkness. All the bottoms should be the same and darker than all the tops. All right sides should be the same and darker than all the left sides, etc. This consistency will do more than anything else to differentiate surfaces lighted by indirect or diffused light.

INTERIORS

Since architectural interiors are often lighted by indirect light, this is perhaps the best place to say a little about the correct tonal rendering of interiors.

Most drawings of interiors include at least a peek of the outdoors and many emphasize the spatial connection or ambiguity between interior and exterior. The most important characteristic of an interior perspective that includes a view of the exterior is that, in the daytime, the interior will be much darker than the exterior. This is true regardless of the number of windows in the room, their orientation, or how brightly the room is artificially illuminated. There is no way to illuminate the interior as brightly as the exterior. The experience will always be that of being within a very dark volume looking out on a much brighter exterior space. This contrast is most pronounced where a dark interior ceiling is silhouetted against the bright sky beyond it.

The color coding in this section is a reminder of the first principle of perspective: that the three sets of parallel planes in a perspective converge to three separate VLs.

- Horizontal planes and the horizontal eyelevel VL into which they vanish are colored red.

- Near-vanishing vertical planes and the near-vertical VL into which they vanish are colored green.

- Far-vanishing vertical planes and the far-vertical VL into which they vanish are colored blue.

This understanding is necessary when finding VPs for sets of "perpendicular" lines.

Tonal Interest:
Shadow-Casting in Direct Perspectives

Tonal interest is the most powerful of the interest categories, the last to be squinted out, and the one that can be seen from the greatest distance. Tonal interest depends on the full range of grays, from pure white to solid black, over broad areas of the drawing. The main source of tonal interest is light, shade, and shadow. Like spatial interest and textural interest, light, shade, and shadows are integral parts of any design.

Shadow-casting is traditionally taught on plans, sections, and elevations from a fixed sun angle. It is much more useful to learn shadow-casting in three dimensions and to experience the freedom of placing the sun where you want and studying and choosing the most characteristic or dramatic shadow patterns.

Learning shadow-casting in perspective means that you will be using the same perspective structure used in drawing the perspective. While there are computer programs that, after you build a computer model of an environment, cast the shadows for you, you still need to learn to cast shadows in the precomputer conceptual drawings you make for yourself.

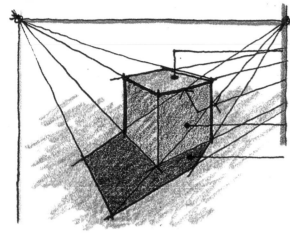

NOMENCLATURE

Sun: a surface lit directly by the sun

Casting edge: any outside corner that separates sun and shade

Shade: a surface turned away from the sun

Shadow: a surface turned toward the sun except that an intervening mass blocks the sun's rays and casts a shadow; the casting edge of an object casts the boundary of the shadow

In rectangular environments there are only two possible relationships between a casting edge and the surface on which the shadow will fall: ⊥ as in lines AB and DE, or ‖ as in lines BC and CD.

⊥ *Shadows* (ABs and DsE)
- vary dramatically in angle and length
- always begin and end shade/shadow systems
- converge to a separate VP on the VL for the plane in which they lie
- always cut across any rectangular environment at an angle

‖ *Shadows* (BsCs and CsDs.)
- are always ‖ to, and the same length as, the line that casts them
- are never connected to the line that casts them
- converge to one of the regular VPs of the perspective framework
- are always ‖ to the edges and joints of the environment

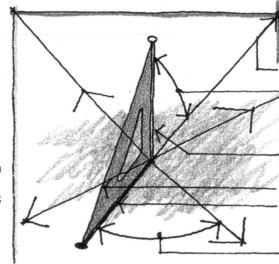

THE SUN'S RAY TRIANGLE

Flagpole VP

Vertical angle of the sun: measured in the vertical plane rising out of the flagpole shadow

Flagpole: a vertical casting edge

Sun's Ray: the hypotenuse

Flagpole shadow: the ⊥ shadow cast on a horizontal surface by a vertical line

Horizontal angle of the sun: measured on the earth's surface as an azimuth related to the compass points

Sun in front of the viewer
- VP for sun's rays is above eyelevel
- most vertical surfaces are in shade with ground shadows in the foreground
- usually best for interior perspectives

Sun behind the viewer
- VP for sun's rays is below eyelevel
- most vertical surfaces are in sun and shadow, with most ground shadows behind the building
- usually good for exterior perspectives

SHADE/SHADOW SYSTEMS

Most complicated shadow patterns are made up of combinations of three simple shade/shadow systems:

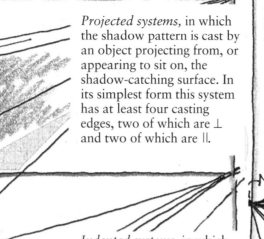

Projected systems, in which the shadow pattern is cast by an object projecting from, or appearing to sit on, the shadow-catching surface. In its simplest form this system has at least four casting edges, two of which are ⊥ and two of which are ‖.

Indented systems, in which the shadow pattern occurs in a recess or indentation in a surface, with the edges of the indentation casting a shadow pattern within the indentation. This system has only two casting edges, each of which casts a shadow that is ⊥ as it angles down the side-wall of the indentation and changes to a ‖ shadow when it hits the bottom.

Step systems, which are the most complex, beginning with ⊥ shadows at each end and alternating relationships from ⊥ to ‖ each time the shadow changes planes.

SHADOW-ANALYSIS CUBE

This cube is made up of three mutually perpendicular planes and three mutually perpendicular struts. The shadow patterns it catches when turned toward the sun represent all the shadow-casting relationships possible in rectangular environments. There are three ⊥ and six ‖ shadow-casting relationships. At any one time, except at coincidence, the sun casts a shadow pattern consisting of three ⊥ shadows and two (of the six possible) ‖ shadows.

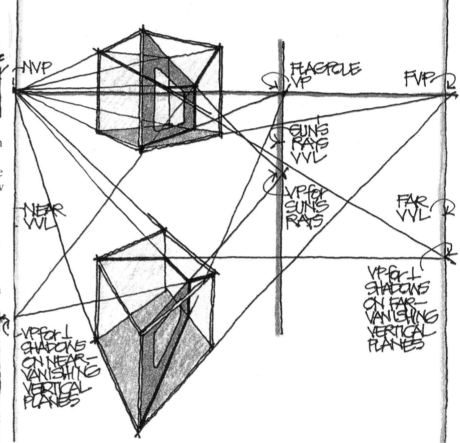

This perspective framework shows the location of all the VPs necessary to cast the shadows in a rectangular environment. As the designer/delineator, you are free to place the sun where it will cast the most characteristic or dramatic shadows, and the best way to do that is to directly choose the angles of two of the three ⊥ shadows. The third ⊥ angle and the VP for the sun's rays are resultants of those first two choices.

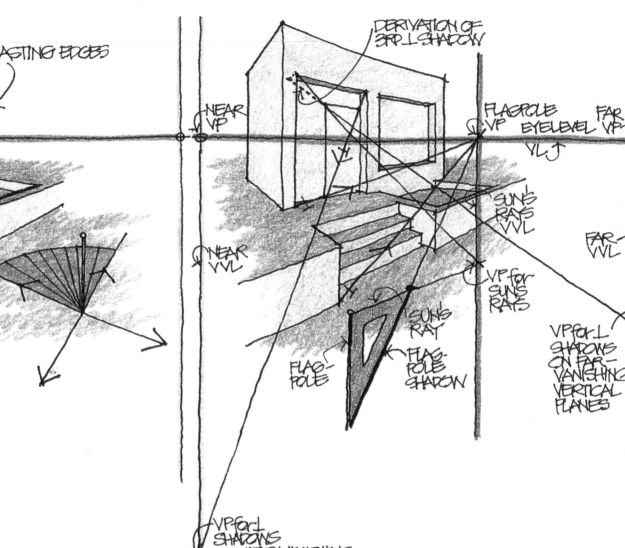

SHADOW-CASTING ON EXTERIOR PERSPECTIVES

1. Choose a general sun direction by deciding which quadrant the sun is in.

2. Make a sun/shade analysis that determines which surfaces are directly facing the sun and which surfaces are turned away from the sun or in shade. The surfaces identified as being in shade should be toned in a light gray because these surfaces will never have sun or shadow on them.

3. Identify the casting edges, which are all the outside corners (including hidden ones) that separate sunlit surfaces from those in shade.

4. Choose the specific sun angle by choosing the angles of two of the three ⊥ shadows.

5. Derive the third ⊥ shadow and establish the VPs for the three ⊥ shadows (on the VLs for the planes in which the shadows lie) as well as the VP for sun's rays (on the vertical vanishing line, or VVL, for the vertical planes of the sun's rays—which is always a vertical line through the flagpole VP). The third ⊥ shadow can often be derived directly in one of the indented shade/shadow systems (as in the doorway recess in the perspective above) or you can draw a shadow-analysis cube in the foreground to verify the derivation. The shadow-analysis cube must be accurate or the shadow angles won't agree.

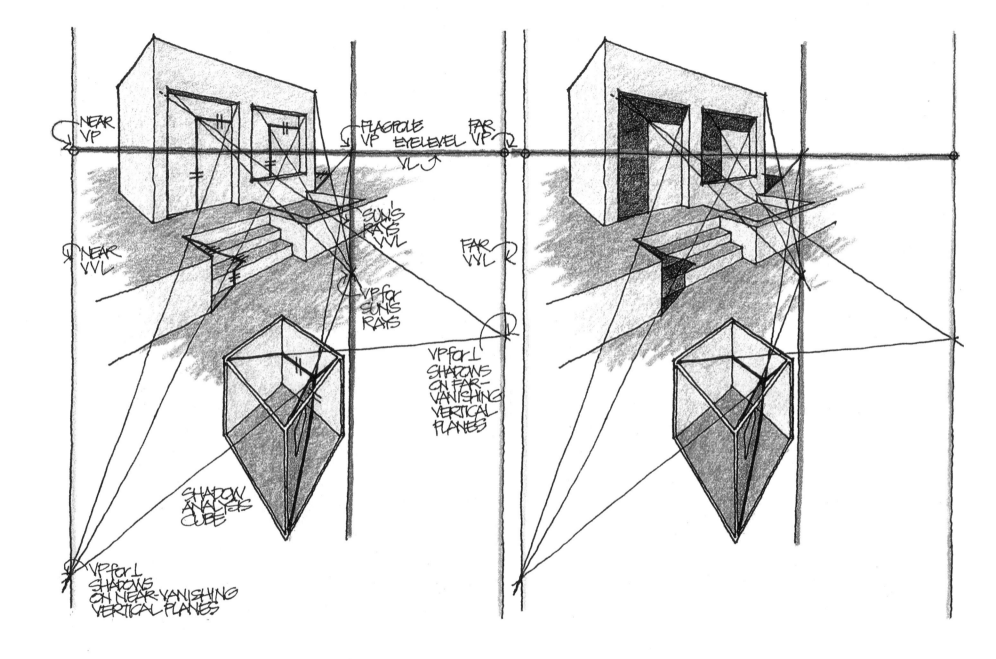

6. Extend all the ⊥ shadows and resolve the shade/shadow systems they initiate with the connecting ∥ shadows.

7. The last step is to render the shadows a darker gray and make sure you understand the shadow-casting perspective framework. After a few times through the procedure you will see that the resulting shadow pattern can easily be changed and possibly improved by slight changes in the locations of various VPs.

The interesting thing about shadow-casting is that shadow patterns look right when they are correct because we have been reading them all our lives.

SHADOW-CASTING ON
INTERIOR PERSPECTIVES

1. Choose a general sun direction by deciding which quadrant the sun is in. Usually it is best to place the sun in front of the viewer so that light and shadow enter the space.

2. Make a sun/shade analysis that determines which surfaces are directly facing the sun, or in sun, and which surfaces are turned away from the sun, or in shade. Surfaces identified as being in shade should be toned light gray because they can have neither sun nor shadows. It is good to tone these shade surfaces right away so the perspective begins to read.

3. Identify the casting edges, which are all the outside corners (including hidden ones) that separate sunlit surfaces from those in shade.

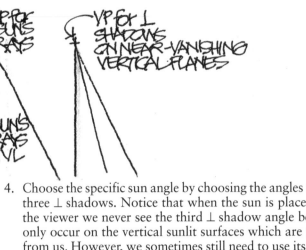

4. Choose the specific sun angle by choosing the angles of two of the three ⊥ shadows. Notice that when the sun is placed in front of the viewer we never see the third ⊥ shadow angle because it can only occur on the vertical sunlit surfaces which are turned away from us. However, we sometimes still need to use its angle, as we will soon see.

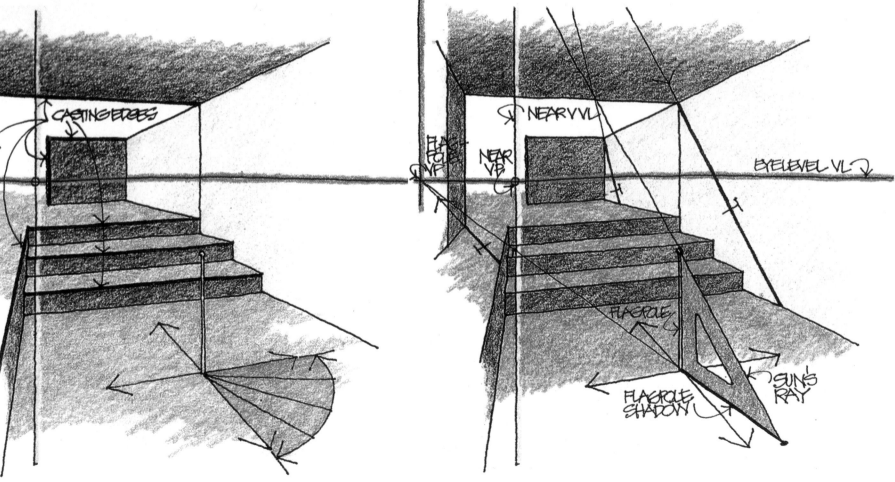

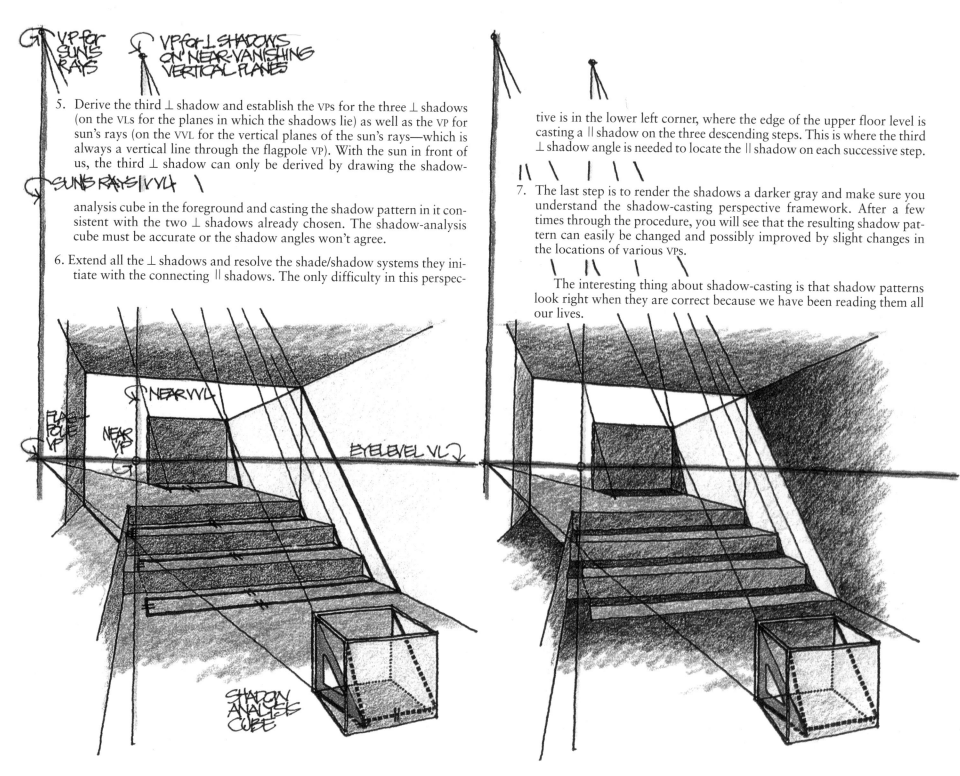

5. Derive the third ⊥ shadow and establish the VPs for the three ⊥ shadows (on the VLs for the planes in which the shadows lie) as well as the VP for sun's rays (on the VVL for the vertical planes of the sun's rays—which is always a vertical line through the flagpole VP). With the sun in front of us, the third ⊥ shadow can only be derived by drawing the shadow-analysis cube in the foreground and casting the shadow pattern in it consistent with the two ⊥ shadows already chosen. The shadow-analysis cube must be accurate or the shadow angles won't agree.

6. Extend all the ⊥ shadows and resolve the shade/shadow systems they initiate with the connecting ‖ shadows. The only difficulty in this perspec-

tive is in the lower left corner, where the edge of the upper floor level is casting a ‖ shadow on the three descending steps. This is where the third ⊥ shadow angle is needed to locate the ‖ shadow on each successive step.

7. The last step is to render the shadows a darker gray and make sure you understand the shadow-casting perspective framework. After a few times through the procedure, you will see that the resulting shadow pattern can easily be changed and possibly improved by slight changes in the locations of various VPs.

The interesting thing about shadow-casting is that shadow patterns look right when they are correct because we have been reading them all our lives.

NIGHT PERSPECTIVES

Many environments we design are used at least as much under artificial illumination as they are in sunlight, yet we seldom study the experience of nighttime illumination.

Today's technology makes the representation of artificial nighttime illumination quite easy. You can quickly and inexpensively get any perspective sketch photocopied onto a dark paper. (You will need to supply the paper, since photocopiers seldom stock dark papers.) Or, as in the examples above, you can get an underexposed blackline Diazo print as an optional base for beginning a night perspective. You will have to persuade the blueprinter that you really want a print run *very* fast, and bring him an example if possible, because the typical blackline print is run slowly enough to burn all the photosensitive chemical coating off the white paper.

Once you get the dark base copy or print, you can simply "turn on the lights," by using light Prismacolor™ pencils to tone the illuminated interior surfaces and washing light out onto lateral surfaces. It is better not to draw light fixtures or light rays—simply render the surfaces they illuminate. This can be seen in the perspective above with its illuminated interior ceilings and walls and the light washing out onto lateral surfaces like the sidewall, roofs, and soffits. Light is also rendered washing out onto steps from hidden sources.

It is usually best to make the rendering as if it were late dusk, not completely dark, so that the buildings stand out slightly against a darker sky. It also helps to assume a little directional moonlight, so that the vertical walls are slightly lighter or darker, depending on their orientation.

Interior night perspectives are just the reverse of daytime interiors. Instead of the interior being relatively dark compared to the bright exterior seen through windows and doors, the exterior will be much darker than the interior. As in exterior night perspective it is better to assume it is late dusk, so that exterior walls of the building can be distinguished against the dark sky. The interior surfaces would be rendered as to their relative illumination, with the ceiling usually being the darkest and the floor the lightest. Although artificial illumination will never light the interior surfaces perfectly evenly, it is better to draw them that way instead of trying to imagine the intricate patterns that various light sources would actually produce.

In the drawings above I used Prismacolor™ Indigo Blue for the skies and tried to grade it from lighter at the horizon to darker toward the zenith. In the interior I colored the artwork in what is supposed to be a gallery a uniform white and avoided any attempt to draw the images on the paintings. This keeps you from becoming a painter and, hopefully, keeps the emphasis on the architecture.

5 Building a Graphic Vocabulary

Perspectives provide a structure for measuring and lighting experiential space and for representing the most basic environmental interest categories. But simply having a structure in which to place the various kinds of interest isn't enough—you must also learn *how* to add interest to your drawings. This should be a process of discovering, acquiring, and developing different ways of drawing additional and textural interest, which can then serve as graphic "templates" that can be added to the drawing. Just as every draftsperson comes to own a set of plastic, cut-out templates for drawing circles, ellipses, and bathroom fixtures, so too do designers acquire a set of drawing templates that allow them to add figures, trees, furniture, cars, material indications, and landscape textures to a drawing.

While *template* serves as an easily understood introductory metaphor, *videotape* is really a much more accurate analogy for the learned, stored and retrievable ability to draw the objects and patterns with which this section of the book is concerned. The videotape analogy is also better because the ability involves mastering a controlled procedure occurring in a particular sequence. Design drawings are graphic records of a series of acts; if you try to discover what was done first, second, and third, and then practice duplicating the process, you will begin to build a memory bank of such videotapes.

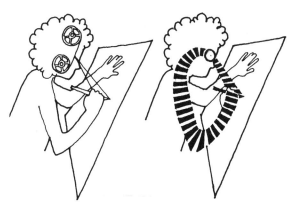

These videotapes include a feedback loop that links the eye and hand and allows a continual monitoring and control of the developing drawing. This kind of continuously adjusted control is called *cybernetics* and in drawing is dependent on the perceptual videotape of how to draw the tree, figure, chair, or leaf texture. Learning to draw is much more correctly thought of as the training of your perception rather than your hand, for only your trained perception has any hope of controlling your hand.

What appears to be incredible drawing ability is simply the replaying of perceptual videotapes prerecorded long ago and stored for convenient retrieval. The videotapes or templates need to be learned and indexed according to their amount of detail (and the time they take to draw) and to their distance from the viewer. For example, your tree-template collection should include a thirty-second tree, a five-minute tree, and a thirty-minute tree, as well as a tree that is 500 yards away from the viewer, a tree 30 yards from the viewer, and a tree 20 feet from the viewer. Additionally, you shouldn't have just one set of tree templates, but rather should eventually include various drawing techniques and several different kinds of trees.

The most valuable templates are time-flexible so that they become visually acceptable quickly but also will benefit from further attention if the time becomes available. I have tried to illustrate this incremental detailing in the following illustrations. It is important to remember that you need an extensive range of alternatives in drawing technique, in what to include or exclude, and in levels of detail. Being able to execute any of the alternatives is the primary source of freedom in drawing.

Speed in drawing is the most impressive manifestation of the freedom and confidence that comes from having a bulging memory bank of perceptual videotapes. The ability to make quick sketches comes from the confident selection from and management of this memory bank.

An experienced design-delineator can begin a representational design drawing within a very limited time frame and hold an incredible number of alternatives open for a significant length of time. And all this is done without gnashing of teeth or frenetic hand speed. To watch it is very intimidating for the beginning design student, who finds it hard to believe that she or he is really only witnessing the synchronized meshing of a network of decisions involving the selection, coordination, and application of perhaps only a few prerecorded perceptual videotapes. Each individual prerecorded videotape in this very small set may have, however, a nearly infinite variety in its specific conformation and in its level of detail. If they are all time-flexible templates, then most of the drawing time can be spent studying the coordination of their placement in the drawing, while detail is added in whatever time remains.

To illustrate how this disciplined freedom works in practice, let's say that I am making a very early conceptual sketch of a building. I decide that the building needs a tree in front of it. The decision to draw the tree is initially no more than that—*tree here*. Decisions about what kind of tree it is, whether it is placed in a raised planter or grows out of paving with the help of a grating, whether or not there is a figure group under the tree, how much of the tree is drawn, and whether or not it casts a shadow can be made later. The tree's importance in the overall drawing and its appropriate level of detail should be continually reevaluated as the drawing develops, and this can be done with cool confidence *if* you have the template collection with which to draw all those alternatives. If you don't have the templates, the whole situation deteriorates into, "Oh wow, how will I ever draw a decent tree right out there in front of the building? It's got to have one but I'll screw up the whole drawing sure as anything. I saw a neat, easy-to-draw tree the other day—let's see, I think the trunk started out like this—oops, Charlie, did you bring your electric eraser tonight?"

One of the best collections of perceptual templates is Tim White's *A Graphic Vocabulary for Architectural Presentation* (1972). *Vocabulary* is a particularly appropriate word. If we use language as an analogy for drawing, we can see perspective as the sentence structure and the figures, trees, furniture, cars, material indications, and landscape textures as the *words* of the language. And, as with language, your expression in drawing is absolutely limited by the extent of your graphic vocabulary.

Fortunately, environmental designers only need to master the drawing of a very limited slice of the visual world. I have been making architectural design drawings for a long time, but my memory bank of perceptual videotapes is embarrassingly meager compared to that of a cartoonist or commercial artist. If you ask me to draw an elephant or a helicopter I'd have to say, "I'm sorry, I don't have that tape."

Designers must develop a very critical, but forgiving, visual appraisal of their own designs and drawings. Through such a cold-eyed evaluation you will probably discover that there is an imbalance in your drawing skill—you probably draw some things better than other things. The continual balancing act required to make your drawings transparently consistent should become one of your endless tasks. Some delineators, even professional cartoonists, don't really draw *anything* with great skill, but they have learned to draw *everything* with a consistency in which nothing stands out as being poorly drawn. The development of a parity in everything you draw, especially objects of additional interest, will contribute more than anything else to the sought-for transparency of your design drawings.

I would suggest that until you have achieved an acceptable balance in your ability to draw the necessary contents and context for your designs, you collect well-drawn examples of figures, trees, furniture, and cars and trace them directly into your drawings whenever it is necessary to make slick, persuasive drawings. Meanwhile, however, you should strive to make your own template/tapes consistent. This cannot be accomplished by tracing; you should rather try to copy your file of collected entourage freehand. Remember that you need to cultivate the ability to draw them repeatedly, not just once, which means you need to develop a reliable, controlled process.

It may seem that making and using templates removes all the creativity from drawing, but creativity in design drawing does not lie in the continual invention of new ways of drawing. Your creativity should be in the design of the environment, not in its delineation. If your reason for making a design drawing is primarily to show off your creativity as a renderer you misunderstand and are misusing design drawing.

Textural Interest

Textural interest is tactile interest—the interest we find in touching various materials or surfaces. While this is the most intimate of the interest categories, demanding direct physical contact for its full experience, the anticipation of potential tactile interest is cued visually like all other interest categories. We remember what a brick floor or a teak tabletop feels like, and the sight of such surfaces prompts that memory.

Drawings can represent tactile interest by prompting our perception in much the same way as distant vision. Drawing techniques represent, with varying degrees of realism or abstraction, the various textures of the natural and built environment. The main source of textural interest is the collection of materials that make up the environment. The increased cost of handmade and hand-installed materials and the concurrent development of modern technology have drastically changed the number of available materials. There aren't nearly as many textures to enjoy or to draw in today's buildings as there once were.

This change can be seen in Ted Kautzky's drawings. Kautzky was a master of pencil tone drawing and his "broad stroke" technique was ideally suited to the architectural materials of his day (stone, cedar shakes, brick, shutters), which were all rich in textural interest. Near the end of his career, however, Kautzky was asked to draw modern buildings, but he found nothing to draw with his drawing technique. He drew everything *but* the building itself, for how can you render white stucco, steel, aluminum, Formica, or glass with a surface-rendering tool like a pencil? This is one reason for the change to line and line-and-tone drawings; our modern materials have very little textural interest and are better represented by edge drawing techniques.

Drawings above from *The Ted Kautzky Pencil Book* by Ted Kautzky.

MATERIALS

The materials of which any designed object or space is constructed are an integral part of the design. The choice of materials should be appropriate to the form and function of the environment, for materials contribute greatly to the sensory experience of any design.

Designers must represent materials realistically so that material choices are an early and continuing consideration in the design process. The inability to draw a particular material may mean that we seldom consider using it—simply because we can't adequately represent it to ourselves or our clients.

Tone or color. In drawing materials it is usually better to represent their texture and configuration and let their relative lightness or darkness be entirely dependent on light (sun, shade, or shadow) instead of trying to represent the material's integral tone or color.

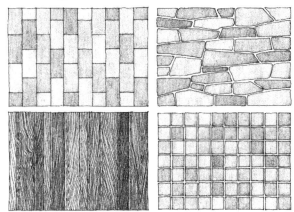

Unit materials. Forms or surfaces made up of individual pieces (masonry, paneling, shingles) should be drawn so that individual units are defined. Toning some of the units slightly darker or lighter achieves this.

Edge configuration. The best place to show a material's texture is at a corner or edge where it can be seen in profile. The joint indentation of a masonry wall, the projecting seam of a standing seam roof, or the overlapping profile of horizontal wood siding tell more about the texture of those materials than any amount of rendering on their surfaces.

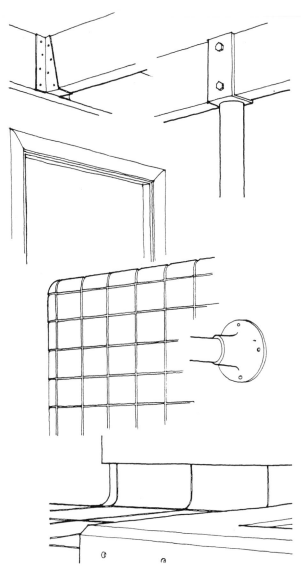

Installation details. Careful attention to a material's realistic application can also help its representation. The drawing of chamfered edges at the top of a concrete retaining wall, the mitering of a wood door frame, and the jointing of a terrazzo floor are examples of installation details that offer efficient clues to the identity of the materials being represented.

REFLECTIONS

While reflective surfaces have no texture of their own, they reflect all the textures and tonal values around them. Glass and water are the most common reflective materials and they are also the most misrepresented of materials. This misrepresentation is unfortunate, especially for glass, since it is one of modern architecture's favorite materials. To represent water or glass viewed from the outside as being either transparent or opaque is to seriously misunderstand their material nature.

Many other materials (stainless steel, aluminum, polished marble or terrazzo, and some plastics) are also reflective, but their reflectivity is limited and need only be hinted at in drawings. Glass viewed from the outside and water viewed from above reflect their surroundings because they are smooth surface membranes separating a relatively dark interior (or underwater) volume from a relatively bright exterior space.

Reflections in glass or water, or on any reflective surface, are easily drawn with the understanding of one simple analogy. You are probably familiar with sterile or highly controlled environments that demand that scientists stand behind a vision panel and insert their hands into rubber gloves that are hermetically sealed to the vision panel. When drawing reflections, just imagine that you are the scientist: reach from behind the glass (or from beneath the water, or from within any reflective surface), grab everything that is out there (or up there), and pull it back through, under, or inside the reflective surface. It is as if you have removed your hands from the gloves by pulling them *inside* the reflective surface, and they now extend, wrong side out, inside the reflective surface.

This is the way to draw the world that is reflected in any reflective surface—as if it existed the same distance *inside* the reflective surface as it actually exists outside. The reflection always pulls the reflected world through the glass *perpendicularly* at 90° to the reflective surface, and it always foreshortens in perspective as if it actually existed behind the reflective surface.

GLASS

The perception of a vertical glass wall, window, or door is always a variable combination of reflectivity and transparency, with the reflections usually being dominant. There are four variables that affect this mixture of reflectivity and transparency.

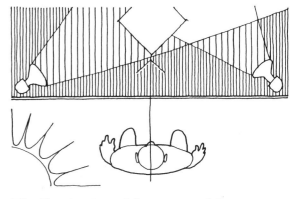

The illumination of the interior. If the interior is brightly illuminated by direct sunlight shining through the glass or even by extremely bright artificial lighting, the reflectivity will be decreased and the transparency increased.

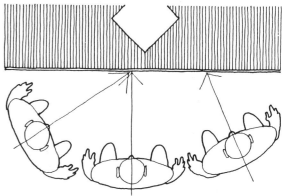

The angle of the viewer to the glass. The glass will be most transparent when viewed perpendicularly. As the viewer's angle to the glass becomes more acute, the glass will become more reflective.

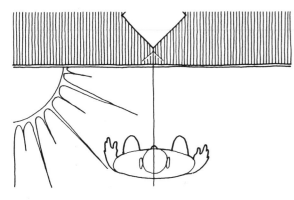

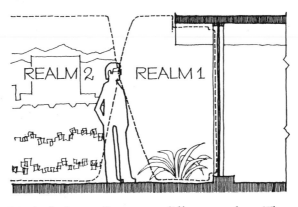

The illumination of the exterior. If the world reflected in the glass is brightly illuminated by direct sunlight and exhibits the full tonal range, its reflection will be stronger and the glass's transparency will be weakened.

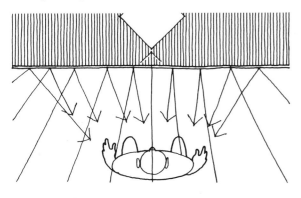

The inherent reflectivity of the particular glass. Artificially darkened and mirrored glass are much more reflective than ordinary clear glass.

Since glass is normally vertically oriented, it is best represented by rendering all the reflections in vertical tones-of-lines—even in a line-and-tone drawing. In pencil tone drawings the reflections should all be stroked vertically to represent the orientation of the reflective surface. Whatever is seen through the glass should be drawn in first, and then the reflections rendered directly on top of them.

Vertical glass reflects two different realms. The first realm is that between the viewer and the glass and includes everything that appears in front of the glass in perspective. The reflection of this realm should have the same tonal values (darks and lights) *as it actually has in the drawing.* The second realm is everything that lies behind the viewer and does not appear in the perspective *except* as reflections in the glass. This second realm is best delineated with receding, progressively lighter layers of space—distant buildings, trees, mountains—rendered as vertical tones-of-lines. Above the reflections of this second realm, beginning a little above eye-level, the sky behind the viewer will be reflected, and this sky reflection will normally be the brightest of the reflections in the glass. In black-and-white drawings this sky reflection should be left white; in colored drawings it should be tinted a light blue.

DRAWING REFLECTIONS IN GLASS

- Pull everything in front of the glass perpendicularly through the glass and toward the VP.
- Draw these reflections as if they were the same distance (foreshortened) behind the glass as they actually are in front of the glass.
- Indicate all reflections on the glass with vertical tones-of-lines since the reflecting glass surface is vertical.
- Tone reflections of objects between the viewer and the glass the same relative darkness or lightness as they are in the drawing.
- Tone reflections of everything behind the viewer as progressively lighter layers of receding space.

WATER

Since water is normally a horizontal surface, water reflections are best delineated by horizontal lines. I recommend rendering water reflections as horizontal tones-of-lines in all the drawing techniques except tone, where the stroking direction of the reflected tones should still be horizontal.

The horizontality of water as a reflective surface eliminates many of the complications encountered in drawing reflections in glass. In normal perspectives there is no vertical convergence to a VP and therefore no foreshortening of the reflections, allowing the reflections to be measured directly. There is also no problem with variable reflectivity/transparency, since the normal viewer's angle to the surface of the water is so acute that the surface remains steadfastly reflective. Nor are there two realms reflected in water. The relationship of the viewer to any reflective water surface is such that nothing *behind* the viewer will ever be reflected. Only the portion of the world seen directly in the perspective is reflected in the water.

There is, however, one slight complication with reflections in water that is not often encountered with glass. Some objects reflected in the water that do not actually touch the surface of the water—like buildings or trees slightly inland from the water's edge. For these you must imagine or mechanically extend the plane of the water's surface to a point directly below the object, and then measure the reflection downward from that point, *not from where the object hits the ground.* Imagine that you simply took the land away, leaving the tree or building suspended in mid-air and then ran the water level back under it. If you measure the reflections in this way they will be correct. The reflecting relationship is between the object and the plane of the reflecting water surface. The land has nothing to do with it.

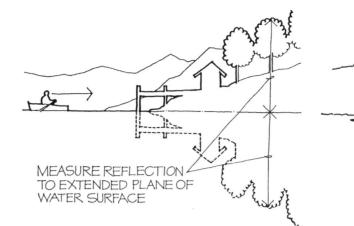

MEASURE REFLECTION TO EXTENDED PLANE OF WATER SURFACE

DRAWING REFLECTIONS IN WATER

- Pull everything above the surface of the water down through the water in a vertical direction.
- Draw these reflections as if they were the same distance below the water as they actually are above the water.
- Indicate all reflections on the water with transverse horizontal tones-of-lines since the reflecting water surface is horizontal.
- Tone reflections the same relative darkness or lightness as they are in the drawing.

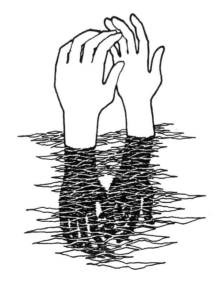

Reflections are the most characteristic and exciting contributions of glass and water as exterior materials in the environment. The reflections in glass double the apparent wall thickness by reflecting the reveal of the opening. Both glass and water can reflect a beautiful natural environment or a respected built environment in a way no other materials can, and your designs and the drawings with which you represent them should reflect this understanding.

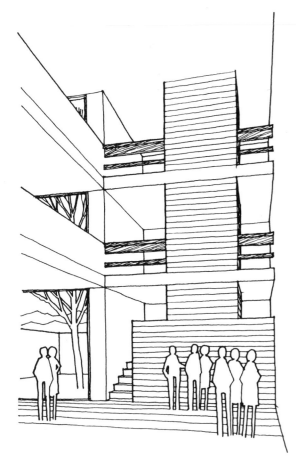

PLACING TEXTURES TO DEEPEN THE SPACE

The determinants that affect the placement of textures in an environment are somewhat different from those that affect texture placement in a drawing. In an environment the most critical determinants are functional. Imperviousness to wear, ease of cleaning, comfort or pleasure in physical contact, acoustic absorption and reflectance, and nonslip floor surfaces are examples of some of these functional determinants. In a drawing there is really only one determinant—how the textures help the viewer to perceive the space—and that means they should always be placed on the farthest space-bounding surfaces.

The placement of textures on the farthest space-bounding surfaces will deepen the drawing in two ways:

1. The gradation of the texture from coarse to fine on the receding surfaces makes us perceive them as existing in three dimensions.
2. The disappearance and reappearance of background surface textures behind untextured foreground objects makes us perceive a continuous, underlying background space.

The difference the placement of textures can make in a drawing can be demonstrated in a two-dimensional plan. Texturing the table and chairs in a dining room accomplishes nothing in helping a viewer perceive the drawing as having depth, but if texture is applied to the floor so that the pattern disappears and reappears beneath the furniture, we perceive a continuous background surface *under* the table and chairs, which produces an illusion of depth.

Additional Interest

Additional interest consists of the additions we, and nature, make to the built environment. This includes trees, plants, other human beings, and all our human artifacts—furnishings, signs, automobiles, etc.

Much of this interest category is frankly ornamental, and past generations of environmental designers unblushingly designed it into their buildings as integral ornament. Early in this century, however, architects condemned all ornament as decadent and superficial, and lack of ornament became one of modern architecture's hallmarks. We are only recently beginning to ornament our buildings once again. The morality and purity we believed we gained by stripping all the ornament from the built environment proved to be as superficial as the decorations we condemned, for we continued to bring this kind of interest back into our environments in the form of scheffleras, Bentwood rockers, and Marimekko prints.

The collection of things that provide additional interest can also enrich the perception of any environment or drawing in the following three ways, each of which should be considered separately.

Specifying the scale. Because the objects that provide additional interest have an established relationship to, and even include, the human figure, they are our primary source of mensurate scale. The scale of the designed environment is one of the designer's traditional means of expression. A space can be designed to look larger or smaller than its actual dimensions and a deliberate ambiguity in the scale of an environment can make the experience of it more interesting. Regardless of the designer's intentions, the actual scale is always specified by the items of additional interest, especially the human figure.

Indicating the use. Items of additional interest also indicate the use of the space. The equipment, furnishings, signs, and the activity of the people in the space should communicate the space's function. A shopping center should have signs for the various stores and lots of shoppers carrying packages and looking and pointing at window displays.

MISUSE OF ADDITIONAL ELEMENTS OF INTEREST

In addition to all the good things that elements of additional interest can add to a drawing, they can also detract from the drawing in the following ways.

ings at left, which show how the same number of elements of additional interest can be placed in the same drawing of an environment, one in a way that covers the space-defining corners and makes the space difficult to understand, and the other in a way that lets all the space-defining corners show and allows the space to be clearly perceived. Planar intersections of great lengths can be covered as long as they aren't obscured near the corners where the enclosure is resolved. We sort of trust them to stay straight behind sofas and bushes if we can see their resolution at either end.

Demonstrating the space. Perhaps the most important contribution items of additional interest make is to demonstrate the space of the perspective. By simply occupying upper and lower levels or distant courtyards, or by disappearing behind other elements in the environment, they demonstrate that certain spaces exist and have a particular height, depth, or configuration. This demonstration of space is highly important and must be carefully integrated with the spatial interest of a drawing, which I will return to at the end of this section.

Obscuring the space. Elements of additional interest must be added to a drawing very carefully so that they promote the perception of the space rather than inhibiting it. Because our understanding of the space depends on the visibility of the space-bounding surfaces (which in turn depends on the visibility of the surfaces' edges or intersections), figures, trees, furniture, and automobiles should never be placed so that they completely hide planar intersections at corners. This can be demonstrated in the draw-

Disrupting the transparency. Earlier I mentioned that one of the designer's goals is to create drawings that are completely transparent—where the viewer looks *through* the drawing to the environment it represents. This is especially critical for items of additional interest. Because human figures, trees, plants, furniture, and automobiles are so familiar to us and normally command so much of our attention and compulsive discrimination, they can very easily dominate a drawing by preempting the design emphasis, or by making the drawing self-conscious.

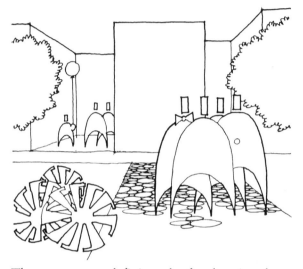

As an example of both pitfalls, let me draw a few figures the way students did when I was an undergraduate. The figures are hardly recognizable to first-time viewers because they are both a redesign and an oh-so-self-conscious way of drawing the human figure.

There were very definite rules for drawing these figures. The heads were always rectangular and disconnected from the body. Some figures were distinguished by a small circle in the center of the body torso, which could be interpreted, I suppose, as either a Dagwood button or a navel. They were unisex except that some had bow ties, and further detail could be added in the form of a circular hand holding a balloon or leading a dog (which I never mastered). We drew great groups of these androids standing around our drawings, and we were proud that we had mastered the reigning graphic cliché. Later I discovered such figures never failed to elicit comments from clients, which is always a sure sign that they are preempting the design and making the drawings self-consciously opaque.

Preempting the design emphasis is easily done by attempting to *design* all, or any, of the elements of additional interest. Because furniture and automobiles, for instance, are already designed, and because we are all familiar with the common designs, styles, and models, any attempt to design an original automobile or piece of furniture will be immediately apparent and can easily preempt the design emphasis of the drawing.

Making the drawing self-conscious is similarly accomplished by drawing the elements of additional interest in a way that demands too much attention. Unfortunately, some of the first "templates" or "perceptual videotapes" acquired by beginning designers are of this variety. They are so-o-o-o clever and cute and their placement at center stage in the drawing makes it very clear that the delineator is more proud of her or his ability to draw a particular tree, automobile, or figure than to design the environment.

RETAINING TRANSPARENCY

There are two approaches to drawing elements of additional interest in such a way that they specify the scale, indicate the use, and demonstrate the space but still remain transparent and never preempt the design or make the drawing opaque.

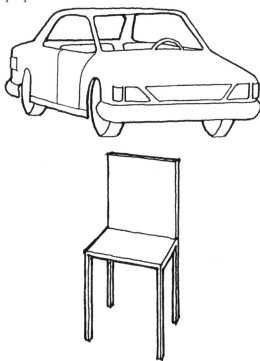

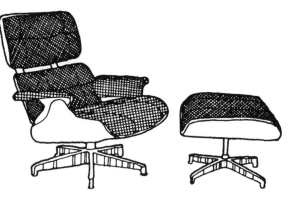

Plato's chair. The first approach is to draw elements of additional interest that are so simple that they make no design statement whatever. With this approach each chair becomes Plato's chair, with the seat, back, and four legs necessary to all chairs but *nothing* else; nothing about this chair distinguishes it from the quintessential chair of chairs. In addition to keeping the elements of additional interest transparent, this approach is also the most efficient way to draw.

Eames's chair. The second approach is to choose particular well-known, well-designed elements and draw them with great accuracy and realism, like an Eames chair or a Volkswagen. This approach requires having a photograph or drawing of the item for reference and always takes a little more time (unless you can trace the items), but in the end it has the same effect. It takes the elements of additional interest out of the realm of self-conscious design or self-conscious drawing so that they do not compete for the viewer's attention.

Credibility. The second approach has another important advantage. If you include one or more well-known elements of additional interest in your representational drawings, they will help to establish the credibility of the drawings. This is particularly true if the selected elements are essential to the environment being represented. If you are designing a gymnasium, for instance, the very meticulous drawing of a side horse, a set of parallel bars, or a basketball goal and its braces will do more to establish the drawing's credibility as a representation of that environment than anything else. And strangely, perhaps, your credibility as a designer is always somehow related, for good or ill, to the credibility of your drawings.

If you are the designer of the gymnasium and your drawings indicate that you don't know what equipment is normally found in that environment or that you are so unfamiliar with it that you can't draw it accurately, what will the client assume about your ability to design the space?

FIGURES

Unlike the other elements of additional interest, human figures have a more basic purpose in design drawings. In addition to specifying the scale, indicating the use, and demonstrating the space, human figures remind designers that their clients are the people who will inhabit the spaces they design, and unless the space is designed to accept the human figure, it may deserve to be uninhabited.

When we stripped the ornamental detail from our buildings early in the last century, we also stripped much of the possibility for humans to physically relate to buildings. Older buildings have moldings, belt courses, chair rails, and all kinds of other elements that you can sit on, lean against, put your feet or elbows on, and generally become physically involved with. Many modern buildings, both in their material choice and their detailing, are, literally and perhaps intentionally, untouchable.

The inclusion of human figures in your design drawings, from the earliest sketches, will remind you that there should be places on which to sit, lean, rest your elbow or foot, or just to touch. If there aren't, all humans can do in the space is stand uncomfortably, which means you probably are designing a very inhuman place.

Most designers will never, and need never, become virtuoso delineators of the human figure. I am still not (and probably never will be) capable of drawing the slick, detailed figures some presentation drawings require without referring to or tracing figures drawn by delineators more skilled than I. Designers need to draw figures competently, but they should never be drawn better or in greater detail than the product or space being designed. Nor should the designer attempt to redesign the human figure; it is a reasonably workable design, or evolutionary

result, and if you redesign the figures in your design drawings, they may preempt the room, patio, or building you were asked to design. Designers are much wiser if they confine their efforts to learning to draw the human figure competently, place it carefully, and design *for* it, instead of trying to redesign it.

As with drawing furniture and automobiles, there are two approaches to figure drawing that give beginning designers much-needed flexibility.

TRACING FIGURES is the safest approach and it is comforting to be able simply to select appropriate figures from a photograph and trace them directly into a drawing. You may need to dismember and reassemble some of them to make them fit the context of your drawing, but if your perspective is taken at eyelevel, standing figures of any scale can simply be hung on that eyelevel.

There are several books that offer a variety of figures for tracing and you should begin a collection of figures that can be traced into your presentation drawings. Although this tracing of figures adds little to your ability to draw figures from scratch, it gives you much-needed experience in placing figures in perspective. Until your skill in drawing homemade figures is as good as your other drawing skills, it is only intelligent to trace well-drawn figures in your design drawings.

MAKING YOUR OWN FIGURES is the only other way of drawing figures and should be pursued concurrently. While you are collecting a "morgue" of well-drawn figures for tracing, you should also be building a similar collection of the prerecorded perceptual "videotapes" that will allow you to draw figures of your own. The building of this second collection is much slower but much more worthwhile because of the freedom it will eventually give you.

The best way I have found to draw homemade figures is to begin with crude design doodles and refine them as you refine the design. This means that you never work continuously on a figure until it is finished. Instead, each drawing of a figure or group of figures is a progression of tracing paper overlays that are refined as the design drawing is refined.

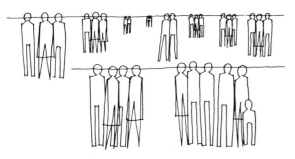

A standing figure in an eyelevel perspective is best begun by drawing a balloon head hung on the eyelevel line and a rectangular body split into two legs by a deep crotch notch. Male and female figures can be distinguished by the shape of the ends of the legs—rectangular for male, resulting from squared-off pant cuffs, and triangular for women, resulting from pointed shoes. With the modest addition of a straight shift dress to the women, such crude figures can sufficiently represent human beings in rough sketches.

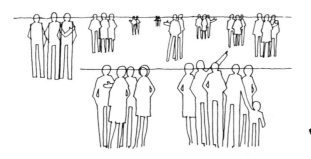

The next level of detail adds indications of arms, either as asymmetrical elbow bulges or extended in talking or pointing gestures. Figures should always be collected into groups and the addition of a gesturing arm on one figure and of chins and slight head inclinations can indicate who is talking and who is listening. Such portrayals of typical social relationships between individual figures can help greatly in indicating the use of a space.

Next come a few indications of clothing details, such as collars, necklines, cuffs, and waistlines, which begin to make the male/female distinctions more sophisticated, as well as some differences in head outlines, which begin to indicate the differences in male and female coiffures.

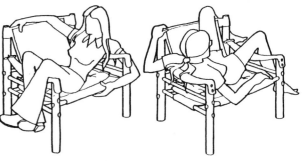

It is also extremely important to physically relate figures to their environment by showing them touching, holding, and sitting or leaning against their environment in various postures. This requires another level of refinement that includes the hands, knee/seat bends, and elbows locked over the backs of seats. Except when inhibited by very formal contexts, humans generally get very physically involved with their environment. We sit all over a chair, throw our legs over the arms and our arms over the back, put our elbows on tables, hang our heels on chair rungs, etc. Figures sitting or standing in primly symmetrical postures are not only more difficult to draw, but also never look like they belong in the environment. I have found that figures drawn in a variety of postures, all in the most direct physical contact with their environment, are much easier to draw and look as though they belong there.

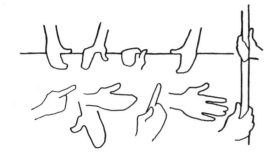

At this level it is best to draw the hands as mittens, indicating only the thumb, which distinguishes us from the rest of the animal kingdom. The thumb, in drawings as in reality, allows us to grasp handrails, chair backs, or door pulls and thus convincingly attaches us to our environment.

The knee/seat bend is necessary in drawing a seated figure and the curves of the kneecaps and the buttocks are extremely important in showing various seated leg postures. The elbow lock is a good way of relating a seated figure to a chair back or a standing figure to a bar-height surface or a guardrail. I think you'll find that if you learn to draw a grasping hand, kneecaps for a number of various seated postures, and various elbow-lock relationships, your figures will look convincing and related to their context even if some of their details are crudely drawn.

The relationship of figures to their context involves bending the torso and the arms and legs so that the figure occupies space or depth. This is a very important advance over the stick figure, which exists in a decal-flat plane facing the viewer and whose body and limbs are always seen in full-length, like one of the rivet-jointed cardboard skeletons we hang up at Halloween. In order to occupy space, one part of the limb or torso must be foreshortened so that it comes at the viewer in space while the other part of the arm, leg, or body is still seen full-length. The ability to draw figures that occupy space is a major step up the hierarchy of detail and makes any figure much more convincing.

Some more refined details of figure drawing may be worth a little more explanation. Because we perceive most about our fellow human beings by looking at their faces, the further detailing of a figure should begin with the head. I recommend adding the following details in the following order:

- chin and nose (to show where the person's attention is directed)
- hair outline (to specify sex and age)
- glasses (to suggest eyes and reinforce direction of attention)
- hair texture (to add textural interest to a figure)

I always recommend stopping short of drawing the eyes and mouth because they are very difficult to draw and they add facial expression, which is in the realm of the cartoonist. Cartoonists usually vary only the mouth, eyes and eyebrows to indicate the full range of human emotions. If you draw eyes and mouths you risk having your figures turn your drawing into a soap opera.

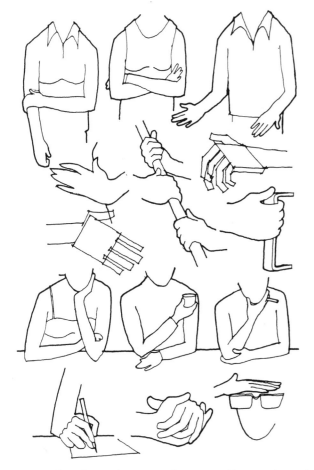

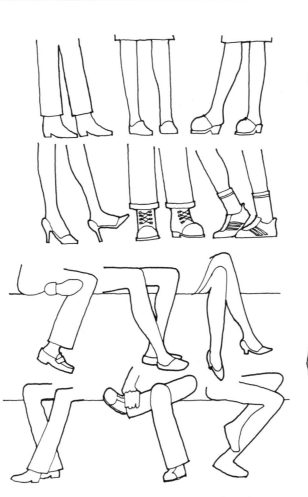

For hands and arms, the ascending order of detail I recommend is:

- mitten hand (to allow grasping of railings, handles, and edges)
- cuff or short sleeve (to suggest clothing)
- foreshortening of upper or lower arm (to make figure occupy space)
- separate fingers (to indicate close-up hands)
- muscle placement on bare arms—biceps attached to inside of upper arm.

Never draw the arms symmetrically.

For feet and legs, the progressive detailing is similar:

- feet (to show facing direction and give figure stability)
- pant cuff and shoe heel (to suggest attire)
- foreshortening of upper or lower leg (to make figure occupy space)
- shoe top, sole, or strap details (to indicate shoe style)
- muscle placement on bare legs—calf muscle attached to inside of leg.

Never draw the legs symmetrically.

Clothing. Certain standard articles of clothing are easier to draw than others and this simpler attire avoids your getting bogged down in the details of a fashion designer. Certain garments can also reinforce the sexual identity or age of a figure. In general, garments that overhang the waist eliminate the need for belts, and the shoulder straps of jumpers and vests are helpful in adding easily drawn detail. The basic garments shown above may not be the latest styles but they allow some variety of easily drawn attire without ever being mistaken for a fashion ad.

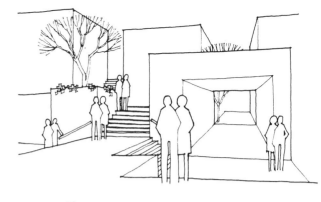

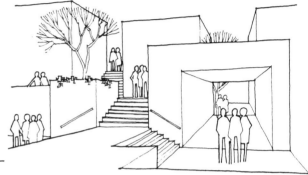

Props. Accessory elements further clarify age and sex distinctions and indicate occupations or functional activities. Canes, balloons, purses, packages, stethoscopes, and briefcases may be a little stereotypical but can be helpful in clarifying a human situation or indicating the use of a space.

Groups. Figures should be collected into groups of various sizes. People are gregarious and, except in the most hostile environment, will stand or sit in conversational groups. Solitary figures will seldom enhance a drawing. Unless you want the drawing to express the alienation of twentieth-century man or to look like a freshman mixer, you should always collect your figures into groups. Groups are easily accepted by the viewer, because they are obviously talking to one another, having come together or arranged to meet in the environment. The lurking about of lone figures, on the other hand, is suspect.

Placement. The placement of figures in a design drawing is extremely important and demands great care. In addition to conforming to the criteria for the placement of other elements of additional interest, figure placement has a few extra pitfalls and opportunities. Figures should be spaced rather evenly throughout the drawing, but always avoid regimentation in the spacing or the numbers of figures in the groups. They shouldn't be evenly spaced like trees in an orchard. There should be figures in the foreground, background, and middle ground, to either side, and on all levels of the space, generally avoiding dead center. Figures can also be placed to demonstrate spaces, particularly sunken spaces like conversation pits, which are almost impossible to show otherwise. The two perspectives above indicate how figures can thoughtlessly hide space-defining intersections (in the top drawing) or let them all be seen clearly (in the bottom drawing).

Overlaid refinement. To demonstrate the progressive levels of figure drawing, here is a group of figures taken about as far as I am capable through several overlaid stages of refinement. Each drawing represents a level of detail that might be appropriate for a particular represen-

tational drawing or for the amount of time available, but each stage requires the underlay studies to reach its level of refinement.

Humanizing elements. Making a space human requires more than just sprinkling a few figures around the environment. There are architectural elements, landscape elements, and pieces of furniture that have special significance for human beings because of familiar, intimate human use. Furniture will be covered separately in a later section, but I would like to demonstrate the potential for physical interaction with certain elements of the environment.

Landscape humanizing elements include fountains, benches, planters, seat-high walls, steps, and trees. To varying degrees these allow and invite human participation.

Architectural humanizing elements include doors, windows, and fireplaces. To varying degrees these include or accommodate the human figure (think of window seats, recessed doorways, or fireplaces with hearth seats).

Designing environments for the human figure and drawing human figures in the environment are inseparably related. They promote one another. Figures are much easier to draw in environments that have been designed for them, and the habitual inclusion of figures in design drawings will inevitably result in a more human design.

TREES AND GROWIES

Trees and "growies" (as they are called by my architecture students at the University of Arizona) constitute an important category of additional interest. Trees have a special relationship to humans because of the shade they give and the fruit they bear, and because our ancestors probably lived in them.

TREES

Trees embellish any drawing because they contribute to all the interest categories: spatial, tonal, textural, and additional. They even hold interest for the other senses in that you can hear a tree when it rustles in the wind and smell a tree when it blooms.

Trees can create a space as a leafy roof or articulate it as a row of columns. They contribute tonal interest by the pool of shadow they cast, and their leaf mass adds both tonal and textural interest. Their branch structure is highly figural, especially that of bare deciduous trees in winter.

Drawn trees can be abstracted into simple graphic conventions, which should be mastered first; but the realistic rendering of specific trees depends on knowing the characteristic branch structure, overall form, and leaf detail of each species. Trees are probably the most demanding single thing a designer needs to know how to draw.

The accompanying drawings begin with simple, abstract trees and progress to the specific trees in my limited vocabulary.

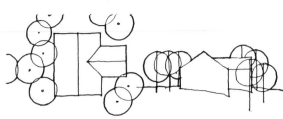

The simplest tree indications are open circles with stick trunks. These are sufficient for rough small-scale sketches.

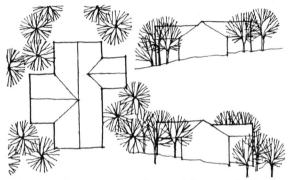

The simplest structured tree fills out the basic "lollipop" outline of the previous tree indication with a single-line branch structure growing from the initial stick trunk. This skeletal branch structure is usually leafless but may have various configurations, as demonstrated in the series of trees below.

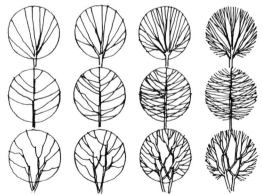

The branch structures all end at a circular or oval perimeter guideline, which is later erased, and the more graceful branches begin low on the trunk so that their length is maximized.

So far, the developing tree templates are flat, two-dimensional "decals" that do not yet demonstrate that they have depth.

Depth in the branch structure is accomplished with a double-line trunk and branches that communicate thickness. The trunk's double-line indication can be continued into the secondary branches.

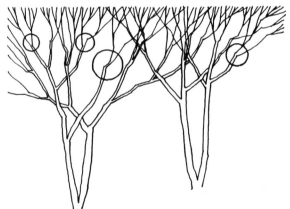

At some point the two lines that have been indicating the two sides of a trunk or branch must become single-line indications of minor, peripheral branches. This transition becomes almost imperceptible and maintains the delicacy of the outer branches while offering the same spatial capability the lower parts of the branch structure have.

The potential of the double-line branch indication lies in crossing double-line branches over one another so that they are perceived as having depth. This crossing of branches requires a little planning of the branch arrangement but this is easily accomplished in even the briefest series of overlays.

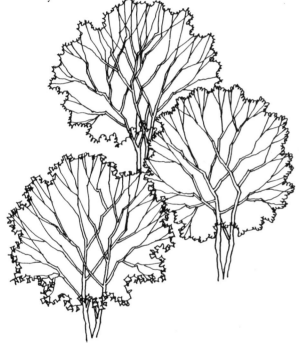

The next level of detail is the more sophisticated delineation of the outline of the leaf mass. Instead of just a simple smooth circle or oval, but without getting into the tedium of drawing individual leaves, we can suggest the shape of the individual leaves with a boundary line drawn around the tree's mass of leaves. A leaf-boundary line can have at least three configurations. It can be made by a line whose deformations are always concave, always convex, or neutral. The concave configuration is appropri-

ate for oak, maple, or holly; the convex for olives, ash, or eucalyptus; and the neutral for nonspecific trees.

In addition to suggesting the conformation of the tree's individual leaves, the boundary line of the leaf mass allows the foliage to be toned or colored while remaining transparent. Buildings and other elements of the environment can be shown right through the transparent light tone or green tint rendering of the leaf mass.

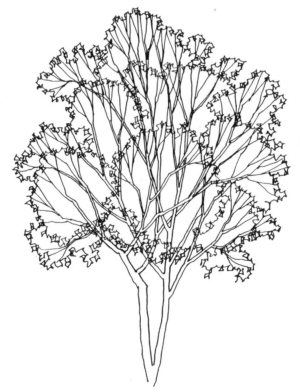

The next step in the developing tree template is the subdivision of the entire leaf mass into smaller clumps of leaves carried by the major branch structures. This is done by simply

extending lines of the same configuration as the leaf-boundary line across the leaf mass to give the appearance of some clumps of leaves in front of others. This step in the ascending hierarchy of detail is relatively worthless unless you follow it up by toning or coloring the various leaf subdivisions differently.

The next step is in some ways a regression: the tree loses its transparency and becomes an opaque object with all attention called to the configuration and subdivision of the leaf outline and no suggestion of the inner branch structure.

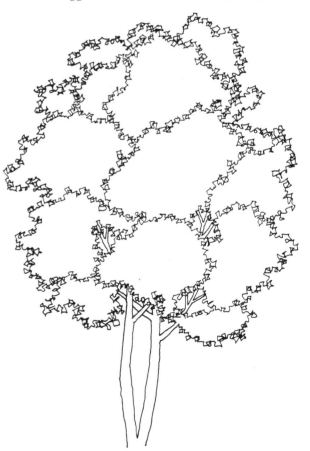

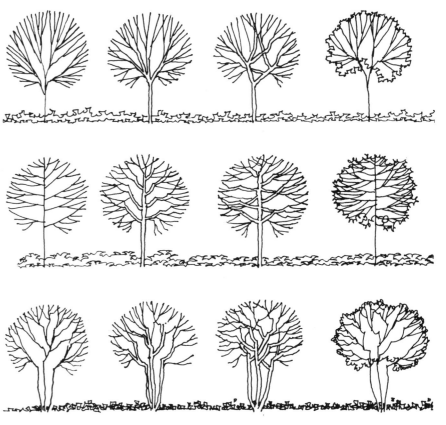

The final step is to draw or suggest the definition of all the individual leaves. This can be accomplished rather efficiently with any of several repetitive hand motions much like those with which the leaf-boundaries were drawn. Such repetitive hand motions must be mastered and prerecorded as perceptual tapes to be retrieved and played on demand.

In building up the individual leaf indication, the entire mass of leaves should still be subdivided by the shading or relative density of the built-up texture. This should be done by shading each clump of leaves individually—from dark at the bottom and one side (depending on the light direction) to light at the top and other side. The light edges of the nearer clump of leaves will then stand out in sharp contrast to the dark side and bottom of the clump behind.

As with all the prerecorded perceptual videotapes, the most valuable tree templates to master are those that have a time-flexible form.

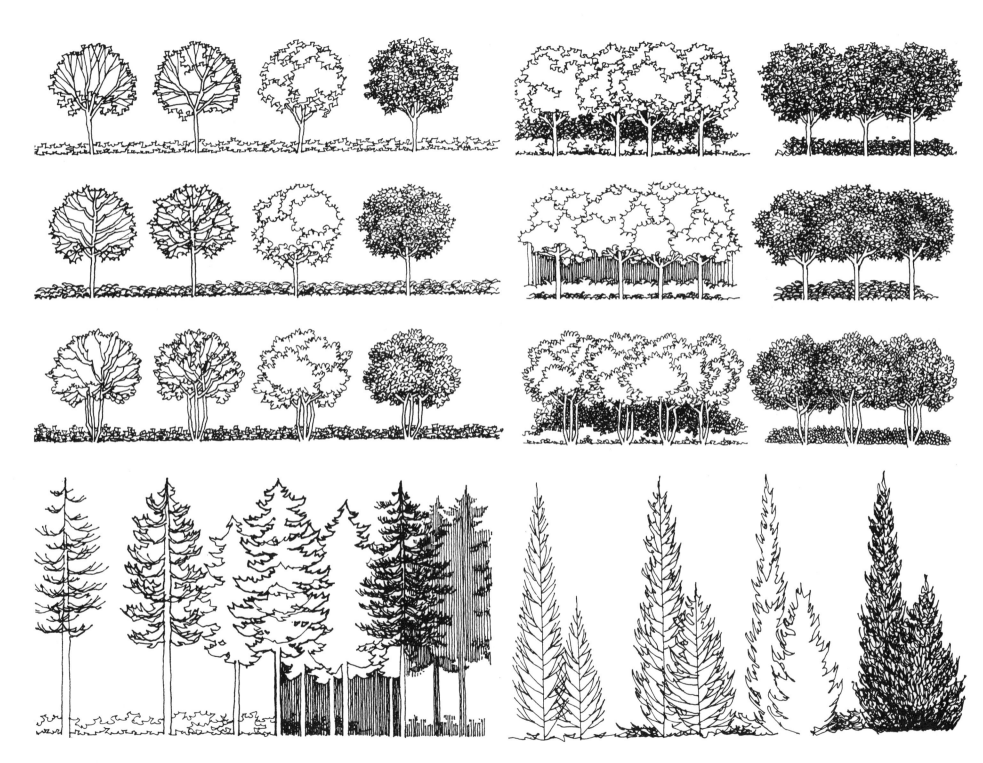

GROWIES

Shrubs and hedges are like trees except that branch structure is of little or no importance in drawing them. Overall form and leaf detail must be mastered and, like trees, drawn shrubs range from simple abstraction to complex realism.

Drawing shrubs and hedges is mostly a matter of building up a texture that represents the leaves of the plant. This may be done laboriously, leaf by leaf, but it is much more efficiently accomplished by developing a continuous hand motion that produces the texture. As with the leaf-boundary lines mentioned earlier, there are, generally, three possible kinds of repetitive hand motions:

CONCAVE

CONVEX

NEUTRAL

Vines and ground covers are even simpler in that they require only the textural indication of the leaf detail. Vines do have a certain form, but it is relatively easy to master.

Drawing vines and ground covers is also a textural build-up. The concave and convex textures are better for ground covers because they give the appearance of foreshortening, which helps the ground covers look flat.

In quick sketching, these textural scribble strokes are the fastest way to add a little textural interest to a drawing. They represent the textural interest provided by landscaping and yet are appropriately noncommittal in the early stages of the design synthesis—before you know which specific plants to recommend.

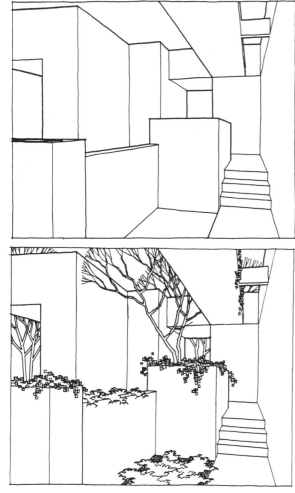

THE PLACEMENT OF TREES AND GROWIES

Where you place trees, shrubs, hedges, vines, and ground covers is extremely important in drawing and design. They can add greatly to all the drawing and environmental-interest categories. They can demonstrate space by disappearing and reappearing behind architectural elements, they can add the textural interest needed in a stark environment, and they can provide the additional interest needed in a stiff orthogonal environment by spilling over edges and delighting the eye with their structure.

FURNISHINGS

Humans have always surrounded themselves with whatever useful and symbolic objects they could acquire. Of all the world's and history's cultures, the affluent societies of the twentieth century are perhaps the most self-indulgent collectors of this material clutter that gives us comfort and pleasure. While environmental designers are often not responsible for the design or even the selection of such furnishings, we must include them in our drawings in order to represent the spaces accurately. In many cases the design of the spaces must be integrally related to the furnishings they will hold and cannot possibly be evaluated without an indication of that integration.

The most important advice I can give about adding furnishings to a drawing is that offered earlier as a general approach for all elements of additional interest: don't attempt to design the furnishings yourself—either choose existing well-designed items or draw completely characterless prototypes. Beyond this warning there are several secondary tips that may help you add furnishings to your drawings efficiently, accurately, and without preempting the design of the space.

DRAWING FURNITURE TO SCALE is sometimes difficult, especially in the foreground of eyelevel perspectives. There seems to be a tendency to draw foreground tables and chairs much lower than they would actually be. I can only guess at the reasons for this depression of the foreground. It may be caused by a compulsion to return to plan view, the drawing board's horizontal position, or a desire to stretch out the foreground furniture so that it doesn't obscure other furniture or figures already drawn. The best way I have found to keep the furniture in scale is to draw a figure standing directly beside the piece of furniture, with the figure's head on the eyelevel line and its feet next to the chair or table. The scale of the piece of furniture will be immediately apparent.

Since all furniture is designed to accommodate the human figure, it is virtually impossible to draw it out of scale when a figure is standing right next to it. You may eliminate the figure in the final drawing after it has served its purpose in helping you draw the furniture.

THE 30"-CUBE MODULE is another help in drawing correctly scaled furniture. The 10' cube we used to structure and measure space can easily be subdivided into 5' cubes and again into 2'6" (30") cubes by using intersecting diagonals. When we reach the 30" cubes we have arrived at a module uniquely useful for drawing furniture—thirty inches is approximately desk height, table height, desktop depth, and the depth and back height of most sofas. Half the 30" height (15") is the approximate height of coffee tables and sofa and lounge-chair seats.

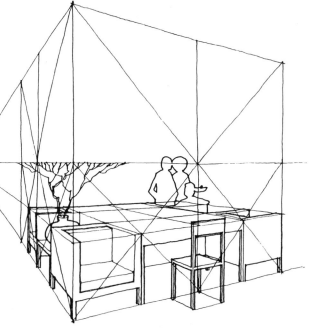

It is very easy to establish a 30" cube anywhere in an eyelevel perspective since thirty inches is half the 5' eyelevel anywhere in the perspective. And once the initial 30" cube is established it can be multiplied in any direction by the use of diagonals, as explained earlier under the section on perspective.

PLAN CIRCLES present another problem that is most often encountered in drawing cylindrical lamps, circular tables, and other furnishings generated by horizontal circles.

In perspectives, all horizontal circles should be drawn flat, not tipped or responding overtly to any projected perspective lines. This is best understood and experienced by drawing a vertical stack of plan circles at various distances above and below eyelevel.

At eyelevel, a circle or any two-dimensional horizontal shape will simply appear as a line. As the horizontal circle is moved up or down from eyelevel, it will begin to reveal its true shape, first as a narrow ellipse and successively as a fatter and fatter ellipse approaching a circle.

There is a phenomenon long noted by psychologists and other students of perception called "constancy," which is a tendency to perceive foreshortened geometric shapes in their plan shape. This tendency can be verified by most drawing teachers because students carry it into their first perspectives.

This tendency to draw all horizontal surfaces tipped up toward the viewer can be hard to break. It takes quite awhile to persuade students that they should draw the perspective as a camera would photograph it—with all the horizontal surfaces foreshortened and lying down—and that our perception of the drawing will perform the constancy phenomenon without the additional help from the delineator.

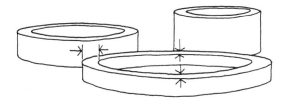

Concentric plan circles can be a particular problem and they are also an excellent vehicle for understanding foreshortening in perspective. The distance between two concentric circles is quite different when foreshortened in perspective; the front and back of the ring between the circles becomes quite thin, while the sides of the circle appear true to their size.

PLAN ANGLES of pieces of furniture can present the same difficulties encountered in drawing circular forms. As with plan circles, the problem is usually created by allowing the furniture to occupy too much space in depth, which results in the furniture appearing as if it were tilted forward. Rectangular pieces of furniture, when they are turned at an angle to the spatial framework of the room, will have their own special pair of VPs on the eyelevel line, and it is important to keep those VPs far enough apart so that the furniture is limited to its true depth in space. This limitation can be further understood by realizing that any square piece of furniture, as it pivots through the 360° of possible plan angles, will always remain within the foreshortened ellipse of its plan circle.

VISUAL FURNISHINGS include pictures, wall hangings, ornamental plants and pottery, sculpture, and knick-knacks. These furnishings have few scale or perspective problems but do present some other pitfalls and opportunities. The furniture we have discussed could be called *haptic*—we relate to it physically by sitting, eating, or writing on it. Visual furnishings are the furniture we experience primarily or exclusively visually, as the name suggests.

These objects should be used for the purpose of enriching or ornamenting a drawing, exactly as they are used in the real environment. They can add textural interest as well as figural interest that may otherwise be lacking in the drawing or the environment.

In real human environments, such objects always have deep personal meaning for the people who select and place them in the space. Portraits, souvenirs, and prized objects of art all obviously have personal associations related to their specific content. Because of this, any representation of content in these objects risks being both distracting and objectionable and will inevitably call unwanted attention to itself. For this reason any indication of this class of furnishings should be of the most abstract, characterless kind.

VEHICLES

Vehicles are also possessions that people are proud of and that inevitably clutter (or ornament, depending on your point of view) the environment. In *Drawing As a Means to Architecture* (1968), I limited the discussion about vehicles to automobiles, and even included some remarks favoring automobiles as symbolic of our personal freedom. While that may still be true, our continued use of automobiles as our almost exclusive means of transportation seems much more self-indulgent and irresponsible than it did then, and my mind has changed to the point where I think we must include bicycles and buses in our discussion, even in a book on drawing.

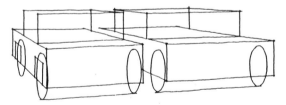

Once again, the two recommended approaches are either to draw a specific model or a completely characterless prototype. Either type can indicate the means of arrival or departure and the area designed for parking without preempting the drawing by calling too much attention to itself. Although bicycles and buses vary little in design, automobiles are extremely self-conscious in their "styling" and the various models

and years are so well known that any new design you might offer is more than likely to attract the viewer's attention.

This means you should trace or copy a specific model from a brochure or advertisement or you should learn to draw completely innocuous cars that simply have four wheels and a body Ghia would never claim.

There are a few tips for drawing characterless automobiles that may be worth mentioning. The form of most passenger cars can be abstracted to a small box sitting on a longer box. Sloping the sides of the upper box begins to make it look like the passenger compartment, and headlights, bumpers, wheel wells, and license plates make the lower box look like the chassis.

Remember that the tops of all modern passenger cars are well below eyelevel, so in an eyelevel perspective an individual automobile or many in a parking lot will lie well below the eyelevel line. Great masses of parking may be usefully simplified by drawing only a descriptive collective outline of their tops; this simplified delineation can also be applied to individual automobiles so that they never call too much attention to themselves.

When adding cars to a perspective, and especially when tracing a photograph or advertising brochure, be very careful that the VPs for the car are on the eyelevel line of the perspective. They often are not because the car was photographed from below or above eyelevel in an attempt to improve its appearance. If the VPs for the car are not on the eyelevel of the perspective, the car will look like it is propped up or is in some kind of skid. Cars are prone to the same distortions furniture is often subjected to—they may occupy too much space or have their VPs too close together (see the previous discussion on plan angles under the furnishings section).

Buses are probably easier to draw than automobiles and are easily made credible by drawing the route sign on their front, the special way their doors open, a bus stop sign and benches, and shelters for waiting riders. I strongly encourage the inclusion of public-transportation vehicles in design drawings because I am convinced that until we learn to draw them we will never seriously consider these desperately needed alternative modes of transportation or propose their accommodation in the design proposals we offer our clients.

Bicycles are more difficult to draw, and I haven't yet discovered how to successfully simplify their delineation. I think the effort to find ways to draw bicycles and to design their parking racks is seriously worth pursuing, however, so that they become as acceptable near the entrances to our buildings as the obligatory planters and trees or the late-model limousine pulled up at the curb.

INTEGRATION WITH SPATIAL INTEREST

I recommended earlier that additional interest be closely integrated with spatial interest, but here I would like to extend the discussion and demonstrate some of the advantages of such an integration. While figures, trees, furniture, and automobiles add a certain interest by just being mindlessly sprinkled around the drawing like cake decorations, that practice does nothing to enhance the drawing as a design communication. I believe items of additional interest should not be added to *decorate* a drawing, but rather only when they can be beneficially and tightly integrated with the drawing's spatial interest.

Some of the best illustrations of this integration involve the use of trees to demonstrate continuous background space. A perspective of an interior courtyard may be difficult to make read as unroofed and open to the sky. The minute you draw a tree standing in the courtyard, however, with its branches disappearing above the ceiling of the enclosed foreground space, it becomes apparent that the tree is occupying an exterior space that extends upward above the roof.

An even more dramatic demonstration of this principle can be shown in a space with several windows of different sizes and positions, including high clerestory windows. If you draw individual trees or plants in each window they will look like individual landscape paintings, but if you draw continuous hedges and large trees appearing in several windows the viewer will perceive a continuous space outside the building.

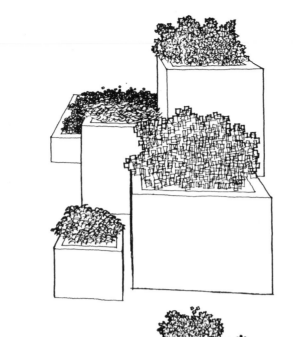

Figures can be integrated with spatial interest in a similar way. A sunken conversation pit may be very difficult to indicate in an eyelevel perspective of a living room, but a group of figures sitting and standing in the pit will make the existence of the sunken space immediately apparent.

The general idea of integrating objects of additional interest into any drawing so that they make its space manifest can be illustrated by drawing a plant in a container. The plant can be neatly trimmed and add no spatial interest, as in the top drawing, or it can add great spatial interest by spilling over and demonstrating the space around each planter, as in the bottom drawing. The foliage should be drawn spilling over the container's edge in such a way that it demonstrates the space in front of, to either side, behind, and above the container.

In the lapping that indicates spatial layers, the nearer object must always be drawn as having thickness; that is, it must be drawn with a double line indication so that more distant lines and textures can be perceived as disappearing under and reappearing from behind it. For the same reason, the nearer object should never be textured since the rendering of the texture will focus attention on that spatial layer and not the deeper layer beyond. Textures should always be applied to the deepest spaces so that they can disappear behind the nearer objects.

6 Drawing's Relationship to the Design Process

The entire subject matter of this book would seem to fall under such a heading. The other chapters present a separate and more general discussion of the context in which the design process occurs, while this chapter concentrates on the activity of designing and the specific relationships it can have to drawing.

All drawing can be seen as communication, and in the previous section I discussed the various ways design drawings can communicate the experience of the environment. This section will look at the various relationships drawing can have to the design process, from simply selling or recording the products of the process to leading or even becoming the process.

These relationships arise from a number of variables that differ for every designer and every design process. The extent of this list of variables makes clear the folly of always using the same drawings in the same fixed order. The variables may be thought of in six categories:

1. Designer's personal model of the process (variations in the model held by the designer for what does or should happen during the activity of designing)

2. Assumed role of drawing (variations in the designer's beliefs and expectations regarding the general relationship drawing has to the design process)

3. Communicative purpose (variations in the purpose of any drawing in the design dialog)

4. Kind of problem or solution (variations in the tailoring of analytical, exploratory drawings to a particular problem, or of synthetic study and refinement drawings to a particular solution)

5. Choice of drawing (variations in the kind of drawing and its relationship to its predecessors and successors in the process)

6. Degree of resolution (variations based on the stage of the design process and the drawing's predecessors and successors—the appropriate level of finish for the drawing)

Because of the kind of eyeminds we have, some understanding of the range and complexity of these variables is mandatory for anyone who uses drawing in the design process. What we show ourselves and the order in which it is shown is extremely important, since vision is the dominant sense in the perception, conception, and decisions involved in environmental design. And if we intend to be clear and persuasive, the choices of which drawings to use and in what order they are shown is critical in our communication with those for whom we are designing.

The preceding list of variables that affect the relationships between drawing and the design process deserve elaboration because the range of each variable is wider than we may realize.

Personal Model of the Process

The continuing proliferation of descriptions and prescriptions for the design process shows no sign of diminishing the healthy variety in what designers actually do when they design. Although architects, landscape architects, and interior designers seem prepared to let all kinds of people from other disciplines try to tell them how they should design and eagerly try suggested vocabularies and analytical techniques, the methodological paradigm (like scientific method in the sciences) that appears to be the desired goal seems as remote as ever. What we have forgotten is that the resistance to any particular method and the abandonment of the futile search for certainty (of which methodological certainty is only the latest version) *is* the paradigm we seek, and we have had it all along.

The design process combines two distinctly different but complementary kinds of behavior. These behaviors each have a tradition and a value system and probably originate in the patterns of the left and right cerebral hemispheres that make us human. These two approaches are very similar to the traditional attitudes and values of art and science, intuition and logic, or the subjective and objective views of the world. They are also much like deBono's "lateral and vertical" thinking, Guilford's "convergent and divergent" thinking, Jones's "black box and glass box" designers, and the right-brain and left-brain functioning described by Ornstein and others.

Objective, analytical, logical behavior needs little advocacy or defense in the design professions or in society in general. Subjective, synthetic, intuitive behavior, however, has few advocates in the recent writing about design, partly because it has nothing to do with language, and one of my purposes here is to argue that it is essential and deserves equal partnership in the design process.

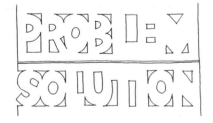

To illustrate the differences between the two behaviors, I would like to propose that the so-called design process is analogous to the joining of two pieces of cloth, one called the "problem" and the other the "solution." The two different behaviors are analogous to two completely dif-ferent techniques for joining pieces of fabric: zip-pering and stitching.

ZIPPERS AND STITCHES

Today's faith in method and our culture's demand for rational explanation give us the pre-vailing model of the design process: the *zipper*. The zipper closes the gap that separates the prob-lem from the solution by connecting separately solved piecemeal congruences in a predetermined linear order just like the sequential meshing of the zipper's individual teeth.

Each step in this linear zippering must be correct and consistent and must remain a part of the final overall congruence, lest gaps develop that might reopen the entire closure. The zipper has a fixed beginning and ending and its narrow linear process solves difficulties in the process by back-ing up linearly and then forcing its way through them. Lateral entanglements, as when the mate-rial becomes caught in the zipper, are to be avoided at all costs.

The complementary model of the design process is the random *stitching* used in darning a sock or in sewing two pieces of fabric together. This kind of closure sews the problem to the solution through a series of actions that rely more on the skill developed by experience than on any for-malized method. While successive stitches are to some extent determined by earlier stitches, the order is never precious and the entire pattern of stitches may include unnecessary or even incor-rect stitches. Unlike the zipper, lateral move-ments are the most valuable, and the first stitches are not anchored on the problem side of the seam, as most zipper models of the process seem to imply, but arise from some intuitive hunch or feeling about a possible solution. This is because the environments we inhabit and from which we gather the experience or knowledge we bring to any problem are made up entirely of solutions. The building you are in now is a "solution" you experience without ever knowing what problem the designer was trying to solve. The problems for which the solutions were generated are never seen and can only be inferred from the world of solutions we experience. We probably only understand design problems in terms of design solutions we know about. The first stitches arise and are anchored on the solution side of the seam we are sewing, and always seek a part of the prob-lem that fits, or can be made to fit, their insight.

The zipper is an efficient management tool, but creativity occurs in spite of it, not because of it. The zipper model of problem-solving solves piecemeal problems one at a time in a prescribed linear order, with the first tooth of the zipper engagement being a single problem to be solved. In contrast, our creative insights occur as disor-derly lateral stitches across the gap in our prob-lem-solving, not alone, but in bunches in an unanticipated order, and the pattern they make in joining any problem to its solution is unpre-dictable, inefficient, and only barely manageable, but infinitely more beautiful and human as a pat-terned whole than any zipper.

LOGICAL LANGUAGE

When we are called upon to explain our design process to a colleague or client, our linear language and our cultural indoctrination assure that we will describe our actions as having been a flawless logical process: a zipper. In our culture this habit begins very early, with parents' demands that children use their newly learned language to produce logical explanations for their actions. "Why are you so late coming home from school?" or "Why did you get your shoes all muddy?" imply that even such ad hoc behavior is to be logically explained. The child hasn't the slightest idea why she got her shoes all muddy except as the unanticipated and incidental result of actions in which she was completely and intensely involved. The pretense that muddy shoes are the result of logical action is absurd, but children and environmental design students learn early that parents, teachers, and society in general expect them to be able to offer rational explanations for their actions.

Thomas Kuhn points out in *The Structure of Scientific Revolutions* (1962) that the history of science is described in textbooks as a smooth linear process—a zipper—leaving out the dead ends and misdirected efforts of whole groups of scientists because their mistaken "stitching" is now an embarrassment to the linear logical model. Much of the recent writing about the design process has been dominated by zipper advocates who model all design activity as a linear process. The word "process" itself tends to carry this implication. It sounds suspiciously like that symbol of our technological age, the production line, and the inflexible standardization implied by such a process and its products is boring and inhuman. There is some indication that the act of writing about cre-

ativity or problem solving, or our language itself, tricks authors into describing the activity as a logical procedure.

THE HITCH

From Osborn to Archer, literature is full of verbal descriptions that gloss over the crucial *hitch* that anchors the process when the design idea is formed. The use of "hitch" is not to be confused with one of its other common meanings—that of an obstacle or stoppage. I mean it in the sense of a hitching post, or a fisherman setting the hook, or a tie or knot that can anchor the subsequent

stitching. I will call this "concept formation"— the period during which the design concept is formed is the most significant point in the process because it signals a profound change in design activity. In my experience, stitching always starts the process and continues until one stitch or series of stitches sews the problem to the solution in a way that feels uniquely right and promises to be a solid anchor for the zippering that will systematically extend the idea and develop its logical rationale. The feeling of correctness is preverbal and is a recognition of a certain congruence that appears in the exploratory drawings or diagrams between the form of solution and the continual restatement of the form of the problem.

Any complete model of the design process must include both the stitching and the zippering, as well as that crucial hitch when the design concept is formed. Concept formation involves a

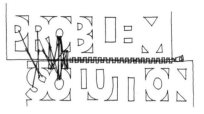

commitment to a particular idea or collection of ideas capable of organizing the subsequent design activity. It represents a change in behavior from searching to testing, or from intuition to logic, as well as from insights into the various individual parts of the problem to an attempt to deal with the problem and its solution as a comprehensive whole. I don't mean to imply that this concept formation and the transition from stitching to zippering occurs only once in the process. It may recur many times and the model of the overall design process for any complex problem will be more like a multiple exposure than a single picture.

THE COMPOSITE MODEL

We now have a composite model of the design process that represents both stitching and zippering as well as the connecting (hitching) transition, and on such a model we can explain the disparate descriptions of the design process in our literature.

CREATIVITY

Authors such as Maslow, Koestler, and deBono are examples of theorists who are mostly interested in the first part of the process: stitching. Such authors concentrate on the kinds of attitudes, activities, and thought patterns that precede creative ideas, assuming that the creative process begins with discovering or generating a unique idea and ends with the birth of that idea. The creativity theorists tend to leave the testing or evaluation of the idea to others or to assume that the quality of the idea is entirely and immediately apparent. They also tend to view the implementation of any idea as being rather automatic, uncreative, and mostly a matter of technique.

DESIGN METHOD

Design methodologists, like Jones and Archer, on the other hand, come directly from scientific method as expressed in Karl Popper's writings. These methodologists begin with the hypothesis and are not interested in how the idea came to exist, but rather in its systematic criticism and refinement. Design methodologists are mostly interested in the zipper end of our composite model of the design process. They assume that ideas just happen or that they already exist in the form of rather obvious alternatives; they believe that what really counts is the application of rigorous testing and criticism to determine the correctness and best form of the idea, or the systematic evaluation of the available alternatives.

ART AND SCIENCE

Real practicing designers and people of recognized creativity in all fields have been curiously silent about how they do what they do. Maslow found evidence that they may not even know how they do it because they are so "lost in the doing" that the coolly detached phenomenological management advocated by Jones in his "designers as self-organizing systems" may not be possible. Another reason designers have seldom tried to describe their personal design processes may be that they know the process

must be self-made, and they have little desire to convert other designers to their way of designing. They might even consider such evangelism arrogant and ill-mannered.

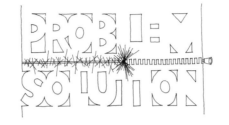

Scientists, on the other hand, have as their goal the logical explanation of the universe. Science sets out to describe how the world works, including creativity, so that verbal or mathematical explanation can be seen as the very essence of science. Further, science is not satisfied with personal speculation or insight, but aims for verifiable principles of universal application.

Viewed in this way, it is ironic that artists are usually the ones accused of ego-tripping, when all they ever offer is the personal witness of their individual experience of the world. Artists seldom seek any universal acceptance of what they do, for they know that whatever value is found in their work springs from its individuality and subjectivity.

One other explanation for the lack of testimony from the stitch end of the process is that doing and saying have fundamentally different goals, rules, and values. The doing of art is equivalent to the saying of science. The artist may find the request for explanation superfluous because the work itself was intended to communicate something about the artist's experience, and when the communication fails it can only be the fault of the artist or an insensitive observer.

While designers may not go around telling people how they design, or seem to exhibit a great consistency between what they say and what they do, most of them try very hard to understand and control what they do when they design. They make a personal model of the process, if not at the conscious intellectual level then perhaps in a more meaningful way by their actual behavior. Their dilemma, or, as I prefer to believe, their good fortune, is that they stand uncomfortably astride of the art/science, stitches/zipper continuum. Their responsibility is to maintain the traditional illogical balance they have inherited by talking like scientists but behaving like artists.

The implications of the stitches and zipper analogy for drawing depend on which end of the model you adopt as being most representative of the design process. All drawings can become valuable stitches, from the most mysterious personal doodles and diagrams, to the graphic techniques illustrated in Paul Laseau's *Graphic Problem Solving* (1975), to tentative perspectives, sections, and plans. Zipper drawings are more formal and tend to be more quantitative than qualitative. There is no place in the zipper for the expressive, exploratory, or experimental drawings that give us those sideways glances so valuable to the early stitching. The mandatory zipper drawings conclude the process and record its results while remaining fixated on the goal. They tend to be the more refined plans, sections, and elevations necessary to establish and relate the various physical aspects of the design, take off its quantities, and instruct its builders. The more detailed implications any model of the design process holds for drawing must be considered on the basis of what role in the process it assumes for drawing.

The Assumed Role of Drawing

The role of drawing is usually implied in the design-process model the designer chooses. In chapter 2, I offered six different roles that drawing can play in the design process:

- selling the product (with full-color perspective renderings)
- neutrally printing out the results of a mental process that occurs separately, privately, and previously (with graphs, charts, matrices, sections, elevations, and plans)
- communicating the process (with networks and critical path diagrams)
- participating in the process (with all forms of drawing, including those newly invented)
- leading the process (with exploratory drawings in which concepts are expected to appear)
- being the process (with drawings that provoke other drawings in a chain reaction)

In chapter 2, I described the first two roles as excluding drawing from the process, but I saved the discussion of drawing's various participatory roles for this chapter. I will discuss the various roles under the heading of the "zipper and stitches" analogy because I want to emphasize the overall process, but all the active roles for drawing will be discussed.

The Communicative Purpose

The purpose of drawing varies according to its succession in the process. The most simple, polar way of thinking about drawing's communicative role is to categorize drawings as either open (exploratory, input-seeking questionnaires), or closed (persuasive, convincing commercials). During the design process, drawing alternates between these poles and only generally progresses from open to closed over the entire process. Along the way there are several other kinds of drawings but most of them may be thought of as either opening or closing the process.

A successful design process is like a dialog in which the roles of communicator and listener alternate frequently and gradually shift in response to the overall form of the process. The pattern below indicates this process.

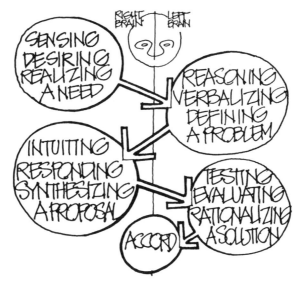

The entire dialog may take place in the privacy of the designer's consciousness, as a conversation between the right and left cerebral hemispheres. In a strongly intuitive designer the sequence may short circuit down the intuitive side without bothering to rationally define the problem or logically test the solution. The need to communicate, rationalize, or defend the solution, however, which is always necessary with a client, assures that the pattern will become a true dialog.

The pattern may also take place as a communicative cycle between designer and client or between designer and consultant; it may also be seen as the overall form of the design process.

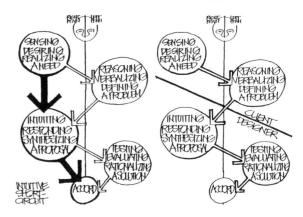

The pattern of the dialog can also be seen as the initial cycle in the dialog between designer and client, in which the designer gains information from the client by questioning, listening, and confirming a correct understanding of the problem. In the second half of the cycle the direction of the communication switches as the designer responds to the information gained in the first half of the cycle with some sort of designed synthesis.

Drawing can participate in any such dialog by recording or translating the input into graphic notes, or it can lead the process by making graphic question marks that solicit input like a questionnaire. After the transfer of information has been completed, drawing can confirm the correctness of the designer's understanding by synthesizing the information graphically—just as a secretary produces the minutes of a meeting for approval.

The role of drawing in the second half of the cycle is more familiar. Here drawing represents a proposed solution or conceptual response to the problem and will be altered until it pleases both the client and the designer. The client's approval completes the cycle and the proposal may now be tested.

The testing may be the designer's inner self-dialog, which is similar in form to the client-designer dialog. Further testing may be by a consultant or other member of the design team. Now the designer has the apparent problem and the consultant has the potential solution. Later in the process the designer may have the apparent problem (e.g., not able to satisfy the clients' needs within the budget) and the clients may have the potential solution (reducing their needs).

After a great number of similar cycles in the dialog, with various participants filling the two roles, the overall process begins to close for the client and shift to the design team. During this time of testing, improving, and refining the concept, the communication follows an overall script developed by the design team from experience in many such previous processes. Drawings shown to the client during this stage function more like journalistic reporting of the now-linear zippering process.

Finally the process becomes zipped tight and fully closed. The only communicative purpose remaining is that of persuading others—bankers, buyers, or building officials—of the quality of the product.

The drawings that record or lead the design dialog must be carefully designed so that their focus and content is appropriate to their purpose. The various communicative drawings of the design process can be thought of as:

Opening drawings, which are designed to prevent premature solutions, open up the design space, and establish the designer's credibility by asking questions and posing tentative alternative choices. These involve directionless exploration of the design space.

Clearing drawings, which are designed to remove various kinds of blocks, misunderstandings, and preconceptions by offering and confirming alternative syntheses of the problem statement.

Stitch drawings, which are designed to make trial closures between the problem and a solution by offering tentative, piecemeal solutions to specific parts of the problem. They search for direction.

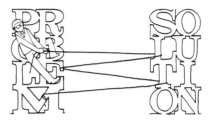

Hitch drawings, which are designed to anchor a particular conceptual solution to the problem by offering various organizing concepts. They establish direction.

Zipper drawings, which are designed to test, develop, and rationalize the solution's relationship to the problem. They study all the aspects of the solution and their relationships to one another. In search of the best final form for the solution, they integrate the solution in the established direction.

Zipped drawings, which are designed to convincingly present the solution by drawing its most flattering views. They extol the destination reached.

Designers must be effective communicators and skill in communication depends not just on convincing logic, persuasive oratory, or even sensitive poetry, but also on skill in asking questions, patience in listening carefully, and perseverance in trying to understand the answers. The design dialog should never close without the help and understanding of all those involved in the process.

Kind of Problem or Solution

The relationships the various drawings have to the design process should depend on the kind of problem or solution. The lack of a consistent typology for design problems is a result of the wide range of problem types and the way that range transforms itself depending on the designer's point of view.

Hospitals might seem to be primarily a functional problem, with the efficiency of the circulation patterns of patients, visitors, doctors, nurses, and other staff indicating plan patterns as the first drawings. Given the same problem, however, a designer with different sensibilities might decide that the hospital's difficult urban site demanded that site plans and elevations studies were the place to begin.

All beginnings are also strongly affected by the confidence a designer feels with successive stages of the process. It is quite different to choose a drawing out of fear or incompetence—because it is familiar and easy—than to begin with the same drawing because you have consciously, deliberately decided it is the best place to start.

The conventional sequence of drawings made during the design process is plans, sections, elevations, and perspectives. As Edward deBono's writing has made clear, the choice of entry into any problem and the sequence in which information is processed is extremely important, because without deliberate choice or random variation we wear a perceptual/conceptual rut that becomes increasingly difficult to avoid.

Some kinds of problems suggest beginning with drawings other than plans. The problem of vertical circulation sorting required in airports or stadia indicates that sections be the first drawings. Filling in an empty site on a historic street or square might best begin with elevation studies. Buildings in which the quality of the interior space is paramount, like churches or restaurants, might lead a designer to begin with interior perspectives; buildings that are to occupy beautiful natural sites might demand that exterior perspectives be the first conceptual drawings.

The conventional order of any set of construction drawings (site plan, foundation plan, floor plan, framing plan, sections, and elevations) is basically the sequence in which a building is built—a logical *zipper*. The conceptual drawings that make the random stitches that initiate the design process should be related instead to the kind of problem being solved. Experienced designers know that it is just as possible to make a plan fill in a concept that begins as an exterior perspective as it is to always make the plan be the generator of the design.

Even after the hitch that anchors the organizing concept of the solution has been made, the first zipper study drawings should be based not on the construction order, but on the characteristics of the particular solution. Solutions based on level changes, sight lines, or earth integration should be studied first in section. Solutions that are based on the way natural light is brought into the building or on a particular palette of interior finishes or spatial sequence would demand interior perspectives as the first study drawings. Solutions based on relationships to an urban context might indicate street elevations as the first drawings, while solutions based on scale, materials, and articulation of the overall form of the building should be studied first in exterior perspectives.

If we become sensitive to the benefits of varying the drawings we choose in response to the kind of design problem or to the kind of solution with which we are working, we will also become more sensitive to what we expect to be shown by the various drawings. For instance, instead of testing a solution by making the conventional construction drawings, we ask ourselves which drawings will best test the success of the solution—drawings that show the way light will come into the space? or drawings that show how the building will appear at night?

Choice of Drawing

In the design process, the choice of drawing may be initially affected by the problem or the solution, but at any particular point in the process the choice must be based on what you need to resolve about the design. While it may be comforting to keep making those drawings that show the best qualities of the design, what is needed is an exploration of what you suspect are the design's weaknesses.

Choosing the most critical, problem-seeking drawings should be based on the preceding variables and a thorough understanding of what kinds of information can be included in the various drawings.

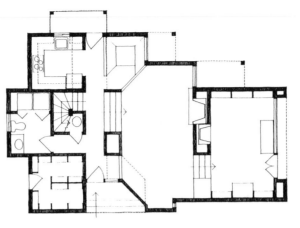
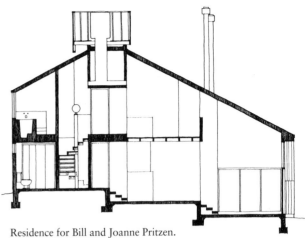

Residence for Bill and Joanne Pritzen.

While plans, sections, and elevations are questionable as representations of the experience of an environment, they are the best conceptual drawings. They focus on the basic relationships of spaces and architectural elements, which is not possible in perspectives.

The distinction between conventional construction drawings and perspectives can be best understood by recognizing the complementary but essential kinds of syntheses they show. Plans, sections, and elevations show a holistic synthesis of the entire building as a built object—a synthesis that is very important and is essential to the logical consistency needed in construction but can never be experienced directly.

Perspectives, on the other hand, even in unlimited numbers, can never show the building as a total object like the orthographic drawings. What they can show, however, is the synthesis of what can be experienced in one place at one time, including the prediction of the further experience of the adjacent spaces. Perspectives are indispensable in testing the success of the ideas generated in the other drawings. They show how many of the designer's attempts to relate various elements will actually be perceived when the environment is built.

The following brief list of each drawing's potential should indicate the range of the drawing's form and content.

PLANS CAN SHOW

- Horizontal functional sorting (zoning, adjacency, separation, and interpenetration)
- Horizontal circulation (pattern and arrangement of the corridors, vestibules, entries, and exits)
- Horizontal functional adequacy (scale, shape, and appropriateness for the functions being accommodated)
- Horizontal formal arrangement (point-, line-, or matrix-generated geometries)
- Vertical architectural elements and openings (characteristics and arrangements of columns, walls, windows, and doors)
- Horizontal orientation and inflection to the larger context (wind, sun, view, topography, and adjacent or distant built environments)
- Furniture arrangement, floor materials, and other levels of detail
- Roof and floor framing
- Horizontal distribution of mechanical, plumbing, and electrical elements
- Horizontal integration of all the above (as in the relationships between the spatial subdivisions and the structural module or between the human circulation and the mechanical distribution)

SECTIONS CAN SHOW

- Vertical functional sorting (stacking, separation, and interpenetration)
- Vertical circulation (pattern and arrangement of the stairs, ramps, and elevators)
- Vertical functional adequacy (scale, shape, and appropriateness for the desired functions)
- Vertical formal arrangement (stacked, staggered, stepped, or clustered geometries)
- Horizontal architectural elements and openings (characteristics and arrangements of spandrels, slabs, parapets, overhangs, stairwells, and atria)
- Vertical orientation and inflection to the larger context (the building's relationship to the site and to the adjacent or distant built environment)
- Natural lighting, wall materials, and other levels of detail
- Wall, floor, and roof construction
- Vertical distribution of mechanical, plumbing, and electrical elements
- Vertical integration of all the above (as in the relationships between stairs and elevators and the mechanical chases or between the column spacing and the stacking of the spaces)

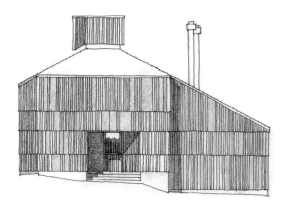

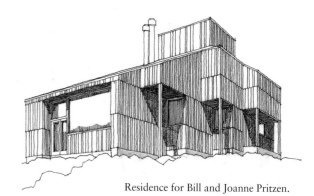

Residence for Bill and Joanne Pritzen.

ELEVATIONS CAN SHOW

- Pattern, scale, and proportions of facades (openings, articulations, and overall composition of a building's facades)
- Contextual relationships to the adjacent natural and built environment
- Shadow patterns and wall materials on the building's faces

INTERIOR PERSPECTIVES CAN SHOW

- Experience of the enclosed environment (the combination of all the visual perceptions possible, including the anticipation of the tactile or kinesthetic experience of touching or walking through the environment)

EXTERIOR PERSPECTIVES CAN SHOW

- Experience of the building as an object (the combination of all perceptions that can be cued or predicted by our visual sense, including the tactile or kinesthetic experience of touching or walking around an object)

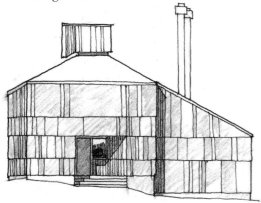

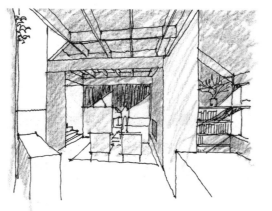

Degree of Resolution

Degree of resolution is a final variable that influences drawing during the design process. Rough, unresolved drawings may not meet clients' expectations if they thought the design was nearing completion, but if the designer correctly prepares clients a great deal of time can be saved by using quick, sketchy drawings with just enough

detail to be able to understand and give interim approval to the design at the appropriate time in the process. Early in the process sketchy drawings actually encourage comment and change and communicate by their tentative quality that the process is open to the clients' input. Overly resolved drawings early in the process may, conversely, put off clients by giving the impression that the process is closed.

The drawings above show the obvious time difference between very resolved and clearly unresolved drawings. The bottom row of drawings are appropriate to the early stages of the process. They would save a great deal of time and, perhaps, communicate just as well, as those in the top row.

There is nothing fixed in the preceding list of variables. They are no more than a framework for a changing set of relationships, but designers should keep these relationships in mind so that their breadth of choice continues to expand. The choices of drawings and the order in which they are made are very important because, although we seem to process visual information simultaneously, the order in which we show ourselves separate drawings will never be without influence. The earlier drawings are always more influential, for they become our point of entry into the problem. The relationships shown in the drawings we choose to make first are assured their share of design attention. The relationships we never see because we haven't made the drawings that would show them, however, are excluded because we have censored ourselves in a way we wouldn't accept if it were applied by any other person or institution.

Most of the recommendations of those who have written about thinking, creativity, or problem solving can be related to the stitches-and-zipper analogy suggested earlier, and the rest of this chapter will be devoted to discussing the various ways drawing can manifest those recommendations. The rest of the chapter is divided into the categories used earlier to describe the various communicative roles drawing can fulfill along the stitches-and-zipper model. What follows, however, does not limit drawing to the role of communicating with others, but includes that intense self-communication between the left and right halves of the brain, when drawing completes the eyemindhand loop that allows the holistic use of all our conceptual abilities—when, to the observer of design behavior, drawing *becomes* the design process.

DESIGN EDUCATION'S IMBALANCE

The ability to form concepts depends on a balanced use of the various opening, clearing, and closing techniques. Design education is often guilty of favoring opening techniques. Some design teaching consists mostly of pointing out an increasingly comprehensive list of design criteria—loading the student with a massive burden of responsibility in the form of problems, concerns, and alternative solutions.

This teaching method often drives the problem and solution as far apart as possible and then simply walks away, leaving the student with only a threatening deadline as a mechanism of closure. For human reasons as well as design reasons, we should spend more time teaching clearing and closing techniques. Students' confidence in their conceptual ability or in the humanity of the profession they are entering is hardly helped by a shattering crit session two days before a deadline.

If we return now to the stitches-and-zipper analogy we will find that any and all drawings can be valuable in the opening, clearing, and stitching phases if they are kept open, sketchy, and ambiguous so that they invite input and interpretation. The hitch drawings and the first zipper drawings must include perspectives, however, if the hoped-for qualities of the solutions are to be truly tested. After the design's ability to communicate the designer's intentions has been rigorously verified in perspective, the process can return with confidence to the orthographic drawings that promote the logical integration of the building as a built object.

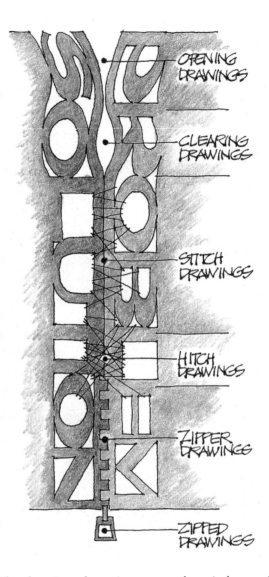

The drawing above integrates the stitches-and-zipper analogy with the various kinds of drawings appropriate to the various stages of the design process.

Opening Drawings

Opening drawings are designed to suspend judgment, prevent premature solutions, and open up the design space.

If design can be thought of as the activity of joining a problem to a solution, then the space between the two belongs to the designer. The extent and quality of such design spaces are extremely variable and designers must often fight to open up an adequate space in which to work. The design space may be almost closed by a number of forces or circumstances and its premature closing may catch the designer like a vise. One of the handiest tools with which to hold open the jaws of the vise is your pen or pencil. Drawing ability can be a great help in prying apart and propping open any narrow design space.

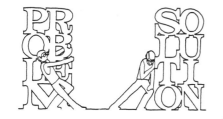

The opening required may be of two kinds: opening the client's and others' minds and opening the designer's mind. The opening can be further divided into pushing back the solution side or pushing back the problem side.

The first thing designers should do is take a very careful look into the design space in which they will have to work—and ask themselves if they really want to be there.

Clients who tell you, "We know what we want, we just need someone to draw it up"; or "I've built three of these developments in California and I know what sells"; or "I just need a set of plans to get through the building department," are also telling you that the design space is virtually closed.

Clients are not the only ones who restrict a designer's moves. Mortgage bankers, government agencies, laws, and society in general all prefer narrow design spaces because they need standard, conventional ways of looking at what, to designers, are opportunities for creativity.

A careful look into a design space should tell you whether there is going to be room for you or not. Young designers tend to be optimistic about any design space, while older heads are extremely wary of, or resigned to, tight design spaces.

What is needed most is an accurate evaluation of the opening potential. It may be a matter of educating the others about the design possibilities or convincing them to appreciate your abilities. In any case, design tradition demands an initial flailing about, just to discover how tight the space really is.

If you make a serious and skillful effort in your first attempts to open the design space, that effort will show in your drawings, and the narrow-minded client or jaded building official will respect your effort, your skill, and your spirit.

Designers themselves often leave precious little room for perceiving a problem freshly or conceiving its solution freely. The limitations of their own experience and their cultural or professional indoctrination may also make the design space narrow. This narrowness is one of the reasons designers need to read, travel, and broaden their education in every possible way. Thankfully, for most designers, preconception is balanced by a healthy procrastination, so that even though they seem to sense a perfect solution right away, they seldom get around to doing anything about it until other, better ideas have begun to occur to them.

The motivation to become a designer and the indoctrination of most design education arouse a certain stubborn openness, or persistence in finding an unusual or imaginative solution. A designer's openness may be distinctly one-sided, however, coming from the designer's application of a preconceived formal solution. In such cases the designer demands a completely open problem side, allowing a drastic restatement of the problem, or an ignorance of certain parts of the problem so that it can fit with a rather rigid, preconceived solution.

The designer's preconceptions may come from several sources:

- over-familiarity with the problem type,
- admired solutions to similar problems, or
- personal preference for certain formal solutions.

Openness, for the designer, may be more a problem of *balancing* the design space—of pushing the solution side open and holding it there, while carefully exploring the problem side with an understanding about how it differs from similar problems.

Many of those who have written about thinking, creativity, or problem solving have recognized the problem of premature closure. John Dewey (*How We Think*, 1909) stated the problem as early and as clearly as anyone:

> The essence of critical thinking is suspended judgment; and the essence of this suspense is inquiry to determine the nature of the problem before proceeding to attempt its solution.

Tactics for opening the design space are all designed to suspend judgment, and most of the recommended behaviors aim at concentrating the designer's and others' attention on the problem side of the design space, so that preconceived or premature solutions can be avoided. Most of the activities are verbal, mathematical, logical, analytical, left-brained operations. Meanwhile, the uninvited, uninvolved holistic right brain may impose its preconceived solution out of utter boredom and frustration.

A far more successful approach, and one of the ways in which drawing can be helpful, is to involve the right brain in *designing* and drawing

alternative ways of seeing the problem, the site, the function, or the context—to make the problem side into its own design problem. The solution side of the problem is thus pushed back by a splitting of the problem side and a relocation of the design space.

While most of the ways of drawing the problem that follow seem concerned with the problem side, or with the relocated design space, they indirectly hold or push back the solution side of the original problem by extending the range of potential solutions and by deepening our understanding of the specific, mandatory criteria for any acceptable solution.

DRAWING THE PROBLEM

The displacement of the design space *within* the problem allows the designer to involve both sides of the brain in designing the problem to be solved. This makes clear the difference between concept attainment and concept formation, discussed earlier in chapter 2. In concept attainment the problem side is always *given*, there is no opportunity for changing it and what is needed is simply a solution that is compliant with this rigid problem statement. In concept formation, the problem side is always extremely variable, depending on the client, the context, and the experience, ability, and resources of the designer; a *congruence* is sought between the problem and a solution and both are developed simultaneously or alternately.

Drawing the problem, then, really becomes *designing* the problem and involves a congruence

within the problem side. Clients and/or users should be involved in the establishment of the congruence because this will allow everyone involved in the design process access to the opening tactics. This involvement in the opening phase will also assure that the congruence reached will reflect a consensus and will be shared by all those involved in the process. This agreement on the problem to be solved is essential, and should be addressed up front, in the open.

There may be difficulties in including the client in this opening of the design space. Clients may not understand the need to pay you to waste time exploring what to them seems an obvious and straightforward problem or in questioning assumptions they have already made and criteria they have already established. Sensing this, the designer may choose to ignore the clients' or users' closed-mindedness and hope to smuggle in an imaginative solution later on in the process after a rapport has been established. You will certainly have to use your own judgment and sensitivity in estimating any client's prejudices, but the earlier you can test the limits of the design space, the better.

One very helpful technique is to frame the opening techniques as a series of questions that you ask the client. The questions should be designed to inquire about aspects of the problem they haven't thought through. The designer then becomes the recorder and synthesizer of this information, while the client is asked to find the information or evaluate alternatives. The designer is thus the innocent questioner, who apparently does not unduly influence the process and obviously does not spend great amounts of time at the client's expense.

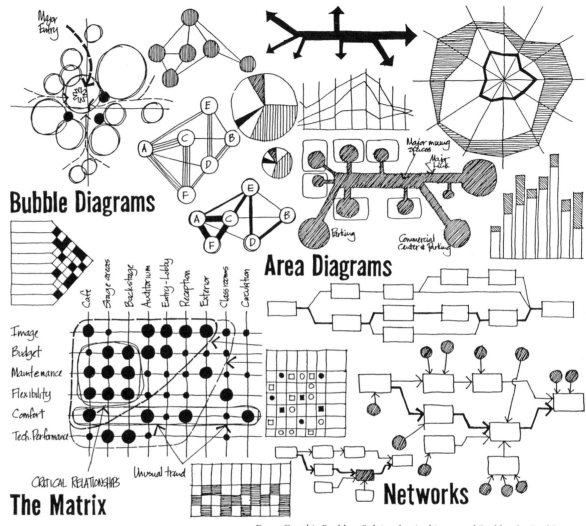

Bubble Diagrams

Area Diagrams

The Matrix

Networks

CRITICAL RELATIONSHIPS

From *Graphic Problem Solving for Architects and Builders* by Paul Laseau.

There are at least six "opening" questions that can help to open the minds of the clients, users, or the designer.

1. *What alternate graphic problem-solving languages should be considered?* There are more graphic languages than you might think and they are rather easily combined and mutated to make entirely new languages.

The traditional drawings will form the base of most problem-solving languages. Bubble diagrams, for instance, have a strong relationship to the horizontal links and separations of plan views. There is tremendous potential, however, for plans of various kinds, which show relationships that are impossible to see in conventional mass/void plan drawings. I have argued earlier *(Drawing As a Means to Architecture,* 1968) that we become prematurely satisfied with our building designs when the formal patterns of the walls, openings, and columns are ordered, because those are the images with which we work. Our evaluative eyeminds may never see the actual functional patterns involved and those more important patterns may remain confused and chaotic.

Beyond the traditional drawings lies a range of other graphics that, while not directly translatable into buildings, represent crucial patterns and relationships involved in the design of any environment—area diagrams, matrices, and networks for example. They indicate comprehensive, ideal relationships and the decision-making and operational sequences that must be considered in the design process.

Paul Laseau's *Graphic Problem Solving for Architects and Builders* (1975) presents and carefully explains the various uses of bubble diagrams, area diagrams, matrices, and networks. These basic graphics can be further enriched by color codes in which different colors represent different functions. Most problems can be benefited by further inventions of graphic languages that represent various parts of the particular problem.

2. *What additional information can be found about this and similar problems?* One of the most obvious ways to open the design space and assure that judgment is withheld is to actively seek further information about the function being designed for, the site, and existing solutions to similar problems. This is one of the roles of programming described in Edward T. White's *Introduction to Architectural Programming* (1972):

> Briefly, in terms of the design paradigm mentioned, programming finds, selects and organizes pertinent facts and translates them from VERBAL to GRAPHIC expression so that they may, in turn, be translated into a physical expression. . . .

The facts that need to be collected are of several kinds. White identifies "traditional" facts as those that are conventionally used by environmental designers and are not arguable. Even these traditional facts must be evaluated for their relevance to the problem at hand and that relevance should be agreed upon by all those involved in the process.

White lists nine categories of traditional facts:

1. Similar projects and critical issues
2. Client
3. Financial
4. Building codes
5. Planning by related organizations
6. Function
7. Site
8. Climate
9. Growth and change

These major categories contain extensive subcategories. For example, number 6, function, contains these subcategories:

a. operational systems—including links beyond the building
b. critical issues in insuring success in systems' operation
c. needs which are supporting to operation (lounge, waiting, toilet, janitor)
d. main operational sequences—"feeder sequences" which support main sequence
e. divisions or departments in the system
f. general departmental relationship affinities
g. number and type of people involved (task categories)
h. operations performed by each type of person
i. systems of people movement
j. systems of information movement
k. systems of material movement
l. work nodes (stations where work is performed)

These categories can be further subdivided. For instance, letter k, systems of material movement, contains:

(1) points of origin and destination (including delivery and pick up)
(2) frequency and pattern (continual or intermittent)
(3) degree of urgency
(4) role in overall operation
(5) form (size, weight)
(6) special considerations (fragile)
(7) operations performed on material (including unpacking and disposal of waste)
(8) storage implications
(9) peak loads

The clients and users must provide much of the information about the "traditional" facts, or certainly participate in the collection. The designer's task is to record and collect the information into categories and translate it into usable graphic form. Such a document is the beginning of a program; in fact, the part of the design space we have called *problem* could be called *program*. The major objection I have to that change in the analogy is that most programmers assume that the program is a rigid antecedent to the solution.

3. *What are the alternative ways of categorizing the problem?* This activity is one of the most crucial in the design process and also one of the most potent as a technique for opening the design space. As discussed earlier in the chapter 2, categorical units can have three relationships to the contextual hierarchy.

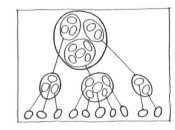

As a part, the problem should relate to the larger physical whole of the neighborhood, city, and region and to the larger temporal whole of its period in time.

- What responsibilities does the design have to the larger system?
- Should the design blend in with the larger environment or stand out as different? to what degree?
- What should the design's response be to the climatic systems of sun, wind, and rain?
- How can the design avoid adding unnecessarily to traffic congestion or air pollution?
- How can the design preserve and extend existing amenities? bike paths? landscaping features like street trees?

As a whole, the problem is composed of various parts.

- What are the alternative ways in which the problem can be subdivided functionally? contextually? sequentially? structurally?
- What are the advantages and disadvantages of the various subdivisions?
- Should these subdivisions remain in the constructed design? Would they foster an understanding of the environment when built?

As a sibling, the problem has relationships to similar environments, designed by others or, perhaps, by yourself.

- What relationships should the design have to similar environments? Should it look newer? larger? more expensive? more imaginative? more traditional?
- Should it share certain characteristics? be identifiable as a member of a set (restaurant, bank, etc.)?
- How should it be different?

It may be difficult to get a client or user to accept alternative ways of categorizing a design problem, because the categories in which we see the world are the stronghold of conventional wisdom. This conventional perception is perhaps even more common in clients who can afford to commission a professional architect, landscape architect, or interior designer, since that very fact demonstrates their success in the conventional world. If you can persuade them to see one or two alternative ways of categorizing the problem, however, it will be worth the effort.

4. *What alternative analogies can be drawn for the problem?* Analogies are well established as creative links in problem solving, and they are equally useful in terms of understanding the problem to be solved. They can help in the categorization of the problem just discussed by clarifying the relationships of the problem and its various parts to other kinds of problems. Alternative analogies are especially helpful in developing new ways of looking at the problem.

- Is the problem of designing a shopping mall like designing a vending machine or a carnival midway?
- Is a new building on an older street like a blood transfusion or an uninvited guest? Is the problem of designing for a multiple client like making a stew, offering a smorgasbord, or serving a very safe, bland dinner?
- Should the problem of designing on a very limited budget be approached like designing a denim muu-muu or a mink bikini? Is the problem of the interior design of an office suite like designing the company's letterhead or letting each employee make a nest?
- Should the landscaping of a patio be thought of as a collection of specimen pieces or as functional furniture that gives shade and adds visual interest?

Drawing analogies may seem redundant but they are useful in the extension of the likeness they

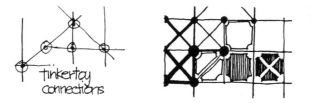

tinkertoy connections

provide. Analogies often contain unsuspected depth that can't be appreciated verbally, especially in the details that make up their physical form.

5. *What alternative entry points into the problem can be established?* Edward deBono *(Lateral Thinking,* 1970) has made it clear that the order in which we gain information in solving a problem has a great influence on the solutions we reach:

> Because of the nature of the self-maximizing memory system of the mind the entry point for considering a situation or a problem can make a big difference to the way it is structured. Usually the obvious entry point is chosen. Such an entry point is itself determined by the established pattern and so leads back to this. There is no way of telling which entry point is going to be best so one is usually content with the most obvious one. It is assumed that the choice of entry point does not matter since one will always arrive at the same conclusions. This is not so since the whole train of thought may be determined by the choice of entry point. It is useful to develop some skill in picking out and following different entry points. . . .*

Usually the common entry points to any problem are the function and the context. One of the simplest ways to vary the entry point is to imagine initiating the design process by looking at the

*These concepts and this material is from the book *Lateral Thinking* by Edward deBono, who is regarded as a leading authority in the field of creative thinking and the inventor of "Lateral Thinking." Toronto: 416-488-0008. web: www.edwdebono.com

problem from the points of view of some of the people who may be involved:

- the owner
- the user, if different
- the builder
- the unfamiliar visitor
- the next designer
- the larger community
- the building official
- the mortgage lender
- the critic
- the fire chief

or to approach the design from one of the narrower concerns that follow:

- structurally
- economically
- maintenance-wise
- formally
- security-wise
- accessibility-wise
- esthetically
- mechanically
- for future growth and change
- according to color, texture
- according to energy conservation
- traditionally

6. *What alternative designs for the design process itself should be considered?* This is an excellent opening technique because it allows you to communicate clearly to your clients or users the general form of the design process and the roles played by the various participants in the process. It also provokes you to consider alternate ways of proceeding based on this particular problem.

The range of options may be suggested by a list of questions.

- In what phases, over time, should the process be conceived? Is there a standard professional description of the designer's services?
- Whose participation and approval should be sought and when? Where are the critical decision points in the process in terms of commitment to a particular design?
- Which aspects of the problem seem most critical? What are the most important decisions to be made from the clients' or users' standpoint? from the designer's standpoint?
- How can a desirable flexibility or contingency be built into the process?
- What will be the most effective ways of communicating during the process? frequent short meetings? infrequent in-depth meetings? memos? drawings?
- Which parts of the process promise to be most profitable in terms of the designer's creativity? early overall conceptualizing? or later critical details?
- Which parts of the process will be most critical for client/user participation? initial goals and criteria? or are they so well established that participation can be concentrated on later, detailed development of the concept?

Taking time to design the process and record it graphically is always worthwhile, even for design projects in school. Planning the way we will use any period of future time, like an appointment calendar or a critical path bar chart, helps guide our efforts and recognizes that getting finished is always part of the problem. The participation of those involved in designing the process also tends to commit them to the successful completion of the process they have helped design.

THE DESIGNER'S CREDIBILITY

In opening the design space, designers may also establish their credibility as problem solvers and demonstrate the breadth and depth of their knowledge and creativity. This establishment of credibility is generally better done graphically because a designer's graphic ability is usually impressive to most clients. The graphic advantage that most designers have over the general public results not so much from our great skill as from the lack of the general development of graphic skills in our culture's educational system. Drawing skill is one of the few communicative advantages we enjoy over most clients and we should use it whenever we need to be persuasive.

In my experience the intelligent and skillful use of drawing can open the design space and involve clients in the continuing dialog of the design process. Abstract plan and section diagrams and sketchy perspectives are excellent for this opening role. The drawings should be like graphic questionnaires or conversation pieces, deliberately ambiguous and subject to alternate interpretations so that they provoke discussion and contribute to the opening of all the minds involved in the process. If you can produce a profusion of these drawings, indicating alternative ways of seeing and solving the problem, you will also communicate that the decision-making process is open to your clients and users and that you welcome and expect their participation— their company in the design space.

CLEARING DRAWINGS

Clearing drawings are designed to remove various kinds of blocks, misunderstandings, and preconceptions. They break the conventional categories we use to think about a problem and clear the design space.

Clearing drawing can be thought of as tactics for clearing up misunderstandings and removing obstructions and residue that may make the eventual closure of the problem to the solution difficult or awkward.

Clearing tactics may be ways of breaking the categories in which the problem is understood or may involve a profound conversion of the way a client or a designer looks at the built environment or the world in general. The best way to clear conceptual blocks is simply to learn to recognize them.

In many design processes there is no time or need to get involved in rethinking everything about the problem. The problem may be simple and familiar and the designer's efforts may be better concentrated on some other part of the process. On the other hand, if the problem is too familiar, or if either the client or the designer is seeking an especially innovative solution, then a thorough clearing of the design space may be necessary.

Most clearing tactics can be thought of as category-breaking, or what deBono has called the breaking of "cliché patterns." As Bruner, Good-now, and Austin made clear in *A Study of Thinking* (1956), the categories in which we perceive or conceive the world at once allow and limit all our cognitive activity. If when designing a house we accept the conventional spatial categories of living room, dining room, bedrooms, and bathrooms, our design will be limited to an arrangement of those categories. If we deliberately break those categories, however, and make ourselves consider other ways of classifying the spaces of a dwelling, we might find several interesting alternatives.

A more meaningful way to think about residential spaces might be in terms of several continuums: public/private, waking/sleeping, noisy/quiet, light/dark, hard/soft, adult/children, or individual/communal. The subcategories into which we break the design problem apart absolutely limit the ways in which we reassemble it.

Two other ways to rattle the conventional categories might be either to undercategorize or overcategorize. Undercategorization for the house could be accomplished by assuming that all functions *could* happen in one undivided space, and then gradually and deliberately adding categories and spatial subdivisions in a carefully considered order.

Overcategorization can be accomplished by taking each space and subdividing it further, as you might categorize the bedroom into sleeping, sitting, and dressing areas, or the kitchen into storage, preparation, cooking, and serving areas. Either variation demonstrates that the conventional categories are arbitrary and should not be accepted as absolute.

Category-breaking in some form is recommended by most of those who have written about the stitch end of the design process.

Another job of clearing drawings is to free the design space of the blocks that clutter it. James Adams's excellent *Conceptual Blockbusting* (1974) has an extensive list of perceptual, emotional, cultural, environmental, intellectual, and expressive blocks. Adams proposes that the first step in clearing conceptual blocks is learning to recognize them. He suggests both conscious and unconscious ways of clearing conceptual blocks. Conscious ways include various checklists, questioning, and striving for fluency and flexibility; for unconscious blockbusting he recommends the techniques of brainstorming (Osborn), synectics (Gordon), and self-actualization (Maslow).

Drawing can be used to clear out three blocks simultaneously: the perceptual block Adams calls "stereotyping—seeing what you expect to see"; the cultural block he describes as "problem solving is a serious business and humor is out of place"; and the perceptual block he calls "inability to see the problem from various viewpoints." By drawing a set of humorous stereotypical solutions of the various people involved in the environment, we can clear out a great many of our preconceptions (see page 200). If we are honest enough to include ourselves as designers in this gallery of stereotypes, and brave enough to show the collection to the other participants in the process, we may have an excellent start in clearing the design space.

Drawing can help in understanding and clearing many such blocks, and the inability to use drawing as a problem-solving language is one of the kinds of expressive blocks Adams discusses. Fluency with various languages and the flexibility to translate from one language to another, including drawing, is central to any design process.

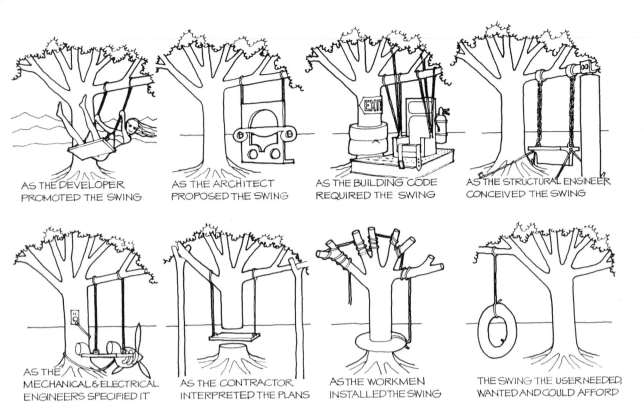

AS THE DEVELOPER
PROMOTED THE SWING

AS THE ARCHITECT
PROPOSED THE SWING

AS THE BUILDING CODE
REQUIRED THE SWING

AS THE STRUCTURAL ENGINEER
CONCEIVED THE SWING

AS THE
MECHANICAL & ELECTRICAL
ENGINEERS SPECIFIED IT

AS THE CONTRACTOR
INTERPRETED THE PLANS

AS THE WORKMEN
INSTALLED THE SWING

THE SWING THE USER NEEDED,
WANTED AND COULD AFFORD

Two of the other blocks Adams has identified (the emotional block of "fear to make a mistake, to fail, to risk" and the perceptual block of "tendency to delimit the problem area too closely") might be loosened by deliberately drawing the most outrageous extensions of the problem we can think of.

And one last graphic effort might simultaneously clear the blocks Adams calls "preference for judging ideas rather than generating them" (emotional) and "taboos" (cultural). Here the idea, recommended by several other writers on creativity, is to set a quota of alternative concepts, several of which include obvious cultural taboos, and delay evaluating them or eliminating objectionable or apparently ridiculous ideas until you have generated and graphically recorded the full quota.

Drawing is particularly helpful in these clearing operations because its actual, physical operation and its manifestation of the idea purges our consciousness at a deeper level because it engages the eyemindhand triad.

If we broaden clearing to include *clarification* we can further our understanding of the problem and prevent premature closure of the design space. This involves the collecting and screening of what White calls "nontraditional" facts. These facts require more discussion and negotiation in the design process because various participants inevitably bring conflicting and antithetical facts. The disagreement is caused by the relational, contingent quality of this kind of information and because, unlike the earlier traditional facts, nontraditional facts do not lie within one particular participant's area of expertise.

This is a typical example of a contradiction in nontraditional facts: (fact #1) people value and respect well-designed, well-maintained environments and their behavior reflects that; (fact #2) people are not to be trusted and if there is any way that an environment can be vandalized or littered, it will be. Because of the controversial nature of such nontraditional facts, it is important that during the clearing phase, disagreements and misunderstandings be cleared up as much as possible.

Tim White (*Introduction to Architectural Programming*, 1972) best describes nontraditional facts:

> There is no clear-cut division that can be made between traditional and non-traditional architectural facts. The classification of a fact as one or the other will depend upon the degree of programming and design DETAIL required for the building type in question, the UNIQUENESS of the building type and the depth and breadth of the KNOWLEDGE of the designer. What is non-traditional for one building or designer may be very common for another.

These nontraditional facts should be screened for relevance and made graphic as White suggests, and their inclusion and arrangement into categories and a hierarchy of importance always should be discussed and decided upon by all the participants in the process. Designers and others probably always harbor a covert set of their own nontraditional facts, which they try to smuggle into the process, but it is always better to acknowledge them openly and graphically and then agree upon them.

Stitch Drawings

Stitch drawings are designed to make trial closures between the problem and a solution by drawing tentative, piecemeal solutions to specific parts of the problem. They search for direction.

Stitches are the first tentative attempts at closing the design space. These first attempts at closure cannot always be delayed through the opening and clearing phases discussed earlier. They happen. Designers cannot *not* have ideas about how to join parts of the problem to parts of the solution; they surface through the cracks in our consciousness and are comforting evidence of the futility of controlling human behavior, especially human thought. Methodological robots might be able to march through the design process with never a sideways glance, or without ever breaking stride into a skip or a dance, but human designers always behave anticipatorily, peeking behind the curtains of whatever model of the design process they say they follow.

CLOSING TECHNIQUES

Closing techniques are not given the attention they deserve in most works on creativity. This lack of attention to closure may come from a hesitancy to suggest conscious, deliberate closing techniques and may carry vestiges of the traditional myth that concepts are *given* not *made* and that all that can be done is to open the mind, clear the blocks, and then just wait patiently for the idea to arrive. After the "problem solver" follows the prescribed opening and clearing techniques, she or he is described variously as "seeing the solution," "arriving at the solution," "discovering the answer," or as coolly choosing between various alternatives.

As a designer, I don't remember those moments as a kind of instantaneous seeing, arriving, discovering, or choosing. I would say that the beginning of the closure occurs when I see, usually in the drawings, a way to make a promising first stitch across the design gap and then feel confident that other reinforcing stitches, only vaguely sensed at the beginning, will soon become possible.

The literature on thinking, problem solving, programming, and creativity varies widely in its recommendations for ways of closing the design space that separates the problem from a solution, ranging from Adams's counsel to "relax, incubate, and sleep on it," to synectics's search for various analogical links to similar problems and solutions in other fields, to deBono's many suggestions for different ways of perceiving and manipulating the problem, to White's methodical development of a detailed program of facts and precepts. As if the range weren't wide enough already I'd like to extend it by adding what might best be called "managed procrastination."

I have found that, after an intense initial effort to understand the problem, the deliberate avoidance of working or even thinking about the problem for extended periods of time is, for me, a very useful technique. Perhaps my tendency to use procrastination as a creativity technique increased after I read that procrastination was the *sine qua non* of creative people; I know it increased with my conceptual confidence and my drawing skill—or perhaps I have some Hopi blood in me. The Hopi see no necessary relationship between how diligently they work in, say, weaving a basket, and how soon the basket is finished. They are simply helping the basket become a basket, which it will do when it is ready, or when the time is right. Most design students are potential Hopi, but the procrastination technique must be controlled by very careful and confident management, because getting finished is always part of any design problem.

Despite the wide variety of advice on how to stitch the problem to a solution, there is broad general agreement that the most successful stitches are made by those who have a solid set of conceptual skills (including drawing) and a good basic knowledge of existing solutions, and who have made an intensely concentrated attempt to "get their heads around" the problem. Beyond this initial agreement the range of suggested techniques quickly diverges and we can only sample it here.

Synectics: The Development of Creative Capacity (1968), by W. J. J. Gordon, proposes four specific classes of analogies that are very clearly illustrated in Paul Laseau's *Graphic Thinking for Architects and Designers* (1980):

> In his book *Synectics: The Development of Creative Capacity*, William Gordon described four types of analogy: symbolic, direct, personal, and fantasy.

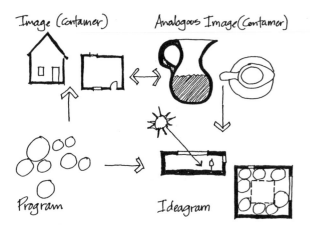

Image (container)   Analogous Image (container)

Program   Ideagram

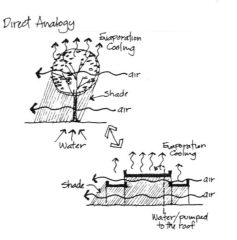

Direct Analogy

Evaporation Cooling
air
Shade
air
Water

Evaporation Cooling
Shade
air
air
Water/pumped to the roof

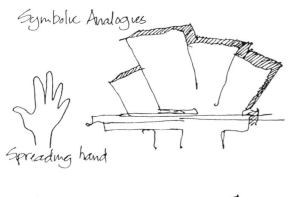

Symbolic Analogues

Spreading hand

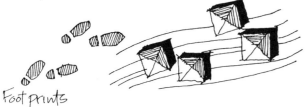

Foot prints

From *Graphic Problem Solving for Architects and Builders* by Paul Laseau.

The example of the pitcher and the house as containers is a *symbolic analogy*, a comparison between general qualities of the two objects. Other symbolic analogies might be made between the spread of a hand and the extensions of a house or between footprints and canopied pavilions which loosely constitute the house.

Direct analogy compares parallel facts or operations. In the above example, the house is designed to have the same cooling characteristics as a tree: shade, evaporation, and air movement.

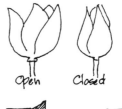

Personal Analogy

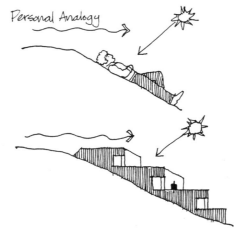

In a *personal analogy,* the designer identifies himself directly with the elements of the problem. Assuming that the prime consideration for this house is warmth and comfort on winter days without large uses of nonrenewable energy sources, the designer might imagine himself to be the house. To make himself comfortable, he might lie close to the ground below the ridge so the cold wind can pass over his head. This can

be translated into a low-profile house below the ridge with trays of space covered by sloped glass skylights to admit the warm rays of the sun.

Fantasy Analogy

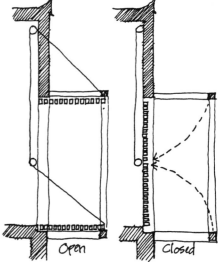

Open   Closed

Open   Closed

The fourth type, *fantasy analogy,* uses a description of an ideal condition, desired as a source for ideas. In the case of our recreational house, the designer might fantasize a house that opens itself up when the client arrives on the weekend and automatically closes up when the client leaves. It could be compared to a tulip that opens and closes with the action of sunlight, or the automatic garage door, or a puppet that comes alive when you pick up the strings. The decks and the roofs over the decks could be like the leaves of the tulip. But how do they open and close? A motor is another energy consumer; is there another way? How can the puppet strings help? The final solution uses ropes and pulleys to raise and lower the flaps. The system is balanced so that the weight of a person on the decks can pull up the roofs, and the drooping of the roofs could pull the decks back up. The decks and roofs would be held in both open and closed positions by spring latches.

The ability to see similarities, make relationships, draw analogies, and make metaphors is perhaps the most valuable creative mechanism. To be able to see how one thing is like another allows designers to stitch to their current design problem *all* they know or have experienced, not just what they may know about architecture, landscape architecture, or interior design.

Edward deBono's *Lateral Thinking* (1970) suggests many techniques for getting out of the rut of what he calls the "vertical thinking" of conventional logic. I have referred to some of deBono's suggestions earlier but a few of his techniques are especially appropriate in stitching:

THE REVERSAL METHOD

Unless one is going to sit around waiting for inspiration the most practical way to get moving is to work on what one has. In a swimming race when the swimmers come to turn at the end of the pool they kick hard against the end to increase their speed. In the reversal method one kicks hard against what is there and fixed in order to move away in the opposite direction.

In the reversal method one takes things as they are and then turns them round, inside out, upside down, back to front. Then one sees what happens. It is a provocative rearrangement of information. You make water run uphill instead of downhill. Instead of driving a car the car leads you.

In Aesop's fable the water in the jug was at too low a level for the bird to drink. The bird was thinking of taking water out of the jug but instead he thought of putting something in. So he dropped pebbles into the jug until the level of water rose high enough for him to drink.

In lateral thinking one is not looking for the right answer but for a different arrangement of information which will provoke a different way of looking at the situation. *

The purpose of the reversal procedure

Very often the reversal procedure leads to a way of looking at the situation that is obviously wrong or ridiculous. What then is the point of doing it?

- One uses the reversal procedure in order to escape from the absolute necessity to look at the situation in the standard way. It does not matter whether the new way makes sense or not for once one escapes

*These concepts and this material is from the book *Lateral Thinking* by Edward deBono, who is regarded as a leading authority in the field of creative thinking and the inventor of "Lateral Thinking." Toronto: 416-488-0008. web: www.edwdebono.com

then it becomes easier to move in other directions as well.
- By disrupting the original way of looking at the situation one frees information that can come together in a new way.
- To overcome the terror of being wrong, of taking a step that is not fully justified.
- The main purpose is provocative. By making the reversal one moves to a new position. Then one sees what happens.
- Occasionally the reversed approach is useful in itself.

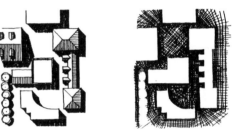

The reversal method suggests several possibilities for design drawing:

- Graphic figure/field reversal can help the designer to see the problem in a new way. The conventional dark/light, mass/void indication can be reversed so that the space is drawn as black and the walls or structure as white.
- It might also be interesting to briefly draw up the worst solution for the problem you can imagine. This effort might help you to see what would constitute the best solution, by contrast.
- It might be interesting to draw what you consider to be the least important aspect of the design and give it your undivided design attention for just a while.

Another technique recommended by deBono *(Lateral Thinking,* 1970) has to do with the importance of the point of entry into a problem:

ENTRY POINT

The choice of entry point is of huge importance because the historical sequence in which ideas follow one another can completely determine the final outcome even if the ideas themselves are the same. . . .

Divide a triangle into three parts in such a way that the parts can be put together again to form a rectangle or a square.

The problem is quite a difficult one since the shape of the triangle is not specified. You first have to choose a triangle shape and then find out how it can be divided up into three pieces that can be put together to give the square or rectangle.

The solution to the problem is shown opposite. It is obviously much easier to start with the square instead of with the triangle which was suggested as the starting point. There can be no doubt about the shape of a square whereas the shape of a triangle (and to a lesser extent of a rectangle) is variable. Since the three parts have to fit together again to form a square one can solve the problem by dividing up a square into three parts that can be put together again to give a rectangle or a triangle. Two ways of doing this are shown opposite.

In many children's books there is the sort of puzzle in which are shown three fishermen whose lines have gotten tangled up. At the bottom of the picture a fish is shown attached to one of the lines. The problem is

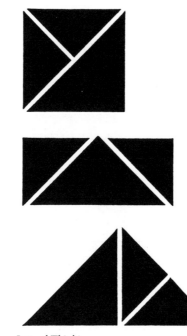

From *Lateral Thinking:*
Creativity Step by Step by Edward de Bono.

to find which fisherman has caught the fish. The children are supposed to follow the line down from the tip of the fishing rod in order to find which line has the fish at the end. This may involve one, two or three lines. It is obviously much easier to start at the other end and trace the line upwards from the fish to the fisherman. That way there need never be more than one attempt.

Choice of entry point is easily translated into a useful design drawing technique by beginning the stitching with drawings that normally come much later in the process, say, a reflected ceiling plan, a window detail, or an interior perspective. Such unusual graphic beginnings can have the same beneficial effects, which deBono describes in geometric puzzles and verbal thinking:

RANDOM WORD STIMULATION

This is a practical and definite procedure in which the true random nature of the input is beyond doubt. If one is a purist one can use a table of random numbers to select a page in a dictionary. The number of a word on that page (counting down the page) can also be obtained from the table of random numbers. With less trouble one can simply think of two numbers and find the word that way. Or throw some dice. What one must not do is to open a dictionary and go through the pages until one finds a likely looking word. That would be selection and it would be useless from a random stimulation point of view.

The numbers 473–13 were given by a table of random numbers and using the Penguin English Dictionary the word located was: 'noose'. The problem under consideration was 'the housing shortage'. Over a timed three minute period the following ideas were generated.

noose—tightening noose—execution—what are the difficulties in executing a housing programme—what is the bottleneck, is it capital, labour or land?

noose tightens—things are going to get worse with the present rate of population increase.

noose—rope—suspension construction system—tent like houses but made of permanent materials—easily packed and erected—or on a large scale with several houses suspended from one framework— much lighter materials possible if walls did not have to support themselves and the roof.

noose—loop—adjustable loop—what about adjustable round house which could be expanded as required—just uncoil the walls— no point in having houses too large to begin with because of heating problems, extra attention to walls and ceilings, furniture etc—but facility for slow stepwise expansion as need arises.

noose—snare—capture—capture a share of the labour market—capture—people captured by home ownership due to difficulty in selling and complications—lack of mobility—houses as exchangeable units— classified into types—direct exchange of one type for similar type—or put one type into the pool and take out a similar type elsewhere.

Random word stimulation is directly analogous to beginning the design process by randomly selecting and then working from a page from Ching's *Architecture: Form, Space & Order* (1979), or from a book on architectural ornament, or even from a book of photographs of electron microscopy. Gyorgy Kepes *(The New Landscape in Art and Science,* 1956) makes the very interesting point that artists and designers, who once had direct access to all the visual stimulation of the world, are no longer seeing the incredibly stimulating visual patterns that are available to scientists. Today there are privileged people peering into micro- and macro-worlds through powerful microscopes, telescopes, and various other devices, and we can only envy the random visual stimulation they enjoy.

If the problem is small in scale or scope, stitch drawings may quickly become the holistic hitches that synthesize entire solutions and anchor the rest of the design process. That kind of complete closure may still be premature, however, and one of the advantages of the deliberate piecemeal approach of programming is the suspended judgment it enforces by its careful consideration of as many aspects of the problem as possible.

The great virtue offered by programming is that the precept diagrams that correspond to the stitches in the present analogy begin to translate the verbal program statements into visual or graphic form. This initial translation and the visual verification of the precept is necessary if the final design is to fulfill the goals expressed by the precept. No one will be giving guided tours or writing guidebooks on the intricacies of the design after it is built. The designed environment will have to speak for itself, and one of the ways to predict what it may say is to begin translating verbal programming ideas into precept diagrams.

To quote once again from Edward T. White's *Introduction to Architectural Programming:*

The organization of data is the essential process for bridging the gap between the PROBLEM STATEMENT and the SYNTHETIC OPERATION that will result in a solution. It is the point where client needs and their relationships with the other facts gathered, analyzed and evaluated are TRANSLATED into the language of the designer.

Needs and other facts at the gathering stage are largely VERBAL concepts. As architecture is a PHYSICAL (visual) expression of the solution to the problem statement it is of value to express as much of the program GRAPHICALLY and DIAGRAMMATICALLY as possible. This diagrammatic translation of the programming facts is the start of the formation of the physical building, as diagrams have DIRECT implications on physical building form.

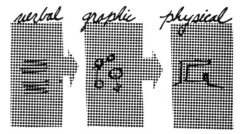

From *Introduction to Architectural Programming* by Edward T. White.

The programmer's ability to design visual, graphic communication of programming data will largely determine the extent to which all the programming NEEDS are met in synthesis.

Example organizational operations are:

1. SORTING and GROUPING of facts into categories based on qualities identified in analysis and according to criteria established by the programmer (sequence of use, relative importance).

2. Sorting and grouping of the EFFECTS on the design of individual building aspects implied by the program data.

3. Establishing a HIERARCHY of determinants which will direct the sequence and intensity of the designer's attention in synthesis.

4. Writing DEFINITIVE precepts describing individual conclusions about the data and proposals about what the final design should accomplish.

    a. Precepts should be SHORT, CONCISE, deal with only ONE issue at a time and be expressed GRAPHICALLY.

    b. Precepts should identify the UNIQUENESS of the problem. The extent to which general or "universal" precepts are written down and contained in the document depends on the PURPOSE of the document. OBVIOUS precepts may need to be included when EDUCATING the client.

    c. Precepts should deal with issues involving building SECTION and ELEVATION as well as plan. This will help to avoid the "extruded plan" difficulty.

    d. An important role of precepts is that of EVALUATORS of directions taken in the conceptualization stages of synthesis. By checking alternative design

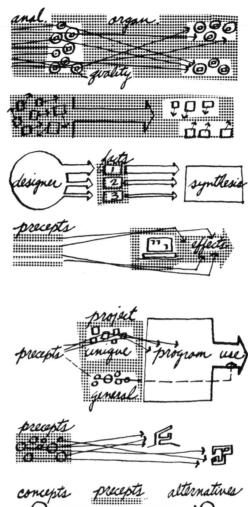

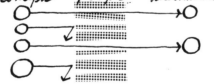

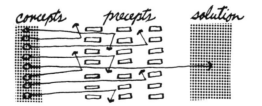

From *Introduction to Architectural Programming* by Edward T. White.

directions against the precepts, the development of INVIABLE concepts can be avoided. Precepts help SCREEN and EVALUATE design alternatives.

Theoretically a comprehensive establishment of precepts at all levels of design synthesis (schematics, development) will result in a CONVERGENCE to the most viable solution to the problem. Hence, the statement, "the solution is contained in the statement of the problem."

    e. The use of precepts can help identify POTENTIAL CONFLICTS in the design problem. This is most clearly illustrated when two precepts COMPETE for a response from a particular building aspect or element where a response to one EXCLUDES the possibility of responding to the other.

    f. PATTERN LANGUAGE (Alexander) is closely related to the precept model. Essentially it proposes synthetic solutions to sub-problems which can be used in designing many different building types. The RESOLUTION of conflicts in the patterns and the SYNTHESIS of them into a whole is left to the DESIGNER.

5. Identifying the ALTERNATIVE CONCEPTS for the design of the building SUGGESTED by the precepts.

6. Putting all the analyzed, evaluated and organized data into USABLE form (presentation). This task has special implications where the program is to be published or where data is to be fed to a computer for sorting or grouping.

Most of the techniques recommended in the literature on creativity can be applied to environmental design, and most of them can be applied graphically, but their value in design drawing tends to be limited to the opening and clearing phases of the design process. When it comes time to begin stitching the design space together most experienced designers have little patience with analytical or analogical drawing. They may continue to use the analytical, analogical, and manipulative techniques in their eyeminds, but they draw sketchy doodles and diagrams based on the traditional representational drawings of their design disciplines. Unless they have deep blockages or hang-ups about externalizing their ideas in drawings, they begin to draw stitches that directly join parts of the problem to parts of the solution.

Stitch drawings are usually plans and sections because those two views show the designed environment's internal relationships most abstractly and efficiently. These diagrammatic plans and sections are usually followed closely, and at times may even be preceded, by thumbnail exterior aerial perspectives (which show the three-dimensional form of the design), and interior eyelevel perspectives (which predict the experience of the built environment). Stitch drawings also usually include sketches of relatively minor details and many verbal notes. Paul Laseau (*Graphic Thinking for Architects and Designers*, 1980) has summed up the characteristics of Leonardo da Vinci's notebooks and illustrates their application in drawings of his own:

1. There are many different ideas on one page; his attention is constantly shifting from one subject to another.

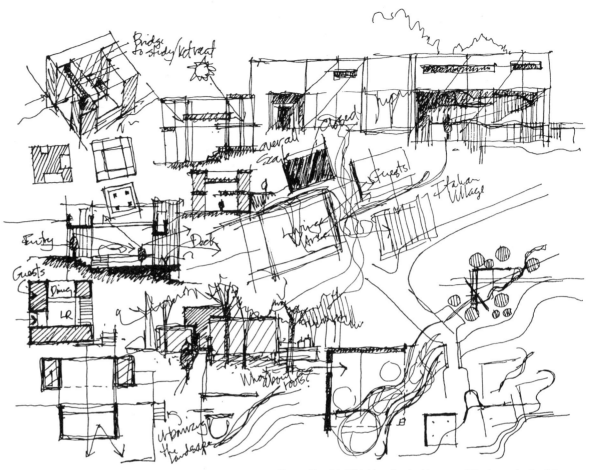

From *Graphic Thinking for Architects and Designers* by Paul Laseau. Copyright © 1989 by Van Nostrand Reinhold. Reprinted by permission of John Wiley & Sons, Inc.

2. The way da Vinci looks at problems is diverse both in method and scale; there are often perspectives, plans, details, and panoramic views on the same page.
3. The thinking is exploratory, open-ended; the sketches are loose and fragmented, while showing how they were derived. Many alternatives for extending the ideas are suggested. The spectator is invited to participate.

Stitches have an undisciplined freedom to range over all our experience and knowledge—of the natural world, of the other arts and sciences, and all of human knowledge—anywhere we can find or make relationships to the problem we are trying to solve. Stitch drawings are characterized by wild variations and alterations of scale and focus, as if the designer were looking through a microscope/telescope/x-ray/time-machine of infinitely variable magnification and focal length. At one moment the focus may be lengthened to include the neighborhood, urban area, or region, and the next be shortened to considerations of the shape and finish of the doorknobs. In addition to their range and flexibility, stitch drawings should have a certain ambiguity, be low in specific information, and prompt a variety of interpretations.

A shift in the analogy we have been using may synthesize what I have to say about the stitch phase of the design process. If we lay down the vertical design space that separates the problem from a solution and fill it with water, we have a river that separates one bank called the "problem" from another called the "solution." And if we bend the river around a central castle we have a moat. If we call the castle the "solutions" and the surrounding land the "problems," the designer's task becomes building ways of joining the problem to the solution by crossing the moat.

The conventional image of this analogy is that we assault the castle with the catapults of reason, the arrows of analysis, feigned withdrawals, and the whole range of methodical siege and assault weapons that we can marshal from the problem side of the moat.

The difficulty with this view of the analogy is that we have it backwards. We are actually on the other side of the moat, imprisoned in the castle of the solutions we already know. We designers do not march up to the moat from the land side to storm the castle—we are already its prisoners! We sally forth into problem-solving land across the *draw*bridges of our design abilities to relate the solutions we know to the problems on the other side of the moat. And drawing is one of the longest and strongest *draw*bridges over which we can cross.

Analysis and programming may extend the abutment that the drawbridge has to reach or scatter stepping stones into the moat leading from the castle, but the moves that finally cross the moat must come from the solution side, because that is where we live.

If we strip the analogy down to simply standing on an island of solutions separated by a moat from the surrounding problem, we can summarize and illustrate the various stitch techniques we have been discussing:

- The analogies of synectics broaden the solution island on which we are standing by adding all the solutions we already know from all our knowledge and experience.
- DeBono's reversal method means doing an about-face and viewing the problem shoreline 180 degrees from the conventional view; his choice of entry point means deliberately examining the 360 degrees of problem shoreline for the most promising entry point; and his random stimulation means randomly probing the bottom of the moat in the hope of finding a ford that can be waded.
- The precepts of programming are stepping stones extending out into the moat from the problem shore.

All techniques are potentially helpful, but in all cases the first plunge into the moat must come from solutions we understand.

HITCH DRAWINGS

Hitch drawings are designed to anchor a particular solution to the problem by drawing various overall organizing concepts. They establish direction for the subsequent zipper.

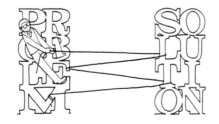

We have reached the most crucial and controversial point in the stitches-and-zipper analogy for the design process. Many of those who have written about creativity regard this as the moment of primary creativity—the creative leap—while many of those who have written about design method discount its importance, and some deny the need or even the desirability of any overall concept or big idea.

THE FORMAL IMPERATIVE

One point of confusion that needs clearing up is this: in the design professions, organizing concepts—ideas capable of ordering the entire design and the remainder of the design process—must be visual, graphic, or spatial. They must have a physical reality. They cannot be verbal statements or mathematical formulas that are translated into some three-dimensional form. While it is true that needs and wishes may initially be expressed verbally and be translated into graphic precept diagrams, or stitch drawings, the translation is the designer's responsibility—in all likelihood the reason he or she enjoys the activity—and the generation of a specific physical form or pattern in response to any design problem is the core of design responsibility.

The recent denigration of "formalism" and "form-giving" is perhaps justified by the abuses of those designers who have littered our environment with willful, self-conscious, formal "statements." We probably don't need many more "form-givers." We have plenty of forms already, but we will always need sensitive designers to apply and recombine the rich formal heritage of the design professions.

Words and numbers may be necessary to the understanding of a problem and useful as description or rationalization, but they cannot be design ideas. *There is no such thing as a verbal design idea, only verbal descriptions of design ideas.* Organizing ideas in environmental design are formal patterns. They are not necessarily innovative, axial, or even geometrically regular, but they must have a memorable pattern *that can be drawn.*

Frank Ching's *Architecture: Form, Space & Order* (1979) is a beautiful collection of historic and contemporary organizing patterns for architecture. One brief look at the richness and variety of these organizing ideas makes it clear that we needn't strain to invent too many new patterns.

Tim White's *Concept Sourcebook: A Vocabulary of Architectural Forms* (1975) is another excellent source of more abstract, less traditional organizing ideas for buildings.

In the past, organizing concepts for additions to the built environment have lasted for centuries. Content to repeat the traditional way of building, builders have been constrained by unquestioned cultural conformity and limited by material and technological necessity. The very notion that each problem should have an innovative solution is relatively new. It may be the product of our cultural and technological freedom, and the *raison d'etre* of the design professions, but it certainly is also one of the reasons for the visual chaos of our built environment.

Today's technological freedom and lack of cultural conformity necessitate an anchor point in the design process, however, whether we view it as an opportunity for radical creativity or merely as a deliberate choice of which formal vocabulary to follow. The formation or selection of such an overall organizing concept is also necessary for design teamwork, where a common goal must be clearly understood by several different people.

THE POPCORN ANALOGY

If you will permit me another simple-minded analogy, the individually conceived piecemeal closures of parts of the problem to parts of a solution—the stitches—can be thought of as individual popcorn kernels. Once a certain conceptual temperature has been reached, such individual ideas can be popped off with relative ease. Undisciplined designers and their clients can soon be up to their knees in popcorn without any notion of how to organize the profusion of separate ideas.

Real popcorn can be strung, bagged, or balled, and these three ways of organizing popcorn illustrate three kinds of organizing concepts. The popcorn string is an analogy for design method as an organizer, while bagging or balling popcorn is analogous to the kinds of organizing ideas sought for in hitch drawings.

The stringing of individual kernels into a popcorn chain used to trim Christmas trees is much like the serial string of operations recommended by design methodologists. The organization achieved is more a product of the linear logic of the method—the needle and thread—than of any overall compositional idea.

The collecting of selected popcorn kernels into a bag is analogous to the traditional exclusive notion of architectural unity. The bag unifies a certain set of ideas by taking them within an exclusive boundary. This kind of organizing idea uses the bag as a discriminatory boundary, concentrating on how the included individual ideas are superior to the excluded ideas, rather than how they are related to one another. This can be demonstrated by shaking the bag, which may drastically rearrange the internal relationships of the selected kernels without changing the outward appearance of the bag. Bags of popcorn are quantitative organizers because all such selective boundaries have a limited capacity.

The making of popcorn balls is analogous to an inclusive way of organizing individual ideas. The unifying element in this case is the caramel or syrup, which can be thought of as an inner structure or affinity the ideas have for one another. This basis of inner integrity, rather than an outer boundary, sets no limit on the size of the resulting popcorn ball, and while the outward appearance changes with each additional kernel, the inner integrity remains. This kind of organizing idea is more qualitative than quantitative and inclusive rather than exclusive.

MAKING THE HITCH

Traditionally, organizing concepts are based on characteristics of the problem or the various sub-concepts or stitches, not on a particular method or procedure. The stitches-and-zipper model of the design process assumes this traditional view.

Another difference in the description of this hitch or anchor point in the design process is whether such organizing concepts are, or should be, thought of as selected, discovered, revealed, or made. (Discovered and revealed ideas were discussed earlier in chapter 2. Selected ideas are a contribution of design method.)

The *selection* of an organizing idea presumes that the alternative ideas are known and broadly shared. If organizing ideas must be *discovered*, the presumption is that although they exist they must be searched for in unexpected places. *Revealed* ideas can only come in moments of inspiration, which can be hoped for but never acquired by direct effort. The *making* of organizing ideas may include a little of all the foregoing, but assumes that organizing ideas should be the result of an active synthesizing effort, unique to every problem, for which the designer is responsible.

Much of the testimony about how creative ideas actually occur holds that they surface into our consciousness unbidden, at times when no direct effort is being made. This would seem most like the revealed or inspired view of creativity, but this may be misleading because the seemingly innocent occurrence of the idea comes only after periods of intensely concentrated conceptual effort and only to persons who have a certain mastery of the subject matter area.

The selecting or finding of organizing concepts also has a validity, in that there is a legacy of such ideas in the design disciplines that is endlessly mined and reinterpreted by successive generations of designers.

Whether organizing concepts are bags or balls, or whether they are selected, found, revealed or made, they can appear in the drawings we make when we are designing. There is nothing magical about their appearance, although one of the great advantages of drawing is that it legitimizes the participation of the unconscious, that great well of wisdom and experience that is normally closed off to verbal or mathematical inquiry.

The "appearance" of an organizing idea or pattern in a drawing will only happen if we have built an extensive knowledge of such organizing patterns and can recognize one when we see it.

To return to the self-model suggested in chapter 2, there is no chance whatever of your recognizing a potential organizing pattern, even if you have created it, if you don't have the perception of a similar pattern lodged somewhere in your experience.

You need not have consciously studied the pattern—you may have walked it or seen it in a book—but it must be a part of your conscious or unconscious experience if you are to have any hope of recognizing it when it "appears."

Such appearances are characterized by their holistic nature—their ability to take over whatever pattern we are working on, whether it be a plan, section, or functional diagram. While we might have been considering only one aspect of the design task, the organizing concept allows or demands that we begin to work with the entire problem as a whole. This comprehensive synthesis realized in the hitch drawings is always beneficial. Too often in design education there is only time for one of these syntheses in the days or hours before the deadline. The many details and relationships that appear for the first time in the hitch drawing leave the designer with an extensive list of unresolved problems to be worked out during the zippering phase that follows.

Those who have written about creativity characterize such moments as occurring when individuals suddenly see how the problem is like something normally not associated with it ("bisociation," Koestler, 1964) and the experience usually includes a profound conversion in their perception of the problem. Others believe that Koestler's "bisociation" and the examples he cites are too pat and simplistic. Howard Gruber (*Darwin On Man, A Psychological Study of Creativity*, 1974) believes the overall structure of the process is more important than the individual insights within it:

As for problem solving, it takes place in a diverse train of activities: reading and observation, imagination and memory, argument and discussion. For all we really know of it, focused problem solving may be a comparatively rare event. The very act of taking up a problem crystallizes a long history of development.

Given a problem-solving process, we may find reflection, sudden insights, and gradual improvement through trial and error. Even the groping trials are not blind or

● IRREGULAR FORMS:

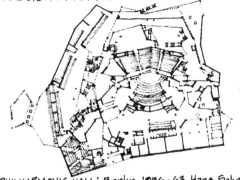

PHILHARMONIC HALL: Berlin 1956-63 Hans Scharoun

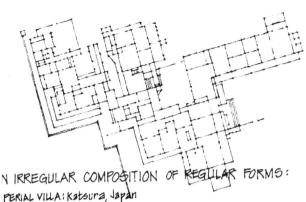

N IRREGULAR COMPOSITION OF REGULAR FORMS:

PERIAL VILLA: Katsura, Japan

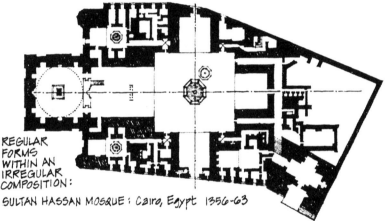

● REGULAR FORMS WITHIN AN IRREGULAR COMPOSITION:

SULTAN HASSAN MOSQUE: Cairo, Egypt 1356-63

From *Architecture: Form, Space and Order* by Francis D. K. Ching. Copyright © 1979 by Litton Educational Publishing, Inc. Reprinted by permission of John Wiley & Sons.

In the design process of mature designers the hitch occurs most often as the recognition of the congruence of a potential pattern with a pattern that is already part of our conscious or unconscious experience. Unfortunately, beginning design students are often asked to produce environmental designs before they have been exposed to the amazingly rich and stimulating heritage of patterns other designers have already used. This practice suggests that one of the major tasks of

random: they emerge from the problem solver's perception of the structure of the problem as he has come to recognize and understand it from his own particular vantage point. Thus, the sudden insight in which a problem is solved, when it is solved suddenly, may represent only a minor nodal point, like the crest of a wave, in a long and very slow process—the development of a point of view.

Although it is presumptuous to compare the process of designing an environment to the development of Darwin's theory of evolution, which is what Gruber is referring to in the preceding quotation, most design processes have more in common with his description than with the examples in most of the literature on creativity. Examples from science seem to dominate most of what has been written about creativity, limiting creativity to what Thomas Kuhn (*The Structure of Scientific Revolutions*, 1962) calls "normal science"—to concept attainment. The concept formation of environmental design is complicated by several characteristics fundamentally different from what Kuhn calls the "puzzle solving" of normal science:

- There are no fixed, verifiable answers to the problems of environmental design as there are in science.
- There is not even agreement on what the problems are, or which problems should be solved, as there is in science.
- Unlike with science, both the definition of the problems and the forms of the solution must be synthesized and remain openly arguable; additionally, the congruence of a problem and a solution should reflect a consensus of all those involved in the process.
- Unlike with science, quantification, mathematics, reason, and logic are only one set of the tools needed in achieving and defending the congruence of a problem and a solution.
- Unlike with science, environmental design always occurs within the real constraints of time and money. The design process is committed to deadlines and budgets that must be met. There is no possibility of not solving the problem.

environmental design is to invent organizing patterns from scratch and in response to each new problem.

The cataloging of these patterns has been traditionally the province of historians and critics who have revealed the collection chronologically in history courses or stacked the deck of examples to rationalize some particular theory. *Architecture: Form, Space & Order* (1979) by Francis D. K. Ching is a refreshingly different kind of collection of these organizing patterns. The

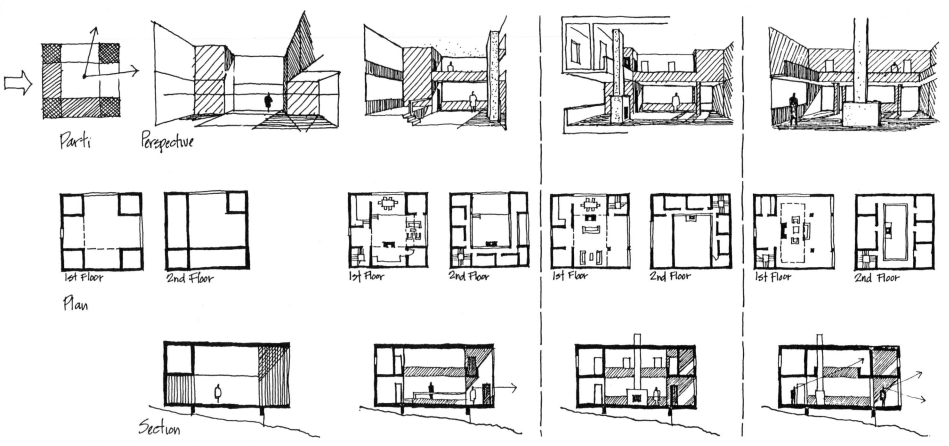

A parti and three different forms of its articulation.

From *Graphic Thinking for Architects and Designers* by Paul Laseau.

examples range over all of history, including buildings as recent as 1978, and over the world, including hemispheres and cultures often ignored by biased architectural histories. The collection is also categorized on a neutrally abstract basis in several ways that directly emphasize formal patterns, and the entire book is *drawn*, which makes the patterns much more usable to the design student because they are presented in the same medium the student will be using in the design process.

When a potential pattern is sensed, drawing *becomes* the design process, because there is now a sensed goal or direction and the drawings are immediately manipulated to see if the congruence can be accomplished—to see if the pattern can be realized.

This need to confirm or work out the pattern gives us the second characteristic of the anchoring hitches in the design process: they are never completely resolved at the moment of recognition. They are only recognized potentials—a betting on the come—and they usually provoke intense design activity. The activity provoked by such potential pattern recognition always includes a certain testing of this crucial hitch that will anchor the rest of the design process. Like testing the security of a knot you've just tied by tugging at it, or setting the hook after a fishing strike, the organizing concept must be tested in two ways: as an object and as an environment.

A quick turning of the idea through the orthographic drawings will evaluate its integrity as a built object, but the testing must include eye-level perspectives if the environmental experience of the concept is to be measured. Paul Laseau's *Graphic Thinking for Architects and Designers* (1980) offers several excellent examples of this kind of testing.

If the organizing pattern passes these tests, it achieves a third characteristic of such conceptual patterns: the commitment of the designer to the remainder of the design process. This commitment is evidence of the congruence between the organizing concept and the designer's goals, wishes, and hunches and may occur in the face of the initial resistance and rejection of other participants in the process. The organizing idea gives meaning to such criteria as integrity and consistency, and allows a sorting of the piecemeal ideas that may have preceded it. All ideas can now be seen as supporting or diluting the main organizing idea.

The commitment of the designer to a particular organizing concept is an exercise of free will. There is nothing "natural" or "necessary" about any of this and the commitment to a design concept is simply another existential choice. Design is always to some degree the imposition of the designer's will on the environment; the organizing ideas of mature designers in particular are usually severely prescribed by certain formal prejudices the designer has developed over the years.

The most surprising thing about organizing ideas is that the recognition, the testing, and the commitment are usually preverbal. The profound conversion of the perception of the problem, the intense preliminary working out and testing of the idea, and finally the complete commitment may occur in the absence of any verbalized rationale. The potential of hitch ideas is sensed in that covert, inner congruence discussed in chapter 2. The quality or correctness of the organizing idea is seen or felt, not reasoned.

Hitch drawings signal a profound change in design activity. Instead of the random, aimless wandering of the previous stitching phase, there is now an established direction, a sensed goal. The difference can be dramatically illustrated by the word association games often played around a table. If the game is begun with a word and the only criterion is to name a new word that has a relationship to the initial or previous word, there will be an interesting progression of associations. Succeeding players can move up to more generic categories, down to subcategories or sideways to siblings or opposites. The relationships may be imaginative or dull as they move over the hierarchy of verbal meanings we share, but their movement will be a directionless odyssey much like the stitches of the previous phase. If the rules of the word game are changed, however, so that two words are given, an initial word and a goal word, with the objective being to build a series of transitional words that "get to" the goal word, the whole character of the game changes. With just a little practice, the goal word can be reached with only a few or even a single transitional word.

The anchoring hitch in any design process always includes a sensed direction. Unlike the analogy of the word game, the direction is not a fixed destination. The goal is only generally sensed—it is never a direct copy of an existing solution. The direction established for the zipper that will close the problem to a solution may be better understood as a set of "rules of the road" that are included with any proper hitch. Interestingly, these rules can be read in the designed environment after it is built. It is as if the designer wrote the rules and then played the game according to those rules, for all to see. The built design stands not as the product of some mysterious process but rather, to the trained perception of a critic or designer, as the record of a design process.

Once the anchoring hitch for a potential solution is secure and the designer begins to represent and evaluate the various forms the solution might take, the most useful drawings will be suggested by the solution itself. If the concept is to provide any particular kind of spatial or kinesthetic experience, then the representative drawings must be eyelevel perspectives. Also, concepts that are based on a desired relationship between the environment and its physical context must be represented in perspectives if their success or failure is to be evaluated. Concepts based on a particular relationship between the environment and the human figure might be best represented in sections. The design solution should always be studied and evaluated with those drawings that best show the success or failure of its conceptual basis. Sometimes the concept is, indeed, primarily a plan concept, in which case the conventional order of drawings is appropriate. To always follow the conventional order, however, will in time narrow designers' conceptual range to plan concepts or mislead them into believing they can adequately evaluate, in plan, concepts that have their basis and best representation in other drawings.

Wherever the design synthesis begins and whatever drawings the designer uses to represent its first stages, the playback potential must be judged at the level of human experience. This means that as quickly as possible the synthesis must reach a stage where this playback of the designer's intention can be tested with eyelevel perspectives. Experienced designers reach this stage within minutes or hours of the first conceptual synthesis. As soon as the concept is externalized in some graphic form or pattern, there is an irresistible compulsion to test "what it will look like" in reality. Inexperienced designers, or those who have difficulty drawing perspectives, often deliberately avoid this experiential testing because they are insecure about their drawing ability.

There is seldom only a single hitch in any design process. There are usually several false hitches, each of which at its moment of conception seems uniquely promising. The unsuccessful hitches may be abandoned for several reasons: they may be rejected by clients or others involved in the process; part way into the zipper stage, they may appear dull, simplistic, naïve, or inappropriate; or they may be beyond the designer's zippering capability at the moment. In any case, they should be put aside for use in some future process.

One of the hallmarks of designers is their regenerative ability to come up with hitch after hitch, with equal enthusiasm and optimism, sure that *this* one will be the answer. The primary creativity involved in synthesizing the ideas capable of organizing the solution to a complex design problem is essential, but no more important than the so-called secondary creativity required to follow the rules established by that anchoring hitch into the zippering phase.

ZIPPER DRAWINGS

Zipper drawings are designed to test, develop, and rationalize the best final form for the solution. They integrate the various parts of the solution in the established direction.

After the commitment to an organizational idea is made, that idea must be fleshed out and made to work. This kind of activity is normally defined as secondary creativity, but the abilities involved require great experience and craftsmanlike skill and are, of all the designer's abilities, perhaps the most difficult to acquire. Beginning designers can often come up with ideas that have great potential, but they botch, dilute, or abandon these ideas because they can't work them out.

In *The Farther Reaches of Human Nature* (1971), Abraham Maslow explains that overlooking this phase of the process is:

> a tendency to deify the one side of the creative process, the enthusiastic, the great insight, the illumination, the good idea, the moment in the middle of the night when you get the great inspiration, and of underplaying the two years of hard and sweaty labor that then are necessary to make anything useful out of the bright idea.
>
> In simple terms of time, bright ideas really take a small proportion of our time. Most of our time is spent on hard work. My impression is that our students don't know this. . . .

One of the romantic myths that clings persistently to design is that good designs evolve naturally and inevitably, with elements effortlessly falling into place and relating to one another in an utterly convincing way. We are taught to abhor designs that look forced or contrived. While it may be true that good designs look natural and inevitable and seldom seem forced or contrived, they are often the products of massive willful manipulation by some of the cleverest of forcers and contrivers. It is the skill with which it is done that makes all the difference.

The skill involved in realizing the potential promised by the hitch is misleadingly glossed over in most of the writing about problem solving and creativity and misunderstood by beginning designers. This secondary creativity is seldom described because it is completely different for each field or discipline and its intricacies would fill several books. The skills involved must be learned "on the job" because they lose their meaning when they are separated from the real context in which they are applied. It is also much more interesting to write about the excitement of generating creative ideas, and most authors wisely avoid boring their readers with descriptions of the tedious push and pull and give and take involved in getting those creative ideas to work. Only through years of experience and deeper levels of understanding will you learn to value, and even be stimulated by, this working out of ideas. Perhaps, however, I can outline this zipper phase without being overly boring.

OVERLAID REFINEMENT

Much has been made over the potential of using computer graphics in the design process. The computer is a marvelous tool for repetitive tasks like education or for the analytical or computational tasks involved in material takeoffs or heat-loss calculations, but at the present state of the art the invention of computers and their contribution to the design process can't compare with the development and usefulness of tracing paper! Simple, ordinary buff tracing paper allows a designer to compare alternate designs directly and simultaneously and improve the later one in relation to the earlier one. The ability to overlay design drawings is an incredible design tool. Wouldn't it be nice, for instance, to overlay your life or your face and tinker with it just a little? You can always lift the overlay if it goes awry and leave the base drawing unaltered. Overlays are "play-like"—as children say, "Let's play like. . . . " The act itself is tentative imagining—not yet for real. The tentativeness, the relatedness, and the involvement of the eyemindhand could hardly be a more appropriate symbol for the design process.

In many ways design begins when the beginning student picks up that first roll of buff tracing paper and overlays a drawing. The essence of the design process is the hopeful, expectant pursuit of a better idea that seems sure to be unrolled with the next overlay. One of the ways you can tell the zipper of the design process is working is that the solution represented in the zipper drawings begins to change with each overlay.

Designers should learn to visualize the design drawing not as a single drawing but as a potential stack of drawings progressing from a very crude sketch at the bottom to a very slick, detailed rendering at the top. When you have the disciplined ability to raise a rough sketch to these various levels, drawing becomes a matter of free choice, depending on the purpose of the drawing and the time available.

It takes a while to develop the skill and confidence to refine a rough sketch and know where you're going with it. And it's always tempting to try to make a drawing halfway up the stack without the supporting underlays. The drawing and placement of figures, trees, and shadows always needs the benefit of overlaid refinement.

One of the mistakes many architectural graduates make is to fill their portfolios, which they take to interviews to show prospective employers, with laborious renderings. Most practicing

professionals expect that graduate architects, landscape architects, and interior designers, given *unlimited* time, will be able to make beautiful drawings. What these prospective employers may be much more interested in is the kind of drawings their apprenticing professionals can make in *limited* time. Employers are usually comforted by the appearance of a few rough sketches in prospective employees' portfolios as evidence that they can draw more ways than slowly.

At some time during the zipper phase of the design process most designers experience a phenomenon called "analog takeover," in which the representational drawings, which are analogs for the developing solution, *become* the design solution. This analog takeover happens earlier with complex projects because their complexity cannot be held whole in the mind. In order to work on the whole problem and its interrelationships the designer must literally go where the drawings are. The only way to work with the solution to the problem after this point is to work with the representative drawings that have become the solution.

This is necessary because at home, after dinner, over coffee, in those relaxed moments when creative insights often occur, the designer simply

cannot remember the relationships between the structural framing, the ductwork, and the necessary clearances at a particular point in the building. This explains the habit many designers have of hanging up the representative drawings of a project all around their drawing board and spending hours seemingly lost in the contemplation of these drawings.

In spite of firm anchoring hitches and skillful zippering, the precise direction and destination of any design process is unpredictable. In a sense, the analog takes over; the design becomes a separate part of Popper's World 3 (the products of minds) and strong enough to change the direction and affect the destination of the process. Although many designers have trouble accepting Louis Kahn's idea of a building's "existence will" or its "wanting to be," most anticipate and welcome shifts in the direction of any design process. In addition to shifts caused by the evolving concepts of the design itself there will be other shifts caused by unforeseen changes in the client's, user's, code's, or lender's requirements, which will affect the process and must be responded to. Confident designers manage these shifts rather than fight them, and their attitude is summed up by Abraham Maslow in *The Farther Reaches of Human Nature* (1971):

> a new kind of human being who is comfortable with change, who enjoys change, who is able to improvise, who is able to face with confidence, strength, and courage a situation of which he has absolutely no forewarning.
>
> . . . what I'm talking about is the job of trying to make ourselves over into people who don't need to staticize the world, who

don't need to freeze it and make it stable, who don't need to do what their daddies did, who are able confidently to face tomorrow not knowing what's going to come, not knowing what will happen, with confidence enough in ourselves that we will be able to improvise in that situation which has never existed before. This means a new type of human being. Heraclitian, you might call him. The society which can turn out such people will survive; the societies that cannot turn out such people will die.

THE SYSTEMS AND THEIR RELATIONSHIPS

The built environment is conventionally thought of as being made up of several subsystems that must be designed and related to one another. Most design environments include:

- functional systems
- spatial systems
- enclosure systems
- structural systems (may not be a concern of landscape architects or interior designers)
- active environmental control systems (may not be a concern of landscape architects or interior designers)

and relationships to larger contextual systems such as:

- climate
- topography
- circulation systems serving the site
- neighboring built environment

The relationships that must be established between each of these subsystems is best understood as lying somewhere on the unity/diversity continuum discussed in chapter 2. We can per-

haps state this more simply as the sameness or difference of the various systems. They may be virtually identical or tightly integrated, or they may be separated in such a way that their distinction has a meaning. Furthermore, each of these systems has its own subsystems. Enclosure systems, for instance, include:

- passive environmental control systems (waterproofing, heating, cooling, lighting)
- visual access systems (views in and out)
- physical access systems (entries, exits, service)
- materials systems (choices of building materials and their relationships)

The most typical sameness is between the functional system and the spatial system. We usually articulate our environments functionally (dining, kitchen, etc.), but this is not always consistent. For instance, family room and living room are not so much clear functional distinctions as they are behavioral or cultural conventions concerned with intimacy and formality. We may eat, drink, read, converse, listen to music, or watch TV in either space. The distinction is based more on with whom we do these things and at what times or occasions.

Difference often occurs between the spatial system, the structural system, and the enclosure system. They may have the satisfying match of the Trulli of Albarabello, in which the spatial unit is the structural unit *and* the enclosure system. More often though, with the economy of today's structural spans, the structural system is equated with the overall enclosure system, and the spatial system is a subdivision, a partitioning off, within this larger envelope. In some buildings all three systems are different, with the structural system extending beyond the enclosure system

SYSTEMS INTEGRATED

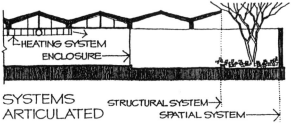

SYSTEMS ARTICULATED   STRUCTURAL SYSTEM→   SPATIAL SYSTEM——→

and the spatial system sometimes extending with it to include exterior spaces and other times remaining as subdivisions within the enclosure system.

The active environmental control system may be integrated with the enclosure system in the form of automatically operated vents and louvers, or wall-integrated air-conditioning units, or mechanical ducts or chases. Alternately, it may be integrated with the spatial system in the form of window air-conditioning units in individual rooms or fan-coil units above the ceiling. The mechanical system is also often tied to the functional system by following the distribution pattern of human circulation through the corridor system of a building. And, last of all, the environmental control system may express itself in an independent pattern of its own, in color-coded clarity.

These subsystems are potentially equivalent and competing siblings that make up part of the larger environmental hierarchy that is being designed. A major part of the zippering of design is the establishment of the relationships among and within these subsystems. The designer may make the subsystems tightly integrated, distinctly separated, or deliberately ambiguous.

The question of whether various parts of the built environment should be treated as being the same or as being different can be applied to virtually everything considered in the design process. Should the windows be made like the doors or expressed as different? How are they the same (both openings in walls) and how are they different (one is for physical access, the other for light, ventilation, and visual access) and to what extent can they be made alike or different? One curious application of this sameness/difference game is that the door hardware finish on the insides of toilet rooms is usually chrome, so that it matches the chrome of the toilet fixtures, rather than the bronze or brass of the other hardware in the building. This distinction respects the integrity of the spaces separated by the door rather than the integrity of the door as an object.

OTHER SYSTEMS

Environmental designers traditionally make drawings that generate, test, and refine the relationships among the subsystems. The drawings with which they represent and study the relationships are biased towards the hardware of walls, columns, floors, roofs, and beams, while the software—the spaces and what happens in the spaces in terms of human movement, light, air circulation, etc.—remains undrawn, unseen, and largely unimagined. Environmental psychologists nag at us because our spaces prohibit or inhibit the human behavior for which they were designed, yet this fault never appears in the drawings we

make. Anything we mean to consider in the design process must be given graphic form, so that it is at least as well understood and habitually used as, say, a framing plan or a reflected ceiling plan. The design process consists of making and evaluating analogs for the congruence of the design problem and a design solution; if our drawings don't represent certain relationships we literally won't see the problem. In response to this failure, the methodological critics of design have tried to talk us out of doing drawings, but after some initial successes, that effort, thankfully, seems to be failing. The better solution is to find a way to represent the various unseen systems in some sort of code so they can be represented, evaluated, and improved in relation to the systems that are already graphically obvious.

THE VERBAL RATIONALE

The other burden that must be pulled along by the zipper is the logical verbal explanation of the congruence between the problem and the particular solution. This rationale must be clearly understood not only by clients, but also by consulting engineers, draftspersons, and the expanding circle of user groups, building officials, mortgage lenders, and people who become involved in the zipper phase of the design process.

Most designers, after a few private trial tugs at the hitch, seek the approval of their clients, users, and collaborators before entering the zipper phase of the process. Consensus approval of the hitch usually includes approval of its initial logic; successive presentations to clients, users, and others whose understanding and approval are needed must include a verbal explanation that is an extension of that initial logic.

Design education, or at least architectural education, fails to place enough emphasis on the importance of successful verbal communication, as pointed out in the recent Boyer report of the Carnegie Foundation:

> We have already discussed our concern that schools of architecture, as a group, inadequately stress the importance of clear, verbal communication. It is difficult to imagine that architects can ever assume leadership in community affairs if they cannot express themselves in jargon-free English in public forums, or to clients. In fact, we found that relatively few studio projects involve sustained contact with clients. . . .
>
> Schools, then, must place far greater priority in preparing graduates to be effective and empathic communicators, able to advocate with clarity for the beauty, utility, and ecological soundness of the built environment.

Zipper drawings are what the American Institute of Architects calls design-development drawings. They are not yet rigid, drafted, working drawings like the construction patterns from which the design will be built. Zipper drawings are still design drawings and they are still exploratory but disciplined now by a particular organizing idea. Their goal is to examine and resolve all the problematic relationships in the design—the trade-offs and compromises that must be made between conflicting design criteria and budgets and building codes.

Because the goal of the zipper phase is to join the problem to a particular solution and its supporting rationale, one of the most helpful strategies is to repeatedly synthesize the whole design.

The time has passed for piecemeal relationships, however elegant. The designer's attention space must expand to encompass the design as a whole, and oscillate frequently and evenly among the various parts. This means that *all* the drawings must be drawn and redrawn, *as a set,* so that the synthesis is continually current. The overworked phrase "getting it all together" describes these syntheses very well and the traditional charettes that precede such deadlines beneficially focus the attention of everyone involved in the process. Both creative and critical powers are heightened by the intense concentration involved, and the more of these conceptual closures that can be achieved in any process, the better.

While I spent a great deal of time earlier knocking the conventional orthographic plans, sections, and elevations as representations of reality or environmental experience, in this part of the process the orthographic drawings are indispensable. With the goal and its direction established by the anchoring hitch, the integrity, consistency, and clarity of the design as a whole (as an object, if it is a building) can be tested with plans, sections, and elevations. Although the experience of the environment will still need to be tested occasionally with eyelevel perspectives, and the three-dimensional quality of certain corners, joints, and transitions will need to be studied in thumbnail perspective sketches, the patterns involved in this phase of the process are best seen and manipulated in orthographic drawings.

CONVENTIONAL PLANS AND SECTIONS

Since the representational drawings of the zipper phase are primarily plans and sections and secondarily elevations, we should take a moment to

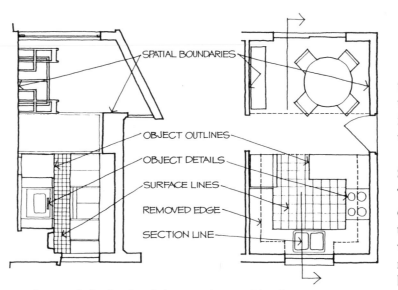

understand the basis of these orthographic abstractions and how they are conventionally drawn.

Plan and section drawings show what would be seen if you cut through buildings or environments and removed the part of the building above or in front of the slice. In these views the lines and planes perpendicular to the plane of the slice do not converge toward a single central vanishing point (as they would in reality) but rather are all perpendicular to the axis of our vision. Perhaps a simpler way of understanding this is to imagine that after the top or front of a building is cut away we put the remaining building in a giant press and compress it into a paper-thin wafer. In a floor plan, the walls, kitchen counters, and furniture would all be mashed flat into the floor and drawn as if they were simply a pattern in the linoleum. A section would be similarly compressed into the back wall, and the wall cabinets or furniture would be drawn as if they were patterned wallpaper on that wall.

LINE-WEIGHT INDICATIONS

The various compressed parts of the building are fundamentally different from one another and

the drawing must tell what they were before the compression. This indication of difference is made with line weight.

SPATIAL BOUNDARIES

The most important lines in a plan or section are the boundaries of the spaces that are cut through when part of the building is removed. These lines indicate the boundaries of the volumes that make up any environment. (Surfaces can be thought of as walls, ceilings, and floors, but it is much more sophisticated to conceive of them as the bounding surfaces of the spatial volumes, the rooms or spaces of an environment.) These important lines should be the heaviest or thickest of all lines.

Sometimes plans and sections are drawn in such a way that the walls, floors, or roof structure appear as solid black. This is a much less sophisticated indication than those that indicate the walls, floor, or roof as consisting of two spatial boundaries, with an in-filling poché that indicates a thickness of separating material.

OBJECT OUTLINES

The next-most important lines, and the next-heaviest lines, are those that indicate the outline of objects within the space of a plan or section. These include attached counters, platforms or steps, and detached articles of furniture. Care should be taken to indicate whether they are attached or not. The outline of a detached piece of furniture like a bed or table should be complete and separate from the spatial boundary indicated by the line of a wall. Even a refrigerator has space behind it (as anyone who has cleaned behind one will discover), and its outline should not die into the wall line like that of a countertop or bathtub.

OBJECT DETAILS

Next in importance and line weight are the lines indicating details of an object. These would include the burners on a stove, the depressed bowl of a lavatory seen in plan, and the recessed panels of a door seen in elevation.

SURFACE LINES

The lightest lines are those that carry no spatial information and simply lie on the horizontal surfaces of a plan or the vertical surfaces of a section. Tile joints or other surface textural indications such as wood grain or carpet are indicated with surface lines.

HIDDEN-EDGE LINES AND REMOVED-EDGE LINES

These two kinds of lines are sometimes shown and sometimes not shown according to traditional practice. Hidden-edge lines are those that occur beneath or beyond the plane shown in the plan or section, like footings beneath a working drawing foundation plan or finished floor or ceiling lines beyond an elevation. (Neither of these indications, especially the footing edges, are useful in design drawings.) In traditional practice these lines are only sometimes indicated.

Removed-edge lines are those that occur in the part of the building that was removed to take the plan or section. Of these, conventionally only those in the plan are drawn. The critical removed-edge lines are those indicating the edges of overhanging planes, like roofs, balconies, and upper cabinets. Both hidden-edge lines and

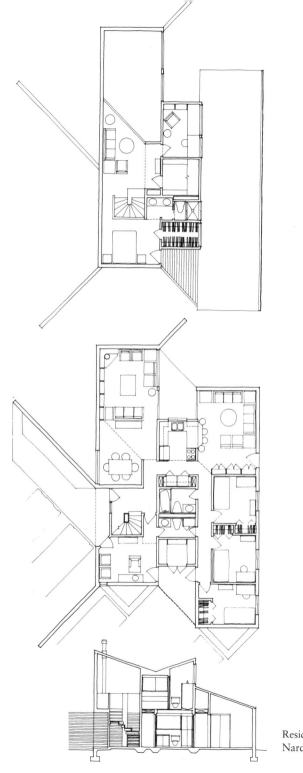

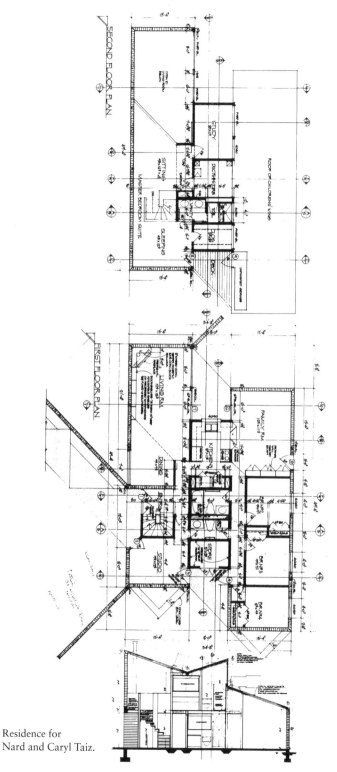

Residence for Nard and Caryl Taiz.

removed-edge lines are dashed or dotted and the same weight as real-edge lines.

SECTION LINES

The last kind of lines aren't actually present in the environment but are abstractions that help the viewer to understand and relate the drawings. The most important of these are section lines, which indicate where the sections are cut through the plan. These lines may also mark where the plans are cut through the sections or elevations, but they are normally cut at such a standard height (somewhere between 4 and 5 feet, going above countertops, below upper cabinets, and through all doors and windows) that there is no need to indicate their exact position. The crucial difference between design drawings and illustrated construction drawings is clearly illustrated by the two preceding drawings.

- Construction drawings describe the exact location, configuration, and dimensions of the walls, floor, and roof and their physical structure and the materials of which they are made.
- Design drawings describe the relative location, configuration, adequacy for human function, and pattern of interrelationships of the spaces formed within the walls, the floor, and the roof.

The emphasis of construction drawings is on the solids, while the emphasis of design drawings is on the voids.

NONCONVENTIONAL PLANS AND SECTIONS

We need to expand our use of plans and sections. In *Drawing As a Means to Architecture* and in an earlier edition of this book I suggested that color codes would be helpful in understanding and

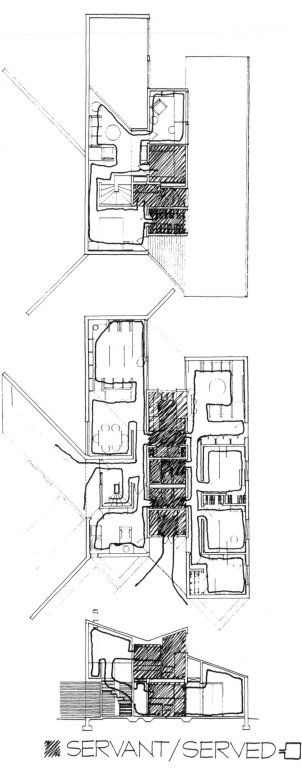

▨ SERVANT/SERVED ▣

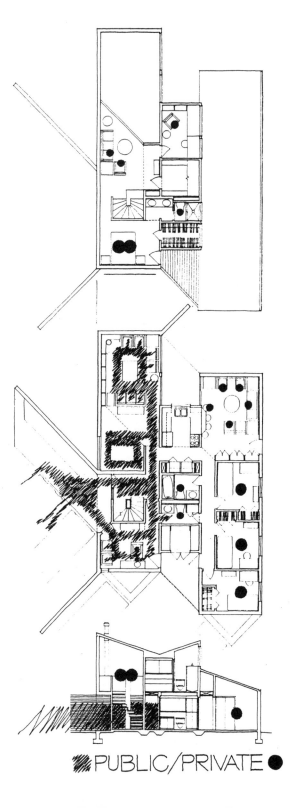

▨ PUBLIC/PRIVATE ●

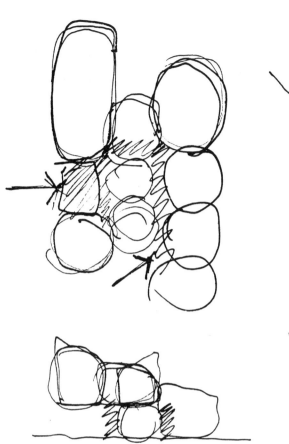

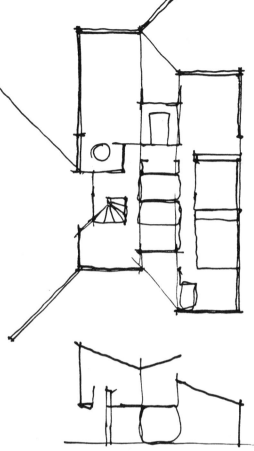

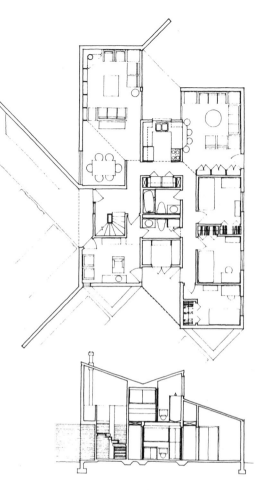

organizing patterns of use and circulation in an environment. I also suggested a set of graphic conventions that could codify the behavior patterns we wish to encourage or inhibit. These could be made a part of our standard set of zipper drawings: we could require students to include a color-coded functional plan or a behavioral plan or section with their other zipper drawings.

There will always be room beyond the standard set of drawings for innovative plans and sections that show qualities and relationships that are not normally drawn, seen, or thought of. The use of drawing in the design process offers at least as much potential for creativity as the design problem itself.

As the zipper progresses, so too should the scope of the design drawings. Plans that begin as bubble diagrams should progress to scaled, single-line drawings of definitive shape, then to plans with walls of realistic and variable thickness, indicating bearing, nonbearing, or plumbing walls, columns, and pilasters. To prove the adequacy of spaces, draw furniture, equipment arrangements, and door swings. You should also include the patterns of flooring-material changes in the zipper drawings. This raising of the level of information contained in the drawings has nothing to do with slickness or finish. All this information can be added to the rough freehand study drawings. The rule is that every time a drawing

is overlaid, the drawing, as well as the design, should be improved and the amount of information it shows the designer should be increased. This increase in density and detail is very important in the zipper phase. It symbolizes and promotes the progress and closure of the process.

The final closing of the zipper is always difficult. By now the designer is so deeply involved in the congruence of the problem and its solution that the total resolution and articulation of that closure sometimes seems impossible. Lack of time always threatens and frequently interrupts the complete closure. I've often thought it would be a good idea to give beginning students a very simple problem and a ridiculously ample time to complete it; just so they can experience deliberate self-closure. This ability to finally and firmly close the process is lacking in some otherwise creative people, but strong, experienced designers have an impressive control and command of this closure. The levels of detail and consistency they can attend to and the range of relationships they can resolve near the end of the zipper is remarkable, and sometimes the most difficult thing for their families and friends to understand is that they find that kind of concentration and hard work extremely rewarding and enjoyable.

ZIPPED DRAWINGS

Zipped drawings are designed to convincingly present the solution by drawing its most flattering aspects. They extoll the destination reached.

If the zipper has done its job well, the design space is now convincingly closed and the designer stands outside this masterpiece like a carnival barker, touting its excellence.

In order to design the drawings and compose the words that will best communicate the solution to others, we must open a new design space within the solution side and leave the problem closure alone. In this new design space we can now consider a new problem: that of persuading or convincing others that the closure we have made is the best possible.

Tim White's *Presentation Strategies in Architecture* (1977) is an excellent study of the factors involved in successfully communicating design ideas. White identifies five critical variables that apply to all kinds of presentations, including zipped drawings. They are extensions of the five Ws of journalistic reporting. The success of zipped drawings, like all successful communication, depends on a careful analysis of and response to these factors.

Usually the five "w's will be unequal in their IMPORTANCE to a presentation. We must determine which of these deserves the most EMPHASIS.

In planning the STRATEGY for a presentation, we must study the impact of the five "w's on the HOW.

From *Presentation Strategies in Architecture* by Edward T. White.

White offers an exhaustive list of questions to be asked in preparing any presentation. This list reveals how many variables are present in even the simplest presentation using zipped drawings. He strongly advocates customizing the design of a presentation based on the answers to his list of questions.

Are there any vital sub-issues within these?

Should we begin with some background material or get right into specifics?

In terms of audience understanding, which information depends on which information?

Must we present an "air tight" sequence of logical decisions or can we simply engage in an informal conversation?

 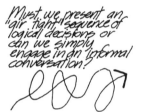

If using slides, should we open and close our presentation with audience eye contact?

How visual should we be in our presentation?

Should we use a multiple projector presentation?

How long can we expect to keep the attention of the audience?

Should we unveil our drawings as they are discussed?

Is there an audience schedule that affects our timing?

TRADITIONAL COMPOSITION OF DRAWINGS

The classic example of a zipped drawing is the traditional Beaux Arts presentation, named for the academic institution that formalized such presentations, the Ecole de Beaux Arts in Paris. Beaux Arts presentations collect all the architectural drawings that represent a design project into one grand composition. These presentations require great skill and hours of painstaking rendering—traditionally ink washes. They have been denigrated for their overemphasis on the supposedly superficial qualities of a design's formal and visual characteristics and have been largely abandoned in architectural education and practice. They did have several advantages, however, especially in design education:

- They allowed designers to add another layer of design by requiring them to carefully compose the representative drawings that made the communication more clear and efficient.
- They led designers to a deeper understanding of their designs and of what various drawings can show and how they best relate to one another.

To give students some experience with the kind of composition involved in such presentations, I use the following assignment (see page 224) in my freshman drawing class, Arch. 112, at the University of Arizona. The problem is to take a given floor plan of a manufactured or precut vacation cabin, site adapt it, and make a formal presentation using the essential representative architectural drawings. The resulting 20" by 30" boards are not only rather satisfying compositions in themselves, but also help the students to understand the characteristics of the various

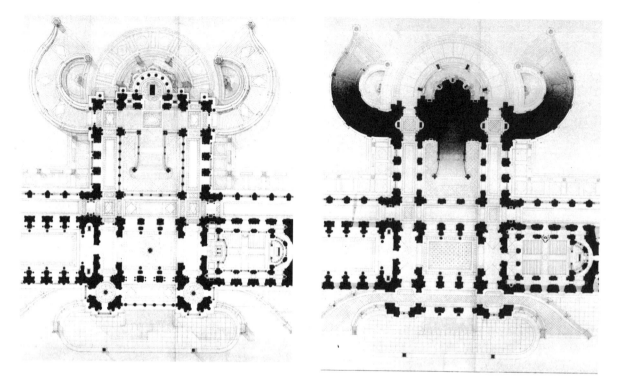

drawings and their relationships to one another.

When we analyze the representative drawings, we will find that some of them are happier in certain positions in the compositions than in others. When a composition is displayed vertically on the wall, it relates to gravity—it has a top and bottom. This makes those drawings that also have a top and bottom, like sections and elevations, want to "settle" to the bottom of the composition. This is especially true when we delineate the band of earth underneath them. Plans and perspectives "float" more successfully than sections and elevations and can be safely placed at the top of collective compositions of drawings.

The strongest relationships between drawings are between multistoried plans, plans and sections, and plans and elevations, usually in that

order. Establishing these relationships between the drawings is more essential than keeping north at the top of the sheet. A single prominent north arrow can explain an unconventional orientation, but having to mentally rotate drawings 90 degrees and relate them to another drawing on the other side of the composition will test the attention span of anyone trying to understand your drawings.

VIEW ALONG
THE SHORE
MOST INTERESTING

WINDOWS
PLACED
AND SCALED
ACCORDING TO
INTERIOR FUNCTION

A VACATION CABIN ON A LAKE   ARCH. 112

Perspectives, especially interiors, are best positioned with the vanishing point near one side of the composition so that the space of the perspective opens up toward the rest of the composition. If perspectives can also be taken in a direction that relates to the orientation of a nearby plan, that is even better.

Because letter forms also relate to gravity, major titles or lettering are more successful if they run along the bottom of the composition, forming a base. Lettering should never call too much attention to itself, and for that reason, open, outlined letters are excellent because they can be an appropriate size without being overly important.

RADIO STATIONS—TUNING THE SET

One last requirement, and perhaps the most difficult one, is that the drawings be consistent as a set. They need to look like they have received an equal amount of the delineator's attention, and they need to be drawn in the same media and technique. The best analogy I have been able to think of for this kind of consistency is that of tuning in a radio station. Early radio stations used to have a whistle that would rise in pitch on either side of the correct frequency. To eliminate such distracting whistles in your presentation drawings you must first be aware of several radio stations (i.e., drawing techniques) and their different positions on the dial. You then will be able to identify the particular one you are seeking. You should have a template for the kind of graphic consistency you want and then bring the whole composition up together—like turning up the volume knob after the station is precisely tuned.

If we want to be persuasive with zipped drawings we must not forget a few things we know about the psychological behavior of human beings. The drawings that communicate the final designed environment should prominently show as many of the other participants' contributions to the process as possible. I am not suggesting that designs should be a hodgepodge collection of all the participants' suggestions, but it is also unrealistic—even undesirable—to pretend that the designer has been the sole source of contributions to the design. The participants will be looking for evidence of responses to suggestions they made during the design process.

The other rather obvious criterion is to present the environment as successful. If it is a shopping center or a restaurant, show it filled with eager consumers or convivial diners. If it is a school, show active children exploring, enjoying, and participating with the environment. Always show the design as you and your clients hope it will be.

The drawings that communicate the results of the design process should also preserve the correct emphasis. The emphasis should remain on the area of design responsibility—architecture, landscape architecture, or interior design. One of the weaknesses of commercial renderings is that they often look more like fashion advertisements or automobile brochures than design drawings. This is because their slickness can make them opaque as design drawings and because their beautiful people and automobiles make us assume that they are a part of the ubiquitous commercial advertising with which we are so familiar.

Correct emphasis also helps to hold the viewer's attention where it should be, just as it focused the designer's attention during the design process.

This drawing shows the correct emphasis for an architectural design drawing. Drawing effort, especially textural interest, is concentrated on the space-defining surfaces, emphasizing the structural elements and the architectural materials. The rendering effort is on the spatial container, with the furniture and trees left as outlines and placed carefully so that they never hide the volume-defining intersections of wall, ceiling, and floor.

LANDSCAPE DESIGN

This drawing shows the correct emphasis for a landscape-design drawing. Drawing effort, especially textural and figural interest, is concentrated on the exterior spaces, trees, and plants. The furniture is kept to a bare minimum and has little design character and the architectural surfaces and the furniture are left as mere outlines.

INTERIOR DESIGN

This drawing shows what might be the correct emphasis for an interior-design drawing. Drawing effort, especially textural and figural interest, is concentrated on the interior space. The furniture, drapes, carpeting, and accessories are selected and drawn with more design character, while the architectural surfaces and the exterior spaces are left as mere outlines. The interior furnishings are also given prominence in their placement and may even cover architectural details or exterior spaces.

EXPLAINING THE DRAWINGS

The standard way of "selling" final designed products to buyers, investors, mortgage bankers, boards of directors, stockholders, or the general public is to order a professional full-color rendering or a meticulously detailed model. While such efforts are always very impressive and make handsome adornments for corporate lobbies or boardrooms, they may tell very little about the building and the main organizing ideas of the design. Presentation drawings should certainly show what the final product will be like, especially experientially, but those images are better understood and more persuasive if they are accompanied by a carefully written verbal description and rationale for the final design, as well as by a narrative describing the process that produced the design.

Designers should use every opportunity to explain the design presented in their zipped drawings, and we should marshal our clearest, most persuasive prose and our best graphic skills to communicate the process—the stitches and the zipper—as well as the design itself. We should run through the zippered logic of the problem and its rationalized solution and perhaps be open enough to allow some peeks at the illogical but creative stitching that anchored the process. A few conceptual diagrams, a color-coded systems model or diagram, or even analogical or precept diagrams can be extremely helpful in telling the story of the problem and the process as well as the solution.

There is another very good reason for the development of a strong, clear, verbal rationale for a designed environment. If the designer has presented the rationale to the clients, they will be able, long after the designer has gone on to

other projects, to explain to those not part of the design process why the environment was designed as it was. One of the great satisfactions in the design professions is to return, after many years, to an environment you designed and find that the rationale for the original design has survived and is now being passed on by people who weren't even involved in the original process. The clear rationale for a solution can even serve a well-designed environment through its awkward middle age, when its design has fallen out of fashion, until it qualifies as worthy of historic preservation.

We should be careful, however, not to make the mistake of the presenter in the Roger Lewis cartoon above. We should be sensitive to the interests and vocabulary of our audience, and we should explain the design as it relates to their interests, using their vocabulary. Too often we behave like the "ugly American" abroad and just shout our English louder instead of making an attempt to communicate in the language of the country we're in. At least half of good communication is careful listening, and by the time we get to the final presentation of our zipped drawings, we should certainly know our client's interests, values, and vocabulary. Any verbal explanation that accompanies our zipped drawings should certainly be in the clients' language as much as our "designers'" language.

ILLUSTRATING THE DESIGN PROCESS

The value of making your own model of the design process and relating your drawing to that process lies in the vitality of those relationships. You should work to improve what you actually show yourself in drawings during the various phases of design—how you illustrate your design process. Drawing can be helpful all through the design process in unexpected, unconventional roles, from initiating the translation of verbal programmatic statements into three-dimensional form to testing the hoped-for qualities of any developing design.

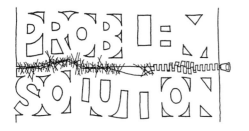

All the tactics discussed in this chapter are worth mastering. A premature closure of any problem to a solution may result in a clumsy seam. The lack of adequate clearing may result in strange lumps sewn into the seam, and the inability to find a hitch to anchor the zipper may not secure the time needed to develop the design in a consistent direction. The failure to convincingly rationalize the closure may result in doubts and questions that undo the entire effort.

The mastery of the various tactics should also maintain a certain balance. An overemphasis on opening tactics, for instance, may drive the problem and solution so far apart that closure is literally inconceivable for a beginning designer. An overemphasis on the abilities at the zipper end of the process may just as easily result in the entire creative effort being spent on closed, persuasive drawings and a polished rationale designed to make superficial solutions acceptable to clients who have been closed out of the process.

7 Combinations

DRAWING AS A PARTNER IN COMMUNICATION

Although the most important use of drawing is during the conceptual frenzy when there is just a design mind and its drawings, drawing also has a leading role to play in communicating design ideas to others. In this communicative role drawing never stands alone, but is always employed in some sort of partnership. These partnerships range from the sophisticated combinations of hand drawing and digital color to the simple combinations with text or conversation.

Learning the potential of the various partnerships in which drawing can participate begins with understanding what each partner can do best, so that their combination is symbiotic. The combinations can then be analyzed as they occur in professional design practice, from client presentations to publications to illustrating normal conversation.

In communicating built designs, the role of drawing changes from showing what the design will be like when built to showing how the design actually turned out. It is pointless to draw perspectives of a built design to show what the experience will be like when the completed design can be photographed. Plans and sections should still be used in publications and exhibitions to describe the integrity and unity of the environment as a designed place or object, and conceptual diagrams can show the generation and development of the underlying concepts that generated it.

In all the combinations, the verbal explanation and rationale for a design and the process that produced it are crucial. Words are the dominant medium of communication in our culture and most people may understand written or oral explanations better than the drawings we show them.

Environmental designers should seek to explain their work at every opportunity, both for their own self-promotion and for the public's education in the value of the environmental design professions. It is most important for designers to master all the combinations of drawing, photographs, and words so that we can be as effective as possible in communicating what we do.

Combining Hand Drawing and Digital Color

by M. Scott Lockard

The most powerful computer-aided presentation drawings are a combination of what the computer can do best and what is still most suitably drawn by the skilled hand. Depending on the project, the time available, and the drawing's role in the design process, combinations of the hand and computer can offer the designer great flexibility.

Modern design offices, most design schools, and even many homes today have hardware and software capable of greatly assisting the designer in generating compelling design images. In many offices, a wide array of graphic tasks beyond CAD work and word processing are routinely performed with the computer. Using these resources to aid in the production of design drawings is generally fairly simple and cost effective.

There are advantages (and a few disadvantages) to using the computer to assist in creating design drawings. The accuracy and flexibility of digital drawings, be they CAD plans or bitmap images, are particularly attractive. Perhaps one of the most important reasons to use computers is that they help you to keep abreast of the production methodologies used by the rest of the architectural team. Too often, the designer is seen as an outsider doing "fluffy," impractical drawings or as someone whose delicate artistic constitution can't handle the rigors of CAD layer-naming standards. However, a well-rounded designer takes advantage of every medium.

Even with the advent of a generation of CAD-savvy architects, the vast majority of design decisions are still made the old-fashioned way: with a pen and paper. In fact, the current scarcity of versatile designers may have its roots in the displacement of hand-drawing (and therefore design) skills by the aforementioned CAD layer-naming standards.

While a working knowledge of AutoCAD or a similar program for modeling is of tremendous value, we will concentrate here on using the computer for coloring and enhancing hand drawings.

In the contemporary design office, we are much more likely to encounter various "computer renderings" than hand drawings. We have all seen the cold and lifeless 3D Studio and Form-Z rendered CAD models that make us say "wow" at first glance but inevitably fail to communicate a true sense of reality and inhabitability. More often than not, the only atmosphere conveyed is one of austerity and artificiality. As in hand drawing, the "natural" things, such as people and trees, are the most difficult things to convey.

When, in addition to this, you consider the many hours spent making the rendering, the "wow" factor is greatly diminished. Further, the lion's share of time required to construct a reasonably rendered CAD model does not go toward improving, exploring, or refining the design, but merely toward the technical processes required for completion (not to mention much staring at progress bars).

The intelligent designer will take great advantage of the computer when it is appropriate and shun it when the return on the investment shrinks. By focusing not on increasing processing speed but instead upon improving one's capabilities in the natural, human-based medium of hand drawing, the "garbage in–garbage out" effect of designing by CAD is more easily avoided. Just as hand drawing increases one's ability to visualize, explore, and test designs, so too should any application of the computer. The computer is simply another tool, and when it is used, it should be as an integral part of the design process.

INTEGRATING DIGITAL COLOR

To be effective, the use of digital color must be integrated with other drawing and design tools. The skill being enhanced and expanded through the computer is "hand drawing." Let it be said very clearly that further development of your hand-drawing skills will always improve and inform your digital-drawing skills.

Several tools and processes are necessary to integrate hand drawing and digital color. They are:

- basic computer/file-management skills
- CAD modeling (optional)
- hand drawing (including perspective structure)
- scanning (digitizing the drawing)
- Photoshop-type layered-graphic software skills

- page-layout software (optional)
- output/viewing devices
- storage devices

A typical process for creating a digitally colored drawing might generally follow the order of this list. Revisions and additions to the hand drawing can be done piecemeal, scanned, merged, and recolored in the digital file, creating small feedback/revision loops in the process. Painting software such as Adobe Photoshop, a scanner, pen tablet, and access to a good printer are necessary.

THE THREE BEST USES OF THE COMPUTER

There are three uses of the computer that benefit the design process by helping to generate effective design drawings.

1. Modeling and view generation (optional) of complex geometry and taking advantage of existing digital information are valuable skills. However, they are certainly of limited use if you lack a fundamental understanding of spatial structure and perspective, and if you have no means to develop and humanize these images.

   Most importantly, using the computer to generate views is always optional. It may or may not be wise to make a computer model for a particular drawing, depending on the time and information available. The base drawing should still be a hand drawing, whether overlaid on a CAD base or not.

2. Coloring and manipulating hand drawings is one of the most natural applications of the computer to the design process and to the process of generating presentation drawings

as well. This is therefore the main focus of this chapter. The examples on the following pages explore the application of digital color to a variety of design drawings.

3. Composition and reproduction of drawings is an important but mostly technical process of outputting all the drawing and color one has input. This will be covered following the discussion and examples of digital color.

CREATING DIGITALLY COLORED DRAWINGS

The digitally colored drawings described in this chapter were each created in three phases. Each began as a hand drawing either laid out by hand or overlaid on a CAD-generated background. The hand drawings were scanned using a desktop scanner and then colored using Adobe Photoshop. In the final phase, they were given overall adjustments, saved in various file formats, and then printed, e-mailed, or imported into other programs.

I. THE FIRST PHASE: GENERATING THE BASE DRAWING

HAND DRAWING: STILL THE FOUNDATION

As mentioned throughout this book, drawing itself is one of the most powerful tools in the designer's arsenal and should be integrally linked to the creation, exploration, and evaluation of the design. If there is such a thing, the ideal design drawing is one that has been integral to the design process and has several possible end uses.

At its roughest level a drawing may only communicate a single idea. As it becomes more refined, it explores and verifies possibilities. It can also convey an atmosphere or mood, summarizing the design from an experiential standpoint. Like a good building, a good design drawing communicates a hierarchy of integrated ideas rather than simply reiterating the program.

CAD BACKGROUNDS

CAD backgrounds, even very schematic ones, can be very useful design tools. When the geometry is complex they are often essential. The primary use of a CAD model is to efficiently generate accurate views of a project.

The beauty of a properly conceived CAD model is that it can begin as a very simple mass and be developed or refined as necessary. Hand-drawn overlays of the model can then be used to refine the design. The model can continue to be refined with updated plots woven back into the hand-drawn studies.

Plotting from a particular view allows the hand drawing to always overlay successive versions of the model, or to be used to explore various design options. Scanned plots or portions can also become part of the digitally colored drawing.

The main considerations when deciding whether to build a CAD model are: (1) how long it will take (often hand construction takes less time); (2) the level of difficult (say, radial) geometry; (3) the accuracy and exactitude of the view required; (4) the usability of other existing CAD data.

THE PAIN OF FAKING IT

It should go without saying that an understanding of perspective is crucial to taking advantage of a CAD background. Divining the horizon and vanishing points on the plot is usually a simple matter—unfortunately many designers are incapable of it.

While the CAD model is a powerful tool in the hands of a good designer, it is also too often a crutch used in place of a basic understanding of perspective. In any design drawing, a lot of detail is designed as it is drawn. The computer should only be used to model as much as is appropriate. Your knowledge of perspective is needed to fill in the blanks.

A couple of points regarding perspective construction bear mention here. Even in the roughest sketch, respect for the horizon and vanishing points must be absolute. More tolerance is allowed in foreshortenings.

Correcting and resolving a faked or poorly constructed perspective is always painful. Nothing gives away an inept drawing more quickly than improper perspective. It conveys not only a misunderstanding (or lack of concern) for spatial structure, but also a level of incompetence on the part of the designer.

Trying to enhance a poorly constructed drawing with digital color is equally difficult. The application of color and light is intended to further describe a space or object, but they will only emphasize inaccuracies in perspective. Pasting in objects such as signs or cars and modifying them to fit the drawing is impossible. Ultimately you run the risk of trying to make a silk purse out of a sow's ear when you use sophisticated coloring techniques on a flawed base drawing.

DRAWING PROCESSES

Whether or not a CAD background is used, the actual approach chosen for a given drawing can have a great effect on the development of the design.

Several specific drawing processes can be extremely useful in advancing the design of a given project. The examples described here each have appropriate applications as part of the design process. Digital color can be applied to almost any hand drawing, regardless of the level of finish.

• Storyboards: A methodology loosely adapted from the film industry, *storyboarding* refers to a series of small drawings that together summarize the entire project. The "story" may or may not be linear. The benefits of such an approach are that it forces the designer to look at all facets of the project, it keeps the focus on the essence of each component, and it allows the evaluation of the composition of views within the project.

Another benefit is that you get more practice really drawing, rather than laboring over details in one view. Also, each drawing naturally informs the others, which may suggest additional design solutions.

Remember that even such rough drawings demand respect for the horizon and vanishing points. They also benefit from a level horizon and straightedged verticals. It is actually quicker to use a straightedge for verticals and, when possible, for vanishing lines than to freehand it. The drawing will also look more "finished" as a result.

• Rough sketches: More expansive, resolved, or detailed design sketches are well suited as last underlays for presentation drawings. The top sketch shown on the next page was done freehand during a meeting, later straightened up in an overlay, scanned, and colored into the fairly polished drawing beneath it.

Again, using a straightedge is quicker and more precise than freehanding. It also adds

This series of storyboards describes a development surrounding a ferry landing. By limiting the size of each drawing, focus was placed on comprehensive development rather than on details. The small size also makes composition and perspective construction simpler. Note that these sketches do not rely on a constructed background, as they occurred so early in the design process that such accuracy was unwarranted. They do, however, respect the horizon and vanishing points. As rough as they are, these drawings can still be digitally colored to increase legibility without a great investment of time. By doing a photocopy enlargement, a good background for a more finished drawing is easily created.

consistency and "legitimizes" the drawing. The other benefit of straight lines is that they are preferable to wiggly ones when you are simplifying selections in Photoshop.

• Finished drawings (renderings): Even with a highly detailed CAD model from which to generate a background, most of the humanizing, natural elements required for an engaging drawing must be drawn by hand. Most CAD figures and cars, not to mention trees, are awful compared with even the loosest hand-drawn versions. There is an inherently lively quality associated with hand drawings that computers are still a long way from approximating. While wonders can be achieved, the effort required to create inspirational drawings with a CAD model is enormous, and it does little to interactively advance the design in the process.

A DESIGN DRAWING SCENARIO

For purposes of illustration, I'll fabricate a reasonable scenario that would benefit from some digitally colored drawings. I'll assume that a design presentation is scheduled in one week, and that in addition to illustrating several features of the project, one "hero shot" perspective is desired. The orthographic drawings that might also be presented will not be addressed here, although the coloring techniques can also be applied to them. Unless you have a strong personal preference, make use of the specific drawing media mentioned.

I have decided to take a storyboard tour of the project, generating six to eight small views in the process. These will be drawn with a black Prismacolor™ pencil or a black Razor Point™ pen at about 5" by 7". A dozen "frames" are drawn on a single piece of white tracing paper. A

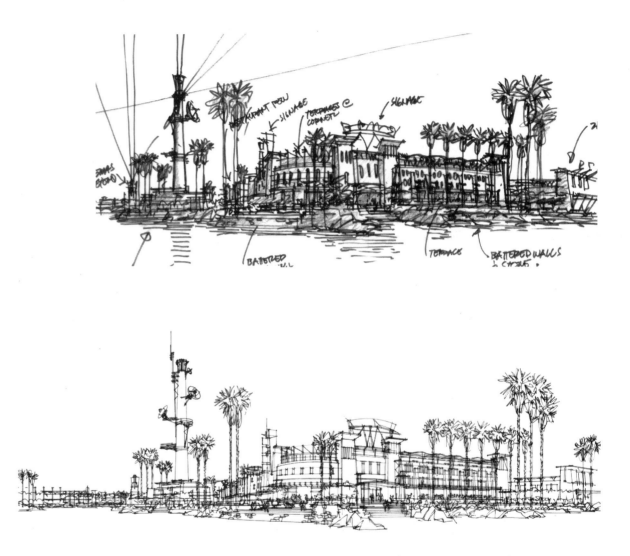

Rough sketches like the one on top can be extremely useful as communication tools, complete with hand-scribbled notes to explain various ideas. This drawing was produced during a design meeting as planning issues were being resolved. The same sketch can be taped down and overlaid a bit more carefully, using a straightedge and triangle to create a good base drawing to digitally color. Reasonably believable perspective structure in the first drawing made overlaying a simple matter.

second piece is overlaid on the frames and the views are sketched out as quickly as possible. (If we had a CAD model, we could assemble a dozen small views to sketch over.)

At this point, undeveloped, unresolved, or weak spots of the design will no doubt become apparent. By sketching an additional overlay on the trouble spots, and by selecting some views over others, we arrive at our eight favorite summarizing views of the project.

The eight sketch views are taped down and overlaid with tracing paper, and the final storyboards are drawn using a straightedge. This refining of the design is part of the process. Little concern is shown over layout lines, roughness, "mistakes," etc. While not done recklessly, the drawings are completed rapidly, in order to maintain a consistency and vitality.

From these views, one or two candidates for the "hero shot" (hopefully) emerge. The best is roughly sketched, or, if you have a CAD model, you can plot the selected view at an appropriate size for a more detailed drawing. This drawing is done with black Razor Point™ on white tracing paper at about 11" by 17". This is a good size for scanning and won't get too mired in detail.

Limiting the size of the drawing is one of the best ways to limit the drawing time required—you'll avoid hours of fussing over imperceptible detail.

II. THE SECOND PHASE: MANIPULATING, COLORING, AND ADDING TO THE BASE DRAWING

Now that the line drawings are done, they must be scanned into the computer. So we must pause for a little primer on scanning.

SCANNING: BEWARE THE DPI QUAGMIRE

Simply put, drawings need to be scanned as grayscale images at about 150 dpi (dots per inch). Different scanners accomplish this in various ways, but the result should be a file in which a single ink line is about 2 or 3 pixels across. Another rule of thumb is that the long dimension of a typical drawing should be no more than about 2000 pixels. This resolution will still look good in a 36"-wide ink-jet-printed poster. For rough, smaller images such as storyboards, the long dimension can be as low as 1000 pixels.

The scanned images should then be adjusted for brightness and contrast so that the background is white but not so much that the gray edges of lines burn out. It is best to make these adjustments in Photoshop rather than on the scanner's screen. There is usually a particular combination of brightening and increasing contrast that works best for each scanner.

There are two dangers often encountered in scanning. One is getting too high a resolution. This is similar to drawing too large a drawing, wherein great amounts of time will be spent coloring at an inappropriate level of detail. This will also invite slow computer performance, crashes, unwieldy file sizes, and a host of other problems. If this happens to you, either proportionally resize the drawing in Photoshop before beginning color or rescan it.

The second danger is undue brain strain over dpi. When dpi is mentioned, we usually are speaking of the capacity of a printing device, not the resolution at which we should strive to work.

When drawing on the computer, you are manipulating pixels. The drawing has a fixed number of pixels. You only need to worry that there are enough pixels to draw what needs to be drawn. The guidelines above should suffice. All you need to know is the fixed number of pixels (d's) at the particular size (i's). These two variables have been fixed and the dpi ratio is therefore defined. (You don't even need to know what it is, as long as the print looks good.)

The easiest way to size an image for printing is to place it into a page-layout program, stretch it (keeping the proportion fixed) to fit the size desired, and let the program do the work.

RIPs (raster image processors) for ink-jet printers, which automatically spread the available pixels over the prescribed size, generally do a very good job in deciding how to print an image. They typically also have "error diffusion" algorithms that effectively break up the pixels into dots appropriate for the printer.

Doing a much worse job are the RIPs that drive color copiers. When printed directly from files, they tend to emphasize individual pixels much more. Unless large numbers of copies must be made, use an ink-jet printer whenever possible.

For large output, the reasonable choice is also an ink-jet, although other options exist. One pleasant paradox in large-sized printing is that high resolution is not necessarily required. The natural viewing distance increases with the size of the drawing and thus the net resolution remains more or less constant.

More discussion of file formats and output issues follows, but let us now look at the digital-coloring process.

COLOR AND LIGHT AS REPLACEMENT FOR DETAIL

Our experience of the physical world is, without a doubt, spatial in nature. When designing physical environments, your first concern should be for the spatial aspects. In fact, part of the process of drawing is to find the most expedient way in which to distinguish elements in space, that is, by their edges. Of course, objects in reality don't have lines around them, but rather are a montage of colored fields corresponding to lit surfaces.

A crucial aspect of our perception of these surfaces is the relationship of their values, but more completely, it is their color. Unless you actually paint (and have time to paint) your images, eliminating all edge-defining lines, you have tacitly agreed to use some shorthand for reality. However, it sometimes is easy to get carried away with drawing details. Using color and light (i.e., painting) is a simpler approach.

The right color and light can often replace vast amounts of drawn detail and do it believably. A well-rendered highlight or glowing edge can often more fully describe a form than precise and elaborate linework. The problem historically has been the impracticality of hauling out the paints and brushes in the middle of a pen-and-paper design session. The use of digital color makes this drawing/painting combination practical.

THE COLOR CONCEPT/COLOR MODEL

Before launching headlong into the coloring of a drawing, you should spend time deciding on the color approach or concept. Often, in a storyboard or rough sketch, this concept can be to some degree a default schtick that communicates the time of day, sun and shade, vegetation, or building-material colors. Even so, it is helpful to have some references, because our mental picture of reality is often quite distorted. The effects of shadow, reflected light, and atmosphere can dramatically change the basic color of a surface in ways we may not immediately recognize.

Making a habit of noticing the real color and using references when possible will keep your drawings from looking like paint-by-numbers.

When time and the finish level of a drawing warrant it, the use of a color model is invaluable. A color model is typically a referent photograph or painting of a scene with color and lighting appropriate to your design. Good sources are architectural magazines and books, travel and photography books, and stock photography catalogs.

Photographs, and the printing processes used to reproduce them, alter and reduce the number of colors that exist in reality. The benefit of this is that it helps you to isolate particular colors and effects of light, such as the color of a shadow in the foreground during a sunset or the color of a highlight on a tile roof when the sun is overhead.

Even though they are artificial, photographs represent reality to us, and the colors they contain are perceived as realistic. The study of lighting, be it in reality or in a photograph, is invaluable if you want to intelligently color your design drawings.

III. THE THIRD PHASE: POST-PRODUCTION, COMPOSITION, AND PRINTING

When the coloring is finished, create a nonlayered version of the file for printing. There are several format choices, but it is easier to keep things straight if you always use the same format. On the PC, the .pcx format is convenient to use. On the Mac, it's the .pict. The .tif(f) format can be used with both platforms, but it sometimes creates problems in page-layout programs. While .tifs can also include alpha channels corresponding to saved selections, they increase the file sizes significantly.

To make a .pcx, .pict, or .tif, choose Save a Copy, then choose the format. This preserves the .psd (Photoshop) file for further work or revisions.

It is often beneficial to make global adjustments to a completed image. Open the flattened image and adjust Levels, Curves, or Brightness/Contrast to improve color density. Some experimentation on the flattened image is usually in order, but take care not to over adjust and lose subtleties. Using levels to adjust density is recommended over using curves because specific values are input and can then be recreated later.

One other important adjustment should be made to the final flattened image. The addition of noise adds a uniform texture to an image, does a great job of eliminating banding in gradient areas, and also helps mitigate any issues of low resolution. A value of 8–15 (uniform, not monochromatic) is usually appropriate. Noise will be more evident on darker images.

At this point, it is often useful to make a copy of the adjusted, noisy file as a .jpg (.jpeg). This is a compressed-file format that will reduce the file size to about 10% of the flattened-image size. This small file can be used for printing, e-mailing, insertion into other programs, etc., and takes up much less hard-drive space than a noncompressed file. However, the .jpg should not be modified and resaved, as it will lose fidelity. If revisions are made to the other files, save a new .jpg from the flattened, adjusted version. You can save .jpegs at various levels of quality. Use the highest one possible, unless something like e-mail or floppy-disk capacities require a smaller file size.

OUTPUT

There are several common destinations for a digital-image file:

- desktop prints
- large-format prints
- transparencies
- on-screen presentation
- e-mail

In each of these cases, the .jpg can be used, although service bureaus may prefer to receive .tifs (in this case, save a copy from the flattened, adjusted image, not from the .jpg).

ANOTHER QUAGMIRE: COLOR CALIBRATION

As with dpi, there has been a lot of well-intentioned but ultimately wasted breath about color calibration. The bottom line is that at the consumer level, it is still difficult to achieve. Most important is adjusting your printer to achieve the results that match your monitor. Giving a print that shows the desired color to your service bureau is the best way to hold them accountable for producing the desired result.

Refer to the previous section on scanning for additional discussion of resolution and output issues.

STORING/ARCHIVING

Digital files, particularly .psd files, are often the biggest single files on anyone's computer. For this reason, it will often be necessary to remove them from the hard drive immediately. Zip™, Jaz™, tape, and CD ROMs are the current standards for doing this. Capacity, durability, and compatibility with others' systems are the primary factors to consider.

Currently recommended is a CD writer, for all of the reasons mentioned above, although there is always the threat of a new standard.

Usually small enough to leave on a hard drive, .jpeg files can be used for most display and printing purposes. See the discussion on computer systems for more information.

TWO IMPORTANT PHOTOSHOP REMINDERS

- Save often, and always after doing something you never want to have to do again.
- After a crash (which will happen), close all programs, then delete any .tmp files. If you don't, the hard drive will literally fill up with these files and cause another crash.

SHORT SUMMARY OF THE DIGITAL-COLOR PROCESS

This summary of the digital-coloring process may clarify the processes shown in the example drawings, which begin on page 239.

Scan the hand drawing as gray scale at about 150 dpi. The long dimension of large images should be about 2000 pixels; that of a sketch can be as low as 1000 pixels. Larger, spliced scans should be limited to a single row if possible. Cut the original drawing level with the horizon, and scan with this edge against the scanner's guide. Tiling in multiple rows invites difficult alignment problems. Open the first scan, expand canvas size to right or left, open the next scan, select all, copy, close, and paste the layer in the first file.

Use a CAD (hidden line) or hand-drawn sketch background. Respect horizon and vanishing points *absolutely*. Approximations can be tolerated in foreshortenings. Use a straightedge whenever possible, including curves (use french curve or

ellipse templates). This adds drawing speed, legitimacy, and consistency and is important in terms of making Photoshop selections simpler.

Modifications can be made to a drawing in a separate drawing overlay. To erase old stuff out from behind revisions, paste onto a new layer, mode set on multiply. Turn one or the other layer (opacity) down to distinguish the two layers, then paint out the bottom layer with white 100% paint. Turn the opacity back up and merge these two layers when done.

Brightness/contrast should be adjusted to create a white background, but don't burn out the grays at the edges of lines.

The scanned line-drawing layer (name it "lines") should be an RGB .psd file. If you end up with lines on a *Background* layer, make a duplicate layer named "lines," then delete the *Background* layer. *Background* cannot be altered in terms of opacity. If the file is not RGB, change the mode to RGB.

Touch up of mistakes, line overruns, etc., should be corrected digitally—don't obsess about finding a perfect line drawing to scan. Use a white 100% paintbrush on the lines layer. This is more reliable than the eraser tool.

Create a new layer (name it "wash") and set it on multiply. This means that anything on a lower layer that is darker will show through, i.e., the lines will remain black when color is put over them. There are also many other modes for layers, so some reordering and experimentation may be beneficial.

The other basic layer (name it "paint") is left on normal, so that there is a means to cover up darker colors/lines when needed. A fourth layer that is often useful is "glow," which keeps feathered colors and gradients separate because they are so difficult to modify smoothly once they're put down.

Additional layers are made from time to time depending on the need to keep items separate or as temporary tests. Layers can be merged together to consolidate items whenever practical. One of the biggest frustrations is putting something on the wrong layer and not realizing it until later, so reducing the number of layers and developing your drawing in the order of lines, wash, paint, and glow is very useful.

Color is applied almost entirely through the gradient, paintbrush, airbrush, and line tools. After initial overall washes, gradients are applied to selections. Selections are made with the lasso tool or rectangular selection tool, not with the magic wand. Unless tolerance is constantly monitored, using the magic wand leaves many white orphan pixels and, more importantly, requires that all linework is closed, leaving distinct selectable areas.

Any even slightly complex selection should be saved (up to 24 selections), and renamed under channels. Use a name you can recognize. Be very careful adding to, subtracting from, and saving so that a complex selection is not accidentally wiped out. Selection borders are made within the thickness of the black lines. As long as you have a selection, you don't need a separate layer to isolate it, which means you don't have the "painting on the wrong layer problem" as much.

Generally, color is built up, lighter or darker, from a middle-ground wash. This is a big advantage over typical media in that "all colors are created equal."

The use of a "color model" is invaluable. Make studying color a habit. Photographs polarize/isolate colors for easier study.

Use gradients (foreground to transparent) of about 25% to build up tones rather than trying to do it in one shot. Gradients are more similar to reality in that no plane is ever of an absolutely consistent color/value across its face.

Use washes to break planes away from general wash color. You will need to develop a few "shticks" such as orange-top/yellow-bottom windows.

In a monochrome tonal drawing just use gray or a single color and white.

The paintbrush tool is for general color application. By setting it at about 25%, tones can be built up. The paint gets no darker as long as the pen is kept down. Pick up and begin again to increase density. Contrast this with the airbrush, which continues to put down more color until lifted.

The line tool is great for highlighted edges, coloring rectangular objects, creating rectangular shapes for backgrounds, window contents, etc. Unfortunately, there is not a gradient line tool or a gradient erase.

The airbrush is mostly for glows, spotlight-type light sources, and fog or cloud painting.

Gratuitous devices such as spotlights (feathered, gradient-filled wedge-shaped selections), photographic lens flares (a filter), streaming headlights (another photographic artifact), paste-in fireworks, etc., can be overused but are sometimes just the thing needed to distinguish a drawing.

Skies are a great candidate for paste-in, but be sure to smudge, blur, and color balance to coordinate/compliment the rest of the drawing. Other typical paste-ins are posters, signs, and Jumbotrons. Use the type tool for signage, and distort it to fit the perspective. There is no need to create a separate layer for pasted-in items (except where they overlap another item, such as with glows) or anything else that has a saved selection, as this isolates them from other things on the same layer. Blurring and color balance are usually needed to match a pasted-in item to its surroundings.

Another semigratuitous but more substantive item is reflections, particularly in water, wet streets (apply some motion blur in a downward direction), and reflective floor surfaces (make a feathered inverted shape, gradient down to transparent). Note that reflections are stronger closer to their origin and in obliquely-viewed surfaces. Often a few well-considered reflections say more about light and material properties than hours of surface rendering can.

The paint layer is for anything that needs to cover darker colors below (including original lines), such as edge highlights, light reflections, and translucent/transparent surfaces. Also, to knock down overly dense linework, use white 100% paint on the lines layer rather than the eraser tool.

The glow layer is to add atmosphere and take care of unaccounted-for light, etc. Often, spotlights are put on glow or on their own layer to keep them isolated/editable. Because it's hard to keep track of the near-transparent pixels and the fact that glows overlap other colors, they need to be isolated.

When you're all done, save it. *Also* save it *anytime you do something you don't want to have to do again.* Then save a copy as a .pcx, .pict, or .tif. Do not flatten your original .psd file. If you save a .tif, you probably don't want to include alpha channels (saved selections) as they will increase the file size. If you want to get a selection into a file, you can always drag it in from the .psd file.

Use this flattened file to make global adjustments in contrast, etc. Levels is the best place to do this because it's quantifiable and can be recreated precisely. Recording the numbers somewhere for recall is useful. Curves is actually much more flexible, but I assume you've not done an awful job that needs so much correction. Levels or curves should be played with on this not-precious file to increase richness and density.

Noise is almost always a good thing to add. It does a great job in obscuring low resolution (note discussion of resolution under the section on scanning). It also eliminates banding in gradients and adds tooth to the drawing. Numbers of 8–15 are common (uniform, not monochromatic).

Save this file so you have a good dense record image. Usually, you'll want to also save a .jpg at this point for use in printing, e-mailing, etc. It takes up 10% of the space and can usually be left on the hard drive. The .psd and other files will at one time or another (often immediately) begin to crowd the drive, and should be archived off on CDs or some other backup media.

ADVANTAGES AND DISADVANTAGES OF DIGITAL COLOR

The preceding examples should have illustrated the numerous advantages to digitally coloring hand drawings. It may be helpful, however, to review and emphasize a few additional factors.

ADVANTAGES

ALL COLORS ARE CREATED EQUAL

The primary advantage of coloring digitally is that all colors are created equal. When using colored pencils or markers, the old standbys of architects and designers, you are always faced with a lot of white paper to cover. Worse, if too dark a tone is built up, it is difficult to lighten it without a lot of work and the possibility of damaging the entire drawing.

With the computer, any color can be applied at any time. There is no difficulty in putting light colors over dark, putting a wash over an entire sheet, changing the hue of a particular region, or altering the contrast of the entire drawing.

It is also possible to paint in a gestural manner, refining later as time permits. The ability to tailor your coloring effort to the time and task at hand corresponds to your ability to draw at different "resolutions" depending on need and time. (Plus, digital color will never leak on your shirt.)

SCALABILITY

The same digital file can be printed in any size. This is, of course, tremendously useful when you are using the same image for a preliminary meeting, for inclusion in a publication, and also for a large presentation. This is a huge advantage over traditional "one original" drawings. There is also none of the generational loss common with copies of originals.

OUTPUT AND PUBLISHING OPTIONS

Digital drawings can be seen on-screen, inserted into a multimedia presentation, printed in a variety of sizes, and made into conventional slides, all from a single file. In the compressed .jpeg format, they can also be easily e-mailed to another party. In a page-layout or on-screen presentation program, digital images can be cropped and re-sized without changing the original file. For composing text alongside single or multiple images, page-layout programs are infinitely superior to the old cut-and-paste methods.

DURABILITY/EASE OF STORAGE

Digital files do not degrade, fade, warp, get loaned out and not returned, eaten by the photocopy machine, or have things spilled on them. If properly archived on a CD, for instance, they take up very little storage space. Backup copies can be made for security and stored in another location.

SHARING OF FILES

Digital files can easily be transmitted on disk to others, shared on a network, or e-mailed.

(continued on page 249)

EXAMPLES OF DIGITALLY COLORED DRAWINGS

The examples on the next ten pages show the range of possibilities for digitally coloring hand drawings, from concept-level sketches to more precise "finished" drawings. It is important to note that the primary purpose of each of these drawings was the development and communication of various design ideas. Their vitality and interest lies primarily in their exploratory, experiential view of a project or concept, and not in a desire to create a perfect rendering.

The tools and processes mentioned for the following drawings refer to Adobe Photoshop. A description of computer-system requirements is included at the end of this chapter beginning on page 250.

Line drawing: Razor Point pen on tracing paper over freehand sketch, using staightedged verticals and eyeballed french curves.

TOKYO TIMELINE:
A MONOCHROMATICALLY TONED DRAWING

This drawing was created to show ideas for a simulator-type theme-park attraction. The space is intended to be vaguely futuristic but a bit run-down, like a real subway. The surfaces in a subway would have to be durable so they would tend to be fairly shiny.

The line drawing above is the last overlay on a series of rough idea sketches for the space. At this point in the process, there were no specific dimensions required, but the overall shape of this queuing area was thought of as circular, conforming to the shape of the ride behind.

A straightedge was used for the verticals, and a french curve was used to fake the circular lines. An almost unacceptable level of distortion is a result of using the last concept sketch as a background rather than stopping to create a more accurate layout by hand or on the computer. This is fine for a concept drawing of a space that has no real dimensions established yet.

Tone is added on the wash layer in gradient-filled selections. People are painted in with 25% paintbrush. Multiple passes are made to darken hair, pants, etc.

Tone complete. White is also used as a wash to create lit coves and to lighten up things that have been overdarkened. The drawing still lacks the glow and sparkle that will be added on the paint layer.

Paint layer: Contains only white painted highlights, white airbrushed glows, and gray (a percentage of black) or white feathered gradient-filled reflections.

The file in Photoshop during painting. Note the order of the three layers. Wash is set to multiply, allowing the darker linework to show through. Others are set to normal. Only grays (percentages of black and white) are used.

Elimination of specific colors makes this type of drawing go quickly. Using an appropriate tint color for the wash layer or tinting the drawing after the fact can enhance the sophistication of the drawing. Try desaturating the image, then adjusting color balance for different hues.

The shapes of the reflected people were just eyeballed for each element or group of people. Some care must be taken to do this "in order" so that the reflections overlap in the proper spatial order. These reflections can be put on the wash layer, but it makes them more difficult to edit. Faded-out gradients are difficult to modify because of all the nearly transparent pixels. For this reason, you might also want to isolate the reflections on their own layer.

The reflections from the people are darkest (or lightest if light) close to their sources and fade out due to imperfections in the floor surface, intruding light, and because of being less oblique to the viewer. The floor has a generally white top to blue bottom; because the distant floor is seen more obliquely, it shows more reflected light. We supposedly see more "through" the reflections to the floor directly in front of us.

The airbrush tool, set to white at a low pressure, may be used to create the glowing lights and also general, almost-invisible ambient glows. The airbrush is very sensitive, and using a separate "glow" layer allows easier revisions. After specific glows from lights were done, a general glow was added at a very, very low pressure in appropriate areas to add ambiance.

Changing the color balance of the image can add an element of sophistication without significant additional effort. The color chosen can be used to reinforce the message or mood of the image, or it can be used to tie a series of images together, be they plans, perspectives, design sketches, or photographs. In this case, blue was chosen for its cold, mechanical connotations.

When completed, the file was saved, and a copy was saved in a non-layered format. This copy was then adjusted for density, using levels or curves. Noise (a filter) was added as a last step to give "tooth" to the drawing and to mitigate any banding or resolution problems that might show up in printing.

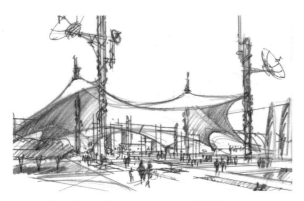

Line drawing: Black Prismacolor™ storyboard-level sketch, using the straightedge whenever practical. Textural "credit" is given for the soft grays in the pencil work. Not too much fuss is made over layout, sketchy, or overdrawn lines.

A night shot means that deep washes go on first, anticipating the addition of light. (Wash layer is set to multiply.) Note the polychromatic palette, implying various colored spot lights. Selections for gradients include tent, sky, and radar dishes.

Highlighting is added on paint layer, with paintbrush, line tool, and airbrush—important on the jewel-like colors for the light sources and edge highlights on the people and trees, keeping in mind the color of the light that would strike them.

CONFERENCE/CONCERT VENUE: BLACK PRISMACOLOR™ STORYBOARD

This sketch is one of a series developed to describe a wide range of programmatic components that were being considered for a large "entertainment destination." Some of the imagery contained in these storyboards is consciously clichéd, or, more forgivingly, archetypal, so that large amounts of verbal explanation were unnecessary.

The tentlike stage is easily understood, but the addition of the light sculpture towers with radar dishes tells a story about uplinking and being connected, which is probably why all these people are here.

As seen above, the drawing began as a daytime sketch of a more expolike environment, with promenades and landscaping. The drawing might also be developed as a day shot or as a contrasting pair, as in the examples of the winter/summer garden later in this section.

Final touch is the spotlights, often overdone, but in the case of a concert venue entirely appropriate. Spots are wedge-shaped selections with feathered edges, filled with foreground-to-transparent gradients. A small glow is added with the airbrush at bright light sources. Note the low resolution of this image (1000 pixels across), which is mitigated and even enhanced by the added "noise."

Line drawing: Black Prismacolor™. Additional texture is created by the grays. A Razor Point™ pen drawing of the same space might look less rich.

Paint layer: Reflections, highlights, and spotlights are added. The spotlight "cones" are kept on a separate layer to ease revision, as they cross other painted areas.

Wash layer: Dark, in anticipation of the addition of light. Major planes are defined and the beginnings of a polychrome palette are suggested.

Pasted-in items are on a separate layer. They include photos on banners, text, and map elements. Experimenting with transparency and layer modes sometimes leads to interesting effects.

TRAVELING LANGUAGE EXHIBIT

This drawing for an exhibit on human language started as a simple black Prismacolor™ sketch. The interest and vibrancy of the space come from color, light, and specific graphic elements. The space also features a dimensional world map that visitors can explore using freestanding "navigation stations."

Stock photographic images were used for the faces on the banners and also served as guides for creation of the maps and some of the other imagery. These images have been distorted, then tinted and screened to create some transparency. It is important that they do not jump out from the rest of the drawing.

Many economical clip-art libraries are available, although it may take quite a bit of searching to find what you want. Usually, it is not critical which image is used. What is communicated is just the idea that an image in the finished space is being suggested. This is also true for television monitors and the like. (See the Taichung image near the end of this section for additional examples of pasted-in images.)

Commercial stock photograph houses have better material but are costly. Often, just studying the right photograph can be instructive enough that you can create small images, such as the brains in this view.

The use of the lens-flare filter can be overdone, but in the case of a spotlit exhibit such as this, it works. A photographic artifact, it adds a level of realism to the drawing.

Final image: Saved via Save a Copy as a .pcx, .tif, or .pic. The lens-flare filter is (sparingly) applied to this flattened image at an appropriate point (where a light might be pointed directly at the viewer). Levels are then adjusted a bit to add some density, and noise is added to give tooth and to mitigate any banding in the gradients.

In this wash layer the separate realms of light and shadow are clear, in this case defined by sunlight. Contrast is high.

In this wash layer light and shadow glow with two opposite colors, but their values are not highly contrasting.

WINTER/SUMMER GARDEN: ROUGH SKETCH

This drawing for a conservatorylike pavilion was colored in two contrasting fashions. The purpose of these drawings was not so much to define the form of the structure as to describe a transformable building that has great appeal as both a shady place in summer and a warm hothouse in winter.

The drawing is a first-pass overlay of a one-shot hand sketch. The roughness of the original drawing is apparent in the line layers, but the painterly application of color mitigates the sloppiness.

The color concepts for the two drawings reinforce the point about the seasons; cool colors are used for the summer shot and warm ones for winter. A particularly striking photograph of Stockholm provided inspiration for the winter view.

Note that some of the original tree linework was painted out with a 100% white to defoliate the winter trees.

Having a reference for such an extreme color approach is very helpful, as some of the colors are hard to believe. Visual clues, like the steam in the winter scene, also help with believability.

The two final images shown here include the paint layer and have had noise added.

In the summer view, the paint layer was used for the glint off the mullions and for reinforcing the bright greens of the leaves and grass, the colorful flowers, and the highlights on the glass.

In the winter view, the paint layer was used to brighten the inside of the pavilion, to make the snow frostier with light-blue highlights, to paint the semi-transparent bare tree filigree, and to airbrush the steam.

In both drawings, some items, such as the steam, were painted on separate layers for ease of editing. Some of these layers were eventually merged with the paint layer.

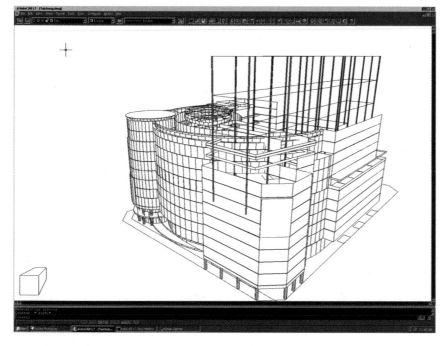

Saved view from 3-D AutoCAD model plotted at a set size. This allows revisions to be plotted at the same scale. The plot serves as background for hand drawing.

Hand drawing with Razor Point™ on white tracing paper. The third vanishing point made this a bit of a pain, but the CAD background provided guidelines for most items.

TAICHUNG RETAIL CENTER:
DESIGN DEVELOPMENT IMAGE

The existence of digital floor plans, circular geometries, and the desire for multiple views prompted the generation of the CAD model. This comprehensive aerial "hero shot" was intended to sum up the design, its setting, and the vitality of the entire development.

An array of visual goodies were used, including spotlights, pasted-in Jumbotron (giant-screen TV) and ad panel images, and streaming headlights. The headlights in particular are interesting as they are a photographic artifact but are not seen as foreign here. We have become accustomed to seeing such things, and they connote movement and reality, even if they are artificial.

The use of a color model, as discussed previously, is invaluable in the depiction of the city background. A photograph is a good reference in a case like this where so much context must be represented. Because it simplifies the palette, a photograph makes it easy to judge the proper hue for a shadow or the nature of a streetlight's glow. As with the headlights, the photograph represents reality for us, even as it artificially simplifies it.

The wash layer has a stock photograph sky pasted into a selection, blurred, smudged, and color balanced to recall the color model. The first washes are over everything except the sky and are quite dark, in anticipation of the addition of light. The lighter blue in the distant background recalls the color model. This color also indicates which elements face away from the setting sun. Faces toward the sun have a pink tint similar to the pink in the sky.

The streaming head- and taillights add drama and the feel of a bustling city. These were created on a separate layer with lines blurred and trimmed to the edge of the street selection. Selections were made for the roofs and then inverted so that glowing light coming up from the street could be added.

Clip art, such as the ad panels and Jumbotron, is pasted into a selection and then distorted to fit. The spotlights are feathered-edged wedges filled with a warm white gradient.

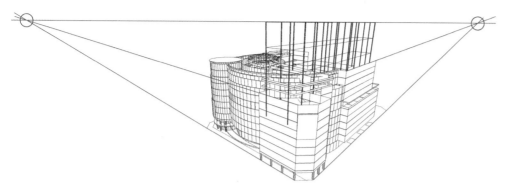

Finding the horizon from the plot: The horizon is level, drawn between the two vanishing points. The use of the third vanishing point is necessary in a situation like this where the entire subject is below the horizon. Interestingly, in a ground-level view of a high-rise, we are more accepting of parallel verticals.

Paint layer: Clip-art photos pasted into ad panels and Jumbotron. Distant city lights, highlights, and other lights are added.

Wash layer: Overall dark wash has building elements broken out and uplit with gradient light. The sky will be enhanced on the paint layer.

Tentative or semitransparent items like the painted trees and spotlights are kept on a separate layer to ease any modifications needed.

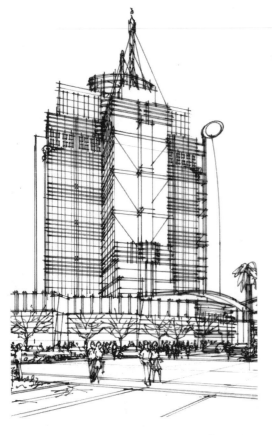

Line drawing: Over super-simple CAD background. At this schematic level, a lot of the visual design is done in the course of drawing the linework.

Wash layer: Very dark, keeping in mind that light will be added to achieve the drama desired.

MUSIC CITY: CONCEPT ILLUSTRATION

The Music City Hotel/Casino project was one of several proposals for a site in Las Vegas. The architectural concept was inspired to some degree by power plants and electrical imagery, including radio-stationlike call letters, skeletal elevator gantries, and catwalks.

Las Vegas being what it is, drama was important, but a sense of something different, perhaps a bit darker and more mysterious, was also sought. The moonlit clouds keep the drawing from being too foreboding and allow the contrast of cool (blue) moonlight with the warm (orange) of incandescent interior lighting.

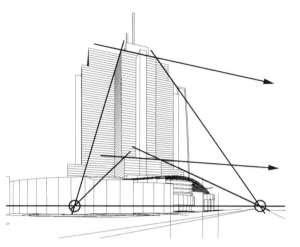

The general X configuration of the hotel tower and the proposed number of floors made this design a candidate for a simple CAD model. The 45° angle also made it easy to establish the other vanishing points.

The text tool is used for the call letters and the signs. The text was made on a separate layer and distorted to fit the perspective of the drawing. Then a little airbrush glow was added. To create a neonlike sign or a contrasting outline, the text is selected, then the selection is contracted 2 or 3 pixels and deleted, leaving just the outline of the letters. This can then be placed over the original type in another color if desired.

The tower portion of this drawing shows the application of various Photoshop tools. As shown in the detail, the line tool is very useful for creating highlighted edges and rectangular patches of color. Unfortunately, there is no gradient line tool.

(ADVANTAGES AND DISADVANTAGES OF DIGITAL COLOR, continued from page 238.)

DISADVANTAGES

NONPORTABILITY

While laptops are portable, using a computer is not the same as rolling out a piece of tracing paper and sketching away. It is possible to use portable scanners and small pen tablets to simulate a digital setup while on the road, but judging color on active matrix screens is difficult. Taking a laptop and plugging into a monitor at the remote location is often a possibility, but Murphy's Law applies heavily to most remote setups. However, a benefit of coloring digitally is that the process can inform the way one sketches and colors by hand when a computer is not available.

EQUIPMENT COST/STORAGE REQUIREMENTS

While computers are ever more ubiquitous, especially in a modern architect's office, having the proper specialized equipment and paying for it are still issues. This is, of course, also true when duplicating a setup for remote use.

While the cost of RAM and hard-drive space has come down dramatically in recent years, your digital graphic files will no doubt be the biggest things on the company server. Having a solid system to back up, remove, and retrieve these files is crucial. These things come at some cost, and may be hard to understand for the system administrator, who is used to archiving much smaller AutoCAD and Word files. Archiving onto CDs is one of the simplest, most cost-effective ways to do this.

The ongoing incremental cost of maintaining an up-to-date system is sometimes worrisome, but keeping a clear mind about what the system needs to do is key. Take advantage of clear improvements and avoid extra "infrastructure" that doesn't serve your purpose.

LEARNING CURVE

While there is a significant learning curve to overcome in using any new technique, many of the skills required for digitally coloring drawings are closely related to general drawing and coloring skills. In particular, using a pen tablet for drawing and painting is much more natural than using a mouse.

Many of the skills required by digital design programs are the same as those needed for general computer use, such as file management, cutting and pasting, etc. If general use of the computer is unfamiliar to you, learning the basic procedures first will reduce frustration when you use a complex program such as Photoshop. Photoshop is primarily a program for photographers and has far greater capabilities and applications than the few used for the drawings shown here.

A FINAL WORD ABOUT DIGITAL COLOR: "FLASH" VS. SUBSTANCE

Conceptual drawings, especially those that emphasize experience, are often criticized for lack of substance or for being too "flashy" or artificial. The questions are, of course, what is the substance of the design? And *what* reality is being created?

The purpose of all design drawings is to explore and communicate aspects of the design. If a flashy Jumbotron and dramatic polychromatic lighting are important aspects of the design, they must be communicated.

Of course, the drawing should never lie about any aspect of the design, but it should emphasize what is important (as should the design itself). If it is most important to communicate that the structural bay is 28 feet square, then another type of drawing is obviously in order.

THE COMPUTER SYSTEM

At the risk of being instantly out-of-date, it might be useful to describe the computer system required to produce the sort of drawings represented here. While there are certainly exceptions and enhancements to any such list, the following guidelines will help to define the main components of the system.

COMPUTER

Naturally, whatever amount of hard-drive space and RAM I could quote here would soon seem quaint and obsolete, so let it be said that, in general, it is worth getting the fastest, biggest, most upgradable system you can at any given time. The drawings here were colored on various generations of equipment, the most sophisticated of which was a 266mhz Pentium II with 128MB of RAM. This was more than enough power to handle these files, but it is possible that next year some unforeseen development could make 128MB wholly inadequate.

You must always remain aware of the weak points in your system. Know what you want to improve, but keep the system as simple as possible. Each time something is added or upgraded, a debugging period is inevitable.

The ever-present PC-Mac controversy will no doubt rage on for some time, but the differences in performance that concern us are, at this point, negligible. The heritage of AutoCAD in most architecture offices means that PCs are more common there, but Photoshop works just as well on a Mac.

MONITOR

While scrolling around the screen makes it possible to work any size monitor, there is no substitute for size when painting digitally. The reasons for wanting to see as much of the "canvas" as possible are self-evident. Most of the preceding drawings were done on a 21-inch monitor at a resolution of 1200 by 1600 pixels. The graphics card used will only display 16-bit color at this resolution, but 16-bit color is perfectly adequate for our purposes and the additional resolution is more than worth it.

Unfortunately, a 21-inch monitor and graphics card can cost as much as the rest of the computer, but there is no question that it is worth the cost.

SCANNER

The scanner is the "gateway to the computer" for any hand drawing, so having one is required. All of the drawings shown were scanned using an HP Scanjet 4C, which has not required upgrading.

The size of the scanner also should be considered. While it is very easy to splice together pieces of a drawing in a single row, the "tiling" of multiple rows usually creates serious alignment problems. For this reason, drawings meant to be scanned on the 4C are generally limited to 14 inches in height. Fortunately, drawings rarely need to be bigger than this anyway, even if printing out E-size posters.

TABLET

Invaluable as a painting device is a pen tablet. It is the most natural and controllable way to paint digitally. Surprisingly, the small 4"-by-6" size is adequate for digital coloring purposes, as you don't want to have to throw out your arm too much in the course of drawing. The small size is also convenient in terms of desk space and is more portable. Generally, the pressure-sensitive capabilities of these tablets are overrated and not very useful (don't plan on using it), but that does not diminish their overall utility.

STORAGE CONCEPT/CD ROM DRIVE/RECORDER

The large files generated by graphics programs quickly eat up even large hard drives, so it is important to develop a strategy for backing up and taking off files. As of this writing, consideration should be given to a CD ROM recorder for this purpose. The media are cheap and easily stored and retrieval is simple. However, a separate drive should be available for day-to-day use, particularly if a lot of read-intensive activities (like games) are used on the system.

Other options include Zip™ and Jaz™ drives and tape backups. If you intend to print through a service bureau, it is important that they can read your media. The advantage of CDs is that they are read only (protecting the original file from overwrites), cheap enough to lose, and readable by others with CD drives, which are extremely common.

SOFTWARE: CAD, PAINTING, PAGE LAYOUT

Software is a lot like language: your native tongue is hard to sublimate. Even though they perform essentially the same functions, competing programs and equipment are still alive and well. Among them are PC and Mac, Form-Z and AutoDesk, and More Taste and Less Filling. For this reason, we will be discussing the specific software that appears to be the best or even only choice for particular tasks. However, you are free to find and use anything else that rolls off your tongue more easily.

That said, it is usually best to use the most prevalent software known for a given task. Problems of file sharing, compatibility, and communication are major distractions when there is designing to be done.

AutoCAD is good for modeling because it is capable of constructing complex geometries, can usually take advantage of existing data, and is something many architects have already. While modeling in AutoCAD can be very simple, we will not address it here in any detail. The main purpose of a CAD model is to give us accurate perspective views that we can then trace over.

Photoshop is probably the only choice for painting in the manner described here. Its main distinguishing feature (although it has many good painting tools), is that it allows you to separate elements onto different layers, which makes editing them far easier. Several other painting programs exist but the tools offered by Photoshop are more than adequate, and it really is the standard.

Beware of programs with a lot of complex capabilities and filters that you will never use. It is far better to master a few simple tools—the computer will never do your creating for you, regardless of how many special features it has. The drawings here were all done using Photoshop version 3.0, and even though several subsequent versions exist, there have been only slight improvements in terms of what is required for our purposes. Some of these improvements come at a cost, such as requiring more RAM.

Some "improvements" even prove to be unwelcome revisions to nicely working features. For instance, versions of Photoshop after 3.0 create a new layer every time something is pasted. This is quite an annoyance if one is trying to limit the number of layers. It is the primary reason I continue to use 3.0.

Page-layout programs are much easier to use for layout than is Photoshop. To avoid the quagmire of dpi calculations, place finished images and text in Pagemaker, Quark, or even PowerPoint. This will give you much more control over output.

OUTPUT DEVICES

Once the drawing is complete, how it gets communicated is the next step. Fortunately, in the past few years, color printing has improved infinitely and become much more economical, especially at an 8 1/2-inch width. Even some wider-format printers have become more affordable, but generally only large offices and service bureaus can afford to buy and keep up printers over 14 inches wide.

Without a doubt, ink-jet printers (such as Epson Stylus) deliver a superior color print (but more slowly) compared with toner-based printers (such as color copiers). Unless large numbers of prints need to be run, a simple desktop ink-jet printer is the best choice for hard copies of digital files.

On-screen viewing is, of course, an option, as is placing files within a PowerPoint or freelance-type presentation. Bitmap or PowerPoint files can be used to make 35mm slides (by service bureaus, usually). Check with the bureau for version/program compatibility. Refer to the section on multimedia presentations for more information.

Combining Drawing with Words and Photographs

Designers, and the design professions in general, should look for every opportunity to publish and display their work, not just for their self-promotion but also to educate the general public about the value of the design professions. These opportunities always involve the combination of words and photographs, with a changing role for drawing.

Once a designed project is built, drawing's predictive role changes to one of describing the outcome. Photographs of the completed project show the experience of being there, so perspectives are no longer needed. Plans and sections help to describe where the photographs are taken and communicate the integrity of the project as a designed object or space. Perhaps most important, conceptual diagrams are needed to show the underlying concepts that generated the design, as well as the process that developed it.

THE ELEMENTS

In considering the various combinations that can best communicate environmental design we must first understand the elements of communication and how they contribute to the combination.

VERBAL DESCRIPTION AND RATIONALE

Designers must realize that their drawings will almost never need, or even be allowed, to communicate alone. Design drawings will normally be described verbally, as a student makes a presentation to a jury or a practicing designer presents to a client. In practice, you will usually verbally present your drawings not once, but many times in the successive phases of the design process. These presentations may be formal or informal and normally include a discussion with questions and further explanations. The discussions will clarify how well the drawings have been understood.

Continuing conversations about various ideas on the project without the drawings, and often by telephone, preclude using the drawings as referents. Thus, the client's remembrance of the designer's verbal description may be more important than the recollection of the drawings. Clients not accustomed to communicating graphically or visually may carry a primarily verbal understanding of the design built from the designer's descriptive words and phrases.

This verbal description—the words and phrases themselves and their logic and eloquence—becomes extremely important. Scholars and authors who have studied designers' communications with clients have found that most famous designers take their descriptions of their work very seriously.

Sometimes what designers say about their work is a continuing explanation of their design philosophy, consistently carried from project to project and reflecting their deepest convictions about design. Others may vary the explanation drastically from project to project, as they do

their design approach. Many prominent designers have a poetic, romantic way of describing their work, and many clients appreciate that kind of explanation. As Stephen A. Kliment writes in *Writing for Design Professionals*:

> Remember who you are. . . . One of the qualities that those who hire you look for is uniqueness and personality, and you cannot project uniqueness unless you define your image and that of your organization. Personality will ultimately creep into your writing. Such attributes as hip, formal, cool, folksy, conservative, and kooky will—and certainly should—show through in what you write.

The client is entitled to understand the rationale for the basic elements and systems of the design and their arrangement, as well as the general configuration and articulations of the three-dimensional form and the selection of materials and colors. Beyond this basic description, designers can add whatever verbal poetry or eloquence they feel comfortable with communicating. Clients appreciate the effort and attention the designer has given to explaining their project.

As part of their professional service, designers owe their clients a careful verbal description of any project they design. This verbal description should be well thought through and persuasively written. It should exist in various forms, from informal, conversational descriptive phrases to an exhaustive, detailed description of the construction and the design process that produced it. I even advocate including a verbal description of the project's design concepts on the cover of the construction documents used to bid and build it,

so that everyone connected with the construction understands the design intentions.

The verbal description of the project should be based on the client's initial programmatic statements about their needs and wishes for the project. It should include as many of their phrases from those early conversations as possible. Responses to those initial goals should be there in the designed environment for all to see, but they may need to be pointed out so they are not overlooked.

Agreement on the evolving verbal description of the design should be an important goal of the design process. As the design evolves and develops, so too should the words that describe it, until the description is understood by all as clear, honest, and, perhaps, poetical. This means that if the clients strongly desire an environment that is "warm and welcoming," considerable time will be spent analyzing and agreeing on what those words mean environmentally.

I previously discussed and quoted Tim White's books concerning the translation of verbal statements into two-dimensional diagrams and eventually a into three-dimensional built form. The verbal description of the finished design project brings the process full circle, helping the owners and users to see those initial programmatic statements in the finished design.

You may say that if the designed environment doesn't reflect or "play back" the responses to the original programmatic statements, it is a failure; that those responses should be readily apparent to the users of the environment; that you should never have to explain how the design has solved those problems. I disagree. I believe designers are entitled to write down a carefully conceived verbal description of any project they design, along with its rationale and the process that produced it. Owners and users may need help in understanding all the qualities of the design. I would even advocate, for most public projects, the publication of a brief folder that contains the verbal description and a few drawings that explain the building. This could be kept in the reception area.

The verbal description should act as a sort of birth certificate for the project, something that legitimizes its existence and is passed down from designer to owner, to successive owners and users of the building, garden, or interior.

Verbal eloquence is generally not a requirement for architects, landscape architects, or interior designers. We tend to be much more left-brained and visual than right-brained and verbal. Writing about our work, or writing about our field in general, is seldom required in design studios or taught in separate courses beyond the general university requirements in English.

For the "Boyer" report, *Building Community*, Ernest L. Boyer and Lee D. Mitgang of the Carnegie Foundation studied the future of architecture education and practice:

In common with many undergraduates, architecture students often display weak oral and written skills. At the start of a fifth-year lecture class we attended, the instructor felt obliged to give a five-minute talk on the difference between "its" and "it's."

"The writing skills of 50 percent of my students are just atrocious," he told us.

"It's not just grammar and spelling," said a faculty member at an East Coast private institution. "They can't construct an argument with a beginning and an end and something in the middle."

Assessing the communication abilities of recently hired interns, a partner of a Washington, D.C., firm told us: "You see students who are well organized and good designers, but can't put two sentences together."

The ability to speak and write with clarity is essential if architects are to assume leadership in the social, political, and economic arenas where key decisions about the built environment are being made, and some administrators and faculty we met are taking those skills seriously. Ball State's architecture program, for example, has a "Writing in the Design Curriculum" program that brings English faculty directly into the studio and prompts both students and faculty to be more mindful of the importance to architects of writing well.

Overall, however, it was disturbing to find how undervalued clear communication is at some programs. At one prestigious school we visited, we read two final theses: one clearly and grammatically written, and a second ungrammatical and nearly incomprehensible. Both papers, however, received identical grades of "A" from the same design instructor. Whatever criteria counted in arriving at those grades, writing ability was surely not high among them.

For all these reasons I recommend that, early in your design education, you take writing, especially writing about your work, very seriously. Make the verbal description of your designs in school part of your responsibility. Write the rationale on your presentation drawings as notes to support your oral presentation in reviews and as an integral part of any project that winds up in your portfolio.

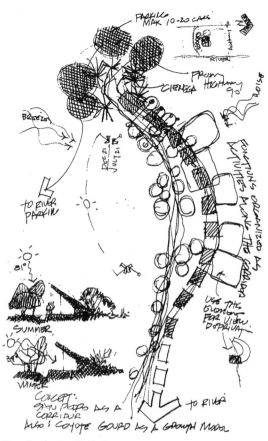

Drawing by Les Wallach.

CONCEPTUAL DIAGRAMS

Since photographs can take the place of perspectives in communicating the experiential qualities of built projects, not having to draw perspectives can free you to draw presentation-type plans and sections to explain the project's integrity as a designed place or object. You also should take the time to make diagrams that explain the conceptual basis and development of the design.

Tucson architect Les Wallach uses conceptual diagrams to design his projects, to help remind his team and the client of the basic concept, and to communicate that organizing concept in the exhibition and publication of his work, as well as in job interviews for subsequent projects.

The diagram at left is the conceptual diagram for Wallach's design of the San Pedro Riparian Center. The freshness and vigor of the drawing is very powerful, making it an indelible image that will guide the whole design-development process. The diagram drives home the idea that the building interprets the San Pedro River as a corridor, with the various functions arranged linearly along an outdoor circulation path that runs alongside and opens onto the river itself.

Notice that the diagram distinguishes functions with various kinds of hatching and that it includes words, arrows, and symbols for the surrounding microclimate. Conceptual diagrams can be incredibly rich in the amount of information they carry. Their primal vigor assures that questions of building style or door swings won't come up until the much more important conceptual matters are agreed on.

PHOTOGRAPHS

Once an environmental design project is built, photographs replace perspectives as the best way to communicate the experience of the environment. You should become your own photographer or develop a working relationship with a professional photographer in order to make a good photographic record of your work. It is important that these photographs be of the highest quality. Never communicate your work in less-than-excellent photographs.

Photographs are always required for submissions to awards programs, and once you have the photographs they can be combined with the eloquent written description of the project. You will then have a publishable package that can be sent to various editors.

Photographs should be taken to illustrate the points made in your verbal description. The two must work together to reinforce each other. The photographer should be given the verbal description ahead of time and be familiar with what you want the photographs to communicate—and you should be prepared to change the verbal description in response to what the photographs are able to show. The photographs and words that describe the design must be just as integrated as the design itself.

ANNOTATED DRAWINGS

Never expect your drawings to stand alone, unexplained. In normal client presentations you must be able to explain the drawings to your clients, answer questions, and clear up misunderstandings on the spot. Problems can arise after the presentation, when clients are left with the drawings but may not remember some of the finer points of your verbal explanation. It is then, when the client is alone with your drawings, that the drawings may have to communicate alone.

This is a job for annotated drawings! Annotated drawings are like an annotated Shakespeare, or the private stage whisper of the author, telling you her or his intentions in the design. If you develop the habit of writing explanatory notes on your design drawings and use the notes to prompt your oral explanations, they will prompt your clients' understanding of the design when you're no longer there.

Les Wallach uses annotated drawings effectively in exhibitions and publications of his work. In the annotated drawings in *spazio e societa*, January–March 1998, Wallach overlaid photographs to make simple line drawings and hand-

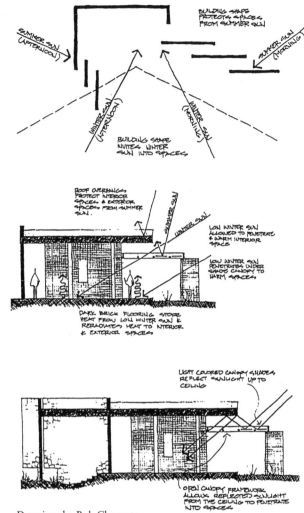

Drawings by Bob Clements.

written notes. Wallach wanted to make sure his design intentions were communicated clearly, so he instructed the perception of the reader. Plans and sections can also be overlaid with annotated drawings, or the notes may be written directly on the drawings. This is particularly helpful in clarifying large, complex orthographic drawings that, to the average person, are like a foreign language.

Photograph by Henry Tom.

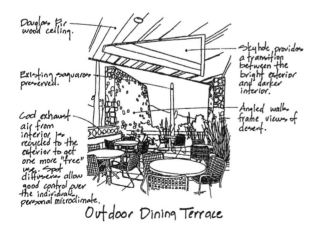

Douglas Fir wood ceiling.

Existing saguaro preserved.

Cool exhaust air from interior recycled to the exterior to get one more "free" use. Spot diffusers allow good control over the individual, personal microclimate.

Skyhole provides a transition between the bright exterior and darker interior.

Angled walls frame views of desert.

Outdoor Dining Terrace

Drawing by John Birkinbine.

LIVE FREEHAND DRAWING

I encourage you to develop the skill, confidence, or both to draw in public. It will make you the leader or "facilitator" of any group meeting where there is an easel or blackboard. Your graphic skills, both your drawing and your lettering, will probably be better than that of anyone else in the room. Even if your graphic skills need a little polishing to accommodate the large scale of the easel tablet, it will be worth the effort.

This open workshop format is useful in many ways and you should become skillful in using it. In early meetings with group clients where you are trying to get to know the building committee, assure them that you are listening to their comments, and encourage a climate of open participation. Taking the role of the graphic facilitator is ideal. By soliciting, writing down, and beginning to translate their comments into two-dimensional diagrams, you will encourage participation and foster consensus. You also will remember the comments better than if you had just listened and taken notes.

Drawing's role in such input sessions can be vital. Beginning to diagram suggestions for adjacency requirements, for instance, can graphically clarify that everything can't be adjacent to everything else. This initiates the prioritizing crucial to developing a workable plan. Drawing can also begin to clarify formal issues, like whether the exterior form of the building is suitably "inviting" or "dignified" or any number of descriptive words on which there may be little agreement.

While you can't really design the entire environment on an easel tablet, you can certainly lead and illustrate productive sessions with your drawing ability. And the one who benefits most from such informal workshops is you. In your role as honest broker you will naturally get to know both the individuals and their opinions and motivations, as well as understand the group and its dynamics. In addition to providing the invaluable content of what is communicated, you will tease out the various preconceptions about the design and begin to get an idea of how you might educate and negotiate to improve the design.

Taking down the client group's ideas and turning them into drawings, live, before their eyes, will very naturally establish you in your rightful role as the translator of their verbal ideas into visual expression.

THE OPPORTUNITIES

Environmental designers should take every opportunity to communicate their work. My generation of designers was generally averse to anything that seemed like self-promotion, and I believe that has contributed to the general public's poor understanding of the value of environmental design. I know that one of the reasons well-designed buildings have difficulty making it through middle age without being awkwardly remodeled or torn down is that their owners and users have no appreciation for what great buildings they are. Perhaps their designers never made the effort to communicate how good their design was.

In this generation of constant commercial hype and political spin-doctors, environmental designers are foolish if we don't take, or *make*, every opportunity to explain ourselves and our work. There is a great range of media available, from the very prestigious and selective to those that are advertising-driven. There are home tours and awards programs, as well as informative, self-published mailers that can let a group of friends and patrons know about your latest projects. We should take advantage of all of these and do it with as much skill as we can muster.

Having considered the various elements of communicative combinations, we can now consider some of the typical ways drawing contributes as a partner with words and photographs, from formal slide shows to informal conversation.

COMPUTER-BASED PRESENTATIONS
by M. Scott Lockard

Designers' presentations of their work have become more sophisticated with advances in technology. Projected presentations that combine drawings, photographs, slides, text, models, and even video footage are easier to create than ever thanks to on-screen presentation programs.

Seamless and easily revisable presentations can now be produced through programs such as PowerPoint and Freelance, using digital images that are either scanned or computer generated. Titling and text is simply typed in and even video footage can be integrated.

Advantages. A major advantage of computer-based presentations over slides is the elimination of the film-processing step. By scanning drawings and photographs you can create projectable images without film.

Film processing is still sometimes necessary for site and existing-conditions photos. While straight scanning of prints is often perfectly ade-

quate, photo CDs are a fairly simple and cost-effective way to get digital files directly from film. However, these images will always require some tweaking and cropping.

Digital cameras skip the film step altogether, and while some are photographically inferior to 35mm cameras, the instant turnaround time can be very helpful, particularly in on-site or charrette situations.

Digitally colored drawings are, of course, perfect candidates for inclusion in a digital presentation. The resulting images are also extremely versatile. Projection can give even very small drawings great impact. Consider scanning and using napkin sketches, bubble diagrams, and the like whenever appropriate.

The most significant advantage of a computer-programmed presentation is that revising and editing of the outline and content is (truly) about as easy as it could possibly be.

Disadvantages. A disadvantage of the computer-based presentation is that it's a bit odd to crowd around a computer screen to view the presentation, unless the screen is quite large and set up with a certain formality. Video projectors, while improving, are less bright and have lower resolution. They're also cumbersome to transport and a bit noisy. You still have to darken the room in most cases, which perpetuates the biggest disadvantage of a slide presentation: a disconnection with the audience.

For the most effective presentation it may still be necessary to reproduce some of your images in large hard copies. Computer-programmed presentations do have multiple options for printing speaker's notes, handouts, and "leave-behinds" from the presentation.

Approach. PowerPoint has some seemingly useful ways to import and format the outline of a presentation, but these features are conceived for verbal, bullet-riddled presentations on health-care benefits or twelve-step programs. For image-rich presentations that rarely have more than a few titles these sorts of tools are too cumbersome to customize.

The best approach is often to do some outlining, making a single point per slide and inserting images as you go. After most of the content is there, cutting and pasting images between slides is simple. Refine the layout of each slide, and resize images and text last. The "slide sorter" view is useful for shuffling and rearranging the whole presentation.

It's possible to create a two-projector show in combination with regular slides, allowing the best projector to handle the slides, and thus get a more dynamic, two-screen show. This of course takes more planning and time. "Animation," the flying, spinning, or zooming effects that can be added to objects, should usually be left altogether. This is often wisest because the creation of last-minute slides or revisions would then require the additional step of animation.

Format. I recommend rejecting the predesigned presentation "looks." It is important to create an appropriate or, at worst, neutral format for your images and information. Beginning with a simple black background is better in terms of letting "floating" images have their own impact than to put one of those ubiquitous blue gradients behind every last thing you show. Creation of a simple title bar is often all that is necessary to tie the slides together. The "looks" were primarily created to put some life into predominantly verbal presentations. Hopefully, your presentation will be too good to suffer such visual distractions.

Importing content. Most common digital formats such as .jpg, .tif, .pcx (PC), and .pict (Mac) can be imported with various video (.avi) and sound (.wav) formats. Note that for complex, precisely timed, or large-display video, Director or Premier is a better choice, but then you have to take on a whole new profession—coordination and timing of music and video can be a nightmare and is often best left to a qualified consultant. For the most part, you should concentrate on the clear, effective, and elegant presentation of your design concepts and not upon the gratuitous packaging of the information.

One issue to understand is that in computer-based presentations, image files are imbedded, meaning that the actual image is included in the file. Note that in page-layout programs such as Quark or Pagemaker, files are usually only "linked," which allows them to be easily updated. As a result, the full size for a computer-programmed presentation can easily be 30–50 megabytes or more for a typical thirty-minute presentation.

Computer system. Depending on the amount of video and audio processing required, the system can be similar to the digital-coloring setup described earlier, with the addition of a frame grabber for video, sound card (resident on many motherboards nowadays), and speakers for audio (if you insist).

SLIDE SHOWS

Now outdated by high-tech computer-based presentations, 35mm slide shows are still a relatively simple and impressive presentation technique. While, like with any projected presentation, you lose eye contact with the audience, slide shows have three great advantages:

1. They focus the viewer's attention on a single image or idea and allow you to lead viewers through a logical linear progression, slide by slide, to the conclusion you are advocating. In presentations of several large boards the audience's attention inevitably wanders away from whatever the presenter is talking about.

2. They homogenize all sorts of disparate media (drawings, models, photographs, text, titles, and slides of various real contexts or activities) into a single seamless medium: 35mm film.

3. Just as with computer-based presentations but much more simply, the slide show can be kept intact or disassembled and stored in a slide collection that retains and files the various slides for future use.

Slide shows also have two serious disadvantages:

1. They require time to photograph all the non-photographic media and get the film developed and mounted. This may not seem like a lot of time, but in the hours and minutes before a deadline it can be huge.

2. They cannot include videotape, and digital images must be made into slides.

If the presentation venue is rather formal with audiencelike seating, and you don't mind darkening the room and losing eye contact, or don't have the expensive high-tech equipment necessary for a computer-based presentation, slide shows can be very effective.

EXHIBITS AND AWARDS

Various professional organizations of the environmental design professions sponsor regular awards programs and exhibits in a variety of venues, usually in conjunction with conventions, and often virtually closed to the public. We admire one another's work and give ourselves awards, which get exhibited very briefly and, perhaps, published in trade magazines or local newspapers, but we are generally ineffective in informing the public about what we do and what we consider our best work.

One reason is the difficulty and expense involved in preparing the traditional project exhibits, which demand descriptions of an entire project in drawings and photographs composed on large presentation boards. Even though many awards programs have recently eased the workload by requiring only a binder of photographs and drawings or just a binder of 35mm slides, the preparation is still daunting.

Because of the difficulty and expense of these rigid requirements, we seldom take the initiative to mount separate exhibitions, and with all the high-tech ways of communicating available today, perhaps the traditional exhibit is no longer worth the effort. But if we forget the laboriously and expensively prepared boards, we can begin to use technology to communicate more effectively in exhibits designed for the general public.

In Tucson an independent interdisciplinary group of environmental designers has mounted

Photograph by Henry Tom.

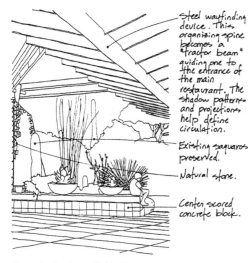

Steel wayfinding device. This organizing spine becomes a "tractor beam" guiding one to the entrance of the main restaurant. The shadow patterns and projections help define circulation.

Existing saguaros preserved.

Natural stone.

Center scored concrete block.

Drawing by John Birkinbine.

two annual exhibits based on determinants of the Sonoran Desert region: sun, shade, color, water, and patterns. Exhibitors prepared single huge images made by "tiling" inexpensive color copies to form the larger image. They also provided smaller line-drawing overlays pointing out the design features that responded to the particular determinant. In the drawing at left we see again an example of the use of shade in Les Wallach's Restaurant and Gallery Complex for the Arizona Sonora Desert Museum.

The exhibit was very successful, made easy for the exhibitors, and more understandable to the general public. Held at the Tucson Museum of Art, it also was a reminder that public venues often are more than happy to make room for interesting environmental design exhibits.

PUBLICATIONS

Once you develop the habit of writing a verbal description of each project you design, preparing orthographic drawings, and having the best possible photographs taken, you are ready to seek publication. The most prominent designers are sought out by editors who sometimes even furnish the photography, but beginning designers and all those not yet famous enough to be courted by the media have to work at getting published.

Begin by researching the publications whom you might like to publish your work, finding out the names, addresses, and phone numbers of the editors who make the publication decisions. Editors are never insulted by your sending them work. They can't possibly keep track of all the bright young designers out there, and sending them examples of your work is usually appreciated.

Just make sure that whatever you send is as good as it can be. The photographs should be as outstanding as the design. A good example of the kind of care that should go into publication of your work is the attention Frank Lloyd Wright gave the preparation of the 1910–11 *Wasmuth Edition* of his work by the famous German publisher. Wright traveled to Europe to personally oversee the publication (although taking along the wife of one of your clients, as Wright did, isn't suggested). Marion Mahony, an architect in Wright's office, did most of the elegant perspectives expressly for that publication.

Tucson architects Les Wallach and Rick Joy (whose Convent Street studios are presented across page) take great care with the drawings that present their work in publications.

Notice how small and simply drawn the site plan and section of Joy's project can be and still communicate quite clearly, while the photographs gain great power by their relatively greater size. This is an important lesson in design. The orthographic drawings are absolutely necessary but they would have gained nothing by being enlarged several times, while the photographs, which communicate the experience of the environment, become very dramatic with enlargement.

CONVERSATION

The most natural partner for drawing is ordinary conversation. You may have noticed that when architects, landscape architects, or interior designers talk about design with one another they draw on something to diagram their ideas. They use napkins, adhesive notes, tablecloths, the tabletop itself, or any white space on any

Photograph by Bill Timmerman.

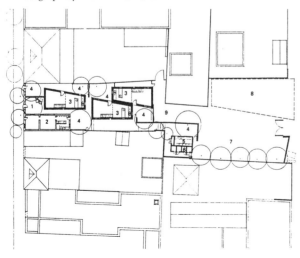

Photograph by Bill Timmerman.

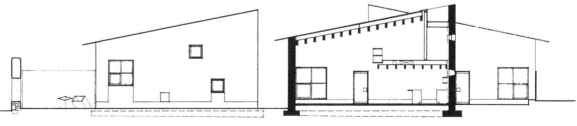

Drawings by Rick Joy.

piece of printed material to illustrate their conversation. During conversation or boring faculty meetings, my former student and fellow teacher, Doug Macneil, used to make incredibly intricate drawings on the tiny covers of matchbooks. Most designers become downright speechless if you take away their pencil or pen.

We should cultivate this habit of drawing professionally, so that we can communicate with our clients more naturally and informally and, when appropriate, impress them with what is surely a unique skill. What is even more impressive is to draw, and even letter, upside down, so that your diagrams, floor plan and section sketches, and even simple perspectives appear right-side up to the client sitting across from you at the conference table or desk.

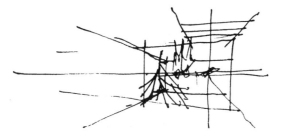

The first time I did this it was purely spontaneous, in the middle of a client conference, and neither I nor the clients noticed right away that I was drawing upside down for their benefit. If you doubt your ability to make simple diagrams and letter simple words upside down, try it. You may be pleasantly surprised at how easy it is, and how easily you can master it with just a little practice.

Bill Stamm, another of my longtime fellow teachers, advocates using our design communication skills deliberately to impress clients. He points out that both doctors and lawyers have an arcane vocabulary that adds a certain professional mystery and helps justify their fees. We need something similar that ordinary folks can't do—it will give us a certain professional distinction and help justify our fees.

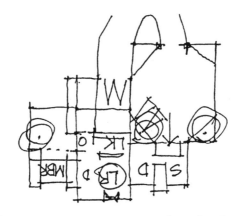

The important point is to explore the development of a personal way of using drawing during your conversations with clients, collaborators, or consultants. There are several benefits in being able to draw better, demonstrably, than anyone else at the table:

- The spontaneity of drawing during design conversations makes the process seem more open, creative, and stimulating, especially if your drawings begin to respond to the suggestions of others around the table.
- Being able to draw during a design conversation makes it clear that you are the designer. You are not presenting drawings that were made by some underling in your office.
- It is clear that you possess a disciplined, creative skill that can certainly be overdone but, if used in a simple, natural way as if to say, "Of course I can draw. It's part of my professional competence," cannot fail to impress.

DRAWING AS A PARTNER IN COMMUNICATION

Although drawing is an essential partner it should always respect the larger purpose of design communication, which is to bring about a clear and thorough understanding of the environment being designed. Unfortunately, stories abound about designers who have either naïvely or purposefully misled their clients into accepting and building a design that they never really understood and, if they had, would almost certainly never have approved.

Drawings, responsibly done and fully understood, are more honest than words and are indispensable in design communication. Before any kind of agreement or approval, it is necessary that the design be completely and clearly communicated.

The German philosopher Juergen Habermas advocates the rationalization that automatically comes from successful communication, "communicative rationality." His thought has much to say to designers about communicating with clients and others about our work. Applied to environmental design, Habermas would hold that designs will always benefit from honest, open communication that ensures that everyone affected by the design clearly understands it and the designer's intentions and has a chance to be heard. This insight mandates a much more serious role for the communication about any design, with the designer not just persuading a client or explaining the design, but seeking clear and complete understanding and responding to the opinions of all those affected. Design drawing is an indispensable partner in this essential kind of design communication.

8 Applications

Books on drawing often neglect to address real situations with actual applications of the techniques they teach, and it is not always obvious to students how and when the drawing skills they are learning can best be applied.

In order for the studio conversations between students and teachers, and between students, to reach their potential, there must be drawings or models of the ideas being discussed.

Without realistic representational referents, like drawings or models, there is no assurance that the student and teacher are talking about the same thing, and what seems to be verbal agreement and approval from the teacher may, to the student's chagrin, change to harsh criticism when the project is presented in the final jury.

It's a good idea to develop the habit of externalizing your design ideas into the form of drawings and models early, and, if you are fortunate enough to have tack space around your drawing board, to pin up your drawings. They will provoke comments from your teachers and fellow students and assure that you get your share of criticism during each design process.

Your beginning drawings may be very crude bubble diagrams in plan or section, or crude perspectives of the overall three-dimensional form or the experience of interior spaces. No teacher will expect accurate, drafted drawings in the early studio crit sessions—rather, they will appreciate and respond positively to your efforts to diagram and sketch your early ideas and they will be happy to suggest how those sketches can be improved.

You will hear all sorts of opinions about when you should start drawing in the design process, and you will have to sort through them to see which are true for you. Some designers advocate not beginning to draw until you know pretty clearly what you want to draw. Supporters of this idea fear that you may unjustifiably fall in love with your early drawings before you really understand the problem. For similar reasons, others believe you should stay with abstract diagrams until most of the conceptual problems are resolved and move to three-dimensional form only after most of the conceptual solutions are agreed upon. There is some wisdom in both of these approaches, and they may be advisable for mature designers who are expert in managing their time.

The problem I have with delaying drawing for the beginning student is that deliberate delay can become an excuse for neglecting the three-dimensional development of the solution and learning how to make the qualitative, experiential drawings that such development requires. If teachers allow students to habitually delay drawing it dooms them as designers because they will never learn to make the drawings that help to nail down a design; consequently they will not wind up in the design departments of the offices that employ them.

The advantages of early drawing in the design studio seem obvious. Studio conversations will tend to be about design ideas that appear early in the process and are tacked up around designers' boards. Additionally, you will be able to see, and made to live with, your proposed solutions and to develop the self-critical eye on which good designers depend.

Furthermore, designers who draw early actually *learn to draw* because they have time and learn to enjoy making the drawings that convincingly, satisfyingly finish a project.

Whether or not you draw early in the design process comes down to your confidence in your drawing ability and what you believe about the role of drawing in the design process. For me, drawing *is* design. I can't imagine designing without drawing and so I begin to draw immediately and expectantly, counting on more ideas appearing in the drawings than I would be able to conjure up with unillustrated thought alone.

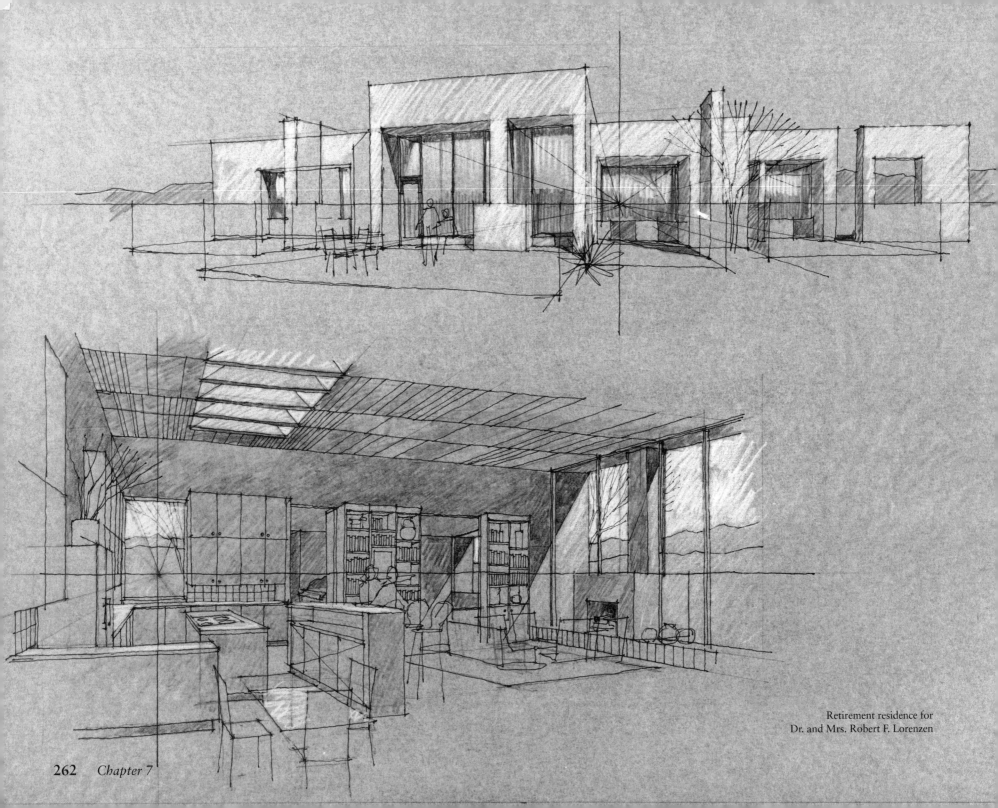

Retirement residence for
Dr. and Mrs. Robert F. Lorenzen

MAKING THE MOST OF YOUR ROUGH SKETCHES

The sketches on these two pages were drawn on buff tracing paper with a Rotring™ extra-fine-point fountain pen and black and white Prismacolor™ pencils. They were then mounted on a tan underlay paper before being photographed for the book. Mounting the tracing paper on colored paper brought out the contrast of the white Prismacolor™ and strengthened the sketches considerably.

   In spite of their rough, unrefined quality, these sketches tell me what I need to know about the experiential qualities of the residence I'm designing. Because the clients are old friends for whom I've designed a previous residence, there is no need to impress them with my drawing ability, and these rough sketches were shown to them (with a little color) as presentation drawings. Notice that, rough as they are, they have an accurate perspective layout, light and shadow, trees, furniture, and figures.

Even in the sketch on this page of a space with no windows, the white Prismacolor™ gives a strong sense of top light coming from the rooftop monitor. This gallery will display the owners' collection of quilts, baskets, and paintings.

LEARNING TO USE THE OVERLAY

Of all the habits that are helpful to student designers, that of using the tracing paper overlay to improve a drawing or design idea may be the most important. The overlay process is also the best model and symbol of the design process because it manifests the self-critical, iterative syntheses that refining a design requires.

The following drawings show what could be the first and last overlays that synthesize a design for presentation to a teacher, jury, or client. For the first overlays I used the same technique I always use for the drawings that begin the synthesis of the design. It is extremely important for a designer to have a special, personal way of making the early design drawings—your designs must look good to you and provoke you to keep drawing and designing.

It is strange, however, to have written several books on drawing without showing you the kinds of drawings I make for myself. The main reason is that drawings that use buff tracing paper as a middletone by adding white Prismacolor™ are very difficult and expensive to imitate in the offset printing process that produces books, but these overlays come as close as offset printing can.

The first complete set of drawings would be drawn over separate piecemeal conceptual efforts, as the initial effort to put the design all together and that first synthesis is extremely important. The drawings are a complete description of the design, including plans and sections as well as experiential perspectives. This synthesis is extremely important because it shows you the whole reality of the design and requires you to consider all the relationships of the proposed solution. Mature designers know that the more times they can accomplish similar syntheses during the design process, the better the final design will be.

The application of tones is one of the most time-consuming tasks in making really strong drawings. The pattern of black, gray, and white tones on this page are made with paper cutouts, one of the quickest, most effective ways to add tone to a drawing on tracing paper to emphasize brightly lit exterior space or sunlit surfaces. An easier alternative is to mount the white and gray cutouts on the back of the tracing paper, but that obviously can't be demonstrated in this book.

As you lay down the rough sketch and the more finished overlay over this page, the pattern of white and gray paper will imitate a technique that can't be duplicated by offset lithography—the addition of opaque, white Prismacolor™ pencil to buff tracing paper. This technique is represented here in a four-color photographic separation, but it can't quite replicate the opaque, waxy, white color applied directly to the back of the tracing paper.

Try this technique by applying the white pencil to the back of all windows in interior perspectives and all sunlit surfaces in exterior perspectives.

This overlay represents the first perspectives drawn to test the subjective quality or eyelevel experience of a design. First perspectives might actually include the width- and depth-plane grid used to layout the perspective. They also generally leave layout lines and cut away some intervening objects, like the stairway in the interior perspective. The perspectives are essentially accurate but remain sketchy. They are complete in that they suggest landscaping, furniture, and figures. See-through "ghosting" and overdrawing are acceptable and add to the sketchy quality. Color and tones are applied vigorously, but in a consistent stroking direction. Instead of being a design statement, color remains traditional and symbolic—blue for skies, green for trees, red for roof, floor, and metal color. In this way the color helps the sketches communicate without raising questions about eventual color schemes. This symbolic use of color saves a lot of time—a few branches and a green smudge (for instance) efficiently symbolize a tree.

This overlay represents the first perspectives drawn to test the subjective quality or eyelevel experience of a design. First perspectives might actually include the width- and depth-plane grid used to layout the perspective. They also generally leave layout lines and cut away some intervening objects, like the stairway in the interior perspective. The perspectives are essentially accurate but remain sketchy. They are complete in that they suggest landscaping, furniture, and figures. See-through "ghosting" and overdrawing are acceptable and add to the sketchy quality.

Color and tones are applied vigorously, but in a consistent stroking direction. Instead of being a design statement, color remains traditional and symbolic—blue for skies, green for trees, red for roof, floor, and metal color. In this way the color helps the sketches communicate without raising questions about eventual color schemes. This symbolic use of color saves a lot of time—a few branches and a green smudge (for instance) efficiently symbolize a tree.

This overlay represents a more finished drawing made over the previous sketch. Note the much more careful combination of spatial and additional interest, elimination of all overdrawing or transparency, and the spatially profiled spatial slices.

Tones—shade, shadows, and color—are more carefully added to this overlay; their application has a consistent stroking direction but remains deliberately sketchy, which saves a great deal of time and maintains the quality of a "process" drawing still open to change.

White Prismacolor™ is still added to the back, but all other colors are added directly to the front. Some designers, like Michael Doyle, use a more finished final overlay on white tracing paper and apply all color to the back so that it doesn't obscure the black lines on the front. The white tracing paper provides a more color-neutral background that can be color-copied using a variety of different-colored backup papers.

This overlay represents a more finished drawing made over the previous sketch. Note the much more careful combination of spatial and additional interest, elimination of all overdrawing or transparency, and the spatially profiled spatial slices.

Tones—shade, shadows, and color—are more carefully added to this overlay; their application has a consistent stroking direction but remains deliberately sketchy, which saves a great deal of time and maintains the quality of a "process" drawing still open to change.

White Prismacolor™ is still added to the back, but all other colors are added directly to the front. Some designers, like Michael Doyle, use a more finished final overlay on white tracing paper and apply all color to the back so that it doesn't obscure the black lines on the front. The white tracing paper provides a more color-neutral background that can be color-copied using a variety of different-colored backup papers.

This overlay represents a more refined drawing made over the original overlay. It has a double-line and poché indication of walls, and a strong distinction in line weight. It demonstrates the functioning of the various spaces with furniture layouts, and trees and growies are more carefully drawn.

You may also want to add a carefully lettered name for the project, your name, and, perhaps, titles for the drawings. Consistent lettering adds a certain unity to the presentation. You should

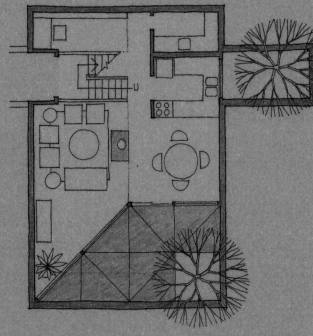

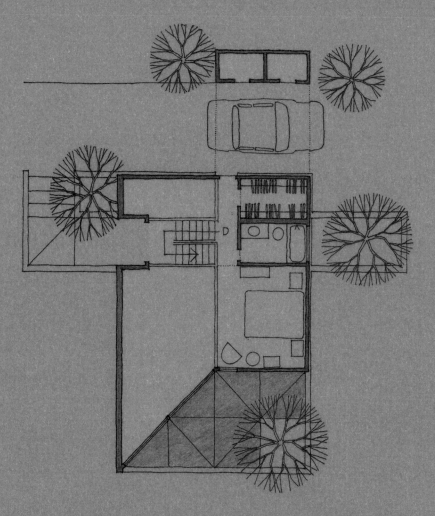

always trace a carefully selected alphabet. Sloppy title lettering or rub-on letters that contrast with the drawings in their precision and formality can be a major distraction. When you are going to be using photocopies for the final drawings, remember that you can print out all the lettering on a laser printer and paste them onto the originals before photocopying.

White Prismacolor™ is again added to the back of the drawing to indicate degrees of spatial enclosure and colored tones are added to the front of the drawing to indicate floor materials and landscaping.

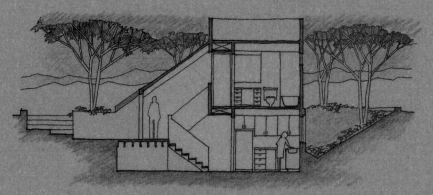

This overlay represents a more refined drawing made over the original overlay. It has a double-line and poché indication of walls, and a strong distinction in line weight. It demonstrates the functioning of the various spaces with furniture layouts, and trees and growies are more carefully drawn.

You may also want to add a carefully lettered name for the project, your name, and, perhaps, titles for the drawings. Consistent lettering adds a certain unity to the presentation. You should

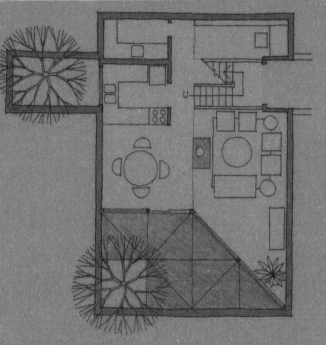

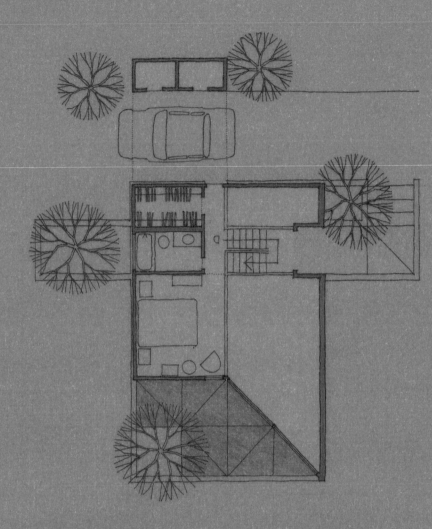

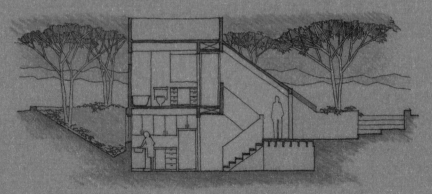

always trace a carefully selected alphabet. Sloppy title lettering or rub-on letters that contrast with the drawings in their precision and formality can be a major distraction. When you are going to be using photocopies for the final drawings, remember that you can print out all the lettering on a laser printer and paste them onto the originals before photocopying.

White Prismacolor™ is again added to the back of the drawing to indicate degrees of spatial enclosure and colored tones are added to the front of the drawing to indicate floor materials and landscaping.

This first sketchy overlay represents the kind of plans and sections you might make to describe to yourself (and perhaps even to a client who didn't need impressing) the qualities of a design as a built object. There would certainly have been earlier plan and section diagrams to get the design process to this point. These drawings, combined with the previous exterior and interior perspectives, make up the first synthesis of a design you believe is worth committing to.

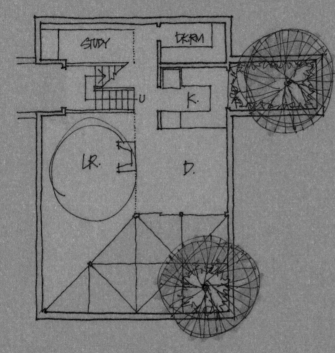

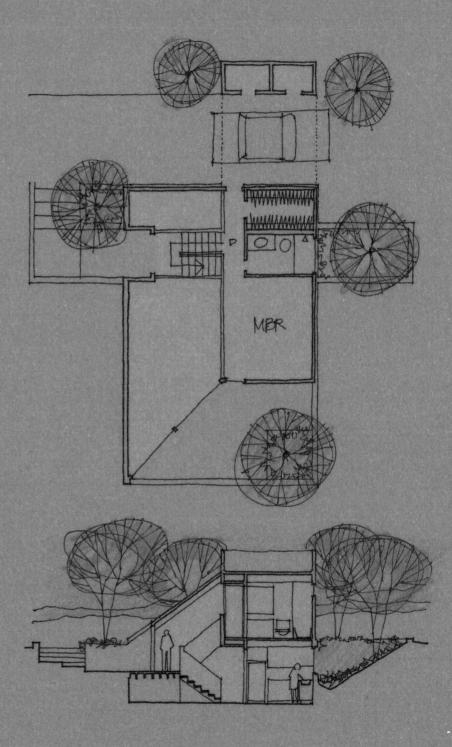

These drawings could have been made freehand over an eight-to-the-inch grid, or blocked out first on eight-to-the-inch tracing paper, but if you use buff overlays you will be able to take advantage of the translucency of the paper by adding white Prismacolor™ to the back of the buff paper.

In these sketches, layout lines are acceptable and the spaces are labeled rather than demonstrated with furniture arrangements. White Prismacolor™ identifies roofed and walled spaces as not fully enclosed and a circle and a green smudge create trees. Color is applied loosely but disciplined by a common stroking direction. Thicker walls are represented by a fatter marker.

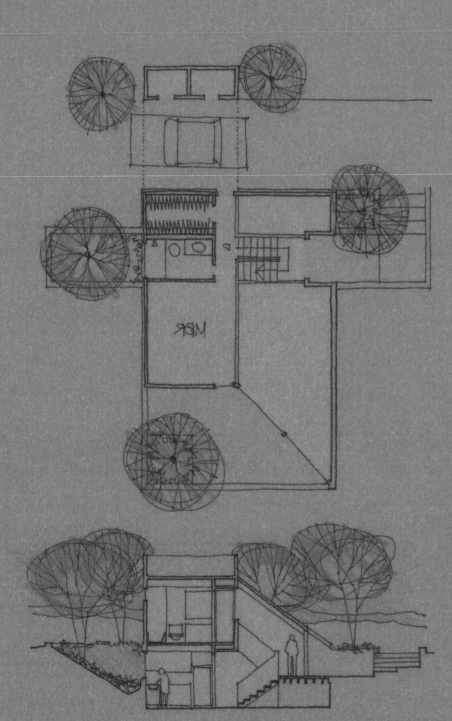

This first sketchy overlay represents the kind of plans and sections you might make to describe to yourself (and perhaps even to a client who didn't need impressing) the qualities of a design as a built object. There would certainly have been earlier plan and section diagrams to get the design process to this point. These drawings, combined with the previous exterior and interior perspectives, make up the first synthesis of a design you believe is worth committing to.

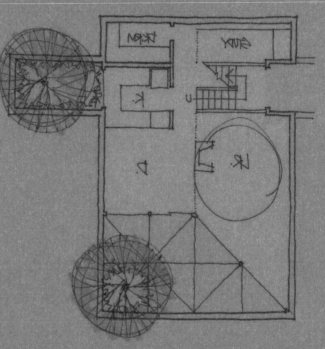

These drawings could have been made freehand over an eight-to-the-inch grid, or blocked out first on eight-to-the-inch tracing paper, but if you use buff overlays you will be able to take advantage of the translucency of the paper by adding white Prismacolor™ to the back of the buff paper.

In these sketches, layout lines are acceptable and the spaces are labeled rather than demonstrated with furniture arrangements. White Prismacolor™ identifies roofed and walled spaces as not fully enclosed and a circle and a green smudge create trees. Color is applied loosely but disciplined by a common stroking direction. Thicker walls are represented by a fatter marker.

As on page 264, the pattern of black, gray, and white paper on this page represents paper cutouts that may be applied to an underlay board on which to mount tracing paper drawings. Another alternative is to apply layers of white or buff tracing paper or white bond paper directly to the back of a tracing paper drawing and then mount it on a black, or very dark, board. Of course this technique is impossible to duplicate in a book like this.

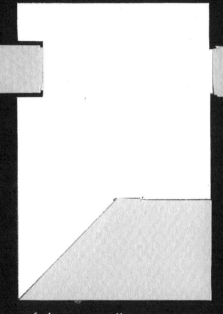

The translucency of the paper allows you to quickly add tonal interest just as you added refinement to the earlier drawings.

In plans and sections you may want to use opaque, white underlays to indicate fully enclosed space and additional layers of tracing paper to indicate partially enclosed spaces that are roofed or walled but not fully enclosed.

As with the previous tracing paper overlays, these white and light-gray paper patterns could also be white Prismacolor™ applied to the back of buff tracing paper. This only takes a few minutes and helps the enclosed spaces read much more strongly.

DRAWING FOR YOUR FIRST JURY

The major problem in making drawings for your first jury is one of self-management, which can be especially difficult because you may be trying to manage a whole new set of skills that you are still in the process of learning. Students typically underestimate the time the drawings will take and often make things worse by choosing some impossibly difficult drawing technique.

Successful management depends on establishing a schedule and trying to meet the schedule's interim deadlines. You should also choose a technique that you can realistically accomplish at your present level of skill. It is also a good idea to surround yourself with examples of drawings in the technique you have chosen, as well as of particular furnishings or entourage you are going to have to draw. If you need special boards, papers, or prints, get them when the shops are open. Good management avoids surprises.

Planning flexibility into your presentation is always a good idea. In spite of your best intentions there will be occasions when something goes wrong or takes more time than you thought it would. Such crises demand the kind of flexible planning that always has a plan B.

Plan B may be as simple as eliminating one or more drawings that aren't absolutely necessary or deciding not to add tones or color to any of the drawings. If the presentation you planned included getting prints, you might forget the prints and just go with the original tracings.

Balancing your drawings is one of the best ways to maintain flexibility. It helps if you can conceive of completing the drawings in layers, so that all the drawings are laid out as open, single-line drawings, including and integrating the entourage or additional interest. Next, all the drawings should be profiled so they read consistently. Then you should consider adding tones to all the drawings, then textures, then colors.

The trick is to have all the drawings look like they received an equal amount of your attention. If your set of drawings is kept in balance they won't look incomplete. One of the giveaways of incompleteness is that some drawings are rendered in great detail while others are barely started or left completely void of entourage. Another obvious clue is the lack of labeling of your drawings. I am not an advocate of over-labeling, but the plans should be readable without your having to name the spaces. Another way to show thoughtful completion is to write out your major concepts in careful prose on the drawings and maybe have a few conceptual diagrams to help explain your ideas.

VERBAL PRESENTATIONS

One of the misleading myths about design and drawing is that "the drawings should speak for themselves." While it is true that the design should be completely and clearly described in the drawings and models, only fools would miss the chance to say something about their designs.

Students' first experience with verbal presentation is usually in a setting called a "jury," where student projects are reviewed by faculty and invited guests. This is a traumatic time for some students who may be inexperienced at making such public presentations. You should prepare for such presentations by carefully composing a verbal explanation. I recommend that you go as far as to write down and memorize the opening paragraphs so that you don't forget to tell the jury the most important ideas of your design. It also helps to write down some of the rationale right on the presentation itself so that you won't forget to explain your concepts for the design.

DRAWING FOR YOUR PORTFOLIO

The years of professional design education go by faster than you would believe, and before you know it you will be graduating and thinking about looking for a job. One of the things your professional employers will want to know is how well you can draw. While some of them who are looking for "production" people will be more interested in your graphic capabilities on the computer, most of those looking for apprentice designers will be more interested in your free-hand drawing ability.

If you save your best work in a consistent portfolio format, you will be way ahead when the time comes to go job hunting. Portfolios larger than 8½" by 11" will give you more flexibility in establishing a format for displaying your work, but you won't need one larger than 11" by 17". Ernest Burden's *Design Communication* is an excellent source for layout examples.

It is important to get your best work photographed before it gets trashed. You can get enlarged prints later, when you can afford them.

Although black-and-white drawings are the easiest and least expensive to reproduce, your portfolio should include tone techniques and color. Be sure that you include examples of your quick sketches and conceptual diagrams.

Employers usually will assume that most graduates of professional schools can draw beautifully if they are given enough time. What they may be much more interested in is employees who can draw quickly, or who at least have more than one gear.

The stitches-and-zipper analogy was intended to be a model that could accommodate most of the opinions and recommendations about what should occur during the design process. But models are never unbiased. Although I have rigorously challenged the validity of linear models, even the stitches-and-zipper analogy winds up looking like a linear procedure. After several years of considering various frameworks, I chose to stay with the so-called *process* and the so-called *problem* and *solution* because of their broad general acceptance and use in design education.

I must now add a brief but comprehensive disclaimer for serious readers. *Problem, solution,* and design *process* are very misleading words if they are taken literally. I would much prefer to replace *problem* with *perceived conceptual opportunity* or *percept*, to replace *solution* with *rationalized conceptual response* or *concept*, to replace *problem solving* with *opportunity seeking*, and to replace *design process* with *design synthesis*. I decided, however, that what I had to say might be difficult enough for my limited writing skills and powers of persuasion without also trying to change the accepted vocabulary.

The Limitations of the Design Process

Of all the misleading phrases commonly applied to design, creative problem solving surely takes the cake. It belongs in that select class of oxymorons, alongside jumbo shrimp, postal service, and military intelligence. Anyone who approaches whatever they do as problem solving gives up creativity at the outset. Creativity is always what you do *besides* solving the obvious or conventional problems. Creative problem solving implies that the problems are already known and that only creativity is needed in finding a solution for the fixed problem—the *compliance* of what I have called *concept attainment*. Real creativity includes seeking, understanding, and responding to design opportunities that have been overlooked by others—the *congruence* of *concept formation*.

The greatest danger of all linear methods or models of thought or creativity, even ones as loose as the stitches-and-zipper analogy, is that they sometimes lead designers to surrender their subjectivity. We are the products of two infinitely wiser processes: human evolution and the experience of our own lifetimes; when our senses veto the products of our linear, rational processes as "inappropriate" or "ugly" we should accept that judgment without question or apology.

Unlike the scales, distances, and speeds of modern physics, which are beyond direct human experience but whose techniques many design methodologists emulate, the scale and complexity of the environments we design can still be represented quite adequately with traditional drawing and modeling techniques. The ultimate evaluation of the environments we design will be made by human beings like ourselves, who have the same perceptual apparatus we have been using all our lives. Our best hope is still what it has always been: to develop our own individual sensitivity to our fellow human beings and to the built environment, and to consider our additions to that environment very carefully, with accurate representational drawings and models that keep the process open to everyone involved.

To deny or censor the evaluation of our senses in favor of the pseudo-certainty of any ritual, however logical, mathematical, or scientific, is a very serious mistake. To believe in any design method to the extent that we are prepared to let it override our own subjective experience is to abdicate our role as environmental designers and our responsibility as human beings.

Afterthought

The oldest known drawings are design drawings. The cave paintings of the Ardeche Valley of France, made over 30,000 years ago, were not made as records of history or as art to impress or influence the viewer. They were made by torch light in the most inaccessible parts of the caves and were often overlays of earlier paintings. They were not drawn with a parallel edge and triangle or a computer, nor are they flat plans or sections. Rather, they are remarkably realistic representations of reality.

Most experts agree that the drawings were intended to *influence the future*. Their makers believed that the act of making graphic representations of successful future hunts would help those efforts be successful.

Design drawings are the direct descendants of these prehistoric cave paintings. They have much more in common with each other than either has with art or drafting. Design drawing has precisely the same intention as these earliest drawings, without the magic. The ability to draw alternative futures and the potential those representations have for helping us build better environments all comes from design drawing.

Photograph by Douglas Mazonwicz.
From *Prehistoric Art* by T. G. E. Powell.

Bibliography

The categorization of drawing books is a continuing problem, as you will discover from the shelving patterns found in any library. The categories of this bibliography are ordered according to the organization of the book, which seems appropriate for design drawing.

My greatest problem with the categorization is where to place my own previous books, *Drawing as a Means to Architecture* (1968) and *Design Drawing Experiences* (2000 Edition). Several books by others appear more than once in the bibliography, but since the categories are my categories, my books wind up in every category, or none. I have decided the latter choice is the more modest, and so you will find only *Design Drawing Experiences* listed under Introductory Books with Exercises. *Drawing as a Means to Architecture,* one of the first books that attempted to relate drawing to the design process, and the initiator of many of the ideas in this book, is so general that it fits in all the categories.

1. Perception

This is a very selective, basic list of books that directly relate perception to environmental design and drawing.

Arnheim, Rudolf. *Visual Thinking*. Berkeley/Los Angeles: University of California Press, 1969, 1971.

Berrill, N. J. *Man's Emerging Mind: The Story of Man's Progress Through Time*. New York: Fawcett World Library, 1965.

Bronowski, J. *The Ascent of Man*. Boston/ Toronto: Little, Brown & Company, 1973.

Gibson, James J. *The Perception of the Visual World*. Boston: Houghton Mifflin Company, 1950. Reprint, Westport, CT: Greenwood Press, 1974.

Gibson, James J. *The Senses Considered as Perceptual Systems*. Boston: Houghton Mifflin Company, 1966.

Gibson, James J. *The Ecological Approach to Visual Perception*. Boston: Houghton Miffin Company, 1979.

Gombrich, E. H. *Art and Illusion: A Study in the Psychology of Pictorial Representation*. The A. W. Mellon Lectures in the Fine Arts, 1965. Paperback ed. Bollingen Series XXXV 5. Princeton: Princeton University Press, 1972.

Gregory, R. L. *The Intelligent Eye*. New York: McGraw-Hill Book Company, 1970.

Hall, Edward T. *The Hidden Dimension*. New York: Doubleday and Company, 1966. Anchor Books ed., 1969.

Hoffman, Donald D. *Visual Intelligence*. New York: W. W. Norton & Company, Inc., 1998.

Ittelson, William H., ed. *Environment and Cognition*. New York: Seminar Press, 1973.

McLuhan, Marshall. *Understanding Media: The Extensions of Man*. New York: McGraw-Hill Book Company, 1964.

2. Conception

The books that follow are selected to demonstrate the range of thought, most of it by nondesigners, that can be related to environmental design and drawing.

Adams, James L. *Conceptual Blockbusting: A Guide to Better Ideas*. 2nd ed. New York: W. W. Norton & Company, 1974.

Allport, Gordon W. *The Nature of Prejudice*. Reading, MA: Addison-Wesley Publishing Company, 1954. Garden City: Doubleday Anchor Books, 1958.

Arnheim, Rudolf. *Visual Thinking*. Berkeley/Los Angeles: University of California Press, 1971.

Bruner, Jerome S., Jacqueline J. Goodnow, and George A. Austin. *A Study of Thinking*. New York: John Wiley & Sons, 1956.

Bruner, Jerome S. *On Knowing: Essays for the Left Hand*. Cambridge: Harvard University Press, 1963. Paperback ed. New York: Atheneum, 1973.

Bruner, Jerome S. *Beyond the Information Given: Studies in the Psychology of Knowing*. Edited by Jeremy M. Anglin. New York: W. W. Norton & Company, 1973.

Churchman, C. West. *The Systems Approach*. New York: Dell Publishing, 1968.

deBono, Edward. *The Mechanism of Mind*. New York: Simon and Schuster, 1969.

deBono, Edward. *Lateral Thinking: Creativity Step by Step*. New York: Harper & Row, Publishers, 1970.

deBono, Edward. *New Think: The Use of Lateral Thinking in the Generation of New Ideas*. New York: The Hearst Corporation, Avon Books, 1971.

Foz, Adel Twefik-Khalil. "Some Observations on Designer Behavior in the Parti." Master's thesis, Massachusetts Institute of Technology, 1972.

Gordon, William J. J. *Synectics: The Development of Creative Capacity*. New York: Harper & Row Publishers, 1961. Paperback ed. Coffier Books, 1968.

Gruber, Howard E. *Darwin on Man: A Psychological Study of Scientific Creativity*. New York: E. P. Dutton and Company, 1974.

Kepes, Gyorgy. *The New Landscape in Art and Science*. Chicago: Paul Theobald and Company, 1956.

Koberg, Don, and Jim Bagnall. *The Universal Traveler*. Los Altos, CA: William Kaufman, 1972.

Koestler, Arthur. *The Act of Creation: A Study of the Conscious and Unconscious in Science and Art*. New York: The Macmillan Company, 1964. Paperback ed. Dell Publishing Company, 1967.

Koestler, Arthur. *The Ghost in the Machine*. New York: The Macmillan Company, 1967. Gateway ed. Chicago: Henry Regnery Company, 1971.

Koestler, Arthur. *Janus: A Summing Up*. New York: Random House, 1978. Vintage Book ed., 1979.

Kuhn, Thomas S. *Structure of Scientific Revolutions*. 2nd ed., enlarged. Chicago: The University of Chicago Press, 1962, 1970.

Levi-Strauss, Claude. *The Savage Mind*. Chicago: The University of Chicago Press, 1966.

McKim, R. H. *Experiences in Visual Thinking*. 2nd ed. Monterey, CA: Brooks/Cole Publishing Company, 1972.

Magee, Bryan. *Karl Popper*. New York: The Viking Press, 1973.

Martin, William David. "The Architect's Role in Participatory Planning Processes: Case Study—Boston Transportation Planning Review." Master's thesis, Massachusetts Institute of Technology, 1976.

Maslow, A. H. *The Farther Reaches of Human Nature*. New York: The Viking Press, 1971. Viking Compass ed., 1972.

Newell, Allen, and Herbert A. Simon. *Human Problem Solving*. Englewood Cliffs, NJ: Prentice-Hall, 1972.

Ornstein, Robert E. *Psychology of Consciousness*. San Francisco: W. H. Freeman and Company, 1972. 2nd ed. New York: Harcourt Brace Jovanovich, 1977.

Pearce, Joseph Chilton. *The Crack in the Cosmic Egg: Challenging Constructs of Mind and Reality*. New York: Julian Press, 1971. Paperback ed. Simon & Schuster, Pocket Books, 1973.

Polanyi, Michael. *The Tacit Dimension*. New York: Doubleday and Company, Inc., 1966. Anchor books, 1967.

Prince, George M. *The Practice of Creativity*. New York: Harper & Row. Paperback ed. Collier Books, 1972.

Samuels, Mike, M.D., and Nancy Samuels. *Seeing With the Mind's Eye: The History, Techniques and Uses of Visualization*. New York: Random House, 1975.

Wilson, Frank R. *The Hand*. New York: Random House, Inc., 1998.

3. Representation

Drawing's Relationship to Experience

Drawing Techniques

Line

Bon-Hui Uy. *Architectural Drawings and Leisure Sketches*. Hololulu: Bon-Hui Uy, 1978.

Bon-Hui Uy. *Drawings, Architecture and Leisure*. New York: Bon-Hui Uy, 1980.

Parenti, George. *Masonite Contemporary Studies*. Chicago: Masonite Corporation, 1960.

Welling, Richard. *The Technique of Drawing Buildings*. New York: Watson-Guptill Publications, 1971.

Tone

Kautzky, Ted. *Pencil Broadsides: A Manual of Broad Stroke Technique*. New York: Reinhold, 1940, 1960.

Kautzky, Ted. *The Ted Kautzky Pencil Book*. New York: Van Nostrand Reinhold Company, 1979.

Oles, Paul Stevenson. *Architectural Illustration: The Value Delineation Process*. New York: Van Nostrand Reinhold Company, 1979.

Tone-of-lines

Guptill, Arthur Leighton. *Drawing with Pen and Ink*. New York: Reinhold, 1961.

White, Edward T. *A Graphic Vocabulary for Architectural Presentation*. Tucson: Architectural Media, 1972.

Line-and-tone

Cullen, Gordon. *Townscape*. New York: Reinhold, 1961.

Jacoby, Helmut. *Architectural Drawings*. New York: Frederick A. Praeger, Publishers, 1965.

Jacoby, Helmut. *New Architectural Drawings*. New York: Frederick A. Praeger, Publishers, 1969.

4. Perspective

Burden, Ernest. *Architectural Delineation: A Photographic Approach to Presentation.* New York: McGraw Hill Book Company, 1971.

D'Amelio, Joseph. *Perspective Drawing Handbook.* New York: Tudor Publishing, 1964.

Doblin, Jay. *Perspective: A New System for Designers.* New York: Whitney Library of Design, 1956.

Ivins, William M., Jr. *On the Rationalization of Sight: With an Examination of Three Renaissance Texts on Perspective.* New York: Da Capo Press, 1973.

Light

Doyle, Michael E. *Color Drawing.* New York: Van Nostrand Reinhold Company, 1981.

Forseth, Kevin, with David Vaughan. *Graphics for Architecture.* New York: Van Nostrand Reinhold Company, 1980.

Oles, Paul Stevenson. *Architectural Illustration: The Value Delineation Process.* New York: Van Nostrand Reinhold Company, 1979.

Color

Doyle, Michael E. *Color Drawing.* New York: Van Nostrand Reinhold Company, 1981.

Oles, Paul Stevenson. *Architectural Illustration: The Value Delineation Process.* New York: Van Nostrand Reinhold Company, 1979.

Welling, Richard. *Drawing with Markers.* New York: Watson-Guptill Publications, 1974.

Tape and templates

Burden, Ernest E. *Entourage: A Tracing File for Architecture and Interior Design.* New York: McGraw Hill Book Company, 1981.

Denny, Edward, and Patricia Terrazas. *Bod File: A Resource Book for Designers & Illustrators.* Arlington: Inner Image Books, 1976.

McGinty, Tim. *Drawing Skills in Architecture: Perspective, Layout Design.* Dubuque: Kendall/Hunt Publishing Company, 1976.

Szabo. *Drawing File for Architects.* New York: Van Nostrand Reinhold Company, 1976.

Wang, Thomas C. *Plan and Section Drawing.* New York: Van Nostrand Reinhold Company, 1979.

White, Edward T. *A Graphic Vocabulary for Architectural Presentation.* Tucson: Architectural Media, 1972.

Introductory books with exercises

Lockard, William Kirby, *Design Drawing Experiences. 2000 Edition.* New York: W. W. Norton & Company, Inc., 2000.

McGinty, Tim. *Drawing Skills in Architecture: Perspective Layout, Design.* Dubuque: Kendall/Hunt Publishing Company, 1976.

Wester, Lari M. *Think and Do Graphics: A Graphic Communication Workbook.* Proof Copy. Guelph, Canada: Guelph Campus CO-OP, 1976.

Drafting

Ching, Francis D. K. *Architectural Graphics.* New York: Van Nostrand Reinhold Company, 1975.

Forseth, Kevin, with David Vaughan. *Graphics for Architecture.* New York: Van Nostrand Reinhold Company.

Martin, C. Leslie. *Design Graphics.* 2nd ed. New York: The Macmillan Company, 1968.

Patten, Lawton, M., and Milton L. Rogness. *Architectural Drawing.* Rev. ed. Dubuque: Win. C. Brown Company, Publishers, 1968.

Ramsey, Charles G., and Harold R. Sleeper. *Architectural Graphic Standards.* 6th ed. New York: John Wiley & Sons, 1970.

6. Drawing's Relationship to the Design Process

Design process and method

This list offers a collection of descriptions and prescriptions of what does or should happen during the so-called design process. Some of the methods exclude drawings from any meaningful role in the process, and hence conflict totally with the basis of this book.

Broadbent, Geoffrey, and Anthony Ward, eds. *Design Methods in Architecture.* Architectural Association Paper number 4. London: Lund Humphries Publishers, 1969.

Broadbent, Geoffrey. *Design in Architecture: Architecture and the Human Sciences.* Chicester: John Wiley & Sons, 1973.

Jones, J. Christopher. *Design Methods: Seeds of Human Futures.* London: Wiley-Interscience, 1970.

Moore, Gary T., ed. *Emerging Methods in Environmental Design and Planning.* Cambridge: MIT Press, 1970.

Conceptual drawing

This category addresses all the drawings involved in opening, clearing, and closing the design space.

Adams, James L. *Conceptual Blockbusting: A Guide to Better Ideas.* 2nd ed. New York: W. W. Norton & Company, 1974.

Ching, Francis D. K. *Architecture: Form, Space & Order.* New York: Van Nostrand Reinhold Company, 1979.

Hanks, Kurt, and Larry Belliston. *Draw! A Visual Approach to Thinking, Learning and Communicating.* Los Altos, CA: William Kaufmann, 1977.

Hanks, Kurt, and Larry Belliston. *Rapid Viz: A New Method for the Rapid Visualization of Ideas.* Los Altos, CA: William Kaufmann, 1977.

Laseau, Paul. *Graphic Problem Solving for Architects and Builders*. Boston: CBI Publishing Company, 1975.

Laseau, Paul. *Graphic Thinking for Architects and Designers*. New York: Van Nostrand Reinhold Company, 1980.

McKim, R. H. *Experiences in Visual Thinking*. 2nd ed. Monterey, CA: Brooks/Cole Publishing Company, 1972.

Porter, Tom. *How Architects Visualize*. New York: Van Nostrand Reinhold Company, 1979.

White, Edward T. *Introduction to Architectural Programming*. Tucson: Architectural Media, 1972.

White, Edward T. *Ordering Systems: An Introduction to Architectural Design*. Tucson: Architectural Media, 1973.

White, Edward T. *Concept Sourcebook: A Vocabulary of Architectural Forms*. Tucson: Architectural Media, 1975.

Presentation drawing

The books that follow are mostly collections of closed, persuasive drawings that come after all the design decisions have been made—what I have called *zipped* drawings. The most hopeful characteristic of this group is its great diversity and also the growing number of books that show in detail exactly how the drawings were made.

Atkin, William Wilson, Raniero Corbelletti, and Vincent T. Fiore. *Pencil Techniques in Modern Design*. New York: Van Nostrand Reinhold Company, 1953.

Atkin, William Wilson. *Architectural Presentation Techniques*. New York: Van Nostrand Reinhold Company, 1976.

Burden, Ernest. *Architectural Delineation: A Photographic Approach to Presentation*. New York: McGraw-Hill Book Company, 1971.

Doyle, Michael E. *Color Drawing*. New York: Van Nostrand Reinhold Company, 1981.

Halse, Albert O. *Architectural Rendering: The Techniques of Contemporary Presentation*. 2nd ed. New York: McGraw-Hill Book Company, 1972.

Jacoby, Helmut. *Architectural Drawings*. New York: Frederick A. Praeger, Publishers, 1965.

Jacoby, Helmut. *New Architectural Drawings*. New York: Frederick A. Praeger, Publishers, 1969

Jacoby, Helmut. *New Techniques of Architectural Rendering*. New York: Frederick A. Praeger, Publishers, 1971.

Kemper, Alfred M. *Drawings by American Architects*. New York: John Wiley & Sons, 1973.

Kemper, Alfred M. *Presentation Drawings by American Architects*. New York: Wiley-Interscience, John Wiley & Sons, 1977.

Oles, Paul Stevenson. *Architectural Illustration: The Value Delineation Process*. New York: Van Nostrand Reinhold Company, 1979.

Pile, John, comp. *Drawings of Architectural Interiors*. New York: Whitney Library of Design, 1967.

Walker, Theodore D. *Perspective Sketches*. West Lafayette, IN: PDA Publishers, 1972.

Walker, Theodore D. *Perspective Sketches II*. West Lafayette, IN: PDA Publishers, 1975.

White, Edward T. *A Graphic Vocabulary for Architectural Presentation*. Tucson: Architectural Media, 1972.

White, Edward T. *Presentation Strategies in Architecture*. Tucson: Architectural Media, 1977.

7. Combinations: Drawing as a Partner in Communication

Not much has been written for the design professions about combining drawing with other media. This list should grow dramatically in the coming years.

Boyer, Ernest L., and Lee D. Mitgang. *Building Community: A New Future for Architecture Education and Practice*. Princeton: The Carnegie Foundation for the Advancement of Teaching, 1996.

Kliment, Stephen A. *Writing for Design Professionals*. New York: W. W. Norton & Company, 1998.

Lewis, Roger K., *Shaping the City*. Washington, D.C.: The AIA Press, 1987.

Tuft, Edward R. *Envisioning Information*. Chesire, Connecticut: Graphics Press, 1991.

Tuft, Edward R. *The Visual Display of Quantitative Information*. Chesire, Connecticut: Graphics Press, 1983.

Wurman, Richard Saul. *Information Anxiety*. New York: Bantam Books, 1989.

Index